PENGUIN BO(

BAREFOOT TO I

Novy Kapadia is a renowned sports journalist and columnist, and taught English literature at Delhi University. Recognized as India's foremost football expert and commentator on leading television channels, he is the author of *The Football Fanatic's Essential Guide Book*, and has contributed to *Soccer in South Asia*, *Fields of Play* and *Enduring Legacy: Parsis of the 20th Century*. Novy has been a consultant to the *Limca Book of Records* from 1990 onwards, and has edited the *Durand Journal*—India's most comprehensive football journal—since 1983. Since 1980, he has covered several international championships, including the World Cup and the Olympics, and all major domestic tournaments.

Novy won the Wills Award for Excellence in Sports Journalism in 1986. He lives in Delhi.

NOVY KAPADIA

BAREFOOT TO BOOTS

THE MANY LIVES OF
INDIAN
FOOTBALL

FOREWORD BY
BHAICHUNG BHUTIA

PENGUIN BOOKS
An imprint of Penguin Random House

PENGUIN BOOKS

USA | Canada | UK | Ireland | Australia
New Zealand | India | South Africa | China

Penguin Books is part of the Penguin Random House group of companies
whose addresses can be found at global.penguinrandomhouse.com

Published by Penguin Random House India Pvt. Ltd
7th Floor, Infinity Tower C, DLF Cyber City,
Gurgaon 122 002, Haryana, India

First published in Penguin Books by Penguin Random House India 2017

ISBN 9780143426417

Typeset in Sabon by Manipal Digital Systems, Manipal
Printed at Replika Press Pvt. Ltd, India

www.penguin.co.in

Contents

Foreword

Many of us call Novy Kapadia 'the grand old man of Indian football'. He is a serious football historian and has been involved with the sport as a writer and commentator for many decades. He has watched from close quarters the epic rivalries in domestic football, India's performance in international competitions as well as all the great players, past and present.

Novy has witnessed the ebb and flow of Indian football—and how it has evolved from an amateur to a professional sport. The game has sustained itself thanks to the passion of some clubs and officials and the dedication of the players. Infrastructure has been lacking and youth development has started seriously only some years ago. To improve our performance, Indian clubs need to become more professional, with greater attention being paid to the development of infrastructure and grass-roots programmes.

There have been many moments of glory for Indian football. And with India set to host the FIFA U-17 World Cup in October 2017, Novy's documentation of the country's rich football legacy through this book could not have come at a better time.

I have known Novy Kapadia since 1991, when I came to Delhi to play for the Tashi Namgyal Academy in the annual Subroto Mukherjee Cup football tournament and the Limca Football tournament for schools. As a football-loving reporter he was always around, watching us play and writing about me and other players in *Sportsworld* and the *Telegraph*.

Later, when I became a professional player and joined East Bengal and then JCT, we came more into contact. Novy and the late Noel da Lima Leitao were the first commentators in IMG's telecast of the inaugural National Football League and the KBL Federation Cup, which were shown on Star Sports in 1997. Novy, because of his background as a professor of English, always spoke with a literary flourish. He added to the images shown on television and provided lots of interesting information, in an era when the Internet barely existed. This combination was very good.

In 2004, we both worked for ESPN in Singapore for the telecast of Euro 2004, which was being held in Portugal. We travelled daily from our hotel to the studios by taxi and discussed football a lot. Since then I have been on several programmes with him on different TV channels to discuss Indian or European football.

Novy Kapadia is well known for his immense passion for football and sports. His detailed knowledge of players, in both India and abroad, and their backgrounds is unparalleled. This book does justice to the many histories of Indian football, with its racy anecdotes about players, clubs and important tournaments, detailed descriptions of matches and the outlining of a long-term perspective. This is a meticulously researched work that makes for a very enjoyable read. I wish the author and the book all success.

Padma Shri Bhaichung Bhutia
Former captain, India
August 2017

Acknowledgements

When I was captain of Young Bengal Football Club in 1974–75, the club secretary gave me a book, *The Indian Football 1975*, compiled and edited by S.L. Ghosh, as a present. I still cherish this gift as it was an eye-opener for me and provided detailed insights about India's glory years in the 1950s. It is still a ready reckoner for Indian football statistics till 1975. Literature on Indian football in English has been limited but has been delightful to read. They have all had an influence on my writing. I am indebted to Jaydeep Basu (*Stories of Indian Football*), Nirmal Nath (*The History of Indian Football*), Boria Mazumdar (*Goalless*), Ronojoy Sen (*Nation at Play*), Debashis Majumder (*The History of the Football Clubs in Calcutta*), *The Grass Is Green*, published by the Goa Football Association in 1999, and the well-produced *Footprints in the Sand: History of Salgaocar Football* (1956–2006) and *The Golden Eagles: 50 Years of Dempo Sports Club* (1967–2017), both put together by Mario Rodrigues and Marcus Mergulhao.

In 2008–09, I wrote for the *90 Minutes* journal, and their editor, Subhransu Roy, kept persuading me to write a book on Indian football and share my experiences with the future generations. I never thought such a book would materialize, till Richa Burman of Penguin approached me in November 2015. Due to my teaching commitments and football commentaries, I was hesitant. But after several meetings with Richa, I agreed.

This book is a labour of love as it involves all my memories and anecdotes of Indian football from 1960 till the present.

My special thanks to Richa, for her patience, guidance and excellent editing, which has given the book its current shape (as in my overenthusiasm, I had overwritten on nearly every topic). I had a special section on women's football in Manipur, particularly on the recent Arjuna Award–winner O. Bembem Devi. But due to a shortage of space it had to be omitted. For the same reason, and to create a balance among the states and different generations, the profiles of some football legends could not be done, much to my regret. My thanks also to Rachita Raj, for her painstaking proofreading, queries and corrections, which helped this book become a fine, finished product.

I thank all the renowned players and coaches with whom I have had numerous discussions for nearly four decades. This book would not have been possible without my many personal conversations with P.K. Banerjee, the late Amal Dutta, Syed Nayeemuddin, Tulsidas Balaram, Chuni Goswami, F.A. Franco, S.S. Narayan, S.S. Hakeem, Subhash Bhowmick, Subrata Bhattacharya, Bhaskar Ganguly, Inder Singh, Harjinder Singh, Sukhwinder Singh, Parminder Singh, Shabbir Ali, Bruno Coutinho, Armando Colaco, Brahmanand Shankhwalkar and Derrick Pereira, Santosh Kashyap, Bhaichung Bhutia, Karim Bencherifa (Moroccan coach of Churchill Brothers, Mohun Bagan and Salgaocar, with whom I did many TV programmes), late Noel da Lima Leitao (we worked as commentators for Star Sports in the NFL, KBL Federation Cup and the 2006 World Cup), Alberto Colaco (former AIFF secretary), renowned statistician and historian Gautam Roy, sports journalists N. Ganesan, Kewal Kaushik, Rupak Saha, Manas Chakraborty, Nirmal Nath, Swapan Sarkar, Jaydeep Basu and several others, the late Gama Qureishi, the late Nawabuddin Zaheer, O.P. Malhotra, N.K. Bhatia, Hem Chand, M.M. Sultan and Dilip Bose (all from the Delhi Soccer Association), the late K.K. Ganguly (Durand secretary), the late G. Sinha and R.K. Gupta (DCM tournament officials), Ghaus Mohammed (a commentator friend), the late Mohammed Taki (of the Indian Nationals) and Hariprasad Chattopadhyay (a statistician).

My deep gratitude to Bhaichung Bhutia for writing an encouraging foreword, and to Praful Patel, president of the AIFF, P.K. Banerjee and Syed Nayeemuddin, for their endorsement of the book. I am immensely grateful to my friend Vijay Lokapally, who was always there to provide timely advice and who wholeheartedly supported my endeavour.

For the photographs I would like to thank my many friends all over India, who responded to our request to send rare photographs, which have embellished the book and added to its appeal. My special thanks to S.S. Hakeem (photos of the Indian Olympics team and S. Rahim); Nilanjan Datta, media director, AIFF (rare and unpublished archival photographs, and of the Indian team from AIFF Media); Mario Rodrigues (AIFF photograph of the Indian team); Gautam Roy (East Bengal and Kolkata football); Nirmal Nath (photos from his book); Sukhwinder Singh (JCT); Shivanand V. Salgaocar, Adlear D'Cruz, Jonathan De Sousa and Marcus Mergulhao (Goa football); Valanka Alemao (Churchill Brothers); Mandar Tamhane and Mustafa Ghouse (Bengaluru FC); Shabbir Ali, P.P. Surender Kumar, Saptaparno Ghosh, Mustafa Pervez, the Durand Football Tournament Society, Leeladhar Singh and Hoshedar Gundevia (Indian Super League) and eminent photographer and friend Mohammed Shafiq. Journalist Bir Yadav and photographer Sanjay Kumar kindly provided pictures of the Durand trophies. Chief librarian of the *Anandabazar Patrika*, Saktidas Roy, and Ayon Sengupta and S.K. Subrramanya of *The Hindu* put together an extensive set of archival photographs for us to choose from, and ABP provided rare newspaper clippings of India's feats in international football.

My special thanks to my nephew Jonathan Page, who, despite a hectic schedule at BBC London, found the time to proofread parts of the text and offer valuable suggestions, and to my wonderful students Charu Lakra, Shriya Rawat, Bhavya Sharma and Aishwarya Sharma, for helping me in proofreading and correcting the mistakes of their English teacher.

I dedicate this book to my father, the late Minoo Kapadia, who inspired in me a love for football by taking me to the Durand and DCM tournament matches, encouraging me to play and discussing football with me almost daily. I also dedicate this work to my mother, the late Soona Kapadia, who developed in me a love for reading, as well as to my late sister, Bunny Page, who bought me my first book about sports with her first pay cheque. The book was on cricket (*The Ashes Crown the Year* by Jack Fingleton), but it inculcated in me a lifelong passion for reading about all kinds of sports, which continues till this day.

Abbreviations

AFC	Asian Football Confederation
AIFF	All India Football Federation
AIR	All India Radio
BFA	Bombay Football Association
BNR	Bengal Nagpur Railway
BSF	Border Security Force
CFC	Calcutta Football Club
CIL	Chief of Inspectorate Lines
CPL	Central Police Lines
DFTS	Durand Football Tournament Society
DSA	Delhi Soccer Association
DSC	District Sports Council
EBR	Eastern Bengal Railways
EME	Electrical and Mechanical Engineers
FA	Football Association
FIFA	Fédération Internationale de Football Association
FSDL	Football Sports Development Limited
GFA	Goa Football Association
HAL	Hindustan Aeronautics Limited
HFA	Hyderabad Football Association
IAF	Indian Air Force
IFA	Indian Football Association
IOA	Indian Olympic Association
IOC	International Olympic Committee
IOS	Infinity Optimal Solutions

ISL	Indian Super League
ITI	Indian Telephone Industries
JDT	Johor Darul Ta'zim
KBL	Kalyani Black Label
KFA	Kerala Football Association
MDFA	Malabar District Football Association
MEG	Madras Engineering Group
MFA	Mizoram Football Association
MLS	Major League Soccer
MRC	Madras Regimental Centre
NFL	National Football League
NIS	National Institute of Sports
NWIFA	North-West India Football Association
PFA	Punjab Football Association
PSEB	Punjab State Electricity Board
RAC	Rajasthan Armed Constabulary
SAF	South Asian Federation
SAFF	South Asian Football Federation
SAG	Special Area Games
SAI	Sports Authority of India
SBT	State Bank of Travancore
SRC	Sikh Regimental Centre
SSCB	Services Sports Control Board
TFA	Tata Football Academy
WIFA	Western India Football Association

Prologue

The 'Brazil of Asia'

India's greatest victory in international football so far, the gold medal at the 4th Asian Games in Jakarta in 1962, almost did not happen. In the opening preliminary league match the Koreans had beaten India 2-0. The road to the final was not easy. India qualified as the second team in the group by beating Thailand 4-1 and Japan 2-0. In the match against Thailand, stopper-back Jarnail Singh, considered Asia's best defender in the 1960s, sustained a head injury after colliding with an opponent and received ten stitches on his forehead. India played with ten men as the substitution rule was not yet applicable. India's most successful coach, Syed Abdul Rahim, made some shrewd changes in the formation. Arun Ghosh played as a stopper, and T. Balaram, one of India's greatest forwards, was shifted to the midfield. Arun Ghosh clicked as a stopper-back for the rest of the tournament.

In the semi-finals against South Vietnam, coach Rahim gambled by playing Jarnail as a centre-forward. He could not be played in defence because of his bandaged forehead, which would have prevented him from heading the ball. Rahim knew that playing Jarnail was a psychological advantage as many Asian players feared him for his hard tackling and intimidating physical approach. Additionally, Jarnail had started his career as a centre-forward and liked to move forward and take shots at the goal. The move worked as Jarnail scored India's second goal after receiving a through-pass from skipper Chuni Goswami. In those days South Vietnam fielded a team that had the experience of playing in France and were a formidable opponent. They levelled the score 2-2 in the fifty-eighth minute. However, Chuni Goswami scored the match-winner after a solo dash and clever dribbling in the seventy-third minute.

On the night before the final, the players were tense and turning and tossing about in bed, unable to sleep. Goswami, along with P.K. Banerjee, Balaram, Jarnail, Trilok Singh, midfielder F.A. Franco and some others, decided to go for a walk to soothe their jangling nerves.

As they were softly descending the stairs they saw a small light glowing in the darkness. P.K. recalled, 'We stopped, scared, thinking it was a ghost. But then we mustered our courage and went down the stairs. There, to our surprise, we saw Rahim sitting, smoking a Charminar cigarette in his cupped hands.'

An astute and sympathetic coach, Rahim realized the tension the players were facing. Instead of admonishing them for not sleeping, he said, 'Let us go and take a walk.'

They walked silently. Rahim said in a husky voice, *'Kal mujhe aap logon se ek tofa chahiye* [I want a gift from you all],' as they returned to the camp. He later said, *'Kal aap log sona jit lo* [Win the gold tomorrow].'

Franco recalled that this was the first time they had heard 'the old man so emotional'. The players did not realize it then but the 1962 Asian Games was Rahim's last hurrah. When the team landed in Kolkata (then known as Calcutta) he was sick and was rushed to Hyderabad for treatment. He was diagnosed with lung cancer.

Many experts consider the 1962 team, with an average age of twenty-four years, as the greatest-ever Indian football side. Noted coach and former international player Subhash Bhowmick even said that with proper physical conditioning, India's victorious squad could have played in the World Cup in Chile held the same year. Ironically, the Indian Olympic Association (IOA) did not think the players had a chance of winning a medal even at the Asian Games, and due to a paucity of foreign exchange, the team's departure was not cleared until the last minute.

The victory was hard-won due to other difficult circumstances as well. At Jakarta, Guru Dutt Sondhi, India's representative to the International Olympic Committee (IOC) had criticized the hosts, Indonesia, for excluding both Israel and Taiwan from the games for political reasons. Thus, from the beginning, the crowds were unwelcoming towards India and there were even violent demonstrations against Indian participants. Jarnail Singh, in conversation with me, often recalled the prevailing atmosphere of hostility. As a devout Sikh, Jarnail always wore a turban, which made him very conspicuous. To avoid the hostility of the passionate crowds, Jarnail had to travel sitting on the floor in the team bus!

In the face of these challenges and while battling his illness, the legendary S.A. Rahim used subtle ploys to motivate the Indian players on the day of the final. In the dressing room, before the match began, the entire squad held hands and sang the national anthem, 'Jana Gana Mana'. They sang it again at half-time. Coach Rahim had instilled great team spirit in the squad, which had left Kolkata for Jakarta on Independence Day in 1962. It was considered a good omen, and because of Rahim's persuasive skills they felt like freedom fighters. The team's fitness levels too were exemplary despite the limited availability of training camps.

Rahim's great ability was being able to create a club-like atmosphere in the national team, with an emphasis on cohesiveness and confidence. His intense practice sessions had many variations, as players were used in different positions, with a focus on individual training with the ball. A teacher in his earlier years, he had invented pithy slogans to motivate his players, like 'Soccer is a passing game and a game of open spaces,' 'Soccer depends upon 2L + 2H [legs, lungs, heart and head]' and 'Follow the opponent as soon as you lose the ball.'[1]

Recalling the final on 5 September 1962 against South Korea, Jarnail said, 'The capacity crowd of over 1 lakh booed us and did not even pay respect to our national anthem. When the ball came in our half, such was the din that the referee's whistle was not audible. When we attacked there was pin-drop silence.'

As most of the Indian contingent had returned home a day before, the team had limited support. Franco, noted for his exemplary work-rate and courage, recalled that the Pakistan hockey team (who had beaten India 2-0 in the final the previous day) were at the ground and cheered for India throughout the match.

Rahim instructed his players to play with courage and commitment and shut out the noise of the crowd. He also asked them to avoid the offside trap as it would be difficult to hear the referee's whistle.

Due to their injuries, Rahim improvised with the playing eleven. Jarnail was used as a bustling centre-forward to harass the Korean defence into making errors. The Indian players were so motivated that some of them overcame sickness and injuries to play in the final. Peter Thangaraj replaced Prodyut Burman, who had played all the matches till then as goalkeeper.

Thangaraj had just recovered from a bout of flu, but played because coach Rahim felt his height gave India a psychological advantage. Trilok Singh, the right-back, was in agonizing pain because of a cut toenail but played with grit and courage. Towards the end of the final match, Jarnail was again bleeding from the forehead but refused to exit the ground.

Rahim used Yousuf Khan as a withdrawn forward, and India played in the 3-3-4 system, which bemused the South Koreans, who had lined up in the traditional 3-2-5 system. India started at a scorching pace, and right-winger P.K. Banerjee scored with a stiff angular shot in the seventeenth minute. Jarnail Singh followed with a measured volley in the twentieth minute. South Korea reduced the margin in the second-half, but India held on and emerged 2-1 to win the Asian Games football gold medal for the second time after 1951.

Although there was no footage of the stunning display by India in the 1962 Asian Games, when the 1963 Durand Cup final took place between Mohun Bagan and Andhra Police, Indian fans knew they would be watching some of the best players in Asia. Tickets for the match, priced between Re 1 and Rs 25, were sold out a day in advance. There were heated debates at dinner tables, in coffee houses and on local buses about whether Mohun Bagan's Jarnail Singh and T.A. Rahman would be able to stop the rampaging

Zulfiqaruddin and Yousuf Khan, or whether Chuni Goswami and Arumainayagam would be able to penetrate the rugged Andhra Police defence.

Fresh from the victory, Indian football was all the rage and the star players were no less than demigods. The ace players of the 1962 final, like P.K. Banerjee, Chuni Goswami and T. Balaram, played attractive, skilful, attacking football, which was a delight to behold. It wasn't without reason that India was then called the 'Brazil of Asia'.

INDIA'S SQUAD AT THE 1962 ASIAN GAMES, JAKARTA

Goalkeepers: Peter Thangaraj and Prodyut Burman (West Bengal)

Defenders: O. Chandrasekhar (Bombay), Jarnail Singh and Arun Ghosh (both West Bengal) and Trilok Singh (Services)

Midfielders: F.A. Franco (Bombay), D.M.K. Afzal (Andhra Pradesh), Ram Bahadur and Prasanto Sinha (West Bengal)

Forwards: P.K. Banerjee (Railways), Chuni Goswami (Captain), T. Balaram and Arumainayagam (all West Bengal), D.E. Ethiraj (Services) and Yousuf Khan (Andhra Pradesh)

Coach: S.A. Rahim
Manager: Nurul Amin (Assam)

Results: 26 Aug: Lost to South Korea 0-2; 28 Aug: Beat Thailand 4-1 (P.K. Banerjee: 2, Chuni Goswami, Balaram); 29 Aug: Beat Japan 2-0 (P.K. Banerjee, Balaram)
Semi-final: 1 Sept: Beat South Vietnam 3-2 (Chuni Goswami: 2, Jarnail Singh)
Final: 4 Sept: Beat South Korea 2-1 (P.K. Banerjee, Jarnail Singh)

Introduction

One winter evening in 1961, while taking a stroll, my father and I walked over to the Old Delhi Railway Station. On the platform—there were no security restrictions in those days—there was a buzz of excitement and a crescendo of noise. Hundreds of men, including the coolies, were chanting, '*Kalka Mail aa rahi hai, East Bengal aa rahi hai, Durand jeetne aa rahi hai.*' I was a child of nine and was intrigued by the chanting, the festive atmosphere, the cheering supporters, and the happy, anticipatory looks on their faces.

The next evening the crowd was even larger. Their chanting reverberated around the entire station, '*Dakshin Express aa rahi hai, Andhra Police aa rahi hai, Durand jeetne aa rahi hai.*' Suddenly the crowd surged towards the train as it slid to a halt by the platform. Some men emerged from the compartment and were immediately garlanded. There were shouts of 'Zindabad!', a bearded man and some others were hoisted on to shoulders by the assembled crowd and, amidst vociferous cheers, carried out of the station. I watched, entranced—to me, it seemed like they were the most popular men in the world. In my childlike imagination they were the real heroes, and I wanted to be like them when I grew up.

The teams that had arrived at the Old Delhi Railway Station—East Bengal and Andhra Police (known as Hyderabad City Police till 1958)—were then India's premier football sides. They were going to play in the Durand Cup, India's oldest football tournament and the third-oldest in the world. Such was the breathless excitement for local Indian football teams, not only in Delhi but in many other parts of the country too.

The players' simple attire (trousers and dark coats) and humble demeanour as they stepped out of the train were quite remarkable. It did not strike me then but now I realize that the great players of these two clubs just blended into the crowds that had come to cheer them. There were no flashy clothes, expensive watches or fancy hairstyles. There was no prima-donna behaviour, and they were happy to mingle and chatter with the hordes of supporters who had gathered on the platform. The only aspect that set them apart from the crowd was their slim, athletic bodies, and that some of them were quite muscular.

When East Bengal walked out, the most popular player was the chubby-faced Ram Bahadur. My father told me that he was India's best midfielder, had played in the Olympics a year ago and was very agile. The strapping, bearded Yousuf Khan was greeted with loud cheers by Andhra Police fans. He was hoisted on the shoulders of a dozen young men and carried triumphantly out of the railway station. Another striking and popular personality in this team was the goalkeeper, Mohammed Salim, with his Tarzan-like physique. They were the middle-class and working-class heroes of Indian football.

Football fans in India today may find it hard to believe that one of the oldest rivalries in world football—ranked alongside such famous rivalries as Real Madrid vs Barcelona, Boca Juniors vs River Plate (Argentina), Celtic vs Rangers (Scotland), A.C. Milan vs Internazionale (Italy), Liverpool vs Manchester United (England) and Al Ahly vs Zamalek (Egypt)—is between none other than East Bengal and Mohun Bagan. A premier football magazine *World Soccer*, in its December 2015 issue, rates the East Bengal vs Mohun Bagan match as amongst the fifty-biggest derbies in world football. And this is despite the fact that the Indian national team languishes at an extremely low spot in the Fédération Internationale de Football Association (FIFA) rankings (they were at no. 163 in the June 2016 list).

All the other listed rivalries are from countries in the top fifty of FIFA's ranking list. The only other Asian derby that is listed is

Esteghlal vs Persepolis of Iran. However, this derby is a relatively recent one, with the clubs playing each other for the first time in 1968. FIFA too has acknowledged this amongst the highest-attended club games in the world.[1] The East Bengal vs Mohun Bagan derby has not only retained its appeal but also increased in popularity since it first began in 1924.

The Beginnings

Football in India began in the nineteenth century, introduced by British regimental teams and missionaries during colonial rule. No exact date is known but it is widely believed that the first organized football match in India was played in 1838 when Etonians beat the Rest of Calcutta 3-0. Then again on 13 April 1854 the Calcutta Club of Civilians and Gentlemen of Barrackpore played a friendly match at the Esplanade grounds near Fort William. Records also indicate that a football match was played in Kolkata in 1868 between teams known as Athenians and the Rest of Calcutta, which was watched by many people. It was organized by a renowned footballer from Eton, Robert Vansittart.

British regimental teams had started playing football in Kolkata and the nearby areas of Dum Dum, Barrackpore and Chinsurah. The Calcutta Football Club (CFC) started in the 1870s but membership was restricted to the upper strata of the British middle class. The tradesmen of Kolkata were annoyed at being left out, and two enthusiastic players, Towfett and Love, pooled their resources together and formed the Trades Club in 1874. Six years later it became the Dalhousie Athletic Club.

Sir Henry Mortimer Durand, the foreign secretary in charge of India from 1884–94, instituted the Durand Cup in Shimla in 1888. It was the first tournament to be established in India, and the third in the world after the FA Cup in England (1872) and the FA Cup in Scotland (1878). The Durand was India's most prestigious football tournament until the National Football League (NFL) was started in 1996–97.

Another tournament, the Rovers Cup, was started in Mumbai (then known as Bombay) in 1891 by British football enthusiasts living there. Initially a competition for the regimental teams, it eventually became an all-India tournament. The first football association to be set up in India was the Indian Football Association (IFA) in 1893, although it was only a governing body for football in Kolkata. Three members of Dalhousie Club, J. Sutherland, A.R. Brown and M.B. Lindsay, donated money to buy a huge shield and started the IFA Shield in 1893. It would be decades before the local people of Bengal became enamoured by football (for details, see Chapter 1: 'Bengal'). Apart from Kolkata, other cities where football developed were the garrison towns of Ambala, Bengaluru (then known as Bangalore), Delhi, Chennai (then known as Madras), Hyderabad, Peshawar and Dhaka (then known as Dacca). The last two cities were then part of undivided India. While British troops and missionaries were present all over India, some states like Gujarat, Rajasthan and Madhya Pradesh did not take to football. There seems to be no apparent cause for this.

The British Army played a major role in popularizing the game in several parts of the country. The unexpected victory of Aizawl FC in April 2017 in the 10th Hero I-League can be traced back to an English soldier Herbert Vaughan of the British Army's Medical Corps, who made football popular in the remote state of Mizoram. In 1944 he was posted in the Lushai Hills and played every evening at the Assam Rifles ground, now known as the Lammual Stadium. Football was being played in Mizoram then but it was Vaughan who taught the Mizos the tactical and technical aspects of the game. On Vaughan's death in January 2016, his Mizo wife and entire family flew down from Spain and Sheffield to fulfil his dying wish: to have his ashes scattered at the Lammual Stadium.[2]

Football gradually became popular in several cities due to local leagues and tournaments in which newly formed Indian clubs also participated. However, three famous victories—Mohun Bagan in the 1911 IFA Shield at Kolkata, the Bangalore Muslims in the 1937 Rovers Cup at Mumbai, and Mohammedan Sporting in the 1940 Durand Cup at Delhi—galvanized spectator interest and inspired the start of new clubs and youngsters to play the game. All three iconic triumphs also had significant political implications. The feel-good factor created amongst the local communities was reflected in different forms of nationalist discourses by various political forces.

The IFA Shield final was widely covered in both the local and national press. It was even mentioned in the international media in both England and Australia. By becoming the first Indian team to win the IFA Shield, Mohun Bagan became a nationalist symbol early on in 1911. Some social historians believe that this victory, of eleven barefooted Bengali boys against the hard-tackling and physically fitter British regimental teams, boosted the zeal for nationalism amongst the colonized people in the state. For Bengal it was also a special victory because the British had announced the shifting of the capital from Kolkata to Delhi that very year. Above all, in keeping with the ethos of the age, it reflected Hindu–Muslim unity in overcoming the representatives of the colonial empire, at least on the football field. Muslim fans spontaneously joined in the victory celebrations of Mohun Bagan on their journey back to north Kolkata, and Urdu newspapers hailed this triumph as shattering colonial myths of racial superiority.

The Bangalore Muslims became the first Indian team to win the Rovers Cup (started in 1891), when they beat Mohammedan Sporting 1-0 in the final in 1937. Despite their name, the Bangalore Muslims were cosmopolitan in outlook, and in the 1937 squad there were four non-Muslims. A special reception was organized in Bengaluru by the local Congress Party members for the winning team. They were felicitated as representatives of secularism and a nationalist ethos that involved both the major communities in the country. The victory was seen as a symbol of Hindu–Muslim cooperation. For the Congress, it strengthened the party's claim that India should remain an undivided and secular country after Independence. The *Bombay Chronicle* reported that its editor, Syed Abdullah Brelvi, told the meeting, 'The most pleasing feature of their victory was that it was achieved by a team which consisted of Hindus and Muslims.'[3]

The first team to break the monopoly of British regimental teams in the Durand Cup was Mohammedan Sporting in the 1940 final.

Just like Mohun Bagan's historic 1911 IFA Shield win, this victory too had massive social and political undercurrents. Mohammedan Sporting's phenomenal successes in the Calcutta League (also known as the Calcutta Football League) and the 1940 Durand Cup occurred when Indian politics was polarized between the Indian National Congress and the Muslim League. The acrimonious communal politics of that era was reflected in the football stadiums, which sometimes became violence-prone, especially in Kolkata.

For the local Muslim population of Delhi, Mohammedan Sporting's victory was a kind of psychological liberation from the humiliation suffered at the hands of the British. Mohammedan Sporting's 1940 Rovers and Durand Cup successes instilled both pride and unity amongst the Muslim community at a crucial juncture during the freedom struggle, when the idea of Pakistan was being mooted. Cannily, Muhammad Ali Jinnah and the Muslim League leaders used this to their advantage. Jinnah, in 1941, referred to this historic triumph when he addressed Muslim students in Mumbai and said, 'The discipline that sports teach must be harnessed for the benefit of the Muslim community as a whole.'[4]

Clubs, Tournaments and Spectatorship

Earlier on, football in India was identity and club-based, unlike cricket, which was based on state loyalties. Although different communities identified with different clubs, teams like Mohammedan Sporting, Mohun Bagan, East Bengal and even the Bangalore Muslims had a pan-Indian identity. While their core groups of supporters were from their home cities of Kolkata and Bengaluru respectively, Muslims from all over India identified with the successes of Mohammedan Sporting. Similarly, the Bengalis who had left their ancestral home in the eastern part of undivided Bengal and had settled elsewhere in India were passionate supporters of East Bengal. The same is now true of NorthEast United FC of the Indian Super League (ISL) that gets a lot of support in Delhi because many students from the North-east study and live here.

The clubs, particularly Mohammedan Sporting and East Bengal, also played their role in national integration as they started importing players from several states. Both these clubs introduced a professional ethos into the game in Bengal. Mohammedan Sporting in the 1930s was ahead of its times, with its emphasis on training in gymnasiums, physical fitness, focus on diet and introduction to playing in boots. They were the first Indian club to match the British teams in terms of strength and physical fitness.

The All India Football Federation (AIFF) was formed in 1937. But the Indian national team did not develop an identity until after Independence, when they played in the 1948 London Olympics, when the AIFF joined FIFA. Unlike the hockey team, which became Olympic champions multiple times during the colonial era, the national football team in the 1930s barely played international matches. And when it did take part and was commended for its performance, soon after Independence, there was negligible media coverage. The first FIFA World Cup was held after the Second World War in 1950 in Brazil. Due to certain circumstances, India had made it directly to the final rounds, but it withdrew after the final draw was made. Apart from other reasons, India stayed out primarily because, for the AIFF, the World Cup did not have the same gravitas as the Olympics.[5]

Thus, the passions of football fans in India were aroused by watching derby matches of the local clubs. These games had many social, cultural and political associations. Even amongst the players, club loyalties were paramount, and this continued throughout the twentieth century, at times to the detriment of the national team.

The duration of matches in domestic tournaments used to be seventy minutes and was increased to ninety minutes only in 1967. Even substitutions in matches were allowed in India for the first time in 1960. P.K. Banerjee maintained that 'adjusting to ninety minutes of football in international matches was always difficult as players of my generation were only used to matches of seventy or sixty minutes' duration in the domestic circuit'.

The paradox of Indian football in the twentieth century was that although there were numerous talented players, several of whom were amongst the best in Asia, the physical conditioning and scientific inputs to develop their strength, stamina and fitness were subpar. Indian players were so highly rated that *four* of them were selected for the Asian All-Stars XI in 1966, where they played friendly matches with first-division clubs from England, like Leicester City and Stoke City. These players were skipper and central-defender Jarnail Singh, goalkeeper Peter Thangaraj, left-back Altaf Ahmed and midfielder Yousuf Khan.

Football was a great leveller of a sport in India as it enjoyed a huge fan following across the class divide. For instance, the Delhi league was the sole means of entertainment for those who could not afford holidays in popular hill stations like Mussoorie, Shimla or distant Kashmir. In Kolkata, it was the working-class and lower-middle-class fans who comprised the frenzied support base of the three big clubs. And due to innovative programmes by coaches like S.A. Rahim, players from underprivileged backgrounds too could rise to great heights, enabling people from all classes to identify with the game (for details, see Chapter 2: 'Hyderabad' and the profile of I.M. Vijayan in the 'Hall of Fame').

It was this huge supporter base that enabled Indian football to survive without sponsorships for most of the twentieth century. The major domestic tournaments like the Durand Cup, Rovers Cup and IFA Shield thrived on ticket sales and money obtained from hoardings on the ground. Tickets cost just 10 paise for the local league in Delhi in the 1960s and 25 paise for the popular Calcutta League. Before the advent of satellite television, there was no telecast of foreign leagues in India; coverage of European football and even the World Cup was very limited. Due to this there were no divided loyalties, and homegrown players were heroes for the local population. People flocked to the stadiums, whether in Kolkata, Mumbai or Delhi, to see local clubs in action. The cost of tickets at the Durand Cup was much more than at the local leagues. Tickets would cost 50 paise, Re 1, Rs 2 and Rs 5. For the semi-finals and final, the price would be doubled. Despite the low denomination of tickets, the Durand organizers would manage to collect Rs 5000–10,000 per day. Gate collection would increase to Rs 40,000–50,000 per day when the popular Kolkata clubs played.

To celebrate its centenary year in 1987, the Durand Cup introduced prize money, the first tournament to do so in Indian football. JCT from Phagwara, the winners of the centenary Durand Cup, bagged Rs 1.50 lakh, and runners-up Mohun Bagan got Rs 1 lakh. Other tournaments followed the trend, and gradually all the main domestic tournaments—the Rovers Cup, IFA Shield, DCM Trophy, Federation Cup and Santosh Trophy—introduced prize money. The financial boom in domestic football started in the 1990s. The then secretary of the AIFF, P.P. Lakshmanan, started the Scissors Cup in Kerala, in which the top eight to ten teams of the country participated in a league-cum-knockout tournament. This tournament increased the economic status of the participating clubs as they got cash prizes for each victory. By 2016, the prize money for the Durand Cup was the highest ever, having been raised to Rs 75 lakh.

To provide international exposure to Indian players, the AIFF started the Nehru Cup international tournament in the 1980s. It was first held in Kolkata in January 1982. Thanks to the pioneering efforts of the secretary, Ashoke Ghosh, it was in this tournament that Indian football got its first sponsor, Boroline, who paid a nominal sum of Rs 1 lakh.

Participating in the tournament were the three famous players who later represented Uruguay at the 1986 Mexico World Cup— talented playmaker Enzo Francescoli, and strikers Amaro Nadal and Jorge da Silva, both of whom scored in their winning final in Kolkata. Nadal and da Silva played club football in the Spanish league for Sevilla and Atlético Madrid respectively. China, South Korea, Italy and Yugoslavia were the other countries taking part in the 1982 Nehru Cup. There was massive crowd interest and the huge gate collection enabled the organizers to make a substantial profit of Rs 3.5 lakh. The Nehru Cup was held regularly until 1997, when it had to be discontinued due to lack of sponsorships.

The Nehru Cup was revived after a decade in 2007, this time with prize money. On the sixtieth anniversary of India's independence, the tournament named after India's first prime minister was held in the capital for the first time. ONGC was persuaded about its potential and paid Rs 1 crore to be the title sponsor. Notably, India emerged champions of this tournament for the first time, beating Syria 1-0 in the final. In the 2007, 2009 and 2012 Nehru Cups the total prize money was $100,000, the highest ever, with $40,000 for the winner and $20,000 for the runners-up. The winner of each game got $2500.

Media Coverage, the NFL/I-League and the Indian Super League

In the 1950s and 1960s, the semi-finals and finals of all the major tournaments in India used to be broadcast live on All India Radio (AIR). Doordarshan (TV) in India came into existence in 1959, and the first telecast was of the historic Republic Day Parade on 26 January 1960. Doordarshan was separated from Akashvani (radio) on 1 April 1976. From the mid-1970s onwards Doordarshan became involved in promoting football in the country.

The most historic coverage was in September 1977, when the New York Cosmos team, including the legendary player Pelé, visited Kolkata and played a match against India's champion club of those days—Mohun Bagan. The match was broadcast on AIR and telecast live on Doordarshan, with a repeat telecast on the national network the next day (a Sunday), so that viewers all over India could have a glimpse of the greatest player of the twentieth century, Pelé of Brazil. The match ended in a 2-2 draw.

Historically, both Doordarshan and AIR have helped to popularize sports, particularly football in India, through live coverage of all major domestic tournaments. Since the mid-1970s Doordarshan has been live-telecasting the final—and on most occasions the semi-finals as well—of these tournaments. Doordarshan often telecasts matches in regional languages like Bengali and Malayalam, but for national-level telecasts, the format used is alternating commentary in both Hindi and English.

In the mid-1990s the AIFF negotiated with various satellite TV companies to develop the game professionally in the country. The inaugural edition of the NFL started in 1997 and was telecast on the Star Sports–ESPN network. AIFF's marketing partners,

International Management Group, had roped in Philips as the title sponsor. In January 1998 the AIFF switched allegiance to the national network Doordarshan because of a lucrative financial deal and the promise of live coverage of 100 matches per year, mostly from the prestigious NFL.

Doordarshan's payment for exclusive TV rights of Indian football was Rs 5 crore per annum, which escalated every year. The deal between AIFF and Doordarshan was initially for five years but was further extended till 2005. The NFL was played on a home-and-away basis in the league format, and matches were held all across India, involving teams from Kolkata, Goa, Mumbai, Bengaluru, Kochi, Chennai and Punjab. During this period—January 1998 to May 2005—live telecasts of the league matches popularized the NFL in the country.

From 2005–09 the NFL (which became the I-League in 2007–08) was telecast live on ZEE Sports and from 2010 onwards on the Ten Sports network. To further popularize football, Doordarshan and all the other channels introduced the concept of repeat telecasts. India has very few stadiums with floodlights and hence matches were mostly held during the afternoon, which restricted viewership. To ensure that fans could watch their popular teams and the clubs got greater visibility, Doordarshan initiated the concept of same-day telecasts later in the evening or night, during prime time.

The sale of TV rights has gradually become a major source of income for the AIFF. Increased visibility on TV has also attracted more sponsors. This has helped clubs to increase their budgets and provide better facilities and pay packages to the players. The legends of the past all worked in public- or private-sector enterprises to supplement their income and secure their future. Payment in domestic football was very minimal. They also travelled by public transport and very few owned cars. As pay scales have risen rapidly in the twenty-first century, the players' lifestyles have also changed. All the top players are now full-time professionals who expect substantial monetary returns for their hard work.

The real peak in remuneration for players came with the start of the Hero ISL in 2014. Having a different format from the

NFL, the ISL is a franchise-based tournament with eight teams. It is supported by the central sponsorship pool, television revenue, individual sponsors for teams, and ticket and merchandise sales. The ISL has brought about a financial revolution in Indian football. As many of the top Indian players began to play for the lucrative ISL teams, their incomes from their clubs too increased substantially.

With the ISL there's been a flood of famous foreign players coming to play club football in India, like the 2006 World Cup–winning team member Del Piero (Italy) and runners-up team member Florent Malouda (France). However, international players have been playing here since the 1940s—the very first was Fred Pugsley from Myanmar (then known as Burma). Majid Bishkar who played for East Bengal and Mohammedan Sporting during 1980–84 had represented Iran in the 1978 World Cup, and Emeka Ezeugo (played for Mohammedan Sporting and East Bengal in the late 1980s) represented Nigeria in the 1994 World Cup. When I met Ezeugo in the US, he was grateful to Indian football and Indian coach Syed Nayeemuddin for developing him.

This Book

Football has been uniquely tied to the subcontinent's history and has closely reflected the social and cultural life of India. Where the rivalry between Mohun Bagan and East Bengal mirrored the regional conflict within Bengal, Mohammedan Sporting was perceived as a unifier of Muslims across the subcontinent. The Hyderabad City Police team were all the rage in Delhi, and it is to their patronage that Karim's in Jama Masjid owes its huge popularity. Poetry and music were composed to celebrate landmark victories, and clever parodies of popular songs were sung to encourage a favourite team at the stadium. Loyalty to certain clubs has run through generations amongst families and could sometimes be deeper than religious identity.

Until the last decade of the twentieth century, watching the best club sides was the epitome of football entertainment in India. The contrast in playing styles also made club football very alluring to watch. The Kolkata clubs had the nimbleness of the Brazilians and often indulged in body feints and clever dribbling. In contrast, teams from Andhra Pradesh resembled the Spanish players of 2008–12, as they relied more on combination and accurate passing to wear down the opposition. Watching Indian football was a pleasure and delight as the top teams had both speed and skill.

My involvement in the game since the 1960s has enabled me to witness some of the most epic matches between the top clubs. And as a sports journalist, I have delved deep into the history of the game and have closely known some of the best players, coaches and administrators. This book will remember and celebrate the glory years of football in India, even as it considers the promise the present generation holds. Young talent is being nurtured by local clubs in many states where the game is popular. The AIFF too has been taking initiatives to provide international exposure to upcoming players. Three U-19 players were sent to train with the French club FC Metz for some months in August 2016. The director of FC Metz, Denis Schaeffer, was enthusiastic and said they wished to be associated with the development of football in India. The U-17 World Cup will be held in India for the first time in October 2017, which perhaps heralds a bright future for the game in the country.

Through personal and objective accounts, I will provide a glimpse of the rich legacy of Indian football. The focus is on the states and clubs that have nurtured top-notch players and the important domestic tournaments that have doubled the heartbeats of fans over the decades. By profiling the great legends, whom I either interviewed or knew personally, and describing the skilful football they played, I hope to bring to life a time when nothing seemed beyond the grasp of Indian players.

It has been a roller-coaster ride for India, with unexpected dips and rises and turns, as is bound to happen in football. But we may now be at the threshold of a new era, where Indians can prove themselves in the world arena, thus claiming the beautiful game as their own once again.

The Major Tournaments

The swinging sixties passed me by. It was the decade of the Beatles, who became an iconic group with an international following, and were trendsetters in rock and roll, popular culture and personal liberation. The Beatles hairstyle, also known as the moptop, was all the rage amongst my schoolmates and friends. But my hair remained relatively neatly trimmed. Whilst several of my friends flaunted fading, tight-fitting jeans, my interest in clothes was limited. I was no partygoer and my life revolved around football—playing, reading about it and watching matches at the stadium, as there was no TV in those days.

Every year, I would long for December as the Durand Cup was held in Delhi that month. It also happened to be our school vacation when we had total freedom and no studies or homework to bother about. All my December holidays followed a predictable pattern. The mornings were spent playing football (or occasionally hockey and cricket) in the vast open spaces just outside the Kashmiri Gate wall, followed by a hurried lunch, and then I was off to my paradise, the Delhi Gate Stadium (renamed Ambedkar Stadium in 1983), to witness the Durand matches.

Like any normal teenager, I too had raging hormones and was attracted to some girls in my school bus (the students of St Columba's School and the neighbouring Convent of Jesus and Mary used to travel by the same bus, which led to many blossoming romances). But when football was on in the capital—the DCM Trophy invariably in October and the Durand in November–December—my interest in the opposite sex faded. I attended no Christmas or New Year parties, as all the thrills of my life were at the Delhi Gate Stadium.

My parents did not mind my unusual adolescence. They later said it kept me fit, out of trouble and relatively inexpensive. The entrance ticket to the popular stands in the Durand Cup was 25 paise for children under twelve years, 50 paise otherwise and Re 1 for the semi-finals and final. The season ticket in the 1950s cost Rs 30, and in the 1960s to the 1970s it was just Rs 50. I used to buy one of these so I could see every match of the tournament.

For us, the Durand was the epitome of great football as the best Indian clubs and institutional sides participated. The DCM Trophy also attracted good club sides, but till 1990 Mohun Bagan disdained participation in a tournament they regarded as commercial. Mohun Bagan president Dhiren Dey used to contemptuously remark, 'We do not play in a tournament which sells towels and bed sheets.'[1] So in the Durand I always had the added attraction of watching India's oldest and most famous club play.

Watching the Durand was a whole experience. After the match was over, analysis and gossip sessions would start (what the Bengalis call an 'adda'). People would huddle in small groups or sit at tea stalls, discussing Indian football. These conversations would go on till late evening, discussing the merits of various players and exchanging anecdotes. Sometimes the players would also join in and that would triple our excitement. I used to lap up all the information and discuss it again with my friends on the way home, or share it with my father when he returned from work.

It was December 1965. Mohun Bagan were aiming to win their third successive Durand Cup and thus become the first Indian side to do so. One morning as I was leaving with my friends to play, our servant came running and told me to return home as my maternal grandmother, who had been suffering from cancer, had expired. I was very attached to the old woman and used to chat with her on returning from school. I rushed home and, on seeing her dead body, wept bitterly.

But by midday I came to know that Mohun Bagan were playing their replayed quarter-final match against Chief of

Inspectorate Lines (CIL) Bangalore that day. How could I miss that game? Bagan ruled the social sentiment in those days, the most formidable team in India. To see players like stopper-back Jarnail Singh—then also captain of the Asian All-Stars team— midfielder Mariappa Kempaiah and forwards Chuni Goswami, Arumainayagam and Ashok Chatterjee was sheer bliss. I started fretting and behaving like a spoilt brat. My mother, who loved me deeply and understood my tantrums well, took me aside and quietly gave me what was then the princely sum of Rs 1.50. She said, 'Stop moping, take this money, eat something as I cannot give you lunch at home. Go and see your match but come back early and do not stop to talk.'

As the entire family gathered for prayers near the dead body, I slipped away unnoticed. Food was cheap in those days so I ate a sumptuous lunch of aloo puri for less than a rupee at Mithan Lal Halwai (the shop still exists today) and then made for the stadium.

I followed my mother's instructions and did not stay to chat after the match. I reached home and tried to melt into the assembled gathering of family members, neighbours and friends. The prayer ceremony had just finished and our jovial priest, the late Ervard Darius Bagli, was about to leave. Seeing me he came over to talk. I froze, thinking he would reprimand me for my absence. But Darius Bagli was a football buff and used to watch tournament matches dressed in his starched white pyjamas, *dagli* and cap (typical Parsi attire). He said in Gujarati, '*Suun thayun Mohun Bagan na match ma?* [What happened in Mohun Bagan's match?]' I happily narrated to him how Bagan had won the match and qualified for the semi-finals. Emboldened, I asked him whether there would be any religious ceremonies when Bagan played Andhra Police in the semi-final. He winked and said, 'Do not worry, I want to watch that match too.'

Minutes later, my uncle, the late Lt Colonel Phiroze Keshwala, confronted me on the veranda. He had fought in the decisive Battle of El-Alamein in the Second World War for the Duke of Connaught's Own Rajputana Rifles, and was a stickler for discipline and punctuality. I braced myself for a dressing-down.

Instead, he said, 'Well, what happened? Did Mohun Bagan get through?' Flushed with relief, I gave a detailed description of the match and the prospects for the semi-final.

Later, as I went into the rooms, my father spotted me and came over. I thought I would be third-time unlucky as he was understandably upset at having lost his mother. But he too asked me about the match results. I gladly narrated Bagan's win in some detail to my father as well. Although I did not realize it then, I had probably taken my first steps in the journey towards becoming a football writer and commentator. I used to watch all the matches with great concentration, so the great moves and dribbling skills remained embedded in my mind. I tried to copy the great players of Indian football and emulate their ball skills—not very successfully, but my memories of them remained intact.

From 1960 to 2016, I watched every Durand Cup final, initially as a fan and then from 1980 onwards as a journalist and commentator. Apart from the Durand, there were a number of other domestic tournaments where the talent of Indian footballers was put to the test and players were picked to represent India on the international stage based on their performance. The Durand (Delhi), Rovers Cup (Mumbai), IFA Shield (Kolkata), DCM (Delhi), Federation Cup, Santosh Trophy (state-level), NFL (now I-League) and the ISL are the major tournaments that are or have been played in the Indian football circuit. Here, I offer a round-up of these key competitions where Indian clubs and states clash and their rivalries entertain excited fans.

In the old British tradition, a blue ribbon was tied to the most important trophies, so the AIFF used to call the Durand, Rovers Cup and IFA Shield the 'blue ribbon' tournaments. The viewership for these competitions gives a sense of the intense enthusiasm for domestic football in India. Crowds in the range of 5000 to 20,000 would turn up for the earlier rounds, right through to the semi-finals. A Durand final was usually a full house, with crowds of 20,000 or 40,000 coming to witness it at either the Ambedkar Stadium or the National Stadium respectively. An IFA Shield final at the Eden Gardens would usually see a crowd of 30,000, and up to 70,000 if it was a Kolkata derby (Mohun Bagan vs East Bengal). The newer Salt Lake Stadium has even seen a crowd of 1 lakh for Kolkata derbies. Even for the crucial matches in the inaugural NFL in 1997, there were crowds of 25,000–30,000 at the Nehru Stadium in Margao, and up to 70,000 at the Salt Lake Stadium when Kolkata clubs were playing.

The Majestic Durand

The Durand was the most prestigious tournament in the Indian football circuit until the late twentieth century. Started in 1888, it is the oldest football tournament in India and the third-oldest in the world. Sir Mortimer Durand instituted the tournament as recreation for British troops; in its first edition, six British regimental teams and two Scottish regiments took part.

Before 1940, the Durand was held in September in Shimla, the summer capital of the British Raj. The matches were played at picturesque Annandale, surrounded by beautiful hilly forests, and the tournament was associated with pomp, pageantry and grandeur. In the final, officers and their wives came dressed in their best. Smartly attired military bands played tuneful marching tunes before the match and during the interval. Pennants of the participating British regimental teams fluttered in the sun. The Viceroy of India would personally hand over the prizes.

The Durand Cup was popularized in the schools of Shimla by inviting students to witness the matches at nominal rates. In addition, the three magnificent trophies—the Durand Cup, the Shimla Trophy and the Viceroy's Cup (now replaced by the President's Cup)—were prominently displayed at Whiteways and Ridley, a prominent shopping centre on the famous Mall Road. Former Delhi state player and national referee K.G. Kakkar recalled the excitement the display of these glittering trophies created. It was in fact these trophies that got him interested in football. His dream was to play in this illustrious event.

Initially the tournament was played only by the army, but over the years civilian teams also started participating. The first

Indian club to be invited to play in the Durand were Mohun Bagan in 1922. However, Indian civilian teams generally fared badly before the superior speed, strength and fitness of the British regimental teams. Realizing this, the Durand authorities came up with a unique idea in 1937, to have a separate tournament for all the teams knocked out in the first round. This competition was known as the Little Durand, or 'Chhota' Durand, and was held concurrently with the main tournament.

Before 1940, there were two exceptional times when an Indian civilian team performed well. The first such team to contest the Durand final were the East India Railways in 1927. Aided by renowned players, the Railways team fought gallantly before losing 0-2 to the York and Lancaster Regiment. In 1936, another Kolkata-based side, Aryans Club, entered the semi-finals and took on the Green Howards Regiment. In a pulsating match with end-to-end action, the barefooted Aryans players gradually wrested ascendancy. Towards the closing stages of the match they got a penalty kick. They converted the kick but for no apparent reason the goal was disallowed. They took the kick again and scored, and again it was disallowed by the referee Fletcher. When they scored on the third attempt and the referee still did not grant the goal, a massive protest erupted and the Indian crowd invaded the field claiming that the British referee was biased. The match was abandoned. The Aryans refused to play the next day and left Shimla in disgust.

For forty-five years various British regimental teams held sway in this tournament (it was not held during the First World War, 1914–19). The first team to break this monopoly were the mighty Mohammedan Sporting team, when they beat the Royal Warwickshire Regiment 2-1 in the 1940 final. This marked a turning point for Indian football.

The Durand is the only tournament in which the winners get three trophies—the Durand Cup, the Viceroy's Trophy (replaced by the President's Cup after Independence) and the Shimla Trophy (from 1904 onwards). A medal with Durand inscriptions is also awarded to each member of the winning and runners-up teams.

Each trophy has a unique history. The original Durand Cup consisted of a silver football supported on an ebony stand, on which were inscribed the names of the winning teams and players. This cup was won by the Highland Light Infantry for three successive years from 1893–95 and thus remained in their permanent possession. Sir Mortimer Durand presented another cup in 1896 and the Black Watch Regiment got to claim possession next by winning the tournament for three years in a row. The generous Sir Durand donated yet another glittering trophy but with a proviso that this third Durand Cup be turned into an annual challenge cup, with a miniature cup being awarded to the winning team. This trend continued for the next sixty-five years. Finally, in 1965, this annual challenge cup was declared as a rolling trophy by the Durand Football Tournament Society (DFTS) and the miniature cup was discontinued. Since then, the winning team get to keep the Durand Cup for one year.

In pre-Independence days, the Viceroy of India used to annually donate a trophy to the winning team. This practice was discontinued in independent India but the first President, Rajendra Prasad, a keen football enthusiast, generously donated a cup to be awarded to the winning team. The President's Cup is artistically designed, with a circular disc mounted on the Ashoka lion capital, around the sloping edge of which are carved lions and chakras at regular intervals.

The Shimla Trophy has a fascinating story behind it. At the start of the twentieth century, in an attempt to popularize football in northern India, it was decided to rotate the venues of the Durand Cup annually. However, by 1903, the residents of Shimla had become hugely attached to the prestigious tournament and the festive atmosphere it created in the town. To ensure the tournament remained in Shimla, a committee of various government employees and the public donated generously to present another trophy to the winning team. It was named the Shimla Trophy. Similar to the Durand Cup, a miniature trophy was awarded to the winners. In 1965 the Shimla Trophy also became a rolling trophy.

Just after Independence there was a suggestion to send the Durand Cup to Pakistan. Due to the Second World War and the turmoil caused by Partition, the tournament had not been held since 1941. The location of the trophies was unknown. Finally, the Durand Cup and the Shimla Trophy were found in the office of the Joint Commander in Chief, Sir Claude Auchinleck. The then home secretary, H.M. Patel, who was also looking after the matters related to Partition, collected the trophies and kept them in the safe custody of the State Bank of India.

The tournament is always held at the seat of power, so since its resumption in 1950 it has been held in New Delhi, the capital of independent India. The President of India carried on the viceroy's tradition of personally presenting the trophies to the winning team. The ceremony associated with the final was organized with clockwork precision.

Six Indian Presidents, from Rajendra Prasad (1950–62) to Neelam Sanjiva Reddy (1977–82), have graced the Durand final and watched the complete match. During half-time they would have tea with the captains. After 1982 this tradition was discontinued due to security reasons. Silver crockery was used during this special ceremony, and the President would chat about football and sports with the team captains, whilst the military bands would be parading on the field in all their splendour and entertaining the spectators. On the day before the finals, the captains would receive special training on how to conduct themselves before the President.

For about four decades, till the end of the 1980s, the greatness of a player and even clubs was judged by how many Durand finals they had played in and how many Durand titles they had won. A select quartet has won this prestigious tournament with three different clubs: Peter Thangaraj (Madras Regimental Centre [MRC], Mohun Bagan and East Bengal), Shyam Thapa (Gorkha Brigade, East Bengal and Mohun Bagan), I.M. Vijayan (Mohun Bagan, JCT and FC Kochin) and Jo Paul Ancheri (Mohun Bagan, JCT and FC Kochin). From its inception until 1972, the Durand was a knockout tournament. In 1973 they introduced the quarter-final league, in which some seeded teams and some qualified from the knockout rounds took part, followed by a knockout semi-final and final. The penalty shoot-out replaced the replay after a draw from 1971 onwards, although sometimes replays were still held. In 1995, after FIFA formally adopted the system of three points for a win, the Durand and all other tournaments in India used this instead of the two-points system followed earlier.

The Kolkata teams have the best record in India's oldest football tournament. Mohun Bagan are sixteen-time winners and eleven-time runners-up. Bagan is the only team to have won the Durand Cup thrice in a row on two occasions, 1963–65 and 1984–86. East Bengal also have an enviable record, winning it sixteen times and being runners-up ten times. They achieved a hat-trick of triumphs in 1989–91.

There have been three phases of domination and competition in the Durand Cup since 1950. In the 1950s and 1960s, the main challenge to Mohun Bagan and East Bengal came from the legendary Hyderabad City Police (four-time champions, thrice runners-up) and fit Services outfits like MRC Wellington and Gorkha Brigade. For two decades between 1968 and 1988, the Durand final was either contested between teams from Kolkata and Punjab, or else between all-Kolkata or even all-Punjab teams. The rivalry was intense, and with massive crowd support in Delhi, the Punjab sides achieved several successes. The Border Security Force (BSF) won the title seven times and were runners-up twice; JCT Mills won five times and were runners-up seven times.

In the late 1990s and early twenty-first century, the Kolkata sides had new competitors with teams from Goa and Mumbai challenging their supremacy—Salgaocar (1999, 2003 and 2014), Dempo (2006), Churchill Brothers (2007, 2009 and 2011) and Mahindra United (the first side from Mumbai to win the Durand Cup; won in 1998, 2001 and 2007). FC Kochin won the Durand in the year of their debut in 1997, a rare feat.

Regimental Teams

When the tournament was revived in New Delhi, civilian teams had started dominating the field. Regimental teams of the Indian Army were getting pipped at the post though they were not

totally eclipsed. In the 1950s and 1960s, about ten teams from
the services, regiments, the Indian Air Force (IAF) and Indian
Navy regularly took part with distinction in the Durand. These
well-known teams were MRC Wellington, Gorkha Brigade,
Electrical and Mechanical Engineers (EME) Secunderabad,
Madras Engineering Group (MEG) Bangalore, Army Ordnance
Corps Secunderabad, Sikh Regimental Centre (SRC) Meerut and
Bengal Engineering Group Roorkee. The Delhi Garrison, formed
for some years after the 1965 India–Pakistan War, created a
sensation by beating mighty East Bengal to enter the semi-finals
in their first year in the Durand.

MRC Wellington was a name to be reckoned with in the
Durand Cup. In the 1950s and early 1960s they were a well-knit,
cohesive unit which could match the best in the land. In 1955, they
annexed the Durand Cup for the first time, beating IAF 3-2 in the
replayed final. D'Cruz, Alfonso and Alwyn scored for the winners.

In 1958, MRC met the mighty East Bengal in a titanic semi-final
clash. The Delhi Gate Stadium was filled to the brim. One of India's
best goalkeepers ever, the giant Peter Thangaraj, was playing for
MRC. He recalls that his teammates believed that if they could
beat East Bengal, they could win the prestigious Durand Cup for
a second time. East Bengal were a formidable unit, aiming for their
third successive Durand final, but a determined and very fit MRC
triumphed 2-1. For the first time since Independence, the Durand
final was contested between two regimental sides. MRC Wellington,
with Thangaraj in their ranks, ousted the spirited Gorkha Brigade
2-0 in the final. P. Mukundan and Abu Backer scored the goals.

Peter Thangaraj was involved in both their Durand triumphs
of 1955 and 1958. He left for Mohammedan Sporting in 1961.
Inside-forward Kuppaswamy, right-winger Kamachi, D'Cruz,
Alfonso and Mukundan were some of the other great players who
made MRC a formidable team some four decades ago. Thangaraj
considered the 1958 MRC side as one of the fittest and finest
military units that he had played for.

In the 1950s, Gorkha Brigade also produced classy players
and were renowned for their enthralling, attacking football.

A prolific goalscorer, Puran Bahadur had the skill to torment opposing defenders and the charisma to attract large crowds. He was the first Indian to score a hat-trick in an international match, against Pakistan in the 3rd Quadrangular Tournament in Kolkata, a match India won 3-1. Captain Moloy Lahiri was a skilful inside-forward who played for India in the pre-Olympics in 1959–60. Gorkha Brigade were a thrilling side to watch and were extremely popular amongst the fans. The Durand organizers were sure of a near full-house whenever Gorkha Brigade played, and the big teams of India feared the side too.

In the 1954 Durand Cup, they were involved in a match that is considered one of the best ever seen on the lush green surface of the Ambedkar Stadium, when they clashed with the formidable Hyderabad City Police. The latter rallied to win 6-3 from being 0-3 in the first-half, but Gorkha Brigade deserves credit for making it such an epic encounter (for details, see Chapter 2: 'Hyderabad').

In 1966, Gorkha Brigade of Dehradun annexed India's oldest tournament with an enthralling display of speedy, attacking football, never surpassed and rarely equalled. They had some memorable victories on their way to their first-ever Durand triumph. In their second-round match, they trounced Leaders Club Jalandhar, which included the famous Inder Singh, by a thumping margin of 4-1. In the pre-quarter-finals, Magan Singh's Rajasthan Armed Constabulary (RAC) Bikaner held them to a 1-1 draw, but in the replay, the Gorkhas trounced them 8-0. In the quarter-final match—played as a knockout round in those days—Gorkha Brigade beat the famous Mohammedan Sporting 4-0. Then they tumbled mighty Mohun Bagan 2-0 in the semi-finals. In the final, they beat the tenacious SRC 2-0.

The skill, speed and goalscoring abilities of Gorkha Brigade were a source of wonder and delight. They played in the old-fashioned 3-2-5 system, but the versatility of the forwards enabled them to back-pedal and bolster midfield when under pressure, and also initiate counter-attacks. Overall, Gorkha Brigade scored 26 goals and conceded 2 during their 1966 Durand run.

Short-statured Bhupinder Singh Rawat became a crowd favourite. He would hover around the goal area, drift into vacant space and use his blistering speed to break through and score with deft placements or diving headers. With his instinct for the goal, he was the poor man's Paolo Rossi. Nicknamed 'Scooter' by his adoring fans, Bhupinder had the galloping speed of a Carlton Chapman or a Syed Rahim Nabi in the box, and the cool finish of Bhaichung Bhutia. Another highly acclaimed player was Amar Bahadur, noted for his silky dribbling skills and immaculate crosses from the left flank. A quality winger, Amar Bahadur was more versatile and quicker than Alvito D' Cunha at his best; he could cut in and score goals as well. Ranjit Thapa, a box-to-box midfielder or playmaker as inside-forward impressed with his accurate passes, powerful long-range shots with both feet and exemplary work-rate.

Ranjit Thapa felt the win against Mohun Bagan in the semi-finals was his side's most memorable match. Initially Bagan controlled proceedings and their stout defence managed to blunt the Gorkha attack. Just before half-time, Gorkhas changed their approach and used one-touch football to launch attacks. Bhupinder Rawat broke the ice with a dream goal. He bravely flung himself in front of the lunging Jarnail Singh and scored with a diving header at the near post of a Birkha Bahadur cross. Midway through the second-half, Gorkha Brigade sealed victory when Nar Singh scored with a snap shot, a rising left-footer that deceived Mohun Bagan's international custodian Prodyut Burman.

The 1966 triumph by Gorkha Brigade was significant in more ways than one. Ranjit Thapa says that sheer willpower and collective endeavour enabled them to overcome the fancied and rich clubs. The team had no coach and senior players conducted practice. Diet money was meagre at Rs 8 per day, per player. After practice, refreshment was limited to Rs 1.50 per head, which got the players a samosa, a slice of bread and a cup of tea.

It was the third and last time in post-Independence India that two teams from the Services would meet in the Durand final. The earlier two occasions were in 1958 and 1955. Gorkha Brigade's triumph was also significant as it was for the first time that a team had won the prestigious Durand Cup without any internationals in their ranks.

Gorkha Brigade won the Durand Cup once again in 1969, when the mercurial Shyam Thapa, famous for his acrobatic back-volleys, scored the winning goal against rugged BSF in the replayed final. A youthful, new-looking Gorkha Brigade scored 17 goals and conceded just 1 on their way to a memorable triumph. That year there were full-house signs in every match of the Durand Cup from the quarter-final onwards.

Since then Gorkha Brigade have reached the semi-final just once, in 1983, losing 0-3 to Mohun Bagan. Sadly, they are no longer crowd-pullers and the array of talented players they produced in the past are not forthcoming any more. The decline is baffling but is perhaps an apt reflection of the receding interest in regimental sports.

In the 1990s the Services Sports Control Board (SSCB), alarmed at declining standards, started the concept of the Army XI, a select team drawn from different regiments which competed in various tournaments. Somehow this concept has not quite taken off. The Army XI is neither as charismatic nor feared as the regimental teams of yore, like Gorkha Brigade, MRC Wellington or MEG Bangalore. In the 1990s, the Army XI entered the Durand only once, when, in the 1991 semi-finals, they lost 0-4 to the ultimate runners-up BSF. In 2005, the Army XI, coached by Stanley Rozario, won the Durand Cup, overcoming Sporting Clube de Goa in the final 5-4 via the penalty shoot-out. This was, however, a one-off success.

The Legendary K.K. Ganguly

When you think of the Durand Cup, you think of Wing Commander (Retd) K.K. Ganguly, the former secretary of the tournament, who, like a mighty colossus, reigned supreme for over three decades and was renowned for his impeccable administration. His success in raising the status of the Durand during his long tenure (1954–88) made him a legend.

A footballer in college, Ganguly joined the IAF during the Second World War and helped in developing and popularizing sports in the IAF. Later he was manager of the Indian football side that finished runners-up to Israel in the 1964 Asia Cup.

During his tenure, he made the Durand Cup the most prestigious tournament in India. It was the dream of every Indian player from Kashmir to Kanyakumari to win the coveted Durand Cup. Often held in the winter months of Delhi, it was Indian football's grand finale. In all offices of the Central government there would be a half-day on the day of the Durand final to enable employees to witness the match. Special buses ran to and from the stadium to facilitate movement of the crowds.

Attention to detail, meticulous administration and tight discipline enabled K.K. Ganguly to make the Durand Cup both successful and glamorous. Strict fiscal discipline also made it a profit-making venture. As the concept of sponsorship only emerged in the 1980s, for most of his tenure Ganguly relied on gate money and effective financial management as a source of income.

His qualities as a far-sighted and quick-thinking official were evident during the 1984 edition, held in the months of October–November. On the afternoon of 31 October at 3 p.m., a Durand quarter-final match was to be played. The concept of satellite TV and breaking news did not exist then and the official media—AIR and Doordarshan—did not make a formal announcement about Prime Minister Indira Gandhi's assassination until evening.

At about 2.45 p.m., I, along with some other journalists, approached Ganguly and asked him whether the match would be played. He seemed hesitant but said there had been no official announcement. A young journalist said, 'The *Times of India* has brought out a special supplement regarding the assassination.' On hearing this Ganguly gave his typical acerbic reply, 'The Durand does not run according to the *Times of India*.' The match was played as per schedule.

Ganguly's greatness was that he accepted an error of judgement and made amends. That evening, when news trickled in that riots had broken out in Delhi and incensed mobs had attacked Sikhs, it became the responsibility of the Durand organizers to protect teams like Punjab Police that mostly comprised Sikh players. So that night Ganguly used military trucks to shift the Punjab Police team and their luggage to safety in the Nehru Stadium.

For the next few days Delhi was like an inferno. Law and order had broken down and there was mayhem everywhere. Shops were closed and the caterer and his staff at Nehru Stadium ran away. But the far-sighted Ganguly had anticipated the crisis. On his instructions, the efficient assistant and organizing committee member P.P. Kundu had driven to the Britannia factory in north-west Delhi and bought loaves of bread, ample eggs, butter, teabags and large quantities of milk worth Rs 5000. The teams trapped at Nehru Stadium thus did not starve. Even the school teams participating in the Junior Nehru Hockey Tournament and staying at the Nehru Stadium hostel during those troubled days managed to get adequate food, thanks to Ganguly's planning and Kundu's generosity.

I first closely interacted with K.K. Ganguly when I was made editor of the Durand journal in 1983. He gave me a brief outline of what was required but never interfered with my work. As per tradition the Durand journal was released on the day of the final, and despite his busy schedule on that all-important day, Ganguly would find time to read the *Durand Annual* and even write invaluable notes and suggestions. The Durand journal was never sold, only distributed amongst sports journalists, VIPs and football lovers; it was posted to all local football associations and given to the participating teams.

Ganguly has several firsts to his credit. He ploughed back the profits of the Durand Cup to promote school football in the country by starting the Subroto Mukherjee Cup in 1960. This timely venture became a trendsetter in the promotion of junior sports in the country. He was also the first to introduce prize money in Indian football, during the centenary Durand Cup in 1987.

~

The Durand is conducted annually by a special society nominated by the SSCB. For three years from 2006–08, due to the organizational and financial support of a sports management company Infinity Optimal Solutions (IOS), the Durand was reinvigorated and reinvented. Osians, a Mumbai-based art auction house and cultural archive, also became associated with the Durand Cup from the year 2006 onwards as a major promoter. Neville Tuli, the founder-chairman of Osians, is passionate about football.

To combat the escalating costs, the DFTS, along with IOS, worked overtime and procured money from sponsors. IOS also spruced up the playing conditions at the Ambedkar Stadium and promoted the tournament as a football carnival. From 2007 onwards they held the semi-finals and finals in the evenings when the stadium was floodlit. They roped in Radio Mirchi and other FM stations to broadcast the results because coverage for domestic football had declined in the local press. A lot of the sponsorship money was ploughed back into the game, with generous perks for the participating clubs. In 2016, the DFTS massively increased the prize money. The winners, Army Green, received a whopping Rs 75 lakh, the highest sum given by a traditional sports tournament in India.

However, with the I-League gaining in importance and being played for nearly six to seven months, the DFTS has been facing the problem of finding the right time-slot to schedule the tournament. Its popularity has waned and the top clubs too have gradually lost interest. Mohun Bagan and East Bengal last played in India's oldest tournament in 2009.

The Rovers Cup

The Rovers Cup, the second-oldest football tournament in India, started in 1891. Always held in Mumbai, the Rovers Cup, along with the Durand Cup and IFA Shield, played a major role in helping establish football in India. As was the trend throughout India, some British football enthusiasts stationed in Mumbai set up the Rovers Club in 1890. A trophy was donated, and the following year a knockout competition was held, mainly for British regimental teams. The First Worcester Regiment won the inaugural tournament and were champions again in 1892.

In 1902 the Bombay Football Association (BFA) was formed and they conducted a league tournament. Colonel Harwood, the president of the BFA, donated the trophy. The Bombay League (now known as the Mumbai League) is named the Harwood League after him. In 1911, the two bodies—the BFA and the old Rovers Cup committee—came together and the Western India Football Association (WIFA) was formed. The Rovers Cup was always held at the Cooperage Stadium (except in 1980–83), from its inception till 2000, the last time this historic tournament was held. It is only in the twenty-first century that this stadium was fully developed into an all-seater venue, so during the tournament temporary stands had to be put up to cope with the crowds. In the initial years the entrance fee was just 25 and 50 paise. The rules were nearly identical to those followed in the Durand.

The first Indian club team to be invited for the Rovers Cup was Mohun Bagan in 1923. This glamorous club from Kolkata had bedazzled spectators in the Durand Cup the previous year, and football fans in Mumbai were yearning to see them play. Mohun Bagan played attractive, attacking football and became the first civilian team to reach the Rovers Cup final, losing to holders Durham Light Infantry 1-4. All their matches were played before a packed stadium and the organizers made a record profit due to Bagan's popularity. Mohun Bagan's success led to the organizers inviting more civilian Indian teams from across the country in subsequent editions.

For the next thirteen years British regimental teams held sway in the Rovers Cup. The first Indian success came in 1937. The Bangalore Muslims became the first Indian civilian club to win this prestigious tournament. In an all-India final, they overcame Mohammedan Sporting 1-0. In 1938 they retained the trophy and became the first Indian team to beat a British regimental side in the Rovers Cup final. They beat the Argyll and Scottish Highlanders 3-2.

By the 1930s the Rovers Cup had become the most important sports event in Mumbai. In the 1941 final, Jawaharlal Nehru—who later became India's first prime minister—was the chief guest at the final between the Welsh Regiment and Mohammedan Sporting. As Mumbai remained largely unaffected by the turmoil of Partition, the Rovers Cup continued throughout the 1940s. Only once in its history, in 1947, the tournament got abandoned due to a mishap.

In independent India, the Rovers Cup will always be remembered for the exploits of the famous black-and-golden-shirted team, the legendary Hyderabad City Police. The Rovers Cup was their launching pad as they won this prestigious all-India tournament five years in a row (1950–54), a success sequence that is unsurpassed in domestic football till date. They continued to have a fantastic record in this tournament after being renamed Andhra Police. Several of their players were Olympians and internationals.

The most memorable match was the 1954 final against Kemari Union of Karachi, who were almost a full Pakistan XI and the first foreign team to participate in the Rovers Cup after Independence. They had several famous players, of whom centre-forward Oomer and left-winger Moosa were later recruited by East Bengal and also played for Mohammedan Sporting. Moosa is the only player to score a hat-trick in a Rovers Cup final; this was for Mohammedan Sporting in a replayed 1959 match against East Bengal. The 1954 final was a memorable, fast-paced encounter between two well-balanced teams, and Hyderabad City Police triumphed 2-1. Dashing right-winger Moin scored the winning goal, with a swinging shot, from almost a zero angle that swerved into the net.

The first civilian team from Mumbai to reach the Rovers Cup final was the Western India Athletic Association (WIAA) staff in 1942. The Mumbai teams were mostly institutional, like Caltex, Burmah-Shell, Tata, Mafatlal Mills, Central Railway and Reserve Bank. They did not pay that much and could not compete with the bigger clubs of other states. In 1958, Caltex Sports Club, spearheaded by ace centre-forward Neville D'Souza (who scored a hat-trick against Australia in the 1956 Melbourne Olympics) and five players from Kerala, became the first Mumbai team to win the Rovers Cup. That year, Caltex were coached by the late S.A. Rahim, who had been especially invited by the WIFA to develop football in the city. Caltex beat Mohammedan Sporting 3-2 in a dramatic final. Over 20,000 fans watched this memorable final but there still remains a doubt about Caltex's winning goal. There was controversy about whether inside-forward John Charles had lunged in the box to gain a penalty, which had been awarded promptly by referee E. Lobo. In the 1950s, all the Rovers Cup matches were supervised by Mumbai-based referees. After this incident neutral referees began to be invited.

The Goan clubs entered this tournament only after 1961, and soon came into the limelight. Vasco Club were the first team from Goa to enter the final in 1966, and Dempo the first to win. In 1974 Dempo defeated local outfit Tata 2-1 in the final. In 1989 Salgaocar won the title in the first all-Goa final of the Rovers Cup when they beat Dempo 1-0.

The Goa-based clubs always got a lot of support in the Rovers Cup as many Goans had migrated to or come to work in Mumbai. The Rovers Cup matches reflected the cosmopolitan nature of the city—the supporters in the stands comprised Goans from Dhobi Talao, Bengali diamond-cutters from Princess Street, the Parsis from Wadia Baugh and Bandra, the Kannadiga hotel and restaurant workers from south Mumbai and the migrants from Punjab, the North-east and Kerala.

The 1980 Rovers Cup held in December was unforgettable in more ways than one. The format for this tournament was changed and the quarter-final line-up offered some mouth-watering clashes: Dempo vs JCT, Mohammedan Sporting vs Salgaocar, East Bengal vs Aryans Club and Mohun Bagan vs Vasco. There were several charismatic players in these teams, and people clamoured to see their heroes in action.

Due to the huge demand, duplicate tickets were sold in the black market just outside the famous Cooperage Stadium. On the day of the first-leg quarter-final tie between Mohammedan Sporting and Salgaocar, there were 10,000 more spectators in the stands than the safety limit. Expectedly, some dilapidated wooden stands collapsed and several people were grievously injured. Incensed, the spectators resorted to arson and violence, which the police had to quell by using tear gas. The tournament was suspended for a few days.

The venue for the later stages of the tournament was shifted to the historic Brabourne Cricket Stadium as Cooperage was deemed unsafe. Both the double-legged semi-finals were gripping encounters, and packed crowds once again thronged the stands. In the first leg of the Mohammedan Sporting vs Dempo semi-final, the Goan team waged a resolute battle and rallied from a 0-2 deficit to level at 2-2. However, in the second leg, Mohammedan Sporting—the 1980 DCM winners—changed their approach play. Using a series of shallow diagonal and short passes, and attacking from both flanks, they dominated proceedings, forced 17 corners, created 10 scoring chances and triumphed 4-0. The other semi-final between arch-rivals East Bengal and Mohun Bagan was a classic. East Bengal trailed Mohun Bagan 0-2, but inspired by the 1978 World Cup ace Majid Bishkar, they equalized with goals by international Harjinder Singh and Iranian striker Jamshid Nassiri. East Bengal won the thrilling second leg 3-2 and moved into the final to meet Mohammedan Sporting for the first time that season.

The final was a tense battle of attrition, as during the transfer season that year Mohammedan Sporting had poached several players from East Bengal. Mohammedan Sporting led by a goal and seemed set to win their second major trophy of the season. But then came Majid Bishkar's moment of magic. The Iranian star equalized for East Bengal with a 30-yard half-volley to the left corner of the net—a shot of rare quality. With his remarkable ball-control, mobility, trapping, shooting and sudden acceleration, Majid was the undoubted Man of the Tournament.

The match ended in a 1-1 draw and both teams declined a replay, so they were declared joint winners of the 1980 Rovers. There was yet another controversy at the prize-giving ceremony. Due to a misunderstanding about who would get to keep the glittering Rovers Cup for the first six months, Mohammedan Sporting boycotted the ceremony and received their individual prizes only the next day. The 1980 Rovers Cup tournament was thus full of nail-biting matches, high drama, passion and vintage entertaining football.

The best foreign clubs to take part in the Rovers Cup were Salahuddin Club (Iraq) and Army Club (Baghdad) in 1982 and 1983 respectively. Both emerged victorious, and on both occasions, beat Mohammedan Sporting 2-1 in the final. Mohammedan Sporting then had the famed Iranian duo Bishkar and Nassiri in their ranks. During this period, since the Iran–Iraq war was taking place, the Rovers Cup final often became an extension of the conflict. These two high-intensity finals, played at the Brabourne Stadium, were watched by capacity crowds of over 40,000 people.

With the start of the NFL, the Rovers Cup too began to face problems similar to the Durand. With escalating costs and sponsorships not forthcoming, the second-oldest tournament in India had to fold up by 2000.

The IFA Shield

This tournament usually heralded the end of the football season in Kolkata. The IFA Shield, India's third-oldest tournament that started in 1893, was invariably held just after the Calcutta League got over and often before the Durga Puja festival. This too was initially a knockout competition and the rules were the same as the other domestic tournaments.

The renowned Mohun Bagan and Mohammedan Sporting were the first Indian clubs to win the IFA Shield (1911 and 1936 respectively). The next to win Kolkata's premier knockout tournament were the lesser-known Aryans Club in 1940. Mighty East Bengal won the IFA Shield for the first time in 1943. In the first IFA Shield final after Independence, Mohun Bagan ousted arch-rivals East Bengal 1-0 to win the title for the second time.

After 1947 British teams stopped participating in the IFA Shield. In 1953, the Indian Cultural League, a Mumbai-based club run by football enthusiasts in the Hindi film industry, became the first non-Bengal team to win the Shield. In the 1960s Mohun Bagan were a formidable team, with Chuni Goswami in attack and Jarnail Singh marshalling the defence. At their peak, these two players were the best in Asia during that era. Consequently, Bagan annexed several domestic tournaments, including the IFA Shield five times (twice joint champions with East Bengal). The

1962 triumph was memorable as they defeated a star-studded
Hyderabad XI 3-1 on a rain-soaked ground.

East Bengal fans are divided over which is their greatest era
in the IFA Shield. Many of the older generation of supporters
rate the hat-trick of victories from 1949–51 as being of supreme
importance. However, the discerning critics feel that the win over
Pas Tehran, then one of Asia's best clubs, is arguably East Bengal's
finest hour in this tournament. It was a historic achievement as
it was the first time since Independence that an Indian club had
ousted a renowned foreign team in a domestic final (Hyderabad
City Police had defeated Kemari Union, Karachi, 2-1 in the 1954
Rovers Cup final).

Pas Tehran were in stupendous form, having scored 8 goals in
3 matches, and were fancied to win. East Bengal's main problem
was how to contain their lethal striker Asghar Sharafi. Prasanta
Sinha, normally a midfielder, played as a central-defender along
with the imperious Syed Nayeemuddin. This makeshift pair
played with great aplomb, and with diminutive right-back Sudhir
Karmakar excelling in anticipations, East Bengal curbed the flow
of Pas Tehran's attacks.

Realizing they could not match the speed of the Iranians, the
Kolkata giants, coached that year by the wily Mohammed Hussain
from Mumbai, altered their tactics. Hussain made East Bengal
slow down the pace of the game and play possession football.
Minutes before the final whistle, the hard-working Mohammed
Habib got injured and was replaced by Parimal Dey. This was the
turning point in the match. Short but stocky Swapan Sengupta
tore down the right flank and sent a measured cross to Parimal
Dey, who trapped and scored the winning goal with a firm, low
grounder, from outside the 18-yard box. East Bengal supporters
were delirious on winning the Shield. They celebrated this epochal
win by lighting paper torches (mashals). Gautam Roy, India's
foremost football statistician, said, 'In 1970, folding paper into a
torch and waving the lit flame was a spontaneous act of joy but
over the years it has become a symbolic gesture by East Bengal
supporters to celebrate their title triumphs.'

Three years later, East Bengal gave another scintillating performance in the IFA Shield against a top-class foreign team, Pyongyang City Club from North Korea. With shrewd coaching by P.K. Banerjee, they registered a memorable 3-1 win against the formidable North Koreans. East Bengal had another golden run in the IFA Shield, from 1972–76, when they won the tournament five years in a row. They inflicted the ultimate humiliation on their arch-rivals Mohun Bagan, trouncing them by a record margin of 5-0 in the 1975 final.

However, fortunes changed by the end of this decade. A revamped Mohun Bagan won the IFA Shield from 1977–79. In the 1978 final they took on formidable Ararat Yerevan of the erstwhile USSR. Ararat Yerevan had recently taken part in the European Cup Winners' Cup (later known as the UEFA Cup Winners' Cup). The fancied Soviet team took an early lead but it started to rain and Bagan adapted better to the slippery conditions. Coach P.K. Banerjee, known for his astute game reading, brought on Bidesh Bose, who, with his blistering pace on the left flank, tormented the Aravan defenders. Lethal striker Mohammed Akbar equalized off a Bidesh Bose cross and, soon, pacy right-winger Manas Bhattacharya made it 2-1. A famous upset win was imminent but Ararat Yerevan rallied to make it 2-2. The trophy was shared.

As the Federation Cup gained in importance from the 1980s onwards, the value of the IFA Shield started to decrease. The tournament organizers tried to bolster its prestige by inviting more quality foreign teams during this period. In 1985, for the first time, two foreign clubs, Peñarol (Uruguay) and 1983 Soviet League champions Shakhtar Donetsk (the USSR), featured in the final. In 1986 Punjab Police became the first team from north India to reach the IFA Shield final. However, in the next decade not many teams from outside West Bengal participated. There were a few exceptions, like the second all-foreign final in 1993 between Pakhtakor (Uzbekistan) and Irtysh Pavlodar (Kazakhstan), and in 1996, when JCT became the first north Indian team to lift the 3-foot-high trophy. The tournament was not held for the first time in 1988 and again in 1992.

The 2001 final is the most controversial episode in the IFA Shield as players from both sides indulged in free-for-all brawls. The Palmeiras players, who had got physical in the semi-final as well, were soon involved in rough and unethical tackles in the final against East Bengal. The well-built Jo Paul Ancheri was brutally kicked by a Brazilian player and the crowd got incensed. The match was abandoned and East Bengal were declared the winner.

East Bengal is the most successful club in this historic tournament, having won it twenty-seven times (the last being in 2012) and were the runners-up ten times. The next most successful are Mohun Bagan, with twenty-one titles and securing the runners-up place fifteen times. The domination of Kolkata clubs in this tournament was curbed in the first decade of the new millennium. The now-defunct Mahindra United (Mumbai), in 2006 and 2007, and Churchill Brothers (Goa), in 2009 and 2010, annexed the IFA Shield. Foreign clubs Finance and Revenue FC (Myanmar) and Bayern Munich's second team won the IFA Shield in 2004 and 2005 respectively.

Due to the changing scenario of Indian football, no time slot could be found for the IFA Shield. Therefore, to keep the tournament alive and preserve its name, it was turned into an U-19 competition in 2016. Some of the junior ISL teams also participate in the tournament now.

The DCM Trophy

In the first few decades after Independence, international football was a relatively unknown entity in India, and exposure to it was negligible. The DCM football tournament, also known as the DCM Trophy, filled this void and became a trendsetter in introducing foreign clubs to local fans. Every year from 1968 onwards they invited two to four clubs to participate, beginning with Ethiopian Airlines and Ceylon XI. The quality of foreign teams improved from 1969 onwards when Taj Tehran participated. In the 1950s, the DCM Trophy invited clubs from Pakistan to participate. Many of these teams, such as the Pak Mughals, had players who had migrated from Delhi after Partition, so for them it was a homecoming of sorts.

In 1980, the genial organizing secretary of the DCM Trophy, G.P. Sinha, told me, 'The primary aim was to give local soccer fans a treat by organizing one of the best tournaments in the country, with representative clubs from each state, improve football standards and provide exposure to Indian players.'

After a period of trial and error in the 1970s, they realized it was pointless getting powerful European clubs like Spartak United and Volga Kalinin (both from the erstwhile USSR) as Indian teams struggled to compete against their robust brand of football. So from 1979 to 1997, barring a few teams from the USSR and Croatia on a couple of occasions, they mostly invited some of the best teams from Iran, South Korea and North Korea, China, Australia, Thailand and Malaysia.

The DCM Trophy was certainly an eye-opener for football fans in Delhi. The foreign teams provided glimpses of how the game had evolved both tactically and in terms of formations. The best example was the highly popular Taj Club of Tehran, the only team to win the tournament thrice in a row, 1969–71. In the 1970 tournament, the quality of their passing and cohesion was mesmerizing and awesome to behold. In both the pre-quarter-final (trounced Punjab Police 3-0) and quarter-final (beat BSF 2-0) they scored all their goals before half-time by using a lot of variety in their attacks, from through-passes to one-touch moves to crosses from the flanks. In the second-half they would just close down the game by indulging in long bouts of ball possession. Often Taj Tehran would retain possession in their own half and then suddenly launch quick counter-attacks, leaving the rugged Punjab teams bewildered. All the defenders of the Iranian team were comfortable with the ball, never cleared wildly and either initiated moves with accurate passes or moved up with the ball. They seemed to win matches without overexerting themselves.

The DCM Trophy had started quietly in 1945, in a public park opposite President's Estate. A local outfit, New Delhi Heroes, emerged champions, beating the British regimental side King's

Own Yorkshire Light Infantry 3-2 in the final. From 1946–48 the tournament was not held due to social and political unrest.

The tournament really took off in 1950 when the glamorous Kolkata clubs started participating. The organizers used entrepreneurial and money power to gradually lure the best teams in India to play. From 1950–60, East Bengal was the most successful team in the DCM Trophy and had a star-studded forward line (for details, see Chapter 1: 'Bengal'). Many experts consider the East Bengal vs Mohammedan Sporting 1960 DCM final as one of the finest matches played in Delhi as the quality of football was par excellence.

East Bengal has the best record in the DCM Trophy overall, winning the tournament seven times and finishing runners-up seven times. From 1968 till 1997 (the last time this tournament was held), foreign teams won this coveted trophy twenty-three times. East Bengal and Mohammedan Sporting are the only teams to have beaten a foreign side in the DCM final. East Bengal won against Dok Ro Gang (North Korea) in 1973 and Mohammedan Sporting beat Bank of Seoul and Trust Company (South Korea) 1-0 in the 1980 final, with winger Debashish Roy scoring the match-winner. In 1976 tenacious BSF held Hanyang University to goalless draws on successive days and in 1979 they drew twice with Citizen's National Bank, becoming joint champions with these South Korean teams in both years.

The DCM Trophy organizers used to generously distribute passes, so the income from ticket sales was never significant. In fact, the tournament ran at a loss for many years, as the cost of getting foreign teams was considerable. The organizers also provided generous remuneration to popular Indian clubs like Mohammedan Sporting and East Bengal. G.P. Sinha once explained why: 'The Calcutta clubs bring in the crowds, create excitement and add to the tournament's stature and popularity. They spend money to buy the best players and mould them into a formidable team.'

In 1980, the effervescent and bubbling S. Guha, the accounts manager of the tournament, told me that it 'consistently ran on a negative balance and the board of directors annually bailed us out'.

Profit was not the overt motive of the DCM Trophy. The owners, Bharat Ram and Charat Ram, were old residents of Delhi and sponsored mushairas, Ram Leela festivals and the football tournament as a form of corporate social responsibility, simultaneously providing entertainment and creating goodwill in north India, their largest market base.

After 1997, the AIFF suggested that the DCM be made a biennial event, which the tournament committee found impractical. Again, scheduling issues and the rising costs of procuring foreign teams made the venture unsustainable. A combination of these and other factors led to the closure of the DCM Trophy, a source of great entertainment while it lasted.

The Santosh Trophy

In 1940 the Dacca Sporting Association, an affiliate of the AIFF, put forth a proposal for an interstate football tournament. Similar interprovincial tournaments had commenced in hockey (national championships started in 1928) and cricket (Ranji Trophy started in 1936). The WIFA pledged to donate a shield for this championship in memory of one of their former presidents, A.C. Hinrichs. Bengal too wished to donate a trophy in memory of the Maharaja of Santosh, who was the first Indian president of their local association. Santosh was a small province in eastern Bengal (now Bangladesh) in undivided India. Although the championship was supposed to commence in September 1940 as a contest for the Hinrichs–Santosh memorial trophy, it did not begin until 1941.

It was decided to start the interstate championship on a zonal basis, to limit expenditure. The winners of each zone would play in the final rounds. The winning team would get the Santosh Trophy, valued in those days at the princely sum of Rs 2000. No records exist of why the name of Hinrichs was omitted. In the inaugural year, thirteen teams from four geographical zones participated. The winning team from each zone met for the semi-finals, whose two winners qualified for the final, held in Kolkata. Bengal won the inaugural tournament, beating Delhi 5-1.

The Santosh Trophy is the only interstate tournament in India at the senior level. For U-19 there is the B.C. Roy Trophy and for U-16 there is the Mir Iqbal Hussain Trophy. Each year the Santosh Trophy is held at different venues and has no fixed months during which it is played. It was once considered the most important tournament for selecting the Indian team for international matches, as the national coach always watched it. Football fans have witnessed some historic moments in this championship, which in a way tells the story of Indian football through the rise of certain states and great players over the years.

In the 1945 tournament, Bengal outclassed Rajputana (now known as Rajasthan) 7-0 with the help of Fred Pugsley, the first non-British foreigner to play for an Indian team. He scored all the 7 goals—a record tally in the Santosh Trophy that is still unbroken. Pugsley was Burmese. In pre-Independence India, eligibility rules were lax and foreigners could play in the national championships. A reputed footballer, Pugsley had walked all the way from Yangon (the Burmese name for Rangoon) to Kolkata in 1943 to escape the Japanese annexation and went straight to the East Bengal club, seeking help. The club officials first nurtured him back to health and he became one of the first foreigners to excel in Indian football.

The renowned P.K. Banerjee launched his football career by first playing in the 1953 Santosh Trophy as a precocious seventeen-year-old right-winger for Bihar. Years later P.K. said, 'I got a paltry sum of Rs 6 as pocket expenses during these national championships but I was impressive in the matches against [West] Bengal. I moved to Calcutta the next season and my football career took off.'

The league-cum-knockout format was introduced in the 15th Santosh Trophy held in Chennai in 1958. The redoubtable Hyderabad team, coached by the legendary late S.A. Rahim, were on the verge of winning the trophy for the third time in succession that year. However, in the quarter-final league phase, Services sharpshooter Moloy Lahiri foiled their dream. He scored a memorable hat-trick, which enabled Services to upset Hyderabad 5-2 and eliminate the holders.

All of India's illustrious forwards have played for the Santosh Trophy and scored memorable goals. Yet, one of the best goals ever scored was, surprisingly, by international defender Arun Ghosh in the 1960 Calicut edition. Mighty West Bengal were struggling against tenacious Assam and needed to win to qualify for the semi-finals. The match-winner was like a bolt from the blue. The Assam defence partially cleared a West Bengal attack and, as the high ball was landing, Arun Ghosh, facing his goal, executed an acrobatic scissors-volley that brooked no denial.

Overall, there was no single region that stood out in the Santosh Trophy in the 1960s. However, in 1969, West Bengal, led by left-back Santo Mitra, produced a memorable display, outclassing all opposition to win the title in style. They routed Goa 4-0, Tamil Nadu 8-0, Andhra Pradesh 4-0 and 6-1 in the double-legged semi-finals and Services 6-1 in the final. West Bengal slammed in 28 goals and conceded just two. The wily inside-forward Mohammed Habib finished as top scorer, with 11 goals, including the first-ever hat-trick in a Santosh trophy final.

A new phase had begun in Indian football by 1970 when Punjab staged and won the Santosh Trophy for the first time, in Jalandhar (then known as Jullundur). In the semi-final they were trailing 0-1 against mighty West Bengal. Then a few minutes before the final whistle, burly striker Manjit Singh latched on to a throw from the left and bulldozed past two of India's finest defenders, Sudhir Karmakar and Syed Nayeemuddin, to score from close. West Bengal got demoralized and lost the penalty shoot-out. It was the first time Punjab had beaten West Bengal. Manjit's dramatic equalizing goal provided the tonic of self-belief and Punjab football went from strength to strength. Over the next few decades, the rivalry between the Punjab and Kolkata club sides became common in important domestic tournaments.

However, few could match West Bengal's striker of the early 1970s for sheer power, the international Sukalyan Ghosh Dastidar. Goa staged the Santosh Trophy for the first time in 1972, with a side that was considered the strongest to have been fielded from Goa so far. They had the international Nicholas Pereira in defence and Sudhir as goalkeeper in top form. The hosts clashed with West Bengal in the semi-finals. In the first-leg match at Margao, Goa was leading 2-1 when, minutes before the final whistle, West Bengal equalized with a booming 40-yard piledriver by Sukalyan Ghosh. West Bengal went on to win the penalty shoot-out.

In the 1974 Jalandhar edition, Punjab won the Santosh Trophy for the second time, routing West Bengal 6-0 in the final. The Punjab team had been training for over a month and had a slick forward line consisting of Inder Singh, Manjit Singh and the brilliant ball player Harjinder Singh. Inder stole the limelight, scoring 23 goals in the tournament, the best-ever individual scoring tally in the Santosh Trophy till date. This win was crucial in popularizing football in Punjab.

In 1983 Goa annexed the Santosh Trophy for the first time, finishing as joint champions with West Bengal—the only time the trophy has been shared. Goa skipper Brahmanand Shankhwalkar gave a sterling display as goalkeeper, and both the final and its replay ended in goalless draws. It was a proud moment for Brahmanand when he went to receive the trophy as it was also his birthday. He later said, 'Lifting the Santosh Trophy in Calcutta was the most memorable day of my life, as it was a historic success and led to Goa football being recognized as the best in the country.'

In 1990, the AIFF experimented with the Santosh Trophy and made it an U-23 tournament. This lasted for only three years and, in the 1993–94 Cuttack edition, the Santosh Trophy reverted to the old format of all states playing at one venue without age restrictions.

Bhaichung Bhutia scored the first-ever golden goal of the Santosh Trophy in a 1995 final, enabling West Bengal to pip Punjab 2-1. Before the match, West Bengal coach Syed Nayeemuddin gambled and dropped international midfielder Gunabir Singh and included Bhaichung as a striker. Till then Bhaichung had played mostly as a midfielder or withdrawn striker. Later, talking about this change of position, Nayeem, noted for his astute game reading, said, 'Bhaichung had the razor-sharp reflexes to be a top-class striker, so I decided to play him upfront as his speed and reflexes could disturb the tough Punjab defence.' The young

Bhaichung justified his coach's faith and scored through a dramatic back-volley. The rest, as they, say is history. After that, Bhaichung Bhutia became a regular striker for his club and country, and the first Indian to play over 100 international football matches.

In 2002, the AIFF changed the eligibility rules for the Santosh Trophy and introduced the domicile rule, under which players had to represent the states in which they were born. The then secretary of AIFF, Alberto Colaco, said:

> The domicile rule was introduced [to] encourage states that developed talented players. Thus, all State Associations could requisition the services of their [local] players, irrespective of which outstation club they played for . . . The Santosh Trophy had become monotonous, and from 1995 till 1999, four successive finals were contested by Bengal and Goa. The leading players in the country were invariably contracted by the top clubs [so] the monopoly of these two states [had to be curbed].

This enabled other states to benefit. Manipur won the trophy in 2002, then Kerala in 2004 and Punjab in 2006 and 2007. West Bengal did not win it again until 2009, although Goa won in 2005 and 2008.

However, overall, West Bengal has the best record in the Santosh Trophy, as they are thirty-two-time champions and twelve-time runners-up. Next is Punjab who are eight-time champions, seven-time runners-up, then Kerala who are five-time winners and eight-time runners-up and finally Goa who are five-time winners and eight-time runners-up.

Since 2012, any player representing an I-League club is ineligible to play for his state in the Santosh Trophy. Due to this, the trophy has lost its glamour and status as the top players of the country do not take part in it.

The Federation Cup

The AIFF started the Federation Cup in 1977 as India's premier, official knockout club championship. The association wished to ensure that the top teams from all states took part; this did not always happen in the traditional tournaments that sometimes invited only the crowd-pulling teams. The tournament was annually allotted to different state associations and the inaugural tournament was held in Ernakulam.

The Federation Cup has always been subject to experimentation and the format keeps getting altered. For the first ten years, there were double-leg semi-finals; this was changed in 1988, when Delhi first staged the tournament. The semi-final became a single knockout match. AIFF's new rule of abolishing goal difference if teams were level on points was applied as well. In the Thrissur edition in 1990, the format was again altered, and the bottom four teams got eliminated from their respective groups.

After another change, the tournament was held on a league-cum-knockout basis till 1995. From 1996–98, the AIFF, with help from their marketing agents IMG, roped in a big-time sponsor Kalyani Black Label (KBL) and the prize money escalated. The format was changed again and it became a major knockout tournament modelled on the lines of the FA Cup in England. Initially the knockout games were conducted on a zonal basis, with the winners meeting the seeded teams in the pre-quarter-finals. Sixty to seventy clubs from all over India entered the Federation Cup during those years—the largest number of participants ever in the history of Indian football.

Once the contract with IMG was over, the glory of the Federation Cup began to decline. Not held for the next two years, the tournament was revived in Chennai in 2001, not held in 2002, but held regularly again since 2003. From 2005–07, the Federation Cup was again staged as a knockout tournament on the lines of the FA Cup. This pattern changed during 2008–12, when the winners amongst the sixteen participating teams directly met in the knockout semi-finals. Each edition from 2003 onwards had a different sponsor, except in 2008 when no sponsor was found. Since 2014, Hero MotoCorp has become the lead sponsor for this tournament.

In the twentieth century, the Federation Cup was invariably one of the first major knockout tournaments of the season, starting in

April or May except on a few occasions. It would provide a clear insight about the composition and forms of the assembled squads and an indication of the teams likely to dominate in the year ahead. However, the time slot for the tournament was changed a few times in the new millennium. This was due to the dilemma the AIFF faced after the I-League gained importance and the Federation Cup lost its sheen with some reputed clubs not competing seriously. From 2010 onwards, the AIFF reverted to staging the Federation Cup prior to the commencement of the I-League. Held just before the Delhi Commonwealth Games, the matches in 2010 took place simultaneously in three different cities instead of a single city.

For the first couple of decades of the tournament, it was mostly clubs from Kolkata, particularly Mohun Bagan, who performed well. Indian Telephone Industries (ITI) Bangalore won the inaugural Federation Cup in 1977 and BSF won in Guwahati in 1979 when the Kolkata clubs did not participate due to the ongoing Assam agitation. With the skilful winger-cum-playmaker Narender Gurung in their team, BSF won the title, beating Mafatlal Mills Mumbai 2-2 and 3-0 in the final. However, it was the 1995 Federation Cup in which history was made in more ways than one. The arrival of JCT of Phagwara as a dominant force in this season had already been made evident when they wrested three experienced internationals from two big Kolkata clubs. JCT not only won this edition of the Federation Cup but, in the process, shattered myths and trampled on existing traditions.

It was always believed that Kolkata teams excelled on slippery ground as their local league was held during the monsoons. In two fine performances, JCT beat Mohammedan Sporting (semi-final) and East Bengal (final)—both matches were played on rain-drenched surfaces on which the Kolkata giants stumbled. Another belief was the superiority of the Kolkata teams in the penalty shoot-out owing to the better technique and greater agility of their goalkeepers. JCT converted six penalty kicks in a row with supreme confidence, which left East Bengal's international custodian Sumit Mukherjee astounded. Coach Sukhwinder Singh did not let his star players I.M. Vijayan and Carlton Chapman take the penalty kicks. Explaining his bold decision, he said:

I knew there would be a lot of pressure on Vijayan and Chapman
who had just got transferred from Calcutta. They were famous and
likely to be booed as they made the dreaded walk to take the penalty
kicks. So after much thinking and discussions with Inder Singh and
Parminder Singh, I opted for a 'sons of the soil policy' and trained
six players from Punjab for the tie-breaker. There was no pressure
on them and I am happy they all converted the penalty kicks.

In that same tournament, it was not just East Bengal that faltered;
Mohun Bagan too lost twice to Air India, while Mohammedan
Sporting lost to Salgaocar. The top Kolkata clubs losing 5 matches
to outstation clubs, in a tournament held in West Bengal, was
unthinkable a few years ago and was an indicator of the changing
times. JCT's stylish victory at the 1995 Federation Cup showed
that Kolkata's monopoly in Indian football would no longer
remain unchallenged. They went on to win the tournament in
the next season as well, having created a competitive side with
Bhaichung Bhutia and talented foreign internationals.

After liberalization, private-sector firms like JCT were oozing
with confidence about future growth; their use of financial
muscle to buy quality players set a trend that was soon emulated.
Mahindra United built a star-studded team in the 2005–06 season,
which did the double of winning the NFL and the Federation Cup.

Despite these changes, the Kolkata clubs have reigned supreme
in the Federation Cup overall. They have won the tournament on
twenty-four occasions: Bagan (fourteen), East Bengal (eight) and
Mohammedan Sporting (two). Mohun Bagan and East Bengal have
met in the final on six occasions, the maximum ever. They finished
joint champions in 1978 and 1980, and on three occasions (1986,
1992 and 1998) Bagan triumphed whilst East Bengal prevailed
over their arch-rivals just once in 1985. Mohun Bagan were the
first to win the title outright thrice in a row, from 1992–94, and
once earlier from 1980–82 (joint champions in 1980).

Mohun Bagan has won four of their fourteen Federation
Cup finals in Kolkata. The most emphatic of these victories
was a 1992 match when with a memorable display of cohesive,

attacking football and slick passing they beat East Bengal 2-0. The goalscorers were midfielder Debasish Sarkar and Chima Okorie, the first foreigner to play for Bagan.

East Bengal's two memorable Federation Cup titles were in 1985 and 1996. In the 1985 final they ousted Mohun Bagan with an extra-time goal by the Iranian striker Jamshid Nassiri. Again in 1996, before a capacity crowd of about 1 lakh people at the Salt Lake Stadium, they beat Dempo 2-1 with prolific striker Raman Vijayan scoring the golden goal in extra time.

East Bengal had not achieved the success they desired in the Federation Cup and their long wait finally ended in 2007. This glamorous club overcame their jinx in grand style, beating Mahindra United 2-1 in the final. East Bengal played glorious attacking football, winning 4 matches in eleven days and scoring 11 goals. Their lethal Brazilian striker Edmilson was the tournament's top scorer with 6 goals in 3 matches. East Bengal beat city rivals Mohammedan Sporting 3-1 in the first round, JCT 3-2 in the quarter-finals and Mohun Bagan 3-2 in the semi-finals.

They also overcame their pattern of beating arch-rivals Mohun Bagan in the semi-final and then losing a final. This time, coached by a former Bagan legend Subrata Bhattacharya, they kept their composure and won the tournament.

From Goa, Salgaocar (four), Dempo and Churchill Brothers (once each) are the only clubs to have won the Federation Cup. Sporting Clube de Goa finished runners-up in successive years, but in dramatic circumstances. In 2005 they lost by a last-minute extra-time goal by Jose Ramirez Barreto, then playing for Mahindra United. The next year they reached the final again but lost on penalties to Bagan. The first all-Goa final was in Kochi in 2014. Churchill Brothers emerged champions, beating Sporting Clube de Goa 3-1.

Englishman David Booth is the first foreign coach to have won the Federation Cup. Under his guidance, Mahindra United annexed the title in 2003 beating Mohammedan Sporting 1-0 in the final in Kolkata. Other foreign coaches to have had success in this prestigious tournament are the Brazilian Robson Mattos, the Belgian Philippe de Ridder, the Spanish Albert Roca and the Englishmen Trevor Morgan and Ashley Westwood. The Moroccan Karim Bencherifa is the only foreign coach to have won the Federation Cup with two different clubs, Mohun Bagan and Salgaocar.

Success in the 2007 Federation Cup helped East Bengal coach Subrata Bhattacharya achieve an important landmark. He joined a select trio who had been victorious training different clubs for the Federation Cup—P.K. Banerjee (Mohun Bagan 1978, East Bengal 1980 and 1985), Amal Dutta (East Bengal joint winners 1978 and Mohun Bagan 1998) and Syed Nayeemuddin (Mohammedan Sporting 1983 and 1984 and Mohun Bagan 1993).

Both Subrata Bhattacharya and Derrick Pereira hold a unique record in Indian football. They are the only two to have won the tournament both as a player and as coach. As a player Subrata won the Federation Cup six times with Mohun Bagan, and as coach for Bagan in 2001 and East Bengal in 2007. As a player, Derrick won back-to-back Federation Cup titles for Salgaocar in 1988 and 1989, and once as the Mahindra United coach in 2005.

The future of the Federation Cup is uncertain. If the AIFF decides to permanently stop the tournament or replace it with a Super Cup, then the winners of the first and last title will be from Bengaluru: ITI Bangalore (1977) and Bengaluru FC (2017). On both occasions Mohun Bagan were beaten in the final.

The National Football League and the I-League

Alarmed by India's declining standards in international football, FIFA sent a three-member committee in February 1995 to investigate and offer possible solutions. One of the suggestions was to set up a semi-professional national league. This was implemented by 1997 and eight teams participated in the inaugural NFL (1996–97) sponsored by Philips. There was a qualifying league from which twelve teams emerged and were then divided equally; from both these groups, the top four teams played in the NFL. In 1998, the league was expanded to include ten teams and matches were played on a home-and-away basis. Apart from prize money, the winners, Mohun Bagan, also got a share of the gate money collected in home matches and so overall earned a hefty sum. Prize money was given to the top six teams, but each participating team had got preparation money as well.

In 1997–98, a second-division national league for eight teams was also started but without a sponsor. To cut costs, the second division was played at three centres: Bengaluru, Guwahati and Cuttack. Two teams got promoted into the first division. Philips terminated their sponsorship for the first-division league after two seasons; then Coca-Cola and later ONGC became the title sponsors.

The format was changed in the 1998–99 edition to curtail costs. The twelve participating teams (including ITI Bangalore and Tollygunge Agragami, Kolkata, who had been promoted in 1997–98) were divided into two equal groups and matches were played on a league basis. The top three from each group played a double-leg final round held in Goa and Kolkata respectively. From 1999–2000 onwards the old format of the round-robin league was restored.

The NFL was able to generate massive spectator interest in the inaugural edition. For crucial matches, crowds of 25,000–30,000 flocked to the Nehru Stadium in Margao, whilst at the Salt Lake Stadium in Kolkata, East Bengal's key matches against JCT and Churchill Brothers attracted crowds of up to 70,000. Even in Delhi, where JCT played several of their home matches, attendance was high and about 20,000 witnessed the key clash against East Bengal in the Ambedkar Stadium.

The final stages of the inaugural NFL were eventful for JCT. In March 1997, star-studded JCT needed a win against Churchill Brothers in their away match in Goa. Before a capacity crowd Churchill Brothers were dominant but failed to score. In a breakaway move, Nigerian international winger Stephen Abarowei scored the match-winner for JCT. Over a week later, Churchill Brothers were leading the charts and were playing against Indian Bank in Chennai. JCT were playing against Dempo simultaneously at the Nehru Stadium in Margao. JCT's brilliant forward line consisting of internationals Bhaichung Bhutia, I.M. Vijayan and Stephen Abarowei were on a rampage and were leading by 4 goals.

However, coach Sukhwinder Singh wondered if this win would be of any use if Churchill Brothers won. As mobile phones had not yet become commonplace, he requested Inder Singh to rush to a nearby STD booth to find out the score in Chennai. Much to his joy, Inder discovered that Churchill Brothers were being held to a 1-1 draw. He stayed on the line till the match was over, then rushed back to Nehru Stadium, where JCT had defeated Dempo 4-1 but were still uncertain about their victory. When a beaming Inder announced the result, it sunk in that JCT had become the inaugural NFL champions. The players went wild, took a lap of honour and some even crawled all over the ground in glee.

The most exciting matches took place in the 6th NFL (2001–02) in Goa. Mohun Bagan went to play their last 2 matches against Salgaocar and Churchill Brothers in April 2002, needing three points to bag the title. In their opening match against Salgaocar, they led 3-0 within half an hour, and their supporters in Kolkata started celebrating by ordering sweetmeats and chingri (prawns) for dinner. However, inspired by the clever passing of Climax Lawrence and Alvito D'Cunha, Salgaocar made it 2-3 by half-time and rallied to win 4-3. Mohun Bagan were shattered and the players demoralized. The situation had reversed. Churchill Brothers needed just a draw in their last game against Bagan to become champions for the first time.

The match was played on a Monday, and the Nehru Stadium in Margao was filled to the brim with Churchill Brothers' supporters. The erstwhile AIFF secretary Alberto Colaco had flown in the referee and assistant referees from Malaysia as he felt the pressure would be very difficult for an Indian referee to handle.

Bagan's Brazilian ace Jose Ramirez Barreto had spent Sunday talking to his teammates, boosting their morale and reviving their confidence. Coach Subrata Bhattacharya also reminded the players of the famous legacy of Mohun Bagan. Bagan started confidently and with a slight tactical switch. Barreto, normally a forward, played in a withdrawn role to bolster the midfield and thwart Churchill Brothers' fierce attacks. Debjit Ghosh was outstanding in defence, with his interceptions and close marking of NFL's top goalscorer, striker Yusif Yakubu of Churchill Brothers. Slowly Bagan weathered the storm and wrested the initiative from Churchill Brothers.

In the second-half, following a Basudeb Mondal corner kick, Bagan's two Nigerian strikers combined to give them the lead in the seventieth minute. Abdul Latif Seriki outjumped Churchill Brothers central-defender Osumanu Husseini and flicked to Abdul Wastu Saliu who headed in. Stung, Churchill Brothers launched numerous counter-attacks. Much to the dismay of the Bagan fans, the Malaysian referee gave five minutes of stoppage time. It was a nail-biting finish. During the additional time Yakubu's header was goal bound but Debjit acrobatically cleared it to safety. Bagan held on 1-0 to win the NFL for the third time.

As the first national league, the NFL was popular amongst both fans and the print and electronic media. Continual, in-depth media coverage put Bhaichung Bhutia, I.M. Vijayan, Jo Paul Ancheri and Bruno Coutinho on the road to stardom.

However, the AIFF could not sustain the momentum gained by the inaugural league. Decline was evident by the fifth edition, when inadequate marketing of key matches and frequently delayed match itineraries led to the NFL losing media and spectator popularity. By the 11th NFL, an average of a mere 4000 viewers had turned up for each match. Despite such setbacks several positives emerged from the NFL: Indian club teams adjusted to frequent travel for away matches, players' salaries grew, the quality of foreign players improved, Mahindra United (champions in 2005–06) and Dempo (champions in 2004–05 and 2006–07) emerged as the new powerhouses, and new clubs like Sporting Clube de Goa and Churchill Brothers made their presence felt. East Bengal and Mohun Bagan reigned supreme in the NFL, both having won three titles each. As a coach, Subhash Bhowmick won back-to-back NFL titles in 2002–03 and 2003–04 (for East Bengal), an unsurpassed feat so far.

The Indian Professional League (I-League) was launched on 24 November 2007 to give Indian football another boost. The title of the new-looking I-League was derived from Japan's successful J-League, which had started in 1993.

The I-League heralded the rise of the Goa clubs. The first six I-Leagues were won by clubs from Goa: Dempo thrice, Churchill Brothers twice and Salgaocar once. When Dempo won the I-League for the third time in 2011–12, five members of their squad, all Goans, were regular members of the Indian team— the first time this had happened. Dempo were such a dominant team from 2007–12 that visiting teams dreaded playing against them. The current Indian captain, Sunil Chhetri, when playing for Mohun Bagan, confessed that the Kolkata teams would be happy if they came away from Goa with one point as they felt it would be almost impossible to snatch three points from Dempo in a home match![2]

In its second edition, Serbian coach Zoran Djordjevic became the first foreign coach (Churchill Brothers) to win India's premier national league. Armando Colaco emerged as the most successful Indian coach of the new millennium, winning two NFL and three I-League titles. Ashley Westwood (England) guided Bengaluru FC to win two titles in 2013–14 and 2015–16.

The I-League saw the decline of the Kolkata clubs. Only Mohun Bagan has won this coveted title, in 2014–15. Overall, in the twenty-one editions of the NFL and I-League, East Bengal finished in the top three on fourteen occasions and were champions of the NFL thrice. However, they have not won a national league title since 2004.

A new set of rules came into play in the I-League where clubs were offered incentives to promote their home matches to the local community. The clubs were unable to take on the task of professionally marketing the league and, gradually, viewership for this premier championship too has declined. There were a number of requirements in the I-League to make Indian football more professional, which are gradually being met. Although most I-League clubs are yet to develop age-group teams, all clubs now have contracts for players and certified coaches (that is, an 'A' or Pro-Licence from the Asian Football Confederation [AFC]).

The Indian Super League

India's youngest football tournament, the ISL, was founded by Football Sports Development Limited, an organization formed by IMG–Reliance and Star Sports. Supported by the AIFF, it kicked off in October 2014 in Kolkata. The ISL, officially called the Hero ISL after its key sponsor, is modelled on the Major League Soccer (MLS) in the US and other commercial leagues in India such as for cricket (Indian Premier League), kabaddi, hockey and wrestling, amongst others. The original eight franchises were named after the places that were awarded the bid: Atletico de Kolkata, Delhi Dynamos, Chennaiyin FC, Goa, Kerala Blasters, Mumbai City FC, NorthEast United FC and FC Pune City.

The ISL is India's most expensive and glamorous football tournament as of 2017, where the involvement of big business houses, cricketing stars, Bollywood actors and European players attracts large crowds and has generated considerable media interest. In the first ISL each franchise had a marquee player, and a total of fifty-six foreign and 112 domestic players were purchased in the first draft, mostly from the I-League clubs. The international players were from fifteen different countries; the maximum from Spain (nine), France (eight) and the Czech Republic (eight). It was for the first time that so many European players were competing in a football event in India, which made the tournament extremely popular amongst the younger generation who have grown up watching European football.

Each season, teams have been hiring over a dozen foreign players, of whom usually six are in the playing eleven. Season one saw the likes of Alessandro Del Piero, Luís Garcia, Joan Capdevila, David Trezeguet and David James feature; season two had Nicolas Anelka, Florent Malouda, Adrian Mutu, Elano Blumer, Roberto Carlos and Simão; and the third edition consisted of renowned players such as Malouda, Diego Forlán, Lúcio, Hélder Postiga and Northern Ireland veteran Aaron Hughes.

The three seasons have also seen legends such as Zico (FC Goa), Marco Materazzi (Chennaiyin FC), Gianluca Zambrotta (Delhi Dynamos), Steve Coppell (Kerala Blasters) and David Platt (FC Pune City) become coaches of the various franchise teams, which has helped in the development of several Indian players. For instance, there is now a finesse in the games of prolific striker C.K. Vineeth, talented midfielder Milan Singh, and wingers Kean Lewis, Romeo Fernandes and Mandar Rao Desai. Their game awareness and positional sense have improved. Similarly, Jeje Lalpekhlua's mobility and shielding has got better. The current Indian coach, Stephen Constantine, has also acknowledged the role of the ISL in developing talent.

Due to these costly recruitments, the annual expenditure of the ISL clubs has been in the range of Rs 35–40 crore. Income from sponsors, ticket sales and hoardings did not add up, so they have been running at losses of around Rs 20–25 crore. But the club owners are optimistic that the franchises will break even after five to seven years.

In each season, the eight franchises played a minimum of fourteen matches. The top four teams qualified for the semi-finals, which were played on a home-and-away basis. Atletico de Kolkata— which has a tie-up with Atletico Madrid—and Kerala Blasters have emerged as the strongest teams so far. Atletico de Kolkata were the champions in the first ISL in 2014 and also in 2016. On both occasions, they beat Kerala Blasters in a well-contested final.

Kerala Blasters have consistently attracted the best crowds in the ISL, and enjoyed the maximum crowd support in the entire third edition. All their home matches were watched by over 50,000 spectators and their average attendance was way above the next best, that of NorthEast United FC in Guwahati. The season finale of 2016 turned out to be a grand sporting event, with over 54,000 people thronging the stadium in Kochi and 4.1 crore fans tuning in on television to follow the nail-biting face-off.

In 2015, Chennaiyin FC rallied to beat FC Goa 3-2 in a thrilling final at the Nehru Stadium in Margao. Chennaiyin FC regularly attracts large crowds of 25,000 when they play at home;

coach Zico for FC Goa has also ensured massive crowd support and identification by recruiting six Goan players and five who have played for Goan clubs.

NorthEast United FC too created a distinct identity, having roped in six players from the region in the second season. They have continued to do so for subsequent seasons. This is smart thinking and ensures they get vociferous support in both their home and away matches as many youngsters from the region work outside the North-east. As of July 2017, about 20 to 25 per cent of India's professional football players are from the North-east, a region that comprises roughly 3 per cent of the country's population.

Overall, the top Indian goalscorers in the three seasons were Jeje Lalpekhlua with 13 goals and Sunil Chhetri with 7.

Impact on Indian Football

The ISL has brought in a lot of changes in the Indian football scenario, some of which are quite positive. For example, the auction in 2015 changed the way transfers took place and the entire process became much more professional. In the first-ever public auction of players, all the eleven Indian participants were sold for well above their base price, purchased by six different teams. Interestingly, midfielders were in great demand, and so Eugeneson Lyngdoh, whose work rate is on par with some of the best medios in the English Premier League, was the first to break the crore barrier. He was bought by FC Pune City for Rs 1.05 crore.

Apart from the bidding sums and the boom in prize money, the ISL has benefited players overall, who are now being treated as professionals. They are paid on time and also receive better training facilities, more exposure abroad for training camps and interaction with foreign coaches and players. These factors have increased the value of footballers in India.

A significant feature has been the visibility and media coverage the ISL has garnered, and the rise in spectator turnout. Initially, the ISL public-relations firm distributed passes to ensure there were reasonably large crowds even in cities like Delhi, Mumbai or Pune, which did not have a fanatical fan base. The ISL also enabled many young football fans to live their dream of coming to the stadiums with painted faces, waving banners and chanting songs. These factors coupled with the rigorous promotion on TV and social media have ensured that the average attendance is over 20,000 despite most matches being played on weekdays. The relentless technology that is turning our society upside down has helped upgrade interest in football. The slot of 7 p.m. for ISL matches is also good for at-home viewers as the matches finish before the serials or news programmes begin. Hence households with one TV set can also follow the tournament. In 2016, the ISL was able to increase its total viewership to 21.6 crore from around 2.07 crore in 2015. These creditworthy figures reveal that the ISL is making an impact and creating new followers of Indian football. Some Indian players are now household names across the country.

Amongst other important initiatives, the ISL has refurbished football infrastructure by relaying the main playing surface at all the stadiums where ISL matches are played, and provided top locker-room and floodlight facilities as well.

ISL rules also demand that each team spend Rs 2 crore for the development of the game at the grass-roots level and build a football academy within five years of formation in their respective states. The ISL sees this as a long-term programme, targeted at children aged six to fourteen. Their ambition is to ensure that by 2018 about 50 lakh children are actively playing organized football.

This is a laudable idea but if so many children are to play, then more clubs, grounds and facilities would be required in several cities. To achieve this aim, the ISL will have to work in tandem with the AIFF and the traditional football clubs, especially those in the I-League first and second divisions. However, at the time of writing, this is a point of contention. From the early trends, it appears that the ISL teams will be getting priority over the traditional clubs.

The AIFF had initially described the ISL as a tournament to popularize the sport in the country, which would never displace the

FIFA-sanctioned I-League. During a visit to India in 2014, former FIFA secretary Jérôme Valcke had asserted that the I-League is the main league of India. A year later, the AIFF changed their stance and hinted at a merger of the two tournaments. In 2016, AIFF president Praful Patel said, 'There will be three seven-month leagues—Leagues 1, 2 and 3—in a hierarchical system from November 2017 onwards.'[3]

All the I-League clubs, including the first-division clubs, were now to play in the second division. According to a regulation in the ISL, none of the franchise teams can get relegated for seven years as the owners are spending considerable money. Therefore in the case of a merger the I-League teams would not get promoted throughout this duration. There were howls of protest over this in the print media, and the proposal was met with massive resistance from the traditional clubs. Complaining of stepmotherly treatment, several successful Goan clubs, including Salgaocar (who celebrated their sixtieth anniversary in 2016) and Dempo (five-time champions of the NFL/I-League), withdrew from the 10th Hero I-League.

If the ISL indeed intends to create a pool of talent for the future, it would need to foster a harmonious relationship with the local football federations and clubs, which regularly discover and nurture emerging players. Some of the franchises are adopting shortcuts like taking over existing academies or filling them with talented players who have already been spotted by officials of other tournaments.

A merger will have significant implications because a massive country like India cannot be represented adequately by the same ten or eleven teams as is being proposed. It is absurd both in terms of geography as well as demographics. This is one of the few areas where the I-League has a distinct edge over the ISL, as teams from smaller states, despite limited means, are able to take part in it. According to the rules as of May 2017, a club has to pay a fee of Rs 15 crore to play in the ISL.[4] If a merger happens, a small club like Aizawl FC from Mizoram, which won the I-League in 2017, would have no hope of ever featuring in the ISL. In practice, the proposed structure would stifle the ambitions of countless such clubs and players who dream to play in the top flight. It is no wonder that Praful Patel has sometimes said, 'The ISL has increased football's popularity in India but has also led to many problems.'[5]

In metros like Chennai or Delhi, which do not have established clubs to support, the ISL franchises have helped create a new fan base, which is commendable. However, in most other places, the fans for the traditional teams number in the millions and should be neither forgotten nor dismissed. For instance, it was believed that the large number of fans for Chennaiyin FC would throng the stadium when a city-based team was representing Tamil Nadu and Tamil pride in the I-League. However, attendance at Chennai City's home matches was meagre. In their match against Mohun Bagan there were more supporters of the Kolkata team than of Chennai City. The Mariner (Mohun Bagan) fan clubs had travelled from Bengaluru and Mumbai to cheer for their team. This reveals the deep-rooted loyalty to traditional football clubs, which should be tapped to the advantage of the sport in India.

As of June 2017, two new clubs have joined the ISL: Bengaluru FC, twice winners of the I-League and runners-up of the 2016 AFC Cup, and the newly formed Jamshedpur FC, sponsored by Tata. The AIFF, in the meantime, has shelved its decision on the merger, declaring that from November 2017 to April 2018 both the ISL and I-League would run simultaneously. The rules of recruitment have also been changed: the ten ISL franchises can now only field five foreigners in their playing eleven and recruit a maximum of eight foreigners.

To put this into perspective, the AFC rankings as on February 2017 showed that amongst the top 100 Asian clubs, the highest-ranked Indian club side was East Bengal at the forty-first position, followed by traditional clubs like Mohun Bagan and the successful Goa clubs. ISL is now recognized by the AFC, so the winner of ISL 2017–18 can play in the AFC Cup next season. But in any continental tournament organized by the AFC, the participating teams can sign on and use only four foreign players, of whom one has to be of Asian origin. It appears that the ISL clubs are now willing to play with fewer foreign players to be able to compete in the AFC. It remains to be seen if they would be able to fare better than the traditional clubs have until now, as matching the best in Asia is an uphill task.

The piper calls the tune and IMG–Reliance have asserted their financial power in the recruitment of players. As the AIFF did not ensure a level playing field for the traditional clubs—through methods such as a salary cap (like in the MLS), budget restrictions or a simultaneous draft—the best Indian players have joined the ten franchises in the ISL draft in July 2017. The departure of 134 of the best Indian players from the first-division I-League clubs has created massive turbulence in the Indian transfer market. The impact of this seismic change in Indian football is evident in the way the historic clubs, Mohun Bagan and East Bengal, have been decimated. Mohun Bagan's star-studded team of the last three seasons (2014–15 to 2016–17) is now bereft of quality players, as they also had sponsorship problems. East Bengal's loss is equally severe. Around twelve of their main players from the 2016–17 season have quit—an unprecedented exodus for the club, which will celebrate their centenary in 2019–20.

The AIFF is now awaiting a report on the I-League and the ISL by Alex Phillips, head of Asia–Europe Affairs, UEFA (presently seconded to AFC). He will conduct research on both the leagues and submit the report to the AFC by the end of August 2017. This report will be discussed after the U-17 World Cup in India.

With the turn of the century, and twenty-five years after liberalization, India's English-speaking middle-class numbers over 12 crore people—more than the population of Britain. Due to non-stop availability of foreign football on satellite TV, there is rising interest in the sport. Observing the trend in schools, Shaji Prabhakaran, former FIFA development officer in India, said, 'A decade ago, most adolescents were keen on cricket, but now increasingly the younger generation is keen to play and follow football. I hope that this trend will increase when India stages the U-17 World Cup in October 2017.'[6]

The ISL is marketed much better than the I-League, and has successfully attracted the Indian middle class to the charm of football. Its entry has shaken traditional Indian clubs and tournaments out of their time warp and forced them to consider reinventing themselves. More finance, slick marketing, greater exposure to the world game and professionalism in club management is needed if the 'sleeping giant' (former FIFA president Sepp Blatter's description for Indian football)[7] is to finally awaken from its Rip Van Winkle-like slumber.

PART I

THE BEAUTIFUL GAME

1

Bengal

Indian Football's El Dorado

History, it is often said, is made more by accident than design. In 1877, when Kolkata was still the capital of British India, a ten-year-old boy named Nagendra Prasad Sarbadhikari was riding with his mother to the Ganges in a carriage. As the carriage was approaching the road near the Calcutta FC ground he noticed a ball game being played by a number of Europeans. Fascinated by the ebb and flow of the game, he pleaded with his mother to stop the carriage so that he could see it for some more time. Whilst watching, the football came towards him and he happily kicked it back into play. This became the first-ever recorded case of an Indian kicking a football.

Enamoured of this game, Sarbadhikari collected subscriptions from classmates at Hare School and purchased a football from Manton & Company, a well-known sports store in Kolkata. The enthusiastic but naive boys purchased a rugby ball and tried playing football with it on their school grounds. G.A. Stack—a professor at the nearby Presidency College—noticed the boys struggling to control an oval ball. An amiable man, Stack helped the boys get a proper football and trained them in the rudiments of the game. This batch of young players formed the Boys' Club, the first football club for Indians.

Earlier in the year some Englishmen had formed the Trades Club, probably the first football club in India, later to become the famous Dalhousie Athletic Club. This club had mostly Englishmen stationed in India playing for them.

It was Sarbadhikari who took the initiative to popularize football clubs amongst the Indian population of Bengal. Soon colleges such as Presidency (his alma mater), Sibpur Engineering College, Calcutta Medical College and St Xavier's College started forming football teams. Within a few years, Sarbadhikari was involved in organizing several clubs like Wellington and Sovabazar in 1887. Several other clubs were also formed, such as Kumartuli, Aryans, National Association and Mohun Bagan in 1889. A club for the Muslims, the Jubilee Club, was established in 1887. This club finally emerged as Mohammedan Sporting in 1891.

The game also spread to the districts. Football clubs came up in towns around Kolkata; like the Town Club in Chinsurah, a small town near the Hooghly river, in 1883; followed by Ripon AC in 1890 and Chinsurah Sporting in 1893. In the industrial town of Hooghly, Howrah Sporting Club was formed in 1889. In Dhaka, the Wari Club was started by a zamindar Surendra Nath Roy in 1898, whilst five rival zamindari families set up Victoria Sporting in 1903. The Calcutta League—the oldest in Asia, and amongst the oldest in the world—was started in 1898. Initially, it had only eight participating teams, comprising either British regiments or civilians. The Indian teams were allowed entry only from 1914 onwards.

Nagendra Prasad Sarbadhikari became known as the 'father of Indian football'. Gradually Indian clubs started achieving success against British teams. The biggest result was when Sovabazar Club defeated East Surrey Regiment 2-1 in the 1892 Trades Cup final. Similarly a year later Fort William Arsenal—a team made up of Indian workers—won the Cooch Behar Cup. The fairy tale continued when Mohun Bagan won the Gladstone Cup in 1905.

From 1906–08 Mohun Bagan started to win the British-instituted Trades Cup. This created a love affair and an intense bond between Bengalis and football. With these triumphs Mohun Bagan instilled belief amongst the local population that they could play on level terms with the English in football. The ultimate victory was when Mohun Bagan lifted the 1911 IFA Shield defeating Yorkshire Regiment in the final and four other English

Clubs in the previous rounds. This victory changed the status of football in Bengal forever.

As passion for the game increased in Kolkata, the British attempted to invite foreign opposition. Archives reveal that the first foreign team that came to Kolkata in 1936 was China's Olympic team. The Kolkata football fans were so eager to witness the Chinese team that tickets, which cost only 6 annas (a rupee consisted of 16 annas then) were sold in the black market for more than Rs 40.

This exorbitant black-market price for a football match ticket can be put into perspective by comparing it to market prices of that time. In 1936 and in the years before the Second World War, 2 maunds (around 75 kg) of rice could be purchased for only Rs 4. So to pay Rs 40 for a ticket to witness a football match was really exorbitant and showed the passion for the game amongst Kolkatans.

A year after Independence another team from China played friendly matches in Kolkata. On 24 September 1977 at the Eden Gardens, 'King' Pelé and Carlos Alberto Torres played for New York Cosmos against Mohun Bagan. After that, many renowned international stars such as the legendary Diego Maradona, the late Eusébio, Gerd Müller, Karl-Heinz Rummenigge, Roger Milla, Oliver Kahn, Diego Forlán, Enzo Francescoli, Valencio Ramos, Rinat Dasayev, Oleg Blokhin, László Kiss and Jorge Burruchaga have either visited West Bengal as celebrity guests or played for their countries in the Nehru Cup tournaments held there.

The foreign stars have all been impressed by the passion for the game amongst fans. However, the maximum passion in Kolkata is for the famous derby match, Mohun Bagan vs East Bengal.

Mohun Bagan

On 15 August 1889, at Kirti Mitra's Mohun Bagan Villa in north Kolkata, the Mohun Bagan Sporting Club was formed. A meeting of eminent intellectuals and landowners was held at this house to start a club to develop sporting activities amongst local Bengali youth. This meeting was presided over by Bhupendra Nath Bose (who became president of the Indian National Congress in 1914) and it was decided to name the club after the villa where the meeting was staged.

Some students of Presidency College, who were also members of the club, invited their professor F.J. Rhow as a guest on the first anniversary of the club. As there were no angling and rifle-shooting activities, Professor Rhow suggested they use the word 'athletic' instead of 'sporting'. The suggestion was accepted and from then onwards the club was renamed Mohun Bagan Athletic Club.

For years there was a special ethos about Bagan; the intelligentsia and aristocrats of Bengal all supported Bagan financially and emotionally. Their aim was to produce strong but principled athletes. A player who failed in a school or college exam was not allowed to play. Smoking and drinking were forbidden in the club house. The youth of Bengal aspired to play for this elite, prestigious club.

In 1900, Sailen Basu, a subedar major in the British Indian Army, became secretary of the club. He improved the fitness of the Bagan players by using physical conditioning methods learnt in the Army. That year Mohun Bagan also got their own field for the first time on the Kolkata Maidan near Fort William (the seat of the British Army in Kolkata), which they shared with Presidency College for the next fifteen years.

The strict training by Sailen Basu paid dividends. Mohun Bagan annexed the Cooch Behar Cup in 1904, 1905 and 1907. In 1905 they also won the Gladstone Cup beating the IFA Shield champions Dalhousie Club 6-1 in the final. They also won the Trades Cup thrice in a row from 1906 to 1908. In all these competitions, they faced British regimental and club sides. Such was Bagan's fame that they were invited to participate in the 1911 IFA Shield, which had then become the most prestigious tournament in Kolkata. The slick trophy presented to the winning team had been ordered from Messrs Elkington & Company in London, and was financed by the Maharajas of Patiala and Cooch Behar as well as two Englishmen.

The composition of the victorious Mohun Bagan team was a good indicator of how enthusiastically upper-caste Bengalis had taken up the sport. The team consisted of ten Bengalis, six of them Brahmins, and one player, Sudhir Kumar Chatterjee, a Christian. Only one player, Sukul, was originally from outside Bengal, his surname a corruption of the north Indian surname 'Shukla'. Though they were from the upper castes, the players were not wealthy; three of them, including captain Shibdas, were employed in government agencies. Not all the players were from Kolkata either. Manmohan Mukherjee was from Uttarpara and Nilmadhav Bhattacharya from Srirampur. Kanu Roy belonged to a wealthy family from Mymensingh in East Bengal while the Bhaduri brothers and Sudhir Chatterjee were originally from Faridpur. These eleven players were the first legends of Indian football.

For the next few decades Bagan did not win a major trophy but one of their players became a legend. The burly defender Gostha Pal in the 1920s became a nationalist symbol in the football field. This solidly built Mohun Bagan defender never won any major titles with his club but his powerful tackles against the physically stronger British players made him a symbol of Indian masculinity. Gostha Pal's robust tackling and powerful kicks exorcised the myth of physical weakness of the Bengalis.[1] Gostha Pal is the only footballer to be honoured with a statue on the Kolkata maidan, and a road was renamed after him.

Mohun Bagan next won the IFA Shield in 1947, thereby fulfilling a prophecy made by defender Sudhir Chatterjee after the 1911 IFA Shield victory. The story goes that the triumphant Bagan players were leaving the ground when a middle-aged person accosted Sudhir. Pointing to the East Yorkshire Regiment colours and the Union Jack aloft on the nearby Fort William, he said, 'This one you have done but what about that?' The supporter was evidently suggesting that since Bagan had lowered the colours of a British regiment, the young men should now join the nationalist movement and drive the British rulers from the country. Sudhir replied that this would occur when his team next won the Shield.

This off-the-cuff and probably flippant prediction came true. Though Mohun Bagan reached the IFA Shield final on a couple of occasions in the 1920s, they regained the trophy only in the year of India's independence, when they beat East Bengal 1-0 in the final. This may be just a coincidence, but during this period Bagan also did not win the Durand or the Rovers Cup.

India's first foreign tour was the 1948 London Olympics, and the captain, Talimeran Ao, was from Mohun Bagan, as were the captains for the next two Olympics: Sailen Manna (1952, Helsinki) and Samar 'Bodru' Banerjee (1956, Melbourne). India won the Asian Games gold medal in football twice, and on both occasions the captains were from Bagan.

After Independence, Mohun Bagan no longer remained a nationalist symbol, but transformed into a symbol of tradition and aristocracy for the residents of Kolkata. Its officials were renowned as men with good political connections, whether with the state government in Bengal or the Central government. An institution unto itself, the club was also a great unifier of people with different political ideologies. Both the Congress politician Siddhartha Shankar Ray (chief minister of Bengal from 1972 to 1977) and the ardent communist Jyoti Basu (chief minister from 1977 till 2002) were supporters of Mohun Bagan. During the 1980s and 1990s, when the rivalry between Congress and the Left Front was deeply entrenched in Bengal, officials of the club would have contrasting ideologies but were united by their affection for the maroon-and-green jersey.

The 1960s were Mohun Bagan's golden period. They had excellent players like Chuni Goswami, speedy outside-left Arumainayagam, centre-forward Ashok Chatterjee, sturdy defenders Jarnail Singh and T.A. Rahman, midfielder Kempaiah and goalkeeper Peter Thangaraj.

Goswami, captain of the 1962 Asiad team, is arguably India's most skilful player ever. His silky dribbling skills and deft placements made him a feared inside-forward. He also played cricket for Bengal and East Zone as a medium-pace bowler and middle-order batsman. Another Bagan legend, the sturdy central-defender

Jarnail Singh, is the only Indian to have twice been captain of the Asian All-Stars team, in 1964 and 1965. During this phase Mohun Bagan won the Calcutta League six times, the IFA Shield four times (1960, 1961, 1962 and 1969), the Durand Cup four times (1960, 1963, 1964 and 1965) and the Rovers Cup twice (1966 and 1968). Thanks to excellent administration they had a settled squad, and the brilliant set of players achieved rare milestones. For the first time, they won the IFA Shield three years in a row, and became the first Indian club to win the prestigious Durand tournament for three successive years as well. They were honoured for the latter by the then President of India, Dr S. Radhakrishnan, at a glittering ceremony at Delhi's Ashoka Hotel.

Mohun Bagan celebrated their platinum jubilee in 1964, with much aplomb and various sporting events. As part of the celebrations, several international teams including Tatabánya FC from Hungary visited India in December that year and played exhibition matches against Mohun Bagan, East Bengal and the Indian team. A cricket match was also organized between the Indian team and the Commonwealth team. The latter included the legendary Sir Garfield Sobers, Colin Cowdrey, Lance Gibbs and Mushtaq Mohammad. In tennis, India's Davis Cup quartet played some matches against Mike Sangster of England, and Bob Hewitt and Martin Mulligan of Australia. A German athletic team visited Kolkata and competed against leading Indian athletes. A hockey team from France played against the Indian team, which had just won the gold medal in the 1964 Tokyo Olympics. Such sporting celebrations have never been repeated in India.

Mohun Bagan's legendary president, Dhiren Dey, was quite a personality. He owned Dey's Medical Stores but his heart was in Mohun Bagan. When the team played outstation matches, he could not bear to listen to the commentary or watch them on TV. His driver would take him to a secluded garden. He would hand over the transistor radio to his driver and sit far away puffing on his cigarettes. The driver would give him regular updates on the match. An efficient administrator, he provided better facilities to the team than they had before. Bagan's own football ground was inaugurated in 1963 and the turf was considered the best in the country. It had a seating capacity of 22,000 people and important matches were held at this venue, such as the 1978 IFA Shield final.

Dhiren Dey's greatest contribution was getting Pelé to Kolkata in 1977. In those pre-satellite television days there was mass hysteria in anticipation of Pelé's visit. Lakhs of people gathered outside the Dum Dum Airport (now Netaji Subhas Chandra Bose International Airport) to greet the Brazilian legend when his plane landed at the late hour of 11.30 p.m. There were also teeming crowds outside his hotel in central Kolkata, waiting to catch a glimpse of the only man to have won three World Cups for his team.

Pelé then played for the New York Cosmos, which also included Carlos Alberto, a member of Brazil's 1970 World Cup–winning team, and Italian player Giorgio Chinaglia. When the match day came, the ground was rain-soaked and slushy. Pelé almost refused to play because of the slippery conditions. However, Dhiren Dey and the Bagan officials begged him to play, even at half-pace. Police officials implored Pelé, saying the crowd would get violent and lynch the Bagan officials if he did not play. The great Brazilian finally relented, but was cautious throughout the match.

On 24 September 1977 Cosmos played Mohun Bagan in front of 80,000 people at the Eden Gardens. Bagan's Mohammed Habib outshone Pelé in that game and assisted in scoring both Bagan goals with his incisive passes. Shyam Thapa in the eighteenth minute and Habib in the thirty-third ensured a lead for Bagan, but Cosmos equalized in the seventy-fifth minute to end the match in a 2-2 draw. At the end of the match Pelé personally congratulated Habib for his inspiring performance.

Decades later, on 27 May 2008, one of the greatest goalkeepers of all time, Oliver Kahn of Bayern Munich and Germany, played his farewell match in front of 1,30,000 people at the Salt Lake Stadium against Mohun Bagan. Kahn was overwhelmed at the response, especially when the main sponsor of the game, Bengal Peerless, gave him a trophy studded with 8640 diamonds.

Mohun Bagan, like Yorkshire in domestic English cricket or like Athletic Bilbao in Spain, was a very traditional club and never recruited foreign players. The club management felt hiring foreign players was against the ethos of the club, formed to nurture talent amongst Indian youth. During the Second World War the legendary Denis Compton, who played cricket for England and football for Arsenal, was stationed in Kolkata and wanted to play for Mohun Bagan, but the club's officials did not relent. Instead, Compton was given honorary membership.

It was only after Dhiren Dey's death in 1990 that Bagan changed their policy. This was also done as there was a paucity of quality Indian strikers. To gain success Mohun Bagan recruited Nigerian player Chima Okorie. This was a historic transfer as Chima shifted from East Bengal to Mohun Bagan for a then-record sum of Rs 5 lakh in 1991. The move was successful as under Satyajit Chatterjee's captaincy Bagan annexed the Calcutta League and Rovers Cup that year.

Creditably, Mohun Bagan have never believed in splurging money to buy players but when required have spent well. The first player to receive Rs 50,000 per season was Shyam Thapa when he left East Bengal for Mohun Bagan in 1977. This was also the start of another golden period for Mohun Bagan. After winning the IFA Shield in 1976–77, they won the Triple Crown— the IFA Shield, the Rovers Cup and the Durand Cup—for the first time in the 1977–78 season. They again won the IFA Shield from 1978 to 1982, making it a series of six consecutive IFA victories. The tournament was not held in 1980. They were also joint winners of the Federation Cup in 1978 and 1980, and won it outright in 1981 and 1982. They won the Durand Cup in 1979 and were joint winners with East Bengal in 1982.

Mohun Bagan's win in the 1999–2000 Coca-Cola NFL is the greatest comeback in the history of Indian football. When their relatively young team, mostly built from Tata Football Academy (TFA) graduates, failed to qualify for the 1st Philips NFL in 1996– 97, the doubting Thomases felt the club was slipping. However, they won the 2nd NFL in 1997–98, relying on many seasoned professionals. Prior to the start of the 4th NFL 1999–2000, Bagan were not even tipped to finish amongst the top six (entitled to prize money ranging from Rs 5 lakh to Rs 40 lakh). Yet they won the league comfortably. This was their second NFL victory and they had the best collection of foreign players ever seen on Indian soil. They recruited five talented foreign players; central-defender Sammy Omollo of Kenya, left-back Dusit Chalersman of Thailand (played for 1997 Asian All-Stars), striker Igor Shkvyrin of Uzbekistan (won the 1994 Asian Games gold medal), winger Stephen Abarowei of Nigeria (played for his country's age-group teams) and Jose Ramirez Barreto of Brazil. The foreigners scored 22 of Bagan's 36 goals, and Igor was top scorer with 11 goals in 14 matches.

This title established Bagan as Indian football's premier club. They became trendsetters again, the first team to have won the NFL—the first major domestic tournament of the twenty-first century—twice.

Still, in recent years there was a slump. Mohun Bagan had not won a major trophy for five years (2010–15), or a national league title (called I-League since 2008) since 2002. Their best showing since then had been being runners-up in the 2nd I-League in 2008–09. The constant changing of coaches and financial crises (chit fund scams in Bengal) had become a source of worry for their fans. But such is the love this club inspires that their fan base never declined.

In June 2015, the fans got something to cheer about when the victorious Bagan team returned from Bengaluru to Kolkata clutching the Hero I-League trophy. Over 2 lakh people greeted their heroes and joined in the spontaneous celebrations all over the City of Joy. Bagan players are again being treated as demigods, just as they were in the heyday of Kolkata football from the 1950s till the 1980s. Bagan's supporters cut across the class divide as they are a mix of IT professionals, media personnel, private- and public-sector employees, and even those of humble origin, like tea-stall owners.

Like in the past, Bagan victory has rekindled interest for the game in Kolkata. East Bengal was the last Kolkata club to have won the I-League way back in 2004. Queries were being raised about declining standards, the poor recruitment of players and inept club management. Doubts had crept in about whether Kolkata would ever regain the glory of their past, but Mohun Bagan's I-League triumph has hopefully heralded the dawn of a new era. Their star players are the Haitian international Sony Norde; Japanese midfield dynamo Katsumi Yusa; and young Indian players: Jeje Lalpekhlua from Mizoram, left-back Dhanachandra Singh from Manipur, goalkeeper Debjit Majumder and right-back Pritam Kotal, both from West Bengal, all of whom can become names to be reckoned with in the future.

In the next season Mohun Bagan further strengthened their squad by acquiring dynamic and well-built, box-to-box midfielder Pronay Halder and the 2006 Trinidad and Tobago World Cup striker Cornell Glen. They came second in the I-League but won the 37th Hero Federation Cup in grand style, trouncing Aizawl FC 5-0 in the final. Bagan scored a record 17 goals in 5 matches, with Jeje finishing as top scorer with 7 goals.

By the end of the 2015–16 season Mohun Bagan had been sixteen-time winners and eleven-time runners-up of India's oldest tournament, the Durand Cup. They are the only team to have won the Durand Cup thrice in a row on two occasions, 1963–65 and 1984–86. They also have the best record in the second-oldest tournament in India, the Rovers Cup in Mumbai: they've entered the final twenty-four times, been champions on fourteen occasions and runners-up ten times. In the prestigious IFA Shield, Mohun Bagan have been winners twenty times and runners-up eighteen times.

The Federation Cup, started by the AIFF in 1977 as India's premier knockout tournament, has been dominated by Mohun Bagan. They are fourteen-time champions and six-time runners-up. They are the only team to have won this prestigious tournament three years in a row, 1992–94. Bagan's former left-back Sankar Banerjee and India's first-ever professional coach, Amal Dutta, have been the most successful coaches in the Federation Cup, each having helped Bagan win the trophy thrice. Syed Nayeemuddin, who won the coveted Mohun Bagan Ratna award on 29 July 2016 for his distinguished services as a player and coach to the club, helped them win the Federation Cup titles twice. Bagan also twice won the Federation Cup with foreign coaches, Robson Mattos (Brazil) in 2006 and Karim Bencherifa (Morocco) in 2008.

There have been some truly outstanding players in the long history of this great club, but due to the constraints of space, I briefly profile nine of them here. Mariappa Kempaiah (1957–65) was an indefatigable midfielder, one of India's greatest ever, who helped in both the defence and the attack. Unfortunately, he died forgotten and with limited finances. Sailen Manna (1942–60) was an exceptional defender in the two-back system, noted for his free kicks and accurate headers. Arumainayagam (1961–68) was a diminutive left-winger, popularly called 'Baby Taxi' for his blistering pace. He had a telepathic understanding with inside-left Chuni Goswami. Subrata Bhattacharya (1974–90) was a skilful defender whose immaculate positioning enabled him to intercept passes for opposing forwards, and he distributed the ball with ease. Chandreshwar Prasad Singh (1966–71) was a hard tackler, excellent man-marker and commanding in the air. Samar Banerjee (1952–58), affectionately called 'Badru Da', was India's first roving striker and excelled as a withdrawn centre-forward, with good dribbling skills and powerful shots. Prasun Banerjee (1974–80, 1982–83) was known as 'the midfield general' and is the first international footballer to become a member of Parliament. Satyajit Chatterjee (1986–2000) was another box-to-box midfielder and helped Mohun Bagan win six Federation Cup titles between 1986 and 1998. He excelled in quick interceptions and initiated attacks with accurate passes. Jose Ramirez Barreto (1999–2004, 2006–12), the Brazilian magician, was Bagan's finest foreign player and difficult to contain because of his sudden acceleration and close control.

There has always been a certain aura about Mohun Bagan, as many famous people have been its fans. Celebrities who were close followers of Bagan were the first President of India, Dr Rajendra Prasad, the first chief minister of Bengal, Dr B.C. Roy, Bengal's longest-serving chief minister, Jyoti Basu, noted Congress leader Atulya Ghosh and famous music composer R.D. Burman.

Many players have also felt a great attachment to Bagan and have never changed clubs, despite not receiving high monetary incentives. Some of these legends—known as Mohun Baganis—include Gostha Pal, Umapati Kumar, Sailen Manna, Chuni Goswami, Arumainayagam, Subrata Bhattacharya and Satyajit Chatterjee. Even some of the foreign recruits like Barreto, Abarowei and Norde are greatly attached to India's oldest football club.

Mohammedan Sporting

This club came into existence in 1891, a decade before the Muslim League was formed. In 1894 they had their first annual meeting, presided over by Justice Syed Amir Ali. Some of the prominent Muslims of Bengal, including the ruling family of Murshidabad and civil servants, attended this meeting. One of the aims of the club was to persuade Muslims to improve their physique and take up 'manly' Western sports.[2] When the club started they did not have a field to practise in so they utilized the playfield of Calcutta Boys' school for the purpose.

The first major tournament they won was the Cooch Behar Trophy in 1909. In 1927 they were promoted to the second division of the Calcutta League. By 1933 they were good enough to be promoted to the first division, winning 8 consecutive matches. They made history by becoming the first Indian team to win the prestigious Calcutta League in 1934 and also the first to win it in their very first year. They continued to break new ground in many ways in the future.

They were in a sense the first pan-India club. Their management, headed by S.A. Rashid and I.G.H. Arif in the 1930s, was professional in outlook and appealed to wealthy Muslims to donate generously. The membership fees were Rs 25–30 per month although not everyone paid up. The secretary of the club during their successful years from 1936–45 was Khwaja Nooruddin, an alderman of the Calcutta Municipal Corporation, who was later elected to the Bengal Legislative Assembly. They recruited Muslim players from all over the country. In 1936 Mohammedan Sporting had nine players

from outside Bengal—defender Jumma Khan (Quetta), Rashid
(Peshawar), Usman Jaan and Aquil Ahmed (both Delhi), Serajuddin,
Saboo, Masoom and Rahim (Bengaluru) and Noor Mohammed
(Faizabad). So they broke the trend of picking up talented players
only from their own state.

Others who played with them included Bacchi Khan (North-
West Frontier Province) and inside-forward Rahmat and midfielder
Mohiuddin (Bengaluru). Anwar from Quetta was the captain
when they won the Calcutta League in 1934, and centre-forward
Rashid the top scorer with 11 goals. A year later they retained
their title, beating city rivals East Bengal and Mohun Bagan on
both occasions. Rashid was again the top scorer with 17 goals out
of a total of 37 in 22 matches.

In 1936 the burly but agile goalkeeper Usman Jaan transferred
from Youngmen FC in Delhi, which further bolstered
Mohammedan Sporting's defence. That year Mohammedan
Sporting became the first team to win the Calcutta League and
IFA Shield in the same season. Despite a serious injury, centre-
forward Rashid finished as top scorer for the third successive year
with 11 goals.

Coached during these years by S.A. Aziz, Mohammedan
Sporting retained the Calcutta League title in both 1937 and 1938.
Their defence was rock solid thanks to Jumma Khan and Bacchi
Khan's firm tackling and first-time clearances. The tall Usman
Jaan in goal cut an imposing figure. During the 1938 season,
Mohammedan Sporting scored a massive 61 goals, with Rahim
finishing as the top scorer with 27 goals.

The popularity of the club reached a peak after they won the
Calcutta League for a record fifth time in 1938. Two Mohammedan
Sporting players featured in advertisements for the Indian Tea
Market Expansion Board, sturdy centre-half Noor Mohammed
and Jumma Khan, who was described as India's best full-back.
The choice of these two players was noteworthy, as till then no
Indian sportsmen had featured in an advertisement. C.K. Nayudu,
captain of the Indian cricket team that toured England in 1932,
first featured in an advertisement only in 1941.

In 1938, iconic poet Kazi Nazrul Islam composed a poem in honour of the team:

> These feet that have so incredibly woven wonders with the football—
> May the power of all of India rise from those very feet,
> May those feet break our chains. And our fear, and our dread—
> May those feet kick them. Allah-u-Akbar![3]

Golam Mostofa also composed a poem to celebrate this milestone. This poem was sung by popular singer Abbasuddin Ahmed and released by the Gramophone record company. The songs and poems added to the lustre and legacy of Mohammedan Sporting.

Mohammedan Sporting was then the most well-organized club in the country, financially sound and alert to the needs of players with regard to training and equipment. They were the only Indian team that could match the fitness level and strength of the British teams. They were the first Indian team to play with boots on wet ground, and focus on a proper diet and physical fitness for their players. Their coach Aziz had designed a lightweight boot for them, suitable to the slippery surfaces in the Kolkata Maidan during the monsoon. The boots were made by local cobblers. Five years of success in the Calcutta League ensured that more and more supporters wanted to watch their matches. The public was charged 8 annas for an enclosure with chairs, and 4 annas for seats in wooden stands. Members of the club had a separate enclosure.

A major factor that contributed to their popularity was their historic 1940 Durand Cup triumph against a British regimental team. This edition of the third-oldest tournament in the world was played in Delhi at what is now the National Stadium. On the day of the final, numerous fans from the Old Delhi area travelled by tonga or cycles to witness this epic encounter. Stories of this famous victory were narrated in the houses and by-lanes of Old Delhi for years thereafter. Legends of the 1940 Durand triumph were passed on orally from generation to generation, thereby ensuring mass identification with this popular Kolkata team.

They became the first Indian club to win the historic Triple Crown—the Calcutta League, the Rovers Cup and the Durand Cup—in 1940. They were also the first team in the history of the Rovers Cup to win the tournament without conceding a goal. They beat the Royal Air Force 8-0 (Karim: 3, Saboo: 3 and Rashid: 2) in a third-round match. They overcame Heavy Battery 3-0 in the quarter-finals (Rashid, Saboo and Karim). In the semi-finals, they beat the Welsh Regiment 3-0 (Rashid: 2 and Rashid Khan). Incidentally, they beat this same outfit, considered one of the best British regimental teams during that time, in the Durand tournament semi-finals also. In the Rovers Cup final they overcame the Bangalore Muslims 1-0 with centre-forward Rashid scoring the match-winning goal.

In 1941 they won the Double Crown of the Calcutta League and the IFA Shield. They scored 110 goals in that entire season and were the first Indian club to cross a century of goals in a single year. In 1942 they retained the IFA Shield beating East Bengal 1-0 in the final. During their dream run from 1934 to 1942, Mohammedan Sporting scored 579 goals, with about 60 per cent of them being netted by their four main forwards; Saboo (117), Rashid (105), Rahim (98) and Rahmat (36).[4] They became so popular that in the early 1940s the Prince of Nepal, a keen player himself, came all the way to Kolkata and trained with this famous club.

The appeal of this club transcended its successes in football. During these turbulent decades, when the two-nation theory was being propagated and the future of British rule was uncertain, there was a sense of unease and displacement amongst the Muslim community across India. Middle class and lower-middle-class Muslims rallied around Mohammedan Sporting. The club became a symbol of Muslim strength and brilliance, and enjoyed an unprecedented fan following from Peshawar to Dhaka and from Kanyakumari to Kashmir. It provided the grounds for pan-Indian Muslim unity in the sociopolitical sphere.

The finances of Mohammedan Sporting took a hit due to Partition. Many wealthy landowners and donors migrated to East Pakistan or West Pakistan, and the financial support that earlier came from Dhaka, Chittagong, Lahore and Peshawar stopped.

After the communal clashes and huge loss of property, Muslims became wary and overprotective of their wealth and no longer donated generously to the club.

After Independence, they were the first club to win the Calcutta League in 1948. This victory came when Kolkata was still tense in the aftermath of Partition violence. Many old-timers have said that their faith in Indian democracy was established due to the unbiased supervision in the 1948 Calcutta League, which enabled their team to win. Football thus became a great social equalizer. In the 1950s players from East and West Pakistan regularly came to play for Mohammedan Sporting. They were the biggest crowd-pullers anywhere in the subcontinent.

Famous film stars Dilip Kumar, Agha and Johnny Walker were fervent fans of Mohammedan Sporting, and whenever possible came to witness their matches at the Rovers Cup in Mumbai. Their captain in 1957, Abdus Salaam, told me that when the club won the Calcutta League that year, Dilip Kumar gave presents and cash awards to the entire squad.

Mohammedan Sporting was also the first Indian side to win a trophy on foreign soil after Independence—the Aga Khan Gold Cup in Dhaka in 1960, beating Makassar Club of Indonesia 4-1 in the final (Oomer: 2, Jaffar and Rahmatullah were the scorers). Inside-forward Rahmatullah, who later settled in the US, scored 10 goals, the highest by an Indian on foreign soil in a single tournament. The record is still unbroken.

By the 1960s Mohammedan Sporting changed its rules and included players from other communities as well. In fact the last great Mohammedan Sporting team—of 1980 and 1981—which won the DCM Trophy, the Rovers Cup and the Calcutta League, had a majority of Bengali Hindu players. This did not affect their support base as the identity of the supporters was with the club.

A major factor for this unflagging support is believed to be the name of the club. As the late Mohammed Taki, a passionate Mohammedan Sporting supporter in Delhi, had once said, 'The club is associated with the Prophet's name, so it arouses passionate feelings amongst us believers.' Taki explained that for the football

lovers of Old Delhi's walled city and all over India, Mohammedan
Sporting was a lifelong commitment.

After Mohammedan Sporting, the most popular team amongst
the Old Delhi fans was Hyderabad City Police (later known as
Andhra Police) due to their exploits in the Durand Cup. Hyderabad
City Police also had several Muslim players but whenever they
clashed with Mohammedan Sporting the loyalties were not
divided. In the 1964 DCM final, Mohammedan Sporting took on
Andhra Police and 90 per cent of the Old Delhi fans supported
the Kolkata club.

In the 1960s and 1970s, the Punjab teams, BSF, Punjab Police,
Leaders Club and later JCT of Phagwara, became the nemesis
of the Kolkata clubs, especially in tournaments in Delhi like the
DCM and Durand. Their robust style of play and hard tackling
often intimidated both East Bengal and Mohun Bagan. However,
Mohammedan Sporting, thanks to their vociferous supporters,
never flinched, and matched the Punjab teams even physically.
This approach also made the team very popular.

There would be a festive atmosphere whenever Mohammedan
Sporting played in Delhi, with their frenzied supporters singing
songs, chanting slogans of encouragement, blowing horns
or whistles and waving club banners. The impromptu songs
were a source of delight. In 1967 when the brothers Ramana
(outside-right) and Pappana (striker) played for Mohammedan
Sporting, fans adapted a popular song from the film *Ganga
Jumna* to chant encouragement. They would sing '*Sawan ka
mahina, pawan kare shor, Ramana kare centre, Pappana kare
score* [It's the monsoon month, the wind bellows, Ramana
centres and Pappana scores].'

For many decades, the annual Durand Cup and DCM Trophy
organizers considered Mohammedan Sporting their best bet for
earning revenue. In the days before sponsorship, ticket sales
were the biggest source of money and Mohammedan Sporting's
popularity ensured capacity crowds every time they played at the
Delhi Gate Stadium. The proximity of the walled city to the Delhi
Gate Stadium also ensured a near-full house.

Gradually Mohammedan Sporting started to decline in the 1970s as regards the recruitment of players and collection of money. They lost the identity of a champion team and only became a tough contender to either East Bengal or Mohun Bagan.

In the following decade, business tycoon Tahir Irfan Randerian became president of Mohammedan Sporting and was determined to spend money and build a strong squad. Prasanta Banerjee recalled that several players returning from the 1980 pre-Olympics were taken secretly to a hideout and offered large sums of money to sign on with the club. The highest-paid Indian player then was Shyam Thapa who got Rs 50,000 per annum when he transferred from East Bengal to Mohun Bagan in 1977. Several star players, some of whom belonged to East Bengal, were offered nearly twice that amount. So, international goalkeeper Bhaskar Ganguly, right-back Chinmoy Chatterjee, defenders Ramen Bhattacharya and Alok Mukherjee, midfielder Prasanta Banerjee, and forwards Surajit Sengupta, Debashish Roy, Shabbir Ali and Mohammed Akbar joined Mohammedan Sporting that year.

In 1981, the team was further strengthened by the inclusion of three internationals from Mohun Bagan: midfielder Prasun Banerjee (now a Trinamool Congress MP) and wingers Manas Bhattacharya and Bidesh Bose. In 1981 they won the Calcutta League after a lapse of fourteen years, as well as several other trophies. The non-Muslim players were welcomed by the club supporters and treated with great respect and affection all over India.

During this time the club changed coaches often. In 1980 and 1981 their coach was former player M.A. Sattar, and in 1983 and 1984, when they won the Federation Cup, it was Syed Nayeemuddin. However, due to another twist in their fortunes these glory years did not last long. Tahir Irfan Randerian suffered huge losses in business because of the Iran–Iraq war and could no longer support the club like before. Most of the club's star players left and returned to either East Bengal or Mohun Bagan.

Mohammedan Sporting waited a long time for their second Durand triumph. After a lapse of seventy-three years they won the Durand again when they beat ONGC 2-1 in the 2013 final. On three earlier occasions—1959, 1980 and 1992—they had been runners-up. All said and done, Mohammedan Sporting has been a successful club. It has won the Calcutta League eleven times, IFA Shield five times, Rovers Cup six times, DCM Trophy four times, and Federation Cup and Durand Cup twice each.

This most-loved club at one time faced a crisis of existence in 2014. Maintaining an I-League team these days means spiralling costs. Clubs like Mohammedan Sporting are unable to survive on club membership and ticket sales alone. As the Prophet's name is attached to the club, they could not have liquor sponsors and others were not forthcoming. In October 2014 club officials announced that the closure of Mohammedan Sporting was imminent, as due to a paucity of funds they could not hire players good enough to field a competitive team. It sent shock waves through their legions of supporters throughout the subcontinent. It seemed like the end of an era was close at hand. Football lovers were distraught that this club which was the first to win a trophy on foreign soil would cease to exist. However, the club managed to survive, but now plays in the second division of the I-League.

East Bengal

The East Bengal club was established after some dramatic circumstances, regional rivalries and perceived insults. During the early decades of the twentieth century, the governing body for football in Kolkata, the IFA, permitted only two Indian, or 'native', clubs, as they were known to play in the prestigious Calcutta League. Most Indian clubs participated in second-tier tournaments like the Cooch Behar Cup and the Trades Cup. East Bengal was formed due to an incident in a Cooch Behar trophy match. On a humid afternoon on 28 July 1920, Mohun Bagan took on Jorabagan club in the semi-finals of the Cooch Behar trophy. For some inexplicable reason Jorabagan excluded their star midfielder Sailesh Bose who hailed from Dhaka. The player was neither injured nor sick, nor was he out of form. Hence there was no apparent reason for his omission.

Jorabagan's vice president and industrialist Suresh Chandra Chaudhuri pleaded for Bose's inclusion but his requests were ignored. Suresh Chaudhuri was originally a zamindar from Mymensingh district. He felt the omission of the player was based on prejudices and was a regional slight. Miffed at this exclusion, Chaudhuri resigned from Jorabagan club and started a new club along with Manmatha Nath Roy Chaudhuri, the former Maharaja of Santosh (the Santosh Trophy is named after him); Sarada Ranjan Roy, the cricketer and principal of Metropolitan College; and Sailesh Bose, Ramesh Chandra Sen and Aurobindo Ghosh. As all the founder members hailed from the eastern part of Bengal they decided to name their newly formed club 'East Bengal'. It was established on 1 August 1920.

During the colonial era many people, especially the zamindars of eastern Bengal, used to stay in Kolkata for administrative and financial reasons. These people felt that the original residents of Kolkata treated them in a derogatory manner, mocking their accent and speaking style, and calling them 'Bangals'. In retaliation, they named Kolkatans 'Ghotis', most likely derived from Kolkatans' regular use of metal pots (*ghoti*) in their daily life. Hence, from the very inception of East Bengal FC, the people from this region started identifying with the club.[5]

In 1921 the club were granted entry into Calcutta League's second division and were promoted to the first division in 1925. East Bengal had been performing well in the local Kolkata tournaments, and initially both Mohun Bagan and Aryans Club, who were members of the Calcutta League committee, opposed their entry. East Bengal officials were further incensed by the haughty attitude of Mohun Bagan and hence their rivalry was established on the football field (for details, see Chapter 10: 'The Great Rivalry'). They first met in a Calcutta League match on 25 May 1925 at the CFC grounds, which East Bengal won 1-0, with N. Chakravarty scoring the winning goal. Mohun Bagan emerged victorious in the return leg.

In the 1930s, East Bengal began to regularly recruit players from other states, just as Mohammedan Sporting did. When East Bengal trounced Mohun Bagan 4-0 in the 1936 Calcutta League—their biggest victory till then over their arch-rivals—all the goals were scored by their outstation players: Murgesh, Lakshminarayan (2) and K. Prasad (all from Bengaluru).

Mohun Bagan's policy of not hiring players from outside Bengal faced massive opposition from other clubs. In 1939 it even led to a walkout from the IFA by Mohammedan Sporting, East Bengal, Kalighat and Aryans. This quartet of clubs formed a rival Bengal Football Association. In 1940, however, a truce was reached and the recalcitrant clubs returned to the fold.

East Bengal rose to prominence from the early 1940s and had a large—though not fanatical—following. According to the eminent sports writer and novelist Rupak Saha, it all changed after the trauma of Partition in 1947.

The short stories of Saadat Hasan Manto and the movies of Ritwik Ghatak chronicle the agony, pain and massive suffering of human beings caused by Partition.[6] The problem of resettlement of the Hindus of East Pakistan was much more complex than for their Punjab counterparts as they wanted to settle only in West Bengal, Tripura or Assam. Many amongst them wanted to stay on in the land of their ancestors. However, from the winter of 1948 communal riots broke out in East Pakistan again, and there was another wave of migration into West Bengal. A number of them were peasants and small-scale farmers who had lost their property and prestige in the turmoil. They were now forced to work as labourers and survive in slums, refugee camps or railway platforms. In 1949, Dr Bidhan Chandra Roy, the second chief minister of West Bengal, mentioned the presence of 16 lakh refugees in his state.

This massive influx of people created a socio-economic crisis. The refugees had hoped for sympathy and cordiality from their co-religionists in West Bengal, but during an economic crisis, religion takes a back seat. The original inhabitants of Kolkata felt the resources of their city were being strained and they maintained a distance from the refugees. There were clashes for jobs and admissions to schools and universities, and rivalries in business. East Bengal club now became a source of identity and hope for people struggling to find their foothold in a new place. The name of the club was a nostalgic reminder of the home they had left behind forever. The joys and agonies of East Bengal FC's fortunes started reflecting their own struggles in daily life. So a political event like Partition played a major role in the evolution of Indian football, developing new social identities amongst the Kolkata clubs.

From 1947 onwards East Bengal, under their efficient secretary Jyotish Chandra Guha, built a formidable team with outstation recruits. All their five forwards were from south India. Outside-right P. Venkatesh (Bengaluru), inside-right Appa Rao (Kakinada, of the then Madras Presidency, now in Andhra Pradesh) and left-winger P.B. Saleh (Kerala) joined in 1947. Inside-left Ahmed Khan (Bengaluru) and centre-forward K.P. Dhanraj were recruited after the 1948 Olympics. Dhanraj was from Hyderabad and then went to Bengaluru to play. Until this time, Mohun Bagan and Mohammedan Sporting were the dominant and star-studded teams. But thanks to their brilliant forward line, named the 'Pancha Pandavas' by fans, East Bengal became the best team in India from 1949 to 1953, scoring an unbelievable 386 goals during this time. In 1948, they defeated the visiting Chinese Olympic team XI 2-0, which further established their prowess.

J.C. Guha had also spotted the barefoot wonder Sheoo Mewalal in the 1940s, but Mewalal wished to play for Mohun Bagan. He later shifted to East Bengal Railway as he needed a regular job. A prolific goalscorer, Mewalal went on to become a regular international, and scored the winning goal for India in the 1951 Asian Games final against Iran.

From 1942–52, East Bengal won sixteen trophies. Their best performance was reserved for the prestigious IFA Shield in 1949, when under midfielder S.M. Kaiser's captaincy they won the shield convincingly. They scored 22 goals without conceding a single one. In the final they beat their arch-rivals Mohun Bagan 2-0, with strikes from P. Venkatesh and Ahmed Khan. East Bengal's centre-forward Dhanraj was top scorer with 10 goals. In the following year they won the shield again under Saleh's captaincy by trouncing Services XI 3-0, thereby becoming the first Indian team to win the trophy back to back. The scorers were Dhanraj (2) and Saleh. Overall, East Bengal scored 17 goals and let in 1 goal. Dhanraj was again the top scorer with 10 goals.

In 1951, defender Byomkesh Bose was the captain and the club was poised for a hat-trick of wins. In the quarter-finals East Bengal brushed aside Maharashtra XI 3-1. East Bengal's goals were scored by Dhanraj (2) and Saleh while Tulsiram reduced the margin. In the semi-finals they stormed past Rajasthan 3-0 with two strikes from Venkatesh and one by Ahmed Khan, and met their arch-rivals Mohun Bagan in the final.

The rivals met on 11 September 1951 on the CFC grounds. East Bengal dominated the proceedings but Bagan's defence held firm. After a hard tussle the match ended in a goalless draw. In the replay, East Bengal attacked from the beginning and ran circles around the rival defence. Venkatesh and Ahmed Khan were impressive. Mohun Bagan's sorties were limited. East Bengal continued their domination in the second-half and eventually won 2-0. Both the goals were scored by left-winger Saleh, and East Bengal emerged as the first Indian team to win the IFA Shield three years in a row.

The Shield was presented to the club in a special ceremony by the governor Kailash Nath Katju at the Raj Bhavan. The club's triumph was hailed by the Football Association, England, who in their annual souvenir nominated East Bengal as the number one club of Asia, on the basis of which they became the first Indian club to be invited to Europe (Romania and the USSR) in 1953. They reached the semi-finals of an invitational tournament in Romania before losing 0-3 to the hosts. The following year they received an invitation to tour the erstwhile USSR, as not only India's but Asia's best club. Back in 1951 they had also beaten Sweden's Gothenburg FC 1-0.

During their period of ascendancy, East Bengal won the Calcutta League six times (1942, 1945-46, 1949-50 and 1952) and the IFA

Shield five times (1943, 1945 and 1949–51). They also won the prestigious Durand Cup twice in a row (1951 and 1952), the Rovers Cup in 1949 and the DCM Trophy in 1950 and 1952.

There is an amusing story about the passion of their supporters at the Calcutta League matches in 1951. In their first encounter, Mohun Bagan were leading 1-0 at half-time (they eventually won 3-0). The famous commentator Berry Sarbadhikari inappropriately stated during the half-time review, 'My team is leading by 1 goal to nil.' East Bengal fans listening to the broadcast objected and the club too complained to the AIR authorities. When the teams met in the replay, AIR replaced Sarbadhikari with Pearson Surita. This change wasn't appreciated by the Mohun Bagan fans. They pleaded to AIR's Kolkata station that Surita not be allowed to broadcast as he was a lucky mascot for East Bengal; every time he was at the mic, Bagan lost. AIR ignored the objection of course and East Bengal won.

East Bengal became the first club to do the 'Delhi double', winning the Durand and DCM tournaments in the same year. In the 1952 Durand Cup, East Bengal overcame Hyderabad City Police 1-0 in the final. A month later in the DCM Trophy, the 'Pancha Pandavas' were in mesmerizing form. Centre-forward K. Dhanraj scored a hat-trick and together they overwhelmed the speedy 58th Gorkhas 4-0 in a one-sided final. They won the tournament without conceding a goal, a feat never repeated in this competition.

The most outstanding East Bengal team was the side that won the 1956 Durand Cup. They fielded some players from Rajasthan and Bengal Nagpur Railway (BNR) on loan. Seeded into the second round, on their way to the final they beat Mughals club, Delhi, 2-1 (Moosa: 2), drew with Caltex Mumbai 0-0, and the next day won the replay 1-0 (Kittu). They drew twice 0-0 with MRC Wellington in the semi-finals but then won the second replay 2-0 (Kanayan and a self-goal). In the final they beat the mighty Hyderabad City Police 2-0 with Balasubramaniam and Moosa scoring. In all their matches, the stadium was full to capacity, as East Bengal had the most attractive forward line in the country.

East Bengal's successes and rise to fame during this period were primarily due to the excellent recruitment of players and efficient management, spearheaded by J.C. Guha. He was secretary of the club from 1945 to 1959 and again from 1965 to 1970. In those days there were no agents or talent scouts. Such was J.C. Guha's love for East Bengal that he would travel to tournaments all over the country to watch players from different teams and persuade the best to join East Bengal. He spotted talented midfielder Ram Bahadur in 1956 and took him to Kolkata. He was impressed by the tenacity and work rate of the precocious inside-forward Mohammed Habib in the 1965 Santosh Trophy, and went to Hyderabad to recruit the trio of Habib, Syed Nayeemuddin and midfielder Mohammed Afzal for the 1966 season. Nayeem has always recalled that his family was so impressed by J.C. Guha's sincerity and humility that they willingly let him give up his job at Andhra Police and join East Bengal. When he went to Nayeem's house in Hyderabad, Guha sat on the floor and shared a simple meal with the family.

After Guha returned to Kolkata, a Mohun Bagan official came to Nayeem's house and tried to convince him to join their club. Sensing that Nayeem might waver, J.C. Guha sent another East Bengal official Ratu Thakurta to Hyderabad. Nayeem decided to join East Bengal. But getting the release order from the Andhra Police department proved to be a tough task. Guha then requested the chief minister of West Bengal, Prafulla Sen, to speak to the Andhra Pradesh chief minister Brahmanand Reddy. After Reddy's intervention, Nayeem got the release order and joined East Bengal.

J.C. Guha's dedication to the cause of East Bengal was amazing. He was an exemplary administrator and ensured that his players got a nutritious diet that included dry fruits and nuts. When any of the outstation players fell sick in Kolkata, Guha would look after them like they were his own sons. When Nayeem contracted jaundice after the 1967 Calcutta League and IFA Shield, Guha and another club official Subir Ghosh visited him daily and helped him recover. Officials like Guha were unique as he neglected his family business and spent most of his time and money on his club's welfare. He would attend morning practice daily, sitting with his umbrella and newspaper and watching the players from early morning to about noon. He would interact with senior players and tell them to conduct the team's practice, as in those days East Bengal did not have a regular coach.

East Bengal played some memorable matches with Mohammedan Sporting in the DCM Trophy. In the 1960 final, star-studded Mohammedan Sporting were favourites against fierce rivals East Bengal, whom they had defeated 3-1 in the 1958 DCM final. However, the smooth skills of East Bengal's centre-forward D. Kannan changed their fortunes. Within fifteen minutes of the commencement of the match, D. Kannan's goal demoralized Mohammedan Sporting as East Bengal led 2-0. He collected a pass near the half line from Balaram, dribbled past defenders Mushtaq Ahmed and Ahmed Hussain, and cleverly lobbed the ball beyond the reach of the Sporting custodian. There was a suspicion of handball in East Bengal's third goal by inside-forward B. Narayan but the referee stuck to his decision, despite fervent requests and appeals by the Mohammedan Sporting players. Irate fans shouted slogans against the referee and some even tried to manhandle him after the match.

East Bengal had four 1960 Rome Olympians in their playing eleven: Tulsidas Balaram, central-defender Arun Ghosh, centre-forward D. Kannan and midfielder Ram Bahadur. In 1960 they became joint champions, with Mohun Bagan, of the Durand, which made them winners of the coveted 'Delhi double' for the second time.

The third and last time East Bengal played against city rivals Mohammedan Sporting in the DCM Trophy was in November 1983, in a match marred by crowd violence. Midfielder Prasanta Banerjee scored for East Bengal in the seventy-first minute, after an exquisite solo run in which he dribbled past a couple of defenders. Piling on the pressure, Mohammedan Sporting scored what seemed a legitimate equalizer by winger Subir Sarkar, off Jamshed Nassiri's back header. The referee Kedarnath Mour had awarded the goal but linesman Shetty put his flag up. The goal was disallowed, much to the anger of Mohammedan Sporting's frenzied supporters, who were present with their club flags and banners. Mayhem broke out as numerous Mohammedan Sporting fans resorted to violence. The police fired tear gas, and later as the fighting spread to the nearby streets, even fired into the air. The match was abandoned and East Bengal were awarded the title.

East Bengal were a formidable team in the 1970 Durand Cup, and the best of that era. Their short-statured but lightning-quick quartet of forwards, Swapan Sengupta, Ashok Chatterjee, Mohammed Habib and Shyam Thapa—with K.B. Sharma used occasionally—played exhilarating, attacking football to overwhelm all their opponents on their way to winning the tournament. Using a 4-2-4 formation they beat RAC Bikaner 3-2 (Shyam Thapa, Habib: 2), SRC 4-2 (Shyam Thapa: 2, Habib and Swapan Sengupta), Mafatlal Mills Mumbai 1-0 (Shyam Thapa) in the semi-finals, and then Mohun Bagan 2-0 (Habib: 2) in the final. Mohammed Hussain of Mumbai was the coach and Santo Mitra the captain.

The DCM Trophy had set the trend in 1968 of annually inviting foreign clubs. East Bengal became the only Indian club with more wins than losses against foreign clubs in home matches. Amongst their most famous triumphs are the 1-0 win against Pas Tehran of Iran in the 1970 IFA Shield final, when Hussain was the coach (for details, see 'The Major Tournaments'); the victories against the North Korean clubs in the 1973 IFA Shield and DCM finals; and the 3-1 victory over BEC Tero Sasana in the 2003 ASEAN Cup final in Jakarta, with Subhash Bhowmick as the coach. With the ASEAN victory, East Bengal became the second Indian club to win a continental tournament on foreign soil. Notably, East Bengal striker Biswajit Bhattacharya was the only scorer from India in the 1984 Nehru Cup, scoring 1 goal against Poland.

Astute substitutions, a clever change of tactics and variation in approach play by the pragmatic coach P.K. Banerjee made the East Bengal team of the early 1970s both successful and attractive to watch. East Bengal could either play defensive or attacking football depending on the situation. They went on to win the IFA Shield for five years in a row from 1972–76.

In the Federation Cup too East Bengal has many historic achievements. They are the only other club to win this cup in their debut year (1978—joint champions with Mohun Bagan) apart from ITI Bangalore (champions in the cup's inaugural year—1977). Their first Federation Cup win was a war of attrition and, like a game of chess, with a focus on tactical discipline. The final was billed as the clash of the coaches: Arun Ghosh of East Bengal against India's most successful club coach P.K. Banerjee, then with Mohun Bagan. This final became famous for Arun Ghosh's clever tactics. He realized that Bagan launched attacks mainly from the left using the blistering pace of Bidesh Bose, who would latch on to through-passes from midfielder Prasun Banerjee and burst through opposing defences.

In both the final and the replay, East Bengal thwarted the rampaging Bidesh by some clever marking. Right-striker Mihir Bose played as a withdrawn right-midfielder to assist right-back Chinmoy Chatterjee in marking Bidesh. A speedy wing-back, Chinmoy ensured that Bidesh did not go down the line and get in penetrative crosses. When Bidesh tried to cut inside and shoot a goal, Mihir was always present to tackle him. With Bidesh restricted, Bagan, the stronger team on paper, faded and made little impact.

East Bengal are also the only side to win the Federation Cup twice in one calendar year in 2010: Guwahati (3 January) and Cuttack (2 October). They are the first club to have entered the Federation Cup final four years in a row, from 2009–12. During this dream run, they won the title thrice and lost just once to Salgaocar FC in 2011. Foreign coaches Philippe de Ridder (Belgium) in 2009 and Trevor Morgan (England) in 2010–12 spearheaded the club's successes during this time.

East Bengal has made sixteen appearances in the Federation Cup final and won the trophy eight times. All their triumphs have been very dramatic. Thrice they won the title in extra time: 1985, 1996 (golden goal) and 2012. In 2009 they won on penalties, beating Shillong Lajong 3-0, after the match ended goalless. That year they won the trophy without conceding a single goal, a feat achieved once before by Mohun Bagan in 1987. Only in 2007 and 2010 did they win the Federation Cup in the regulation ninety minutes.

The 1980 Federation Cup final was memorable for several reasons. It was the first time it was held in Kolkata, and the fans awaited it with eager anticipation. The transfer season had been quite acrimonious as Mohammedan Sporting had poached several stalwarts from East Bengal. Many star players had switched allegiance to Mohammedan Sporting, lured by lucrative contracts offered by its president Tahir Irfan Randerian, a tycoon with business interests in shipping and tea.

East Bengal had also got three new recruits that season, the Iranians Majid Bishkar, Jamshid Nassiri and Mohammed Khabazi. In 1979, I was one of the coaches for the Delhi University team, for the North Zone inter-university championships in Aligarh. The hosts, Aligarh Muslim University, were dominating because of the exceptional play of the Iranians. I found out that Majid had played in the 1978 World Cup and had come to the university to study. On reaching Delhi, I rushed to the Daryaganj house of East Bengal's local manager and ardent fan, H.S. Mamik. He immediately contacted the club in Kolkata, and soon he and the club officials went to Aligarh to sign up the three players.

This time P.K. Banerjee coached East Bengal and Arun Ghosh looked after Mohun Bagan. After the transfer season, P.K. Banerjee had only three weeks to develop a cohesive squad consisting mainly of youngsters: just two established players, sturdy defender Monoranjan Bhattacharya and diminutive Mohammed Habib; and the three new Iranian recruits. This was the first test for the fresh teams in front of their demanding fans. The critics felt this makeshift team would falter. However, thanks to Majid's brilliance, Nassiri's goal-poaching and P.K.'s clever coaching, the weakest-ever East Bengal side reached the final. In the semi-final they overcame Punjab Police 3-0.

Mohun Bagan with their brilliant quartet of forwards—speedy Bidesh Bose, new recruit Francis D'Souza, Xavier Pius and Manas

Bhattacharya—were expected to win the final easily. But P.K. used retractable wingers and made Majid play as a central midfielder. So East Bengal's unusual 4-5-1 system and the team's commitment kept Bagan at bay.

The 1980 Federation Cup was P.K. Banerjee's finest hour. For a decade, the carping critics had been saying that P.K. only managed star-studded teams and enjoyed success as a coach because of this. But he proved his detractors wrong, and with his clever man-management, eye for talent and astute tactics, developed a competitive East Bengal squad. Ultimately arch-rivals East Bengal and Mohun Bagan were declared joint champions when the final match held at the famous cricket stadium Eden Gardens (Salt Lake Stadium had not been built then) ended in a 1-1 draw. The 1980 Federation Cup title was won by arguably the weakest East Bengal side to ever play in this tournament. The victory was an ultimate tribute to P.K.'s motivational skills and coaching prowess as well as the genius of Majid. East Bengal were joint champions in both the Rovers and Federation Cups in the 1980–81 season.

In the 1990 Durand Cup, coach Nayeem's emphasis on conditioning led East Bengal to explode the myth that Kolkata teams were inferior to Punjab sides in fitness. In the semi-final, they were held goalless by BSF till ninety minutes. However, in thirty minutes of extra time, they gave the normally rugged BSF defence a torrid time. Bikash Panji was in full cry on the right flank and Krishanu Dey supplied his usual clever passes. Striker Kuljit scored a hat-trick to enable East Bengal to win 3-0 and enter the final where they beat Mahindra United 3-2 to win the trophy.

Another great East Bengal–BSF match was the 1993 Durand semi-final. The match was drifting towards a goalless draw as shadows lengthened at the Ambedkar Stadium. Coach Shyamal Ghosh introduced the precocious teenager Bhaichung Bhutia to try something new. The move clicked. Bhaichung scored with a dramatic, acrobatic back-volley, much to the rapturous delight of the capacity crowd, and East Bengal won 1-0. This was the goal that made Bhaichung famous and made the fans, media and officials realize that here was a special talent.

Amongst the best clubs in India, East Bengal has been a dominant force in numerous tournaments. They have won the Calcutta League title a record thirty-eight times (till 2016), while the next best is Mohun Bagan with twenty-eight titles. They are also the only team to have won the Calcutta League twice without conceding a goal in 1972 and 1991. They also have the record of annexing the local league title twice by winning all their matches in 1975 and 1977.

In the two renowned domestic tournaments in Delhi, East Bengal has an outstanding record. They have won the Durand Cup sixteen times and been runners-up ten times. They first won it in 1951, and their last Durand victory was in 2004 when two blistering, long-range goals by midfielder Chandan Das enabled them to beat Mohun Bagan 2-1 in the final. East Bengal's achievements in the DCM Trophy are also unsurpassed. They won this trophy seven times and finished runners-up seven times.

East Bengal has won the NFL thrice: in 2001 (with Monoranjan Bhattacharya as coach) and back to back in 2003 and 2004 (Subhash Bhowmick was coach on both occasions).

They last won both the prestigious IFA Shield and Federation Cup in 2012. The latter was a glorious birthday present for their British coach Trevor Morgan. He had won the Federation Cup twice with East Bengal, a record he shares with P.K. Banerjee (1980 and 1985). In 2012, Morgan made some shrewd substitutions. As both the semi-final and the final drifted into extra time, he brought in attacking midfielders Sanju Pradhan and Lalrindika Ralte (the latter being another inspired selection who joined that season). Ralte scored the match-winner against Churchill Brothers (1-0) in the semi-final and set up the winning goals against Dempo (3-2) in the final.

Like Mohun Bagan, East Bengal has consistently had some extraordinary players in its roster. I offer here brief profiles of nine. The legendary Ahmed Khan (1949–59) was a skilful inside-left in the 2-3-5 system, whose ball control and passing were brilliant. He played for eleven consecutive years and never got more than Rs 3000 per season. His marriage to a Hindu nurse was like a fairy tale. He was once admitted to hospital due to an acute asthma attack. Anjali, a nurse, had looked after him and their romance blossomed. Sudhir Karmakar (1969–76, 1980–81) was named the Best Defender of the Millennium at East Bengal. Only 5 ft 4 in. tall, he excelled with his clean tackles and interceptions. Ram Bahadur (1957–67) was a midfielder with such amazing reflexes that he was voted the Best Midfielder of the Millennium at the club. Prasanta Sinha (1964–71), a left-half in the 3-2-5 formation, played as a central-defender and curbed the forwards of Pas Club (Iran) in the 1970 IFA Shield final. Parimal Dey (1964–70, 1973) scored the winning goal in the 1970 IFA Shield Final, and impressed with his dribbling, receiving and ball control. Manoranjan Bhattacharya (1977–90, 1993) appeared for a record fourteen successive seasons for the club. He often overpowered opposition strikers with his strength, biting tackles and positional play. Bhaskar Ganguly (1976–79, 1982–88) was known as the king of the penalty area for his acrobatic saves, determination to foil an attack and never-say-die attitude. Though short in height, he had a tremendous spot jump, good gripping and a flexible body. India's captain in the 1982 Asian Games, he started his career with Mohun Bagan and also played two seasons for Mohammedan Sporting. Sukumar Samajpati (1961–66, 1968) was famous for his skill and close control on the right flank. Majid Bishkar (1980–81), whose name was corrupted to 'Bhaskar', represented Iran in the 1978 World Cup. Majid's passes were incisive and he scored goals from amazing angles and distances. He is still considered the best-ever foreign player to play for an Indian club.

Other outstanding Kolkata players of the 1970s were goalkeeper Tarun Bose, wingers Bidesh Bose and Surojit Sengupta, left-back Shyamal Banerjee, stopper-backs Shyamal Ghosh and Tarun Dey, midfielders Gautam Sarkar and Samaresh 'Pintu' Chowdhury, and utility player Sudeep Chatterjee.

See in 'Hall of Fame': Sheoo Mewalal (centre-forward), Shyam Thapa (forward), Chuni Goswami (inside-left/forward), T. Balaram (winger/ inside-forward), Mohammed Habib (forward), Arun Ghosh (defender), Jarnail Singh (defender), Peter Thangaraj (goalkeeper), P.K. Banerjee (coach), Amal Dutta (coach) and Subhash Bhowmick (coach).

2

Hyderabad

The Fountain of Sporting Talent

Hyderabad brings to mind the colourful shops of Charminar selling jewellery, rare Basra pearls, perfumes and bangles that coexist alongside the towering skyline of Cyberabad and the resplendent new international airport. A very plural city, Hyderabad is a synthesis of many cultures living in harmony. Just like the people and the language, its food is also pluralistic. It blends aromatic Mughlai cuisine with the spice of the Telangana region, and it is in biryanis that Hyderabadi cuisine has carved a niche for itself. It is believed that around forty varieties of biryani are made in Hyderabad, some delicate and flavoured with saffron, others with cream and milk. Most meat dishes and curries, except the biryanis and kebabs, include vegetables so the basic diet is healthy and nourishing. Even traditional sweets like Badam ki Jali (a thin cake made of almonds) and the famous Khubani ka Meetha (apricots and cream) have a nut and a fruit as their base.[1]

In keeping with its cosmopolitan character, Hyderabad has produced outstanding international players in many sports and from different communities. Sports buffs can rattle off names like Mohammad Azharuddin and V.V.S. Laxman (cricket), S.P. Misra and Sania Mirza (tennis), P. Gopichand and Saina Nehwal (badminton), and many others from basketball, boxing, athletics, cycling, sailing, table tennis and volleyball. But old-timers will know that in the decades after Independence, Hyderabad was known for its football.

Like in many other Indian cities, British forces introduced the game of football to the twin cities of Hyderabad and Secunderabad.

Crack teams of the British Army in Secunderabad Cantonment were the main practitioners of the game. At first, the local people were mere spectators at the matches played by the British forces. Their interest in the game gradually grew, but just as the game was about to take root amongst them, there was a sudden setback. The aristocracy and the upper classes frowned upon the game of football. Added to this, the religious-minded also issued statements urging people not to take up the game. A pamphlet published in Urdu early in the twentieth century stated, 'Those who play football become unfit for performing religious rites. They cannot make good patriots. Football is a good-looking evil which sucks the blood of the players, breaks their hands and feet, and invalidates them forever.'[2]

Due to this furore, participation in football dipped. It was now up to the educational institutions to clear these misconceptions about the game. Kenneth Burnett, principal of the Nizam College, wished to prove that the controversy was unnecessary and unfounded. An Englishman, it was he who organized the first non-military and non-white football team from amongst the students of Nizam College. All Saints High School, St George's Grammar School, Asafia High School and Dar-ul-Uloom High School also began to encourage their students to play football.

The credit for forming the first private club goes to Vilayat Hussain, who was the Director of Posts in the Nizam's government. He brought together Nizam College graduates to form the team. Chirag Ali was the most renowned player of this club and soon came to be respected even by the British regimental players for his skill. The Nizam College conducted two tournaments, one of them open only to the educational institutions and the other to the regimental and other clubs in Hyderabad. Crowds of about 4000 people turned up even for the ordinary matches.

The Nawab of Tarband vigorously promoted the game, just like the Nawab Moin-ud-Dowlah popularized cricket. The Maharajas of Kakinada and Rajahmundry also provided support. Two football-loving principals of Nizam College, E.A. Seaton and Burnett, were largely responsible for popularizing the game in the city. Although the purely local teams made little impact on the rigorously trained and more practised British regimental teams, several Hyderabad players began to assert themselves.

Hyderabad's first all-India football tournament, known as the Majeed tournament, was staged in 1910. For three years, this tournament was a major success before it was abandoned because of differences between the City Police and the Hyderabad Army.

The Hyderabad Football Association (HFA) came into existence in 1939, on the initiative of its first secretary S.M. Hadi. Its first president was Ghulam Muhammad, financial adviser in the Nizam's state, who later became governor general of Pakistan.[3] From the next year onwards, all football activities began to be conducted by the association. The Hadi tournament for schools and the 'B' division tournament for smaller clubs were started. In 1942 Hadi became president of the H.F.A. and S.A. Rahim the secretary.

Hyderabad began to participate in the National Championship for the Santosh Trophy from 1944 onwards. Hyderabad players first came into prominence when four of them were chosen for the camp to select the Indian team for the 1948 London Olympics. Two players, left-back Norbert Andrew Fruvall and K.P. Dhanraj were selected, though only one of them could go.

Soon after Independence, a sports-loving police officer and visionary Shiv Kumar Lal became the president of the HFA. With him and S.A. Rahim at the helm, football in the city of pearls made excellent progress. Rahim was always planning something or the other to improve the game in Hyderabad. He conducted a number of coaching classes for footballers and trained scores of coaches. His zeal resulted in several clubs taking to football. In the 1950s there were nearly seventy-five clubs, about 1500 registered players and about forty qualified referees.

Shiv Kumar Lal had a big hand in shaping the most famous team to emerge from this city, the legendary black-and-yellow-shirted Hyderabad City Police. During the Nizam's reign they were known as the City Afghans. His role in developing football infrastructure, recruiting players and acquiring finance for the game was exemplary. In an era when sponsorship and TV rights were unheard of, Shiv Kumar Lal ensured the local association had funds by regularly organizing the league, several tournaments and quality matches. In 1954, the touring Russian football team played 2 matches at the Fateh Maidan Stadium (now known as the Lal Bahadur Shastri Stadium), against an India XI and an HFA XI. Both games drew capacity crowds and ensured that the local association collected adequate funds through ticket sales.

Named after him, the Police Stadium in Goshamahal is a shining monument to the zeal and enthusiasm of Shiv Kumar Lal. Constructed in 1956, it was the hub of football activities in Hyderabad. It was here that India's 1962 Asian Games and 1960 Olympic teams were trained by Rahim and it was here that the 1957 National Championship was staged when the home team won the Santosh Trophy for the second time. He was president of the HFA since 1953, as well as the Andhra Pradesh Football Association after it was formed in the late 1950s. He also held senior positions in the AIFF and the Andhra Pradesh Sports Council, earning the moniker 'Mr Football'. Despite the demands on his time as the Additional Inspector General of Andhra Police, Shiv Kumar Lal took a personal interest in football and actively promoted the game.

Known as 'Maulvi Sahib' (a respectful address for a gentleman) during his lifetime, Rahim remained secretary until his death in June 1963. These were the two best decades of Hyderabad football and so after his death Rahim came to be regarded as 'Baba-e-Football' (father or grand old man of football).

There have been so many footballing legends from Hyderabad that a full book can be devoted to them. The twin cities of Hyderabad and Secunderabad have produced fourteen Olympians and twenty-one international footballers who represented the country in the Asian Games. Footballers from Hyderabad were selected for the Olympics in 1948 (London), 1952 (Helsinki), 1956 (Melbourne) and 1960 (Rome). In the 1956 national team—India's best performance till date, having finished fourth—eight players were from Hyderabad. In the 1960 team, there were seven. Five of these players—Peter Thangaraj, S.K. Azizuddin, S.A. Latif, Noor

Mohammed and T. Balaram—played in two Olympic Games. Till about fifteen years after Independence no other city had so many Olympians or international players as did Hyderabad in one sport.

Six players from Hyderabad have captained India. Aziz led the victorious Indian team in the 4th Asian Quadrangular at Dhaka and again in the 3rd Asian Games at Tokyo. Syed Nayeemuddin was captain when Indian won the bronze medals in both the Merdeka Tournament and the Asian Games in 1970. Nayeem and Syed Shahid Waseem (the latter is the son of coach Rahim) captained India's junior teams in two different Asian Youth Championships. Nippy inside-forward Mohammed Habib and striker Shabbir Ali, who was known for his aerial manoeuvres, were the captains in the 1972 and 1983 pre-Olympics, respectively. Shabbir also led India when they became joint champions for the first and only time in the Asian Youth Championships in Bangkok in 1974. In 1984, midfielder Victor Amalraj was captain of an Indian team in the President's Cup at Dhaka.

The city has given India nine national coaches—S.A. Rahim, G.M. Pentiah, S.A. Salaam, Ahmed Hussain, S.S. Hakeem, Mohammed Afzal, Syed Nayeemuddin, Shabbir Ali and Mohammed Habib. Three referees from Hyderabad—G.M. Pentiah, M. Azam and S.S. Hakeem—have been inducted into the FIFA panel. Azam had the distinction of supervising the 1974 Asian Games final in Tehran between Iran and Israel. S.S. Hakeem has supervised 33 international matches, a record still unbroken in India. This included the Asia Cup finals on three occasions, two Asian Games, pre-Olympics and World Cup qualifiers.

Hyderabad City Police

In the 1940s, teams in Hyderabad had no coach and all the responsibility fell on the captain's shoulders. In the case of Hyderabad City Police, formed in 1941–42, it was captain Norbert Andrew Fruvall who recruited star players like S.K. Azizuddin, S.A. Latif, S.K. Moinuddin, Noor Mohammed, Sheikh Jamal, Anthony Patrick, G.Y.S. Laiq and Susaih (Jr). He moulded his players into a disciplined unit and decided on their tactics. A strict disciplinarian, Fruvall was the only sub-inspector in his team; the other footballers were mostly constables or head constables. Fruvall was a high-jump champion at school and had a great spot jump even though he was not particularly tall. A versatile athlete, he excelled in pole vault and even represented the Hyderabad City Police in cricket, scoring several centuries in the local league.

A famous game in which Hyderabad City Police caught the imagination of spectators was the Ashe Gold Cup final at Bengaluru in 1943. They overcame the Royal Air Force, which included England's Denis Compton (who played football for Arsenal and was a middle-order batsman for England). They were trailing by a single goal but rallied to win with two late penalties by Fruvall.

Fruvall was also captain of the first official state football team that participated in the National Championship in 1944. Known to his fellow players as Captain, he was selected to represent India at the 1948 London Olympics. However, the AIFF was still in its fledgling years and had limited finances. Monetary support from the Government of India, still struggling from the turmoil of Partition, could not be expected. Hence the players were asked to pay for their own travel. Fruvall was unable to raise the requisite amount and the HFA was unable to help. So, much to his dismay, he could not make the trip to the Olympics despite being selected. K.P. Dhanraj, who used to play club football in Bengaluru, thus became the lone representative from Hyderabad at the 1948 Olympics.

By the time of his retirement in 1951, Fruvall had developed Hyderabad City Police into a brilliant side. When Rahim took over its coaching in 1950, he consolidated it into one of the most popular and feared teams in the country. The team was noted for its cohesive attacking play, never-say-die attitude, superb technique, fitness and clever use of set pieces.

It was the 1950 Durand Cup final—the first in independent India—which established Hyderabad City Police as a force to be reckoned with. In that memorable final they trailed Mohun Bagan 0-2, till ten minutes before the final whistle, when an inspired Laiq scored two goals and equalized in the last few seconds. This dramatic comeback electrified the crowds, who ran into the grounds and lifted him up. Some enthusiastic fans even kissed their hero, and one, in his exuberance, bit him on the cheek. The injured hero had to nurse his wound for a week and missed the replay, which his team won 1-0. This victory heralded the arrival of Hyderabad as a football centre to rival Kolkata, and the emergence of Rahim as a high-calibre football coach. In 1950–51, Hyderabad City Police set a record for the number of trophies it won. Besides the first-ever Rovers and Durand Cup double, it annexed thirteen all-India tournaments.

Players from Hyderabad City Police were very popular and were admired by people of all communities for their mental and physical toughness. Their never-say-die spirit is best exemplified by the courage of goalkeeper G. Eraiah in the 1951 Durand Cup. In a match against Gorkha Brigade, late in the second-half a penalty kick was awarded against Hyderabad City Police. Gorkha Brigade's international Dhan Bahadur took a powerful kick to the right of Eraiah. The agile Eraiah, diving sideways, effected a save but the ball slipped out of his hands and Dhan Bahadur kicked goalwards again. The vigilant Eraiah had meanwhile dived forward and gathered the ball, but Dhan Bahadur's kick had landed on the goalkeeper's arm. Eraiah had saved his side and there was tremendous applause from the packed crowd. A little later, he began to feel some pain in the arm. When Fruvall, the captain of the team, came near him, Eraiah sought his permission to leave the field. Not knowing what had happened, the captain ordered him to carry on. Eraiah carried on and made a couple more daring saves. It was only after the game was over that it came to be known that Eraiah had sustained a fracture. He could not even lift his hand and the doctor, who had to strip his entire shirt, found that a part of the broken arm-bone was jutting out. Fruvall hugged Eraiah and, with tears in his eyes, sought his pardon.

During his coaching sessions Rahim always tried to make his players innovative and analytical about the game. This was best witnessed in the 1954 Durand. Hyderabad City Police reached

Delhi after winning the Rovers Cup for the fifth year in a row, beating Kemari Union of Pakistan 2-1 in the final. They became the first Indian side to win any major domestic tournament for five successive years (1950–54). They were greeted with much fanfare in Delhi. However, they were jolted in their opening match against the speedy Gorkha Brigade. With international Puran Bahadur as skipper, the Gorkhas attacked relentlessly and led 3-0 in the first ten minutes of the match.

An upset was on the cards, but the shrewd Hyderabad City Police players had an innate self-confidence in their abilities. They changed tactics and started playing crosses from the flanks to capitalize on their height advantage. The ploy worked. Centre-forward Doraiswamy played with great determination and reduced the margin at the stroke of half-time. During the interval, coach Rahim talked to the players and further fine-tuned their approach play.

In the second-half, Hyderabad City Police used accurate diagonal passes and high crosses into the box with telling effect. Gorkha Brigade crumbled under this onslaught and conceded 5 goals. Hyderabad City Police emerged 6-3 winners with Doraiswamy scoring 4 goals, including a hat-trick, while right-half-back—as midfielders were then known—Anthony Patrick and right-winger Moin scored 1 each. In those days matches in India were seventy minutes long, so Hyderabad City Police had scored 5 goals in the thirty-five minutes of the second-half. The ability to change their game plans during the course of a match, variety in attack, and tenacity made Hyderabad City Police a unique and exciting team to watch (there was a popular saying that Hyderabad/Andhra Police never lost in a replay). Those who watched that match—like former Durand Cup secretary general K.K. Ganguly, Delhi soccer officials and my late father—swore that they had never witnessed such a spirited display either before or after.

In the quarter-final of the same tournament, Hyderabad City Police once again showed remarkable fitness and zeal to rally and win in the last quarter. Laiq was again the hero and this time the passionate fans rewarded him in another way. Mighty Hyderabad

City Police were trailing by 2 goals against the IAF team, with just fifteen minutes left for the final whistle. Spectators began to make their way out. Moin scored a goal twelve minutes before close, yet the spectators believed that IAF would leave the field victorious. With six minutes to go, Laiq found the net and put the teams on equal terms. Their excitement rekindled, the spectators now knew that this equalizer would give Hyderabad City Police a boost while IAF would be demoralized. They rushed back to the stands. The indomitable policemen scored once again, following a through-pass by Laiq, and moved into the next round. Elated at this magnificent turnaround, some passionate fans rushed on to the field and congratulated Laiq. One of them thrust a five-rupee note into his hands. This was published in a Delhi-based paper the next morning. At the time of writing this book, the late Laiq's family still preserves a cutting of the news item.

The team was extremely popular amongst crowds all over India and had supporters in every city. Their support base cut across regional and religious lines. Hyderabad City Police became renowned as the poor man's team, the champion of the masses and the answer to Kolkata's rich Big Three: Mohun Bagan, East Bengal and Mohammedan Sporting. They were an institutional side and players received negligible monetary compensation. The players in those days received a pittance of Rs 40 per month as salary. Noor once said, 'Often at practice we had just one football and for refreshments afterwards a cup of tea, but our hard practice, will to succeed and the excellent coaching from the late Rahim Sahib enabled us to become a successful team.'

When the Hyderabad City Police came to Delhi in the winter months to play in the Durand, the players wore their long, brown woollen overcoats—part of their uniform—as protection from the bitter cold. Since their first Durand in 1950, the team always stayed at the Karim Hotel as their preferred food was on offer there and due to its proximity to Jama Masjid. Beddings and mattresses would be spread out on the floor where the players slept. Despite being one of the best teams in India, the Hyderabad City Police players accepted such rudimentary facilities as many of them were of humble origins.

Rated as the finest restaurant in Delhi for Mughlai food, Karim Hotel became famous due to the team's patronage. Fans flocked to the hotel to gossip and exchange views with the down-to-earth star players of this team. Whilst lingering there, the fans would order food from the restaurant. The reputation of its mouth-watering dishes spread far and wide by word of mouth. The rest, as they say, is history. For any gourmet, Karim Hotel is now a landmark in the capital. Creditably, the owners of Karim Hotel acknowledge the role played by the Hyderabad City Police football team in popularizing their restaurant. Alimuddin Ahmed of Karim Hotel flew to Hyderabad to attend coach Rahim's funeral in 1963. Till date, the Karim Hotel management gives a 50 per cent discount to the former players of the team and to members of Rahim's family.

Unlike most institutional teams Hyderabad City Police did not fade away after one generation of outstanding players started retiring. By 1956–57, stalwarts like goalkeeper Eraiah, Sheikh Jamal, Doraiswamy and others had retired, but the various coaching schemes initiated by Rahim in the city kept producing a vast array of talented players. The 1957 Hyderabad City Police team was also famous. Newcomers like prolific striker Zulfiqaruddin, tireless midfielder Yousuf Khan and crafty winger Mohammed Yousuf all slotted into the team with ease. That year Hyderabad City Police beat East Bengal 1-0 in the Durand final and Mohammedan Sporting 3-0 in the Rovers Cup final.

By 1960 the older stalwarts had mostly left, and the team also acquired a new name. When on 1 November 1956, the map of India was redrawn across linguistic lines, Hyderabad became the capital of the new state of Andhra Pradesh. Within a couple of years, the team was renamed Andhra Police. The players changed, the name changed, but the team continued to inspire fear as their success rate in domestic tournaments was astounding. The astute coach Rahim had a good eye for talent and groomed players to replace the ageing stars. He judiciously chose players who would fit into his system.

Hence by the early 1960s there was a new-look Andhra Police football team. The goalkeeper was the acrobatic Saleemuddin, popular with the crowds because of his Tarzan-like physique. The team adopted the three-back system. The defenders were Azam, Kaleem and the talented Syed Nayeemuddin, a classy left-back. In the midfield was the majestic Afzal with his booming left-footed shots, and the frail but tenacious Saleh (Jr), an excellent man-marker, the poor man's Nobby Stiles. The bearded Abdullah, the crafty Mohammed Yousuf and bow-legged Jaffar were the wingers. Yousuf Khan and Zulfiqaruddin were the inside-forwards and senior members of the team. Edward and later Satyanarayan played as a withdrawn centre-forward. The squad was cohesive, with remarkable team spirit and fitness.

In 1960 Andhra Police annexed the Rovers Cup, beating East Bengal 1-0 in the replay after a thrilling 2-2 draw in the first match. A year later, they won the Durand Cup with Zulfiqaruddin netting the winner against Mohun Bagan. In 1962, they were joint champions of the Rovers Cup with East Bengal, and runners-up in the IFA Shield. In 1963 they won the Rovers Cup, beating East Bengal 1-0 in the final, but Mohun Bagan defeated them in the Durand final. In 1964 they were runners-up in the DCM Trophy.

Between 1950 and 1963, Hyderabad City Police/Andhra Police won the Rovers Cup in Mumbai nine times. They became champions every time they reached the final—a unique feat. During the same time span, they won the Durand Cup four times and were runners-up thrice. They also won the competitive Hyderabad League for eleven consecutive years, an all-time record which may never be broken.

In 1965, Andhra Police and their B team, Central Police Lines (CPL), met each other in the final of the DCM Trophy. Andhra Police won with Zulfiqaruddin scoring twice. It was the last major trophy this formidable team would win. The next year, talented Nayeemuddin, Afzal and Mohammed Habib left their team and joined East Bengal. The great coach Rahim had died three years earlier. In his absence, there was no follow-up action on players, so the flow of talent declined and quality players stopped emerging.

No replacements were found for Nayeemuddin and Afzal. Zulfiqaruddin and Yousuf Khan were ageing.

There was one last flicker of hope when in 1967 they reached the Durand semi-finals. Some of their matches in this tournament were reminiscent of their glory years. In the pre-quarter-finals, for two days they were held to a draw by the spirited MEG Bangalore, spearheaded by ex-international Ethiraj. In their third match, MEG Bangalore led 2-0 at half-time. With the ageing Yousuf Khan initiating attacks from defence, Andhra Police increased the tempo and staged a comeback to win 3-2. Next up were reigning champions Gorkha Brigade, noted for their speedy attack. In this match Andhra Police cleverly slowed down the game and played patient possession football to frustrate the holders. Despite losing key defender Rashid Khan—injured after tackling Gorkha Brigade's international midfielder Ranjit Thapa—the gallant Andhra Police held on for a memorable 3-1 win. In the semi-finals they held ultimate winners East Bengal (with their three erstwhile teammates, Nayeemuddin, Afzal and Habib in its ranks) to a goalless draw but lost 0-1 in the replay.

Their last hour of glory was the 1970 DCM Trophy final. The final was during the holy month of Ramzan. Except for inside-forward Satyanarayan, ten of the players were Muslims. Many of them were in the twilight of their careers, like goalkeeper Saleem, defender Shafiq, wingers Jaffar and Abdullah, and the legendary Asian All-Stars XI player, Yousuf Khan. Despite playing the formidable Iranian champions Taj Club of Tehran, the Andhra Police players maintained their fast.

They played heroically and led 1-0 till the seventy-fifth minute, when the mighty Iranian club (Asian club champions the same year) equalized and later won 3-1. When asked how the team lasted without food and water, Yousuf Khan said it was the pre-dawn diet of nihari (beef or mutton kept all night on a simmering fire along with spices and served with gravy and tandoori rotis) and Khubani ka Meetha which gave them the energy to play.

It was the end of an era; a page of history had been turned forever.

The Glory Years and After

During the 1950s football was the most popular and watched sport in Hyderabad. The standard was also very high, and fifteen teams from this city would annually participate in tournaments across the country. Hyderabad football got international recognition and fame in the inaugural 1951 Asian Games in Delhi. Three players from the Police team were selected for the Indian squad which won the gold medal, beating Iran 1-0 in the final. These were defender S.K. Azizuddin, midfielder Noor Mohammed and inside-forward G.Y.S. Laiq. Another milestone was reached in 1952 when S.K. Moinuddin, Aziz, Noor Mohammed and Laiq represented India at the first Quadrangular Tournament in Colombo, which India won. The first three also represented India at the 1952 Helsinki Olympics.

Hyderabad won the Santosh Trophy, the symbol of national supremacy, in 1956–57 and 1957–58, both times led by full-back Aziz; they won it again as Andhra Pradesh in 1965. In both finals in the 1950s they beat Bombay (now known as Maharashtra). In the 1956 replayed final, T. Balaram excelled for Hyderabad scoring twice in his team's 4-1 win. On the basis of this performance he was picked for the 1956 Melbourne Olympics. His combination with Zulfiqar on the left flank was devastating. S.A. Rahim was coach on both occasions and he was assisted by Sheikh Jamal, the centre-half who had just retired.

It was Rahim's dream to win the Santosh Trophy by beating mighty West Bengal in the final but that did not materialize in his lifetime. Two years after his death, Andhra Pradesh and West Bengal met in a Santosh Trophy final for the third time, and finally the south Indian state prevailed. Twice in the past—in 1950 and 1951—Bengal had beaten Hyderabad in the final. In the 1965 final in Kollam (then known as Quilon), Andhra Pradesh, led by Zulfiqar, drew the first match 1-1, with the skipper scoring a dream goal by flicking the ball over legendary international defender Jarnail Singh's head and volleying it into the net. In the replay, Habib making his Santosh Trophy debut scored the match-winner. G.M.

'Barefoot Wonders': The Indian team at the 1948 London Olympics. (Standing, L to R)
K.P. Dhanraj, Mahabir Prasad, S.A. Basheer, Sunil Nandy, K.V. Varadaraj (goalkeeper),
T.M. Verghese 'Papen' and trainer-coach Balai Das Chatterjee. (Sitting, L to R)
S. Mewalal, Ahmed Khan, Talimeran Ao (captain), S.V. Raman (India's goalscorer)
and Sailen Manna.

The Indian team at the 1948
Olympics, training at Pinner in
Middlesex.

The Indian team entering the ground at Illford for
their first-round match on 31 July at the 1948 London
Olympics.

MONDAY, HS - 02.08.1948

Olympic Football

INDIA WASTE TWO 'PENALTY' KICKS

A Last-Minute Goal Gives Victory To France

LONDON, JULY 31.—After missing two 'penalties'
India went down by a last-minute goal on the ground of
the Ilford Amateur Football Club in the first round of the
14th Olympiad association football competition.

FRANCE took the lead in the first half but India equalised after
strong frequent attacks on crossing over.
But for the two wasted 'penalty' kicks—one of which the
French goalkeeper saved brilliantly, and the other shot over—and
a number of missed chances India would have won the match.
Eight of the India team played barefooted and this did not put
them into any difficulty.

India won the toss and had the
advantage of a rather strong run at their
backs. Tight of the wide did not
wear boots but that did not hamper their
kicking ability.
France came near to scoring after 3
minutes. Their outside-right, after a
nice run on the wing, centred across the
goal but India's goalkeeper cleared well
from centre-forward Palouch.
Both teams played the short-passing
game and although the approach work
was good, many chances were lost by
hurried shooting near the goal.
Both the half-back lines kept a tight
grip on the opposing forwards.
France took the lead in the 30th
minute when outside-left Courdin cut in

India's Hope Centres On Hockey

Today's Attractions In Olympics

LONDON, AUG. 1—India's team of
cheerful, wonderfully fit Olympic athletes
was today taking full advantage of the
Sunday lull in exciting games.
One batch had scratched a cricket team
together and was playing the local North-
wood Cricket Club near their dinner
billets.
Another group was in the West End of
London "seeing the sights" and a third

A report in *Hindusthan Standard*, Kolkata, 2 August 1948, about India's match against France at the
Olympics. (Courtesy: *Hindusthan Standard*)

The Indian squad at the 1956 Melbourne Olympics, who reached the semi-final. (Top row, L to R) M.K. Nandy, M. Kempaiah, Neville D'Souza (hat-trick scorer), P.K. Banerjee, K.C. Paul, Zulfiqaruddin, M. Kannayan. (Middle row, L to R) T.A. Rahman, T. Balaraman, S.S. Narayan, Peter Thangaraj, S.A. Salaam, S.A. Latif, Ahmed Hussain. (Sitting, L to R) S.K. Azizuddin, J. Kittu, D. Ray, S. Banerjee, K. Ziauddin, coach S.A. Rahim and Noor Mohammed. (Courtesy: Nikhil Nandy)

The Indian team before their departure to the 1960 Rome Olympics. (Standing, L to R) O. Chandrasekhar, Chuni Goswami, Simon Sunderaraj, Arun Ghosh, F.A. Franco, Peter Thangaraj, P.K. Banerjee, K. Ziauddin (manager) with his son Pervez, S.A. Rahim (coach), S.A. Latif, S.S. Narayan, Jarnail Singh, Yousuf Khan and Tulsidas Balaram. (Kneeling, L to R) M. Kempaiah, S.H.H. Hamid, S.S. Hakeem, D. Kannan, Ram Bahadur and Dev Das. (Courtesy: S.S. Hakeem)

The gold medallists: The Indian team before their departure to Jakarta
for the Asian Games on 15 August 1962. (Standing, L to R) Ethiraj,
O. Chandrasekhar, Yousuf Khan, Peter Thangaraj, Prodyut Burman,
P.K. Banerjee, S.A. Rahim (coach and manager), Chuni Goswami, Arun
Ghosh and Jarnail Singh. (Kneeling, L to R) Trilok Singh, D.M.K. Afzal,
Ram Bahadur, Arumainayagam, Prasanta Sinha, F.A. Franco and
T. Balaraman. (Courtesy: *The Hindu* archives)

The Indian team's 1955 Russia tour. (L to R) AIFF
president Pankaj Gupta (in spectacles), K. Ziauddin,
later AIFF president, and coach S.A. Rahim.
(Courtesy: S.S. Hakeem)

HS - 02.12.1956

Olympic Football

INDIA MOVE INTO SEMI-FINAL

N. D'SOUZA PERFORMS A HAT-TRICK

MELBOURNE, DEC. 1.—India scored their first success
in Olympic football here today when they defeated
Australia by 4 goals to 2 in the quarter-finals, after being
level at 2-2 at half-time.

Centre forward Neville D'Souza scored the first
three goals for India, achieving a 'hat-trick', while
Kittu scored the fourth.

A report in *Hindustan Standard* on
2 December 1956, after India
beat Australia 4-2.
(Courtesy: *Hindusthan Standard*)

HS - 05.09.1962 —STANDARD Photo

India Win Soccer Gold Medal

KOREA BEATEN IN CLOSE TUSSLE

From PANKAJ GUPTA

DJAKARTA, SEPT. 4.—It was a great day for
Indian football here in Djakarta today when India
defeated Korea by the odd goal in three and won the
gold medal for the second time in the history of Asian
Games football.

A report in *Hindusthan Standard*, 5 September
1962, about India winning the gold at the
Asian Games. (Courtesy: *Hindusthan Standard*)

K.K. Ganguly, the legendary secretary of the
Durand football tournament, here as manager of
the Indian team, receiving the 1964 Asian Cup
runners-up trophy from the President of Israel,
Zalman Shazar. (Courtesy: DFTS)

The glittering Durand trophies:
Durand Cup, President's Cup
and Shimla Trophy.
(Courtesy: Sanjay Kumar)

The Andhra Pradesh Police squad, winners of the 1961 Durand. Standing second from left is
Zulfiqaruddin, third from right is S.A. Latif, and sitting second from right is Saleh (Jr).
(Courtesy: DFTS)

The JCT squad, winners of the 1992 Durand. (Standing, L to R) Coach Sukhwinder Singh,
assistant coach Parminder Singh, and manager and legendary striker Inder Singh.
(Courtesy: Sukhwinder Singh)

The East Bengal team, winners of the 1956 Durand, with President Dr Rajendra Prasad, a football enthusiast. Standing from left are T.A. Rahman and J. Kittu; sitting from right is M. Kempaiah and next to him is Kannayan. (Courtesy: DFTS)

The 1965 Mohun Bagan squad that won the Durand for the third successive year—the first Indian club to do so—with President Dr S. Radhakrishnan. Standing sixth from left is Chuni Goswami, ninth is Jarnail Singh; kneeling third from right is Arumainayagam, next is Prodyut Burman, and seventh is Ashok Chatterjee. (Courtesy: DFTS)

The Gorkha Brigade team, winners of the 1966 Durand, with the vice president, Dr Zakir Hussain. It was the first time they won the title. Sitting first from left is Ranjit Thapa, second is Bhupinder Singh Rawat, and standing second from left is Amar Bahadur. (Courtesy: DFTS)

The players of JCT, who won the 1983 Durand. From left the players are Narender Kumar, G.S. Parmar and Sukhwinder Singh. (Courtesy: DFTS)

The famous eleven players of Mohun Bagan who won the 1911 IFA Shield, beating East Yorkshire Regiment 2-1 in the final.

The beginning of the famous Kolkata derby, East Bengal vs Mohun Bagan, in May 1925. A report in the *Statesman*. (Courtesy: Gautam Roy)

Celebrated actor and football lover Dilip Kumar being introduced to the East Bengal players in a Rovers Cup final. (Courtesy: Gautam Roy)

Football legend Pelé playing for the New York Cosmos in an exhibition match against Mohun Bagan in September 1977.

A Kolkata derby match, the maroon-and-greens against the red-and-golds.
(Courtesy: Gautam Roy)

The passion for football: Fans clamber on to a
scaffolding or stand on bicycles to watch a football
match in Kolkata. (Courtesy: Mona Chowdhury
[left] and Nilanjan Datta [right])

Passion for the club surpasses all: East Bengal
fans wave the club colours.
(Courtesy: Gautam Roy)

East Bengal fans started lighting torches to
celebrate a victory. Here, with coloured
powder and placards.

Salgaocar were the first team from Goa to play in an outstation tournament, the 1962 DCM tournament. They were invited for tea with the sports-loving prime minister, Pandit Jawaharlal Nehru, at his residence in October 1962. (Courtesy: Salgaocar)

Ramesh Redcar, captain of Dempo, leads the team before the 1974–75 Rovers Cup final. Dempo were the first team from Goa to win the title.

The victorious Dempo squad with the Rovers Cup in 1975. (Courtesy: Dempo)

The Kerala Police team, with coach T.K. Chathunni, winners of the 1990 Federation Cup—the first time they achieved this feat. (Courtesy: T.K. Chathunni)

Pentiah, along with Aziz, was the coach of Andhra Pradesh when they won the Santosh Trophy in Kollam.

Many players from Hyderabad were versatile all-rounders and could play in more than one position. Yousuf Khan's display in the 1963 Rovers Cup is the best example of this. Andhra Police's regular stopper-back in the three-back system, Kaleemuddin, was injured. There was no proper replacement so Yousuf Khan, who normally played as a withdrawn forward or attacking midfielder, slotted in as stopper-back throughout the tournament. His exceptional anticipation and calmness under pressure ensured that the Police won the Rovers Cup for the ninth time. Yousuf Khan was so exceptional in every match that he was unanimously chosen as the best defender of the tournament ahead of established internationals Jarnail Singh (Mohun Bagan) and Arun Ghosh (BNR). Syed Nayeemuddin, who started his career in Hyderabad, was equally versatile. He was initially a left-back and then played as central-defender in the four-back system when India won bronze medals in the 1970 Merdeka Tournament and the 1970 Asian Games. He often played in midfield during his stint with Mohun Bagan and excelled with his sublime ball skills and impeccable technique in trapping, heading and passing.

Mohammed Azam, a dour defender, did not get much recognition and acclaim as he played in the same era as the incomparable Aziz. Azam and Aziz started their careers together at National Sporting and later both played for Hyderabad City Police. Azam's international appearances were limited; he played against Russia for both the Indian XI and the HFA XI in 1954 and played for India just once against Pakistan. In 1959, he was shifted to CPL Hyderabad and it was with this new team that his versatility came to the fore. He led his team to victory in the inaugural Nizam Gold Cup in Hyderabad in 1959. A year later he shifted to striker (centre-forward in those days) on the advice of Rahim. He was hesitant but soon blossomed in this position and finished as top scorer in the local 'A' Division championships in 1963. He also scored a hat-trick for CPL Hyderabad against East Bengal in a Rovers Cup match.

Such was the depth of talent in Hyderabad football in the 1950s and 1960s that dozens of players went to other centres in the hope of better prospects. This was a paradox in Hyderabad football even during its heyday. Only two institutions offered jobs, Hyderabad City Police and the local Road Transport Corporation. Private clubs with limited income played a major role in developing talented players but they could not retain players as they lacked the finances to pay regular salaries. Hence many star players from this region shifted their allegiances to other states where their football talent was amply rewarded.

Amongst them were such illustrious international players as Tulsidas Balaram (East Bengal), Peter Thangaraj (MRC Wellington, Mohammedan Sporting, Mohun Bagan and East Bengal), Ahmed Hussain (Mohammedan Sporting), D. Kannan (East Bengal), M.A. Salaam (Mohammedan Sporting), Rahmatullah (Mohammedan Sporting), S.A. Latif (Caltex Mumbai) H.H. Hamid (Mafatlal Mills Mumbai and Mohammedan Sporting), Yamani (Mohammedan Sporting), B. Narayan (East Bengal and Central Railway), S.S. Hakeem (IAF), Kankidas (East Bengal and Central Railway), Dhan Singh (Mohammedan Sporting) and Victor John (Mohammedan Sporting).

The brothers Mohammed Habib and Mohammed Akbar (East Bengal, Mohun Bagan and Mohammedan Sporting), Najam Lateefuddin (East Bengal and Mohammedan Sporting) and Shabbir Ali (Tata Sports Club, East Bengal and Mohammedan Sporting) excelled in Mumbai and Kolkata in the 1970s. Victor Amalraj (East Bengal and Mohun Bagan) and Mohammed Fareed (East Bengal and Mohammedan Sporting) did well in the 1980s. Najam Lateefuddin was the son of Moin. He and Akbar started their careers on a contract basis with Andhra Police, before being lured away by the Kolkata clubs. They were the last batch of famous players from Andhra Police to move to Kolkata.

Another feature of Hyderabad football during its glory days was mutual respect and communal harmony. Rahim set the trend and others followed. Mohammed Ghousuddin, coach of Osmania University, was one such dedicated official. When

Osmania University participated in the all-India inter-varsity championships in Tirupathi in 1957, Ghousuddin took the players for blessings to the Lord Venkateswara temple on a free day. Despite being a devout Muslim, he went for the darshan along with all the Hindu players in the team and even ate the prasad with them inside the temple. Ghousuddin was such a dedicated official that he even cooked meals for the players. Funds were limited and each player was allotted only Rs 4 per day. To ensure that his players were fed well, he carried bags of rice, vegetables and kitchen items with him and, with the help of a local boy, provided daily nutritious meals for the entire squad.

It is a truth stranger than fiction that football in this state of rich talent depended so completely on the enthusiasm of one man, the far-sighted coach and administrator S.A. Rahim.

After his death in June 1963, the excellent schemes he initiated soon started fading away. The training and coaching programmes, especially for teenagers, were abandoned altogether. Apart from attending to organizational and administrative matters, Rahim was able to spot young talent, train them and shape them into quality footballers. His successors coached mechanically and could not inspire and motivate younger players, nor could they spot latent talent amongst junior players.

When Rahim conducted training camps he ensured the trainees were provided with ample refreshments, for which the Andhra Pradesh Sports Council provided grants of up to Rs 3000. This grant was also stopped as there was no follow-up. The refreshments were an incentive for lower-middle-class trainees whose parents could not afford regular nourishing food. So, slowly, attendance at the Regional Coaching centres in Hyderabad thinned.

Rahim's commitment was so strong that he implemented programmes that even professional European clubs did not do till much later. In the 1950s, inter–primary school tournaments were held annually in which over fifty teams took part. Within a decade of his death this tournament stopped. Even participation in the inter–middle school, inter–high school and inter-college tournaments dwindled. The state associations used to conduct these tournaments but after Rahim's death they ceased due to lack of promotion and interest. Earlier, football in Hyderabad went on for most of the year. There were the first-, second- and third-division league championships and ten other knockout tournaments. Players got match exposure and developed their temperament and skills. Gradually these were stopped due to a paucity of funds. Therefore, in the 1960s and 1970s many promising youngsters just faded away.

It fell upon private clubs to spot talent and nurture it but they lacked the resources. Slowly, age-group development programmes disappeared from Hyderabad as the clubs just concentrated on building their 'first eleven' teams. As talented players stopped emerging, the standard of the clubs also declined. It became a Catch-22 situation. By the 1980s the DCM Trophy in Delhi only invited Hyderabad XI to participate, instead of the fifteen teams that used to be invited earlier.

The final blow came in the 1980s, as the Andhra Pradesh Football Association became riddled with factionalism. After a series of court cases and despite an attempted truce, the officials started suspending clubs for minor violations. Many of the clubs—Eleven Hunters, Merry Go Round, City College Old Boys, Hyderabad Sporting and Hyderabad Arsenal, which were the nurseries of the game in the state—gradually either ceased to exist or were marginalized. The state league was not held for years due to infighting. For fourteen years, beginning from 2000, Andhra Pradesh did not field a team for the Santosh Trophy. Football in the state has now almost come to a standstill. Many of the younger generation are unfortunately unaware of Hyderabad football's rich legacy.

With the formation of Telangana in June 2014, the Telangana Football Association became the thirty-sixth local state body to be affiliated to the AIFF. Creditably, some initiatives have begun to be taken, and in September 2015, a new club, Fateh Hyderabad football club, was launched. Fateh Hyderabad made their debut in the second-division I-League in the 2015–16 season and it is hoped that this new venture is the first step in reviving football in the city. Hopefully football can be resurrected in both Telangana and Andhra Pradesh—a region that, half a century ago, produced some of India's greatest footballers.

See in 'Hall of Fame': Noor Mohammed (midfielder), Yousuf Khan (attacking midfielder), S.K. Azizuddin (defender), S.A. Rahim (coach) and Syed Nayeemuddin (coach).

3

Goa

Fiesta, Feni and Football

A visiting British priest, Father William Robert Lyons, brought football to Goa in 1883. He arrived in Siolim, in Bardez taluka, from Udupi in neighbouring Karnataka (then known as Mysore) to recover from a bout of illness. He soon got involved in the activities of a local church and liked Goa enough to settle there. He founded St Joseph's School at Siolim. Father Lyons introduced sports and football into the school curriculum.

Like many of his fellow missionaries in British India, Father Lyons saw sports as integral to a Christian education. It was believed that, 'Christianity is a life that has to be lived . . . and to be a Christian one has to strive after perfect manliness, strength of body, strength of intellect, strength of soul.'[1] Sports was the 'soft power' of British colonialism. Regular participation in games like football inculcated values like fairness, honesty and obedience amongst Indians as well as made them appreciate the British value system, although it played out differently in Goa football due to the Catholic Church.

A decade later, in 1893, Antonio Francisco de Souza from Siolim introduced football at a private English school in Assolna, in Salcete taluka, where he was the headmaster. Priests who were being ordained in seminaries at Rachol (chief centre for training local priests in Goa) also started playing football. By the nineteenth century two-thirds of the population of Goa had become Christian, and the Catholic Church was in the hands of local Goans. So when priests tried to popularize football in the village parishes, the game was easily accepted by local people. This is how football became entrenched in rural Goa and quickly spread in towns and amongst the educated elites. However, the game was not confined to Christians; it spread amongst the local Hindu population as well.

The first reference to a football match played in Goa was in Panjim in 1900, at the Largo de Conceiea. It was witnessed by the state's governor general. Within the next decade, football was being regularly played in Panjim, Taleigao, Saligao, Assagao, Mapusa, Calangute, Margao, Vasco da Gama and Colva. The first club in Goa was formed in the coastal village of Colva in Salcete in 1905 and was called the Boys Social Club. Teams of many educational institutions competed with village teams and clubs like Vasco da Gama, the Goa Hindu club and Clube Coutinho Cabral in various competitions.

The first interstate football match in Goa was played in 1905 between St Mary's College, Mumbai, and Panjim Boys. The first international match in Goa was held in 1923 between the British Army Officers and Sergeants and a team of Portuguese Sports Amateurs at the police grounds in Panjim. The ground was covered with flags and banners and the police band played the national anthems of both countries. A large crowd, including women in fashionable dresses witnessed the Portuguese Amateurs win this game, which did not have any local players. Local tournaments were started soon after. The first all-Goa football tournament which included entrants from both North Goa and South Goa was hosted in 1930 by the Hindu Sporting Club of Mapusa.

On 6 October 1939, the Associação de Futebol da India Portuguesa was formed to improve the conduct of tournaments and to properly organize football in Goa. Foreign clubs and teams from Mumbai started visiting the state. A Goa selection team also visited Mumbai for friendly matches in 1940. In the early twentieth century Goans had started leaving for Mumbai as the city provided more opportunities for employment. By 1921 it was estimated that nearly 50 per cent of Goans lived away from home in East Africa or British India. Goan migrants in other cities formed football teams, which came to Goa to compete and also establish fraternal ties. By the 1940s, the best migrant team, Young Goans from Mumbai, toured Portuguese India. By the mid-1950s the number of Goans working and living away from home was three times greater than those who stayed back. The large number of expatriates encouraged the game by forming club teams and so football became an integral part of the Goan identity.

In the 1950s, the Portuguese dictator Oliveira Salazar used cultural bonding to show that Goa was in no way part of India. His regime used football to impress upon Goans the advantages of colonial rule and their sociocultural link with Portugal. Thus major teams in the Portuguese Empire visited Goa to play matches. In 1955, Ferroviario de Lourenço-Marques from Mozambique travelled to Goa and played a 2-2 draw against a representative team. They won the return match against a selected team from Goa 5-1. The team Port Trust of Karachi was also invited to play. The famous Benfica team visited the state in 1959 and played 3 matches, winning all of them with ease. These matches further popularized football in Goa, and thus on 22 December 1959, the Associação Futebol de Goa was founded, which later became the Goa Football Association (GFA). A Portuguese, Lt João Luis Aranha, became its first president.

The first famous Goan clubs, Salgaocar and Dempo, grew out of industrial organizations formed by the export of iron ore reserves. These clubs were formed as advertisements for the company: for goodwill and self-aggrandizement. Initially the most successful of the Goan clubs was Salgaocar, founded in 1955 as Vimson Football Club, which had four Portuguese players. However, the oldest first-division football club in Goa is Vasco Sports Club founded in 1951.

The first Goan, albeit from Mumbai, to play for India was the centre-forward Neville D'Souza in the 1956 Melbourne Olympics. D'Souza scored a hat-trick in India's memorable 4-2 win over Australia. Four years later another Goan from Mumbai, midfielder Franco, represented India in the 1960 Rome Olympics and was a member of the national squad which won the gold medal in the 1962 Asian Games. Another Goan, also from Mumbai, striker

Derrick D'Souza, played for India in the 1959 Asian Cup qualifiers and again in the 1964 Merdeka Tournament. Derrick was India's joint top scorer in the 1964 Merdeka, with three goals along with Chuni Goswami.

After liberation from colonial rule in 1961, football was used as a medium for a range of political messages. Initially Dayanand Bandodkar, the state's first chief minister and president of the Maharashtrawadi Gomantak Party, wanted Goa to merge with Maharashtra and Marathi to be its official language. Bandodkar became the vice president of the GFA in 1962 and started the all-India Bandodkar Tournament, where teams from all over India came to play. He donated a huge sum from his personal wealth for a solid-gold statuette trophy. It would be worth Rs 30 lakh in 2017 and is arguably the most expensive trophy in India. Bandodkar had the interests of Goans in mind and had mobilized the lower classes and lower castes. But in their fear of losing status, the upper-caste Hindus allied with the Christian population and, in the 1967 referendum, the idea of a merger with Maharashtra was rejected.

However, the Bandodkar Tournament still went ahead and was first played in 1970. Leaders Club Jalandhar emerged winners, beating Salgaocar 1-0 in the replayed final. In the following year Vasco Sports Club became champions beating Dempo 1-0 in the final. In this tournament the famous quartet of strikers, Andrew, Bernard, Catao and Dominic of Vasco, known as the ABCD of football, emerged. After the 1971 Bandodkar Tournament, Andrew D'Souza and Menino Figueredo of Salgaocar became the first Goan players groomed in Goa to represent India in an international match against a visiting Russian team.

An influential official, B.M. Parkkot, took over Goa's oldest club Vasco in 1964–65 and made them a successful team. They became the first Goan club to reach the Rovers Cup final in 1966, before losing 0-1 to Mohun Bagan, and they won the Kerala Trophy in 1968 beating EME Secunderabad 2-1 in the final. Parkkot did not have political but football ambitions. He became GFA president (1968–72) and lobbied the AIFF to make the GFA independent and a fully constituent member. The AIFF finally agreed, and to celebrate this, the GFA hosted the Santosh Trophy in 1972.

By the early 1980s Goa announced itself as a major footballing power in the country with two back-to-back national-level titles, under the guidance of coach T. Shanmugham. Goa first won the Santosh Trophy in 1982–83 when they were joint winners with Bengal. The next year, in the floodlit Nehru Stadium in Chennai, Goa annexed the Santosh Trophy outright in grand style without conceding a goal in any match. Their midfield comprising Arnold Rodrigues (adjudged the player of the tournament), Herbert San and Mauricio Afonso played imaginative football. In the final they beat Punjab 1-0 with striker Camilo Gonsalves scoring the solitary goal.

In 1987 Goa became a fully fledged state of the Indian Union, and by 30 May 1988 the foundation was laid for the Fatorda Stadium (also known as Jawaharlal Nehru Stadium) in Margao, which hosted the Nehru Cup in 1989.

At the start of the new millennium, it was Goan clubs that won the first six editions of the I-League, inaugurated in 2007–08. Dempo have won the most I-League titles (2007–08, 2009–10 and 2011–12), followed by Churchill Brothers (2008–09 and 2012–13). The other Goan club to have won this prestigious title is Salgaocar in 2010–11, when Dempo finished third. Churchill Brothers have finished second on two occasions, and third and fourth on two others in this competition.

Even as football stagnated in many states in India due to factionalism in the local football associations, the standards of the game have improved by leaps and bounds in Goa. The GFA is considered the best in the country in terms of organization and visionary planning. A former president of the AIFF Priya Ranjan Dasmunsi used to often joke that if all the state associations were as progressive as the GFA, Indian football standards would improve rapidly.

The GFA was the first state association to digitize all football records and to get their first-division league sponsored. It was amongst the early ones to realize that the nucleus for development of football standards was youth development and promotion of the game in rural areas. The GFA launched their Youth Football Development programme in 1998 with financial support from Kanan Devan, a subsidiary of the Tata Tea Company.

Before this Goan players mostly emerging from inter-village tournaments did not receive any structured training, so their basics tended to be weak. At the turn of the century, the GFA started six training centres in North Goa and seven in South Goa for U-12 and U-14 boys.

Creditably, the GFA has always taken a very holistic approach to the development of football. For several decades, since jobs in companies provided them security, Goan footballers—with some exceptions like Joseph Rathnam and Joao D'Mello—shunned coaching as a career. Hence the GFA became the only association in the country to fully sponsor candidates for the AFC coaching courses. Many stalwart Goan players eventually became qualified coaches and have made their presence felt. The GFA also developed referees in their state.

While football in Goa has improved due to the initiatives of the progressive GFA, its leading football clubs have played a significant role. The story of Goan football is also the story of Salgaocar, Dempo and Churchill Brothers.

Salgaocar Sports Club

This famous club started as Vimson Football Club in 1955, patronized by Vasudev M. Salgaocar, who was emerging as a business tycoon. The V.M. Salgaocar Group is today amongst the most widely known industrial conglomerates in Goa, exporting iron ore to some of the world's largest steel mills and holding business interests in travel, health and hospitality. In 1956 Vimson FC was absorbed by the Salgaocar Group and renamed Salgaocar Sports Club.

At the time of liberation from colonial rule, Salgaocar was the champion club of Goa. Therefore in October 1962 the DCM Trophy invited them and they became the first team from Goa to participate in an outstation tournament. There was a lot of excitement to see Salgaocar play in Delhi, as it was felt that the Portuguese influence would be visible in their style of play. Their visit created such a stir that Prime Minister Jawaharlal Nehru hosted a tea party for the team at his residence.[2]

Salgaocar started their DCM campaign against rugged Punjab Police in a second-round match and drew goalless on the opening day. They won 2-1 in the replay and reached the quarter-finals. However, they were beaten 0-2 by Mysore XI. The Salgaocar team that toured Delhi in 1962 was managed by James Fernandes of Margao, and included legends like defender Cândido Abreu and forward Wilson Mazarello.

Good performance in the DCM Trophy encouraged Salgaocar to regularly play in competitions all over India. Their first-ever outstation victory was in the Nagpur Rovers Cup (different from the Mumbai edition) in 1971 when they ousted Punjab Police 1-0 in the final. Salgaocar's performances as a team improved when former international midfielder T. Shanmugham took over as coach in 1979. Shanmugham was a member of the Indian squad that won the gold medal at the 1951 Asian Games in Delhi.

T. Shanmugham was Salgaocar club's longest-serving coach, from 1979 till 1996. Despite much more lucrative offers from the Bengal clubs during his tenure, he never left. Shanmugham belonged to the Bengaluru school of football, where the build-up in attack was always elaborate with a series of short passes—at times very intricate, but effective. He exemplified this style of football which shunned physical contact and frenetic pace. As a midfielder, Shanmugham was a cerebral player. His game was based on interceptions, sound technique and astute passes. He changed the style of football in Goa, especially Salgaocar FC. This process was accelerated once S.S. Hakeem—who also coached the team during 1983–85—left and Shanmugham assumed total control of the club.

Hakeem was a 1960 Rome Olympian and assistant coach of the Indian team at the 1982 Asian Games. He belonged to Hyderabad and, during his brief stint as coach, tried to make Salgaocar play a mixture of short passing and frequent cross-field passes. As coach, Hakeem's greatest contribution was discovering the clever defender Derrick Pereira and making him an international player within a short period. A precocious and talented player, Derrick was casual in his approach in his formative years. Like many youngsters he frequented the bars in Goa and was often seen playing cards with his friends after practice sessions. Hakeem, who had just retired from the IAF as squadron leader, was a strict disciplinarian. This was a trait he had also inherited from his father S.A. Rahim, arguably India's greatest-ever football coach. An avid reader, Hakeem visited the markets regularly to buy news magazines. He would invariably spot Derrick on the way. Derrick paid no heed to the warnings that he received from both Hakeem and Shanmugham.

Finally Hakeem took drastic action. He gave an ultimatum to the Salgaocar management that he would leave the club if Derrick continued with his undisciplined lifestyle, as team spirit was being affected. Derrick was summoned, chastised and told to get his act together. A subdued Derrick agreed. A keen psychologist, Hakeem then won over Derrick by telling him if he focused on the game, he would represent India internationally. The prediction came true. Derrick not only played in the 1986 Seoul Asiad but emerged as one of India's best defenders in the 1980s. A man of pleasant disposition, Derrick always acknowledged Hakeem's role in shaping him as a player. Derrick had a long and successful playing career with Salgaocar. He always kept himself fit and was rarely cautioned by referees. He then obtained his 'A' Licence and Pro-Licence coaching degrees and became a successful coach with a number of clubs.

In 1987 Salgaocar became the first Goan club to enter the Federation Cup final, India's premier knockout tournament. They lost 0-2 to Mohun Bagan. They had only two foreigners in that side, Nigerian Valentine Ezeugo and Iranian junior international Abolghasem Kosagavar, while the rest of their players were all from Goa. Well-known Goan players in Salgaocar's team were legendary international custodian Brahmanand Shankhwalkar (the first footballer from Goa to get the Arjuna Award, in 1997), stalwart defenders Derrick Pereira and Norbert Gonsalves, and international midfielders Savio Medeira and Lawrence Gomes.

A year later Salgaocar became the first Goan club to not only win the Federation Cup but also to win a tournament in Delhi. Hitherto, Goan clubs used to struggle in the Delhi winter and were not expected to win. Salgaocar defeated tenacious BSF 1-0 in the Federation Cup final. Mario Soares, the youngest player in the team, scored the match-winner off a pass from Valentine Ezeugo. Soares was just nineteen years old when he scored the match-winner and is, as of June 2017, the youngest player to have scored in this tournament's final.

Salgaocar's first-ever Federation Cup triumph was a testimony to their fitness and tactics. Due to the tight schedule of the tournament, they played 6 matches in eight days, winning twice on penalties. In the final, coach Shanmugham's game plan clicked. He said:

> Our tactics of keeping the ball on the ground helped us win. I told my boys not to play in the air, as the taller BSF players are better in aerial duels. Also, I asked my midfielders not to allow the BSF players to hold on to the ball for long. I am glad my players stuck to the plan and we deservedly won. It was also a triumph of our physical fitness.

Overcoming the Delhi jinx too was vital for Salgaocar. Shanmugham said:

> In the 1980s, clubs from Goa did not travel well. They only performed well in a familiar environment like in Goa and the Rovers Cup in Mumbai. I had to make them believe in themselves, that they could perform well anywhere.

In 1989 Salgaocar lost the services of seven players in the inter-club transfer to the newly formed, big-money spenders MRF of Goa. However, in their opening quarter-final league match of that year's Federation Cup, Salgaocar beat MRF 1-0 with a goal by Bruno

Coutinho. The victory was a great morale booster for Salgaocar and they went from strength to strength. In the semi-finals they beat the glamorous Mohun Bagan for the first time with goals by Ignatius Dias and Bento Andrew. They went on to retain the trophy, beating Mohammedan Sporting 2-0 in extra time, with Ezeugo and Coutinho scoring the winning goals. In 1990, Salgaocar entered the Federation Cup final for the fourth year in a row but lost 1-2 to Kerala Police at Thrissur.

Salgaocar next won the Federation Cup in 1997, upsetting East Bengal 2-1 in the final at the Salt Lake Stadium, Kolkata, with Coutinho scoring twice including the match-winning golden goal. This was arguably their finest victory in the Federation Cup, as it was the first time they had beaten a Kolkata club on home soil. Bruno played as a withdrawn striker, so that Salgaocar often used a five-man midfield.

However, Salgaocar's greatest hour was in the last year of the twentieth century. Coached by Shabbir Ali from Hyderabad, they emerged champions of the 3rd Coca-Cola NFL in early 1999 with a tally of 23 points. They also scored the maximum number of goals, 17 in all. Then on 15 November 1999, Salgaocar beat Churchill Brothers in an all-Goa final 1-0 to win the Rovers Cup. About three weeks later on 4 December, they beat East Bengal 3-2 via penalties to lift the Durand Cup. The match had ended in a goalless draw. Salgaocar thus became the first club from Goa to win the Rovers Cup and Durand Cup double crown in one season. On 6 December, Salgaocar annexed the prestigious Super Cup (a play-off between the reigning National League champions and the Federation Cup champions) at the Ambedkar Stadium, Delhi, with Alvito D'Cunha scoring the match-winner in the eighth minute of extra time. By winning three major trophies within the space of twenty days, Salgaocar showed that Goan football had come of age. The era of supremacy of the Kolkata teams appeared to be dwindling. Shabbir Ali had a very successful stint as coach of Salgaocar, winning eight titles.

In the 1990s it was Salgaocar's defence and midfield which was quite exemplary and helped them dominate Indian football. After Shanmugham, they were initially coached by T.K. Chathunni and then by Shabbir Ali. They had the agile Juje Siddi in goal, and their remarkable and consistent back four consisted of Roberto Fernandes, Francis 'Saby' Coelho, Franky Barreto and Roque Pereira. Both Fernandes and Barreto were regular members of the Indian team. They excelled in the 1997 Nehru Cup at Kochi when India, coached by Syed Nayeemuddin, reached the semi-finals for the first time. A year later both performed excellently in the 1998 Asian Games in Bangkok as well. Tall and lanky Fernandes had a style of play similar to the great Brazilian right-back and World Cup–winner Cafu, and excelled whilst overlapping. He was at his best in both defence and attack against Japan, a match India narrowly lost 0-1. Japan's French coach, the experienced Philippe Troussier, complimented Fernandes for his excellent display in this game.

Shabbir used a diamond formation in midfield, with the Nigerian Habib Adekunle as the holding midfielder and Salgaocar legend Coutinho playing as an advanced midfielder or withdrawn forward. Thrust was provided on the right by Jules Alberto—who was being ordained to be a priest but then opted to be a professional footballer—and by Sabir Ali Mondal or Dharamjit Singh on the left. João Santos of Brazil was the lone roving striker.

In the twenty-first century, however, Salgaocar have not fared as well as expected. In the 10th ONGC-sponsored NFL in 2005–06, they were even relegated to the second division but got promoted the very next season. They again finished at the bottom of the table in the inaugural I-League in 2007–08 but rejoined the main league in 2009–10. Although they have not won many titles during this period, they were involved in two great high-scoring matches, which will be remembered forever and are a lasting legacy to their thoughtful, short-passing approach play and never-say-die attitude—qualities instilled in them by their longest-serving coach, T. Shanmugham.

Incidentally, both these matches were against Mohun Bagan at the Nehru Stadium, Margao. On 11 April 2002, in a round-21 match of the 6th Tata NFL, Bagan, needing a win to secure the title, got off to a scorching start and scored thrice in the first half-hour, with goals by Jose Ramirez Barreto (second and fifteenth minute) and midfielder Basudeb Mondal (twenty-eighth minute). They seemed to be cruising to victory but then came the great Salgaocar comeback spearheaded by the silky ball skills of the highly talented Alvito D'Cunha. The Liberian striker Sunday Seah made it 1-3 in the thirty-second minute and Alvito converted a penalty kick in the forty-second minute. Spurred by this revival, Salgaocar mounted relentless pressure in the second-half where goals by Seah and junior international Alex Ambrose helped them secure a famous 4-3 win.

The second match took place five years later on 22 December 2007. Thanks to a hat-trick by their Nigerian striker Felix Chimaokwu, Salgaocar again rallied from being 1-3 down to make the score 4-4 midway through the second-half. However, midfielder James Singh scored the match-winner for Bagan in the sixty-ninth minute, and the famous maroon-and-green shirted Kolkata club etched out a remarkable 5-4 win.

In September 2011, there was a brief resurgence in Salgaocar's game when they again won the Federation Cup in Kolkata, upsetting East Bengal 3-1 in the final. This time the Moroccan Karim Bencherifa was their coach. Earlier in May, they won the 4th I-League title, also under Bencherifa. Salgaocar did well in the business end to pip East Bengal, who were table toppers from the outset, and emerge triumphant. It was their first and only I-League title so far.

Over the years Salgaocar have produced some excellent players who had distinguished international careers—like goalkeeper Brahmanand; defenders Nicholas Pereira, Norbert Gonsalves and Derrick Pereira; midfielders Savio Medeira, S. Venkatesh, Lawrence Gomes, Climax Lawrence, Jules Alberto, Dharamjit Singh and Jatin Bisht; and forwards Alvito, Coutinho, Bento Andrew, Ignatius Dias and Roy Barreto. This club has always encouraged players with potential and never discarded them quickly after a few mediocre performances, as was often done by the leading Kolkata clubs.

Dempo Sports Club

In 2017, Dempo SC celebrated their golden jubilee and released an excellent historical book about the club, *The Golden Eagles*. However, they had started as Bicholim Football Club, a well-known first-division side in the 1960s. Bicholim was taken over by the company Dempo Souza in 1967 and renamed Dempo Souza SC. They became Dempo when the industrialist Vasantrao Dempo bought his partner Michael Souza's stake in the club and formed his own team.

Dempo were the first Goan team to win the Rovers Cup in Mumbai in 1974–75, under the guidance of the great coach Joseph Rathnam. Led by midfielder Ramesh Redkar, Dempo defeated Tata Sports Club in the replayed final, when striker K. Williams converted a penalty kick in the closing minutes of the match. The penalty kick was awarded when speedy striker Francis D'Souza was tripped in the box by the Tata defender Joaquim Barreto. Since then Dempo has won the Rovers Cup on four other occasions—in 1978, 1979, 1986 and 1990. In 1978, striker Francis D'Souza was again the hero of Dempo's triumph. On his birthday he scored both the goals against Orkay Mills Mumbai. That year Dempo were coached by the Englishman Bob Bootland and were in peak physical condition. They played in the 4-3-3 system, trouncing Sesa Goa 6-1 in the pre-quarter-finals with some fluent attacking football. In 1986, they beat East Bengal 2-1 in the semi-final and Mohun Bagan 2-0 in the final. Dempo's current coach, diminutive international midfielder and the best playmaker of his generation, Mauricio Afonso, starred in those triumphs.

Mauricio Afonso was Goa's Paul Scholes, short-statured and wiry, a bundle of energy in the middle and an astute passer of the ball. His football intelligence was supreme as he was always available for a pass, linked up well with his forwards and was a good snatcher of the ball. From childhood, he was besotted with football and neglected his studies. His mother was tolerant and supported her son's passion. His physical trainer at school, Cajetan Rodrigues, also recognized his talent and improved his basic skills.

Like many players of the 1970s generation in Goa, his career started with his village team CRC Chinchinim. But Mauricio was not a laid-back person and his ambition led him to try greener pastures. He switched to Salcete FC as they had better coaching facilities. In 1981–82 he received an offer from Salgaocar and played three seasons for them. He then opted for Dempo in 1984 and stayed with them for fifteen seasons until he retired. His football skills and passing ability were shaped by coach Joseph Rathnam.

In 1983 he attended the national camp in Delhi and was selected for the President's Cup in Dhaka, Bangladesh. The late Yugoslav coach Milovan Ćirić admired Mauricio's all-action game, positive attitude and sincerity in practice. Ćirić made Mauricio a regular in the national team and he played for India from 1983 to 1989. During his career Mauricio played for four national coaches: Ćirić, Arun Ghosh, P.K. Banerjee and Syed Nayeemuddin, all of whom appreciated his game. The highlight of his international career was playing in the 1984 Asian Cup final rounds in Singapore.

Mauricio belonged to an era when most players in Goa were amateurs. His income came from his job at Dempo, not from his football prowess. But unlike many of his contemporaries who stagnated once they got a permanent job, Mauricio was motivated by a personal desire to excel. This quality made him work diligently and achieve consistency. After retirement, he obtained his coaching degrees and was Dempo's assistant coach, especially during its glorious era under coach Armando Colaco.

Striker Francis D'Souza, known for his blistering pace, is the other outstanding player from this time. A real trailblazer, he was a child prodigy who at just twelve years of age played for his school team. He joined Dempo in 1975 at Rs 400 per month, but refused a permanent job as he was confident of earning substantial money through his football skills. In 1976 and 1977, Francis played for India in Indonesia (for the Marah Halim Cup) and Kabul (for the Independence Day Cup) respectively. In 1979 Bagan secured his services for Rs 83,000 per season, with all facilities including five air tickets to Goa. In his first match for Bagan in the 1980 Federation Cup at the Eden Gardens in Kolkata, he scored the fastest goal in the

tournament's history. He scored seventeen seconds from the start
of play against Salgaocar, whose goalkeeper was Brahmanand.

At his prime, Francis was one of the most intelligent and
quicksilver strikers in the country. In 1983 the great coach Syed
Nayeemuddin said, 'Francis was one of the best forwards of his
time in Indian football for his superb goalscoring ability and body
feints,' He later played for Mohammedan Sporting and Dempo
again, before qualifying as a coach and joining the Sports Authority
of India (SAI). Unfortunately, repeated injuries marred his career,
but the lean and wiry Francis set the trend of professional contracts
in Goan football.

In the 1990s Dempo won the Scissors Cup thrice, in 1992,
1994 and 1996. Their most memorable Scissors Cup triumph was
in 1994, when striker Marcus Carvalho's hat-trick enabled them
to beat Mohun Bagan 3-0 in the final. This win halted Bagan's
record unbeaten sequence of 42 matches that season.

Always progressive in their approach, Dempo experimented
with foreign coaches Bob Bootland (England) in 1978, Francisco
Gonçalves de Silva, or Tico (Brazil), in 1997–98 and Ahmad Sanjari
(Iran) in 1999–2000. For the inaugural Philips National League in
1996–97, Dempo hired a Peruvian, Walter Ormeño, who had coached
in Mexico. They were the first to recruit Brazilian players Anderson
Ribeiro, João Soares and Marcelo Antônio in 1997–98 for the 2nd
NFL. In the 1970s they enrolled stylish midfielder Herbert San from
the remote Andaman and Nicobar Islands. During that period, Goan
clubs mostly relied on local talent but Dempo procured outstation
players like international goalkeeper K. Sampath (MEG Bangalore),
midfielder M. Prasannan (Kerala) and forwards Prem Sahi and
Pratap Khatri (Gorkha Brigade). Dempo's longest-serving players
were internationals Camilo Gonsalves and Mauricio Afonso.

Despite their successes in the Rovers Cup, Stafford Cup and
four successive triumphs in the Bandodkar Trophy from 1982–
86, Dempo's real claim to fame came in the NFL and I-League
in the twenty-first century. They won the NFL/I-League on five
occasions in a span of just eight years. Most of these titles they
won in style. Registering their first NFL victory in 2004–05, they

won its last season in 2006–07, after which they immediately clinched the inaugural I-League in 2007–08.

In the 3rd I-League 2009–10, Dempo finished with 54 points from 26 matches, a whopping 11 points ahead of their nearest challengers Churchill Brothers. Again in 2011–12, they won the 5th I-League with a record haul of 57 points from 26 matches, scoring 59 goals. Nigerian Ranti Martins and Dempo teammates Mahesh Gawli, Anthony Pereira and veteran goalkeeper Sandip Nandy are the four players who have won the NFL/I-League five times. However, ace striker Ranti's contribution in helping Dempo procure these five titles is unprecedented.

In 2004–05 Ranti scored 15 of the 28 goals notched up by his club. Again in 2006–07, he was top scorer for Dempo with 16 goals. Dempo won the inaugural I-League title on goal difference from Churchill Brothers, and as usual Ranti scored the most goals, netting 12 out of a tally of 35. When Dempo emerged champions for the fifth time, in 2011–12, Ranti was the league's leading marksman with 32 goals. Overall, Ranti scored 146 goals in his 164 appearances for Dempo in the NFL/I-League, and thrice won the Golden Boot as top scorer.

This slim but wiry Nigerian striker who came to Goa as a precocious teenager is the silent assassin, a lurking menace who suddenly accelerates and scores with crisp knee-height shots and placements. The credit goes to Dempo's coach Armando Colaco for spotting Ranti's talent and nurturing him for so many years. He first came into the limelight during the 2004 Durand Cup in Delhi. In those days, a club was allowed to field only two foreign players in a domestic tournament. Dempo had signed Cristiano Júnior from East Bengal that season, a highly accomplished and skilful striker. They had Majek Bolaji in defence and all the media at Delhi thought that Armando would field both Bolaji and Cristiano. However, much to everybody's surprise, on match day Cristiano remained seated in the stands and the unknown Nigerian Ranti Martins went out to play. Many in the media questioned Armando's decision. An astute judge of a player's ability, Armando had spotted Ranti's lethal finishing and wanted to give him an extended run to see if he could cope with pressure. Armando was proved right.

The Brazilian striker Cristiano Júnior tragically died after a clash with Mohun Bagan's onrushing goalkeeper Subrata Pal in the 2004 Federation Cup final in Bengaluru. Ranti now became Dempo's chief striker and he responded in style. At the 7th NFL in February 2005, he scored a vital hat-trick against reigning champions East Bengal to help a depleted (due to injuries) Dempo win 3-2. This match was the turning point in Dempo's fortunes as victory against the champions gave them the self-belief and self-confidence that they could be serious title contenders.

Dempo is the only relegated club to have won the NFL. They finished last in the 4th NFL in 1999–2000, winning just 1 match and scoring 12 goals in 22 matches. The disillusioned management nearly disbanded the team. However, persuasion by the fans prevented such a drastic step. The football budget was enhanced and Dempo was promoted to the top flight by the 7th NFL. Former player Armando Colaco was appointed coach in 2002, and under his tutelage, Dempo has come of age in Indian football. They won the 'double' in 2004–05: Federation Cup and NFL. In the 2006–07 season they won the Durand Cup as well as the NFL.

Armando's keen ability to spot and nurture talent helped Dempo's fortunes tremendously. In the 2005–06 season, the Brazilian Beto was used as an advanced midfielder and developed a telepathic understanding with striker Ranti. They formed the pivot of Dempo's attack, with Beto the provider, ably supported by Climax Lawrence in the midfield, Clifford Miranda and Anthony Pereira on the flanks, and Ranti the finisher. If required Peter Carvalho was slotted in as a defensive midfielder. Beto and Ranti became the most lethal combination in Indian football for the next seven years. This coincided with the period of Dempo's dream run.

Armando also persuaded Mahesh Gawli, who played for Mahindra United (now defunct), to join Dempo. The transfer made him India's highest-paid defender. With Gawli in the team Dempo performed exceptionally well and became the first Indian club side to reach the AFC Cup semi-finals in 2008.

On their way to the semi-final Dempo beat clubs from Oman, Lebanon, Bahrain and Singapore, all countries higher than India in the FIFA rankings.

Above all, during the NFL and I-League matches Armando kept the squad free from pressure by taking them to the beach or dinner at their favourite restaurants. Pre-season training was always at one of the beaches. Such relaxation was a favoured ploy of Brian Clough, manager of Nottingham Forest, winner of the European Champions Cup in 1979 and 1980.

Dempo's golden run of eight years (2004–05 to 2011–12) will be remembered not just for their successes but also for their pleasing approach play. Like Spain's 2010 World Cup–winning team, Dempo believed in retaining possession and rotating the ball to wear down the opponent. When they lost the ball, they resorted to high pressing to win back possession, earning them the nickname 'Barcelona of India'. Armando ensured that whoever joined Dempo fitted into this playing style, which guaranteed continuity and success.

Armando's coaching philosophy was greatly influenced by Joseph Rathnam, Dempo's coach for nearly a decade from 1970 onwards. During Rathnam's tenure Dempo annexed the prestigious Rovers Cup for the first time in 1975 and, in later years, the Stafford Cup (Bengaluru), the Nizam Gold Cup (Hyderabad) and the Bordoloi Shield (Assam). Praising Rathnam's person-management skills and his affectionate treatment of the players, Armando has written: 'When some players said they were injured and [were] in no position to take the field, Rathnam emerged from his room with a magical potion, applied it to the injured part and the players felt better. That's the kind of impact he had on players, even if we learnt later that, sometimes, [the magic potion] was toothpaste.'[3]

In the twentieth century Dempo had some outstanding internationals like the crafty midfielder Mauricio Afonso, defenders Nicholas Pereira and Mahesh Lotlikar, midfielders Ramesh Redkar, Thomas Khushboo and Joseph Machado, lethal strikers Francis D'Souza (younger brother of international referee Melwyn D'Souza), Dionisio Trinidade, Camilo Gonsalves (represented India at the 1986 Seoul Asian Games), Mario Soares,

Marcus Carvalho and Francis Silveira. In the twenty-first century,
some of Dempo's outstanding players have been internationals—
Climax Lawrence (a tireless and intelligent midfielder), astute
defenders Mahesh Gawli, Samir Naik and Valeriano Rebello,
defensive midfielder Peter Carvalho and wide midfielders Clifford
Miranda and Anthony Pereira.

Churchill Brothers

Churchill Brothers is India's only family club. In 1975, the
Alemaos—six dynamic and enterprising brothers from the remote
Varca village in South Goa—had a dream of forming a football
club which could rival the best in the land. Their intentions and
ambitions were huge but the road to success was arduous. To form
a top-class club, the brothers knew they had to spend big money.
So they diversified into various branches of business like owning
trawlers, fishing and hotels. At Margao they set up Raisa, the finest
Chinese restaurant in Goa. As their first love was football, they
invested their family wealth into the game. The village club Varca
Sports Club, of which the eldest brother Churchill Alemao was
president, progressed from the third division to the first division
of the Goa League in 1994.

A stroke of luck led to the formation of Churchill Brothers.
In the early 1990s, the MRF academy team, launched with much
fanfare in 1988, faded away. Several talented players lost their
jobs. Seizing this opportunity, the Alemao brothers roped in the
talented players from MRF and formed a new club in 1991. After
much discussion they decided to name it after the eldest of the
family, and since it was supported by the six brothers, it became
Churchill Brothers.

Soon after they set up, Churchill Brothers changed the scenario
of Goan football. Until then the leading clubs of Goa had set up a
type of cartel and had a tacit understanding of not poaching each
other's players for a period of three years. The players would thus
lose out monetarily. Unlike the other teams that are supported by
well-established business groups, the Alemao brothers ploughed

back profits from their newly set up business ventures into their football club. The generous brothers started to pay lucrative salaries for players' services, becoming the first club in Goa to do so. The diminutive but talented midfielder Aqeel Ansari was lured away from Mohun Bagan, the dashing Manipuri Somatai Shaiza from East Bengal and lanky, long-haired defender Naushad Moosa (a long-throw expert) from Mumbai. Midfielder Somatai, left-back Rattan Singh from Manipur and lethal striker Percy Mwase from distant Zimbabwe were in the Churchill Brothers squad for the 1st NFL in 1996–97. Percy was also the first from his country to ply his trade in India. They also roped in Nigerian striker Chibuzor who had been rejected by the Kolkata clubs. Commenting on this, Churchill Alemao said, 'Getting Aqeel and Soso [Somatai's nickname] to play in Goa was quite a catch. Till then Goan players left for Kolkata but there was no movement in the reverse direction. We showed that with good money payments we could rope in the best talent in the country.'

With his bold recruitments and generous contracts, Churchill Alemao decisively ushered in professional football in the state. Other Goan clubs followed suit. Soon other North-eastern players started exploring Goa as an option for a football career instead of just the Kolkata clubs. In the history of Goan football, 1996–97 was significant as a bullish trend started, from which even talented Goan players benefited. There was a tug of war between Dempo and Churchill Brothers for the two nippy and skilful forwards Marcus Carvalho and Francis Silveira, who were both being offered Rs 7 lakh each, an amount unheard of in earlier seasons in Goa.

Initially there was criticism that by hiring outside players, Churchill Brothers were hurting the chances of Goan players. The Alemao brothers, however, retorted that the presence of quality foreign and outstation players improved the standard of football in Goa. Defending this policy, Churchill Alemao said, 'I don't have a company to offer jobs to players. All Goan players ask for jobs whereas outside players are ready to play on a yearly contract, which suits us fine.'

Contrary to popular fears, the family never neglected local talent. Churchill Alemao's intense devotion to the game ensured that he kept scouting around for bargain buys or quality players to improve the team. As he could not compete with the big budgets of the Kolkata clubs or the institution-based Goa teams, he decided to recruit young graduates from TFA and groom them into better players. So players like Mahesh Gawli (arguably India's best defender in the twenty-first century), midfielders Noel Wilson, Kashif Jamal and Lalrindika Ralte, to mention a few, started their careers with Churchill Brothers. Some established Goan players also agreed to play on annual contracts. The famous goalkeeper and Arjuna Awardee Brahmanand Shankwalkhar, international defenders Franky Barreto, Danzie Ferrao and Denzil Franco, and midfielders Mario Soares and Hercules Gomes have worn the colours of the club.

Churchill Brothers also got foreign coaches for the NFL. Their first foreign coach was Danny McLennan of Scotland, who had coached in Asia and Africa since the 1950s and joined the club in 1996. McLennan had a major impact on Churchill Brothers. They became Goa League champions for the first time in 1996 and won the title again in 1997. He revolutionized training methods and his emphasis was to try and create thinking players. He improved the player's work rate, movement of the ball and getting space to receive passes. Their preparation for the Philips League was also very professional. Instead of tiring his players out in several tournaments, McLennan opted for more intensive practice and less exposure. The team thus peaked for the Philips League. Fancied and star-studded JCT were defeated 2-0 at Ludhiana, and mighty East Bengal were upset 0-1 at the Salt Lake Stadium, Kolkata.

In the inaugural eight-team Philips National League they topped the table from the first day till they stumbled on the last day, a 1-1 draw against the lowly placed Indian Bank from Chennai. Churchill Brothers needed just a win but could only draw and JCT pipped them to the title. It was the start of two tumultuous decades, during which Churchill Brothers emerged as a dominant force in Indian football and were always in the news, sometimes for controversial reasons.

Goa's youngest big club, their long wait for a major title came to an end at the 2007 Durand Cup in Delhi. Known as 'chokers', they had come close to winning a major title on several occasions but had stumbled at the final hurdle. Thrice they were runners-up in the NFL, in 1997, 2000 and 2002; thrice in the Rovers Cup in 1997, 1999 and 2000; and once at the 2001 Durand Cup, the 2002 IFA Shield and 1997 Dubai International Tournament.

Churchill Brothers annexed the 120th Osian's Durand Cup in November 2007, beating Mahindra United 1-0 in the final. This win also exorcised the ghosts of their 0-5 loss to Mahindra United in the 2001 Durand final, when defender Osumanu Husseini was shown the red card early in the match and the team crumbled while playing with ten men for the remainder of the match.

Never in the history of the Durand Cup has one club depended so much on one man, as Churchill Brothers did then on skipper Odafa Onyeka Okolie, who scored 11 of their 14 goals in 5 matches, about 80 per cent of the goals his team scored. His 5 goals in 1 match against Central Railway (Mumbai) is a Durand record. Churchill Brothers' triumph was unique as they were without their inspirational Moroccan coach, Karim Bencherifa, who was in Singapore for personal reasons. He watched the matches online and gave constant instructions via his mobile phone to assistant coach and former player Mario Soares—not unlike Mahavir Phogat instructing his wrestler daughter Geeta over the phone in the superhit Hindi film *Dangal*. It was on Karim's insistence that in the second-half of the final, Odafa shifted to midfield to curb Mahindra United's sustained pressure.

Maintaining the same squad for successive years except for some additions, and an emphasis on fitness, helped Churchill Brothers achieve success. This family-owned club made their second tryst with destiny when they annexed the 2nd ONGC I-League 2008–09, setting several new records in the process. Churchill Brothers finished with a record tally of 53 goals in 22 matches. Lethal striker Odafa, with an impressive tally of

26 goals, finished as top scorer for the third year in a row. Their
Serbian coach, Zoran Đorđević, became the first foreigner to
guide a team to success in the national league in India. That year
they became the third club from Goa to annex the national league
title; previous winners were Salgaocar and Dempo. Churchill
Brothers also set a unique record. They had not lost on home
soil to an outstation team for seven years. Their last defeat was
to Mohun Bagan in the deciding match of the 6th NFL 2001–02,
where they'd just needed a draw but lost 0-1.

Leaving the statistics aside, Churchill Brothers' victory
heralded the dawn of a new era. This was the first time that a team
had won the national league with so many players from Manipur
and Mizoram in their playing eleven, a trend seen in all their 22
matches. Some of these players were Thokchom Naoba Singh,
Reisangmei Vashum, Robert Lalthlamuana, Khanthang Paite,
Gouramangi Singh, Govin Singh and Chitrasen Chandan Singh.
By then only Gouramangi was an established player in the Indian
team, whereas the others were junior internationals. Later Vashum,
Robert and Govin also played for the senior Indian team. Churchill
Brothers' international stopper-back, the Manipuri Gouramangi,
said 'Our time has come.' The statement was prescient as since
then, all the I-League clubs have regularly acquired players from
the North-east. For giving a boost to football from this region,
Churchill Brothers deserves due credit.

Churchill Brothers went on to win both the Durand Cup and
the IFA Shield in 2009 and 2011. However, at the start of the
2012–13 season, their young team was succumbing to pressure.
Two of their internationals, long-serving defender Gouramangi
and midfielder Lalrindika Ralte, had been poached by other clubs,
as had their long-serving goalkeeper Arindam Bhattacharya. Their
squad was no longer deemed a strong enough contender for the
national league title. With the support of the Alemaos, technical
director Subhash Bhowmick ventured into new territory and
procured the services of defender Bilal Najjarine and lethal striker
Akram Moghrabi from Lebanon. However, at the beginning of
the 6th I-League, they lost the round-1 match 1-2 to arch-rivals

Dempo, and in a round-6 match they were trounced 0-3 by title aspirants East Bengal.

It was at this stage that Bhowmick's Midas touch got to work. Realizing that the problem was psychological he rallied his squad in a clever and unconventional manner. He never talked about title aspirations to the team before or after any match. He just got them to enjoy each match and play to the best of their abilities. The transformation in attitude worked wonders. Oozing with confidence, the team now played fast-paced, attacking football and won some matches by thumping margins. They overcame Sporting Clube de Goa 8-4 in a thrilling round-11 match and trounced Shillong Lajong 6-0.

Demolishing East Bengal 3-0, their primary rivals, in an away match at Kolkata was a major psychological boost for Churchill Brothers. But they had to overcome several hurdles, including loss of key players, in the middle of the I-League to have a shot at victory. Churchill Brothers were leading the table with 38 points from 16 matches. They had scored 40 goals, the maximum amongst the 14 teams until then. Their defence—ably marshalled by Bilal, international Denzil Franco and Dharmaraj Ravanan—had also conceded just 14 goals. Bilal, along with East Bengal's Uga Okpara, was the best central-defender in this I-League. Unfortunately he got a lucrative offer from the Gulf and departed after 15 rounds. Churchill Brothers recruited quickly to strengthen the defence so that their winning streak continued. The club had some tough I-League matches left and they also played in the AFC Cup, whose group matches started in February 2013. Soon after, Moghrabi left as well and was replaced by the Afghan striker Balal Arezou.

Bhowmick creditably maintained an atmosphere of calm professionalism. He ensured that the team paid attention to detail and changed strategy whenever needed. The best example of changing tactics was during the decisive match against Mohun Bagan. Churchill Brothers were trailing by a solitary goal, when a visibly tiring Beto was replaced in the sixty-fifth minute by the bustling Arezou. The team switched to a 4-3-3 formation, with Arezou on the left, Sunil Chhetri as striker and Henri Antchouet providing speed on the right.

The ploy worked and Churchill Brothers not only equalized the score but dominated proceedings. If not for Bagan goalkeeper Shilton Paul's heroics, they would have emerged as winners.

Coached by Mariano Dias and guided in choice of players by the wily Bhowmick, Churchill Brothers were a revelation in this competition. They scored a club record tally of 56 goals and procured a record 55 points in 26 matches, finally annexing the league title. Of the 56 goals they scored, 35 were by foreigners. Brazilian playmaker Beto scored 13 goals, the Gabonese striker Henri Arnaud Antchouet scored 12 and, before he left, Akram Moghrabi scored 9 goals.

Amongst their Indian players, India skipper Sunil Chhetri who had joined in February on loan from Sporting Lisbon scored the vital equalizer against Mohun Bagan, which clinched the title, the match-winner against Pune FC to end a 5-match winless streak as well as 2 brilliant goals against Dempo to gain a vital point. Bineesh Balan, thrustful on the right, was in great form and scored a memorable hat-trick in the 8-4 win over Sporting Clube de Goa. No wonder Bhowmick remarked, 'My team is my star. Till death I won't forget my players.' Setting a unique record, their charming and dynamic CEO, Ms Valanka Alemao, became the first woman to guide a team to a national title in Indian football. With this victory, Churchill Brothers established themselves as a major force and the most consistent team in the country.

Churchill Brothers have always been iconoclasts in Goan football. The family's passion for the game is such that the Alemao brothers use their business contacts to find out about players available in different countries. But there may be a flip side to this passion too. A number of coaches and players have complained that the family interferes with team selection and puts pressure on players before crucial matches.

The headquarters of Churchill Brothers is in Novangully, a small ward of the village Varca, in the Salcete taluka. Churchill Alemao and his family reside in a typical ancestral Goan bungalow with a large balcony, surrounded by lush foliage. A glimpse of the sitting room reveals the family's craze for football. Wall-to-wall shelves have been built inside, with numerous cups and trophies placed on them, and still more in the large showcases in the corners. Flags, emblems, jerseys and souvenirs are either strung on the walls or placed all over the museum-like room. Their passion for their team is extreme and there are massive arguments if the team lose a match. As one of the brothers Joaquim Alemao said, 'We do not mind suffering a loss in the business, but when the team has lost, we become upset and things go awry at home.'

Over the years the enthusiasm of some of the brothers has waned but Churchill Alemao has remained steadfast. His love for the game is so intense that for the 2012–13 season, he sold some of his land for over Rs 25 lakh, in order to procure the services of stars players like defender Bilal Najjarine and striker Akram Moghrabi. Their presence in the team helped in the club's second I-League victory. The club also improved the infrastructure and facilities for their players. Some years ago, at the behest of Bhowmick, they built a cosy club house amidst sylvan surroundings. Their outstation players can stay there in comfort, with recreational facilities and home-cooked food. It is remarkable that despite increasing monetary demands, the Alemao brothers have kept their club afloat for over a quarter of a century, often by depriving themselves of comforts and luxuries.

By creating a family-like atmosphere for their players, who are treated with great love and respect, Churchill Brothers have been able to foster team spirit and loyalty in a fiercely competitive environment. This was exemplified by a phone call that Churchill Alemao received after clinching the I-League title in May 2013. The congratulatory call was from Lebanon; it was their classy defender, Bilal Najjarine. Despite having left, Najjarine spoke in a voice full of emotion. Their former goalkeeper Arindam Bhattacharya not only joined the victory celebrations at the Alemaos' mansion but gifted Valanka with her favourite sweet dish, six tins of the renowned rasgullas of K.C. Das, Kolkata.

See in 'Hall of Fame': Bruno Coutinho (attacking midfielder/forward) and Brahmanand Shankwalkhar (goalkeeper), Armando Colaco (coach).

4

Kerala

The Many Paradoxes

When you think of Kerala you think of one-storey houses ensconced in lush greenery, the deep blue of the sea and sky merging on its palm-lined beaches, and several boats cruising its backwater canals. Famous for its Ayurvedic treatments, plantations of tea, coffee and spices and rich wildlife, Kerala draws a significant number of the world's tourists through the year. Its long Malabar Coast borders the Arabian Sea for nearly 600 km.

A prosperous state, Kerala scores high in terms of social indices—particularly in the Human Development Index, literacy rate and sex ratio. From the 1970s and early 1980s, a number of people began to migrate to the Middle Eastern countries, and today remittances from the Malayali expatriate community there contribute considerably to the state's economy.

In sports, Kerala is famous for its many well-contested boat races, which attract passionate crowds. It took several years for these boat races to be recognized as legitimate water sports. Volleyball, another popular sport in Kerala, is often played on makeshift courts on sandy beaches along the coast. Jimmy George from Kannur, arguably the most successful volleyball player ever to represent India (active 1974–86), was considered amongst Asia's ten best players. The late K. Udayakumar, sound in defence, was another volleyball superstar from the state.

Kerala's contribution in athletics is immense. From the first Malayali athlete who represented India at the 1924 Paris Olympics to the ten who took part in the 2016 Rio Olympics,

Kerala has been a wellspring of sporting talent. At least one athlete from Kerala has represented India in every Olympics from 1972 to 2016. These include legends like T.C. Yohannan, Suresh Babu, Shiny Wilson and M.D. Valsamma.

The legendary P.T. Usha came closest to winning an Olympic medal in 1984; in the 1986 Seoul Asian Games, she became the first Indian to win four gold medals in a single Asiad. Anju Bobby George, silver medallist in the long jump in the 2005 World Athletics Championship, was later upgraded to gold in January 2014 due to doping charges against the winner. Most of the other Kerala-based athletes have won medals in the Asian Games.

Football in Kerala has had ardent followers and has produced brilliant talent. The game was very popular in the Malabar region, perhaps because of the Muslim population which took to the game in large numbers inspired by Mohammedan Sporting. The Kerala Football Association (KFA) joined the AIFF in 1957, a year after the state of Kerala was formed, combining the Malabar region with Travancore and Kochi. The KFA played a positive role in developing the game by organizing local leagues and holding coaching camps. It also organized several popular all-India tournaments, which helped sustain and develop many clubs and institutional teams in the country. Viewership for the game was always considerable, and due to intensive competition, many quality players emerged. Kerala has given India a few Olympians and several internationals.

The plethora of tournaments in Kerala encouraged the formation of numerous clubs, supported by the local population and local businessmen who vigorously promoted football in the state. As these clubs could thrive and prosper by just playing in the different district tournaments, very few of them played or became popular outside the state. Yet, there were some teams that took part in several national-level tournaments and left their mark.

The first team to create a sensation was the Malabar District Football Association (MDFA) XI in the 1954 Rovers Cup, in Mumbai. They started by beating a well-knit team from Kolkata, BNR. Next, they took on mighty holders Hyderabad City Police.

Instead of being overawed MDFA played with flair. Egged on by the Malayalis who had gathered at the Cooperage Stadium, they led 2-0 within twenty minutes. An upset was on the cards, but Hyderabad City Police recovered their composure and scored thrice in the second-half to progress with a 3-2 win. However, the discerning critics noticed the talent in the MDFA team. Noted sports columnist Bobby Talyarkhan wrote in glowing terms about the silky skills of centre-forward J. Anthony, 'Not since the days of Mewalal at his best, have I seen a centre-forward as J. Anthony, who can pass, dribble, sell the dummy and shoot with both feet from any angle and right on target.'[1]

Another MDFA player to impress was sturdy defender T.A. Rahman, who later represented India at the 1956 Melbourne Olympics. MDFA's success at the 1954 Rovers Cup also started a trend of exodus of players to clubs in Kolkata and Mumbai. Rahman went to Rajasthan Club Kolkata, and J. Anthony joined Mohun Bagan.

Another well-known club from Kerala were Premier Tyres of Kalamassery, who had many skilful international players in the 1970s, like strikers Xavier Pius, Mohammed Najeeb, C.D. Francis, winger Dinakar and right-wing-back Premnath Philip. They were a delight to watch and won the prestigious Darjeeling Gold Cup in 1977. The institutional side Kerala Police briefly became one of the top teams in India. At their prime they had nine internationals in their squad, including I.M. Vijayan and Sharaf Ali, and they won the Federation Cup in both 1990 and 1991. They were also runners-up in the prestigious DCM Trophy in 1990, losing to Kyung Hee University of South Korea 4-5 in the penalty shoot-out in the final.

Kerala's pride and joy was FC Kochin, who developed a strong regional identity by providing an opportunity to local talent and training them well. They came into existence in 1997 and were considered India's first professional football club. In their very first year the club hired a Scottish coach, George Blues, and roped in KBL as a sponsor. These were new trends in Indian football in the last years of the twentieth century. They were the first team in India to publish pamphlets and brochures about the players and their performances. They formed a star-studded squad with some legendary names in Indian football: I.M. Vijayan, Jo Paul Ancheri, Raman Vijayan and Carlton Chapman, in addition to three Nigerian players and the best young talent from Kerala.

Consequently, when they played in the DCM and Durand tournaments in Delhi, Malayalis who had settled in the capital or come there to work flocked to the Ambedkar Stadium in large numbers. Even non-sports journalists from Kerala never missed an FC Kochin match, and an extra press enclosure had to be created at the stadium. I.M. Vijayan was at his peak in 1997 and his artistry and attacking flair made them a very attractive team to watch.

Kerala's most glamorous club, FC Kochin soon won numerous fans throughout the country. Such was their reputation that they were seeded directly into the quarter-final league of the Durand Cup. They started their 1997 Durand campaign on 6 October by beating seven-time former champions BSF 2-1, with I.M. Vijayan scoring a brace. Two days later, they trounced a disjointed Mohammedan Sporting 5-0 with I.M. Vijayan scoring thrice. Raman Vijayan and B. Deepu scored once each. They topped the group on goal difference, despite losing their last league match 2-3 to Air India.

On 12 October they played a thrilling semi-final with holders JCT, considered one of the most memorable matches in the history of the Durand Cup. JCT rallied from 0-3 to make it 3-3 and the match seemed to be drifting to a draw. Then came a moment of magic from I.M. Vijayan. His team earned a free kick some 35 yards from the JCT goal. Vijayan's brilliantly executed free kick curled in the air and zoomed past the helpless JCT custodian Arvind Kumar. The sheer audacity of this long-range free kick drew gasps of admiration and sustained applause. Many experts consider it as the finest free-kick goal seen at the Ambedkar Stadium. FC Kochin won the high-scoring match 4-3.

A couple of days later they upset star-studded Mohun Bagan 3-1 in the final, becoming the first club from Kerala to win the prestigious Durand Cup. Vijayan also scored in the final and finished as top scorer in the tournament with 8 goals from 5 matches. FC Kochin ended with 16 goals in 5 matches, a record at that time. This win in their first-ever national tournament was laudable as they were plagued by injury problems prior to the tournament. International Jo Paul Ancheri had a knee injury and was out of action for three months. FC Kochin won the 1997 Durand Cup with just fifteen fit players.

FC Kochin's focus on developing local talent not only saved expenses but also made them very popular in the state. Promising local players like K. Anson, A.S. Firoz, Mohammed Shafiq and K.T. Ranjit developed by playing alongside established international and seasoned Nigerians. Many were hopeful that FC Kochin would be Kerala's answer to the mighty Kolkata clubs.

Owing to their popularity in the 1997–98 season, FC Kochin were given direct entry into the ten-team 2nd NFL. However, they could not cope with the pressures of a long-drawn-out league involving 18 matches on a home-and-away basis, as they lacked depth in their squad. Ancheri returned to full fitness gradually and as the season wore on the team was affected by injuries. They finished fourth with 29 points from 18 matches. Somehow FC Kochin never fared well in the NFL as they again finished fourth in both 1999–2000 and 2000–01. In the 5th NFL, they were trailing front runners East Bengal by just 2 points at the end of round 14. However, their form slumped and they bagged just 5 points from the remaining 8 matches to finish fourth. The absence of I.M. Vijayan and Ancheri (on pre–World Cup duty) and the suspension of Liberian striker Sunday Seah for two crucial matches had weakened their side.

In the 6th NFL they were relegated. Kerala's glamorous club finished second-last with just 17 points and then they slowly faded into oblivion. There were rumours about misappropriation of funds and the club was not financially viable. To preserve their professional careers, star players I.M. Vijayan and Ancheri shifted to other clubs in 2002–03, and FC Kochin crumbled after that.

After FC Kochin had folded up, a group of businessmen from Kochi and Ernakulam formed Viva Kerala in August 2004, as they wanted a Kerala team to participate in the NFL. Viva Kerala qualified for the inaugural I-League by finishing second in the second division in April 2007. However, in their first venture into the ten-team I-League they finished ninth, and were relegated. The next season they were promoted back to the first division for the 3rd I-League in 2009–10. At this time, expenses increased as all I-League clubs had to hire an AFC-certified ('A' licensed) coach and Viva Kerala was bought over by Chirag Computers. Their name was changed to Chirag United Club, Kerala. They played for a couple of seasons, but in the 5th I-League in 2011-12, they were relegated and folded up.

Another Kerala outfit to briefly emerge as a strong side in 2004 was State Bank of Travancore (SBT). They had several good players like strikers Mohammed Rafi, Abdul Naushad and Abdul Hakim, winger Asif Saheer and midfielders N.P. Pradeep and Anil Kumar—some of whom were internationals. SBT were seeded to the quarter-final league for the Durand Cup that year and did well by beating Assam Rifles 3-1. However, they lost to Mohun Bagan 1-3 and were eliminated. In the 9th ONGC NFL, they got promoted but lasted only one season. SBT finished with 18 points and got relegated to the second division.

Historically, the cuisine, climate and genetic factors have been beneficial for sports in the state. Except for I.M. Vijayan, many players from Kerala were from a middle-class background and were well fed in their formative years. The state's staple food—comprising fish, seafood, meat, vegetables, rice and tapioca, made with a combination of coconut products and spices—is very nourishing. This protein-rich diet enabled Kerala to produce players who were tall, well-built as well as technically sound.

However, in a great paradox, most quality players from the state became famous when they left to play in outstation clubs. Some clubs or institutional teams like Premier Tyres, Alind Kundara, Kerala State Road Transport Corporation, AG's Office, Young Challengers and Titanium until the 1970s, Kerala Police and FC Kochin in the 1990s, and Viva Kerala in the early twenty-first century enjoyed short spells of glory, but were not successful for long. Barring these, private clubs never flourished in Kerala, so star players always sought greener pastures. Kerala has thus come to be known as a nursery for developing football talent and supplying quality players to outstation clubs and the Indian team.

Indian football also owes a big debt to Kerala's organizational skills and the multitude of national-level tournaments held in all the districts of this lush green state. Top teams from Goa, Punjab, Mumbai, Bengaluru and sometimes Kolkata participated, and capacity crowds witnessed most of the matches. In the days before internet, mobile phone and even fax, the coordination between the tournament organizers was commendable as they ensured the schedules did not overlap much.

These impeccably organized tournaments served a dual role. They gave an opportunity for young players in Kerala to compete against the best in the country. Meanwhile outstation teams— especially those from Punjab—which did not have a strong local league, flourished because of regular participation in these tournaments. Nine national-level tournaments were organized every year in Kerala and all survived on gate-money receipts and local sponsorship. The most glamorous of these was the Chakola Cup in Thrissur. The winners got a huge cup, which was one of the costliest football trophies in India. The KFA Shield was held in Changanassery. These tournaments were so popular and such crowd-pullers that the superstar Raj Kapoor inaugurated one of the editions of the KFA Shield.[2]

Calicut was always passionate about football and so, within years of its inception in 1952, the Sait Nagjee tournament became a thriving competition. Initially, Hindustan Aeronautics Limited Bangalore (HAL) won this prestigious tournament, always witnessed by large crowds, three years in a row, from 1952–54.

The far-sighted organizers wanted to make this the best tournament in India, and it was often called the Durand of the south. The Sait Nagjee and the Rovers Cup were the first tournaments to invite teams from abroad, namely, Pakistan. The Karachi Kickers were popular and successful, winning the Sait

Nagjee trophy in both 1955 and 1956. After 1971, teams from newly formed Bangladesh became regular participants too, and Abahani Krira Chakra won in 1989. Alind Kundara is the only local team to have won this tournament, in 1967, and Mohammedan Sporting and JCT (Phagwara) have been the most successful, winning it four times each.

With the inception of the Scissors Cup in the 1990s, the glamour of the Sait Nagjee declined. It permanently lost its appeal once the NFL started in 1997. It was not held for many years from 1995 onwards. When it seemed this historic tournament would be consigned to the history books, some passionate football lovers revived it in 2016, with teams from Europe, South America and the Argentine U-23 team participating. Ronaldinho of Brazil became the tournament's brand ambassador.

How did all these tournaments in Kerala survive? No TV rights were sold and sponsorship was limited. Money was obtained from generous patrons and from hoardings on the ground. The maximum collection was made, however, from ticket sales. Makeshift floodlights were often installed so that matches could be played in the evenings and spectators could come after work. People in all the cities in Kerala were fascinated by the game and willingly bought tickets.

To ensure the coffers remained full, tournament organizers also indulged in a bit of chicanery. There used to be several drawn matches and replays. If the teams of popular players like Inder Singh (Leaders Club and JCT), Manjit Singh (BSF), Shyam Thapa and Amar Bahadur (both Mafatlal Mills) and Bernard Pereira (Orkay Mills Mumbai) were involved in the drawn matches, there were capacity crowds even in replays. Sometimes well-contested matches ended in a stalemate but often the organizers ensured draws, after a tacit understanding with both teams.

Ex-national coach Sukhwinder Singh, who played for both BSF and JCT in the Kerala circuit, explained the modus operandi of these drawn games to me. He said that early on in the second-half, a senior official of the tournament organizing committee would stand at a vantage point and wave a white handkerchief.

That meant that a truce had to be called, and the teams would slow down, curb the intensity of their attacks and settle for a draw, conceding a goal or two if required. The crowd thought the heat and humidity had taken its toll and both teams would play better in the replay. Thus all were satisfied. The organizers made more money and the clubs also got some extra cash that was often shared amongst the players.

The Santosh Trophy was first hosted in Kerala in 1955, in Ernakulam. Capacity crowds witnessed each game, the organizers made maximum profit, and two great stars—T. Balaram and Chuni Goswami—were discovered in these championships. The AIFF realized that they had discovered a gold mine. Since then the Santosh Trophy has been organized thirteen times in different cities in Kerala, and each time it was a grand success.

For Kerala, winning the Santosh Trophy became like the chase for the Holy Grail. Their record in the trophy is enviable. They first won the title in 1973 and their last triumph was in 2004. In a span of thirty-one years they were five-time champions and seven-time runners-up. During that period, Kerala's success in the Santosh Trophy became associated with regional identity and pride, a type of subnationalism. This was evident in the vast coverage they got in the regional media and the frenzied reactions of their fans. Kerala's love affair with the trophy reached a peak in 2002, when they were hoping to win back-to-back titles. The eloquent M. Peethambaran, their most successful coach for the trophy, tried to inspire his players by saying, 'Even the World Cup isn't as important as winning the Santosh Trophy for Kerala.'

The Nehru Cup international tournament was organized twelve times from 1982 to 1997. To watch the international stars in the Nehru Cup, fans from all over the state came to attend matches whether at Kochi, Thiruvananthapuram or Kozhikode. During India's semi-final versus Iraq in the 1997 Nehru Cup at Kochi, the crowd was so massive that some had to sit on the grass near the touchline on either side. It was a violation of FIFA rules to allow spectators on the field of play but seeing the crowd's enthusiasm, the match commissioner allowed the game to go ahead. The

AIFF even allotted India's group matches and a quarter-final in the Millennium Cup held in January 2000 to Kochi. The 9th South Asian Football Federation (SAFF) Cup was successfully staged at the Greenfield Stadium, Thiruvananthapuram, in 2015–16. Large crowds witnessed the semi-final (India beat Maldives 3-2) and dramatic final (India ousted Afghanistan 2-1 after extra time).

A distinctive feature of the game in Kerala is the seven-a-side tournaments that began around the 1950s. These are played on very basic fields, and matches are of about thirty to forty minutes' duration, so it is not taxing for players. Many Kerala-based players, and nowadays even foreigners representing local clubs, supplement their income by playing in such tournaments. Established players, who receive appearance fees, may take part in up to 3 matches a day and their daily income varies from Rs 5000 to 7000. The playing area is smaller than a regular field and players can flaunt their dribbling skills. The crowds sit close to the touchline and these tournaments have a special flavour. Money is collected from the assembled crowds mainly through tickets, and betting on the results also takes place.

The seven-a-side tournaments are supported by local businessmen, who consequently help in providing education to the underprivileged in the area. These tournaments are unauthorized but have continued as they bring revenue to the KFA. For instance, a medium-level sevens tournament in mid-2017 made an income of Rs 50 lakh, and after expenses the net profit was around Rs 20 lakh—a considerable sum in Indian football.

To their infinite credit, football fans in Kerala have never been overtly parochial. Unlike in other states, the loyalty of the fans has not been towards particular clubs but to the game itself. For instance, the 1974 Sait Nagjee Trophy final was contested for three days between an Indian XI (probables for the 1974 Asian Games) and the rugged RAC Bikaner. The first two matches ended in draws and the organizers and spectators did not want to enforce the penalty shoot-out rule. So there were replays. On all three days the stadium was packed, and finally on the third day the India XI side prevailed.

Inder Singh always maintained that he was more popular in Goa and Kerala than in Punjab. In Kerala they used to call Inder Singh the 'Football Magician'. Besides Inder Singh several other players from Punjab were household names in Kerala. A tailoring shop near the Corporation Stadium in Kozhikode had a full-length painting of the lean and lanky RAC striker and 1974 Asian Games skipper, Magan Singh Rajvi, to attract customers. Many star players got discounts when they shopped in Kerala. Some shops in Ernakulam still keep photographs of the Olympians T.A. Rahman and Chuni Goswami. The latter had impressed with his sublime ball skills when he first played for Bengal in the 1955 Santosh Trophy in that city.

This non-partisan approach to football is something unique to Kerala and deserves to be lauded. This was evident in the 4th Scissors Cup semi-final in Kannur on 23 November 1995, when JCT took on the local favourites, Kerala Police. Displaying scintillating attacking football, JCT outclassed Kerala Police 3-0 with I.M. Vijayan scoring twice and former Nigerian junior international Stephen Abarowei once. Midway through the second-half, the match as a contest was over when Vijayan netted his second goal. For the rest of the match, the crowd cheered and applauded JCT's attacking football. The local team was not booed. JCT's success was largely due to their two Kerala imports, Ancheri and Vijayan, and this may have been a factor in the support they got. However, by and large, fans from Kerala have appreciated skilful players from all communities. In the final on 25 November, JCT upset fancied Perlis club from Malaysia 1-0, with the mercurial Vijayan scoring a dramatic long-distance match-winner in the eighty-seventh minute. The elated fans in Kozhikode danced in glee and took out a procession chanting 'JCT zindabad!' or the equivalent in Malayalam, waving JCT banners.

In the twenty-first century, with the advent of globalization and broadcasting of international football on satellite television, the composition of football fans in India has undergone a change. With the advent of the ISL there are now better facilities at the stadiums, and women are visible in large numbers in matches in

Shillong, Aizawl, Bengaluru and Kolkata. However, decades ago, football fans in the country were mostly working class or lower middle class, and amenities at the stadium were elementary. Kerala was then the only state where women attended football matches in large numbers. Players from Punjab remember the adulation they received from female fans in the state in the 1960s and 1970s. When the 1997 Nehru Cup was organized in Kochi, a separate stand was made to accommodate the large number of women viewers.

Such is the love for soccer in Kerala that they often organize football film festivals. Sometimes it is on a large scale like the week-long festival which was organized in Malappuram as a New Year treat in 2006. Seventeen international films were shown, including the famous *Giants of Brazil, Bend It like Beckham, The Two Escobars, Miracle of Bern, Escape to Victory, Pelé Forever, Shaolin Soccer, Maradona, The Hand of God* and others. This film festival was organized by a cultural forum, Malappuram Manassu, and was inaugurated by the former cultural affairs minister of Kerala, A.P. Anil Kumar, on New Year's Eve. The festival was very well attended.

The Great Olympians

Kerala has produced seven Olympians: T.M. Varghese, popularly known as Thiruvalla Pappan (1948 London Olympics), P.B.A. Saleh and J. Anthony (1952 Helsinki Olympics), T.A. Rahman (1956 Melbourne Olympics), S.S. Narayan (1956 and 1960 Rome Olympics), and M. Devadas and O. Chandrasekhar Menon (1960 Rome Olympics) in the golden era of Indian football. Each one of these players was a legend.

The powerful forward line popularly known as the 'Pancha Pandavas', which formed the core of the East Bengal team immediately after Independence, included Saleh (for details, see Chapter 1: 'Bengal'). Considered the greatest attacking combination ever in Indian football, older generations of East Bengal fans still get nostalgic when talking about this forward line. A talented and speedy winger, Saleh was a delight to watch at his peak. His trapping was impeccable; he could cut in and take shots at the goal and also headed the ball well. Saleh helped India win the 1951 Asian Games gold medal. He combined brilliantly with his East Bengal teammate Ahmed Khan in the opening match against Indonesia which India won 3-0. Saleh and J. Anthony were the first footballers from the Malabar region to play in the 1952 Olympics.

During his tenure with East Bengal, Saleh won every major trophy in India and created a record by annexing the prestigious IFA Shield three years in a row, from 1949–51. Saleh captained the team in 1950 and in 1951, and scored the two winning goals in the replayed final against arch-rivals Mohun Bagan. Overall, he scored 55 goals for East Bengal but left the club in 1954 when he got a secure job in the Calcutta Customs. He then played for the Customs team.

Saleh was a compassionate human being. During his stay in Kolkata he always shared a room in a hotel with his best friend Appa Rao from Madras Presidency. In the troubled days before Partition there were riots in Kolkata in 1946. Infuriated mobs spared no one and even football stars were not safe. Some fanatics mistook Appa Rao for a Muslim and started attacking him. Saleh shouted for help but also rushed into the fray and saved his friend despite being severely beaten himself.

J. Anthony represented India in the 1952 Olympics before he played for his state team. He played for India in the 2nd and 3rd Quadrangular tournaments in 1953 (Yangon) and 1954 (Kolkata), where he scored the match-winner for India in the 2-1 win over Burma. A precocious centre-forward, he could play effectively from any angle. His body swerves were a delight to behold. He played for Rajasthan Club from 1951–53 but could not cope with the pressure. He left to join MDFA Kerala in 1954, where he was rediscovered in the domestic circuit. He played briefly for Mohun Bagan and then moved to Caltex Mumbai, where he settled, as several players from his region were part of this team. These included left-winger K. Pavithran who played for India in the 1958 Tokyo Asian Games. J. Anthony was a unique player. Despite starting his career as a centre-forward he played as left-half for Caltex, which became the first Mumbai outfit to win the Rovers Cup in 1958 by beating Mohammedan Sporting 3-2 in a memorable final.

M. Devadas was a crafty inside-forward who started his career with Lucky Star Kannur. He later moved to Mumbai and played for Tatas. Devadas represented Kerala in the Indian squad at the 1960 Rome Olympics.

Three of Kerala's Olympians were defenders. T.M. Varghese was a sturdy full-back in the 2-3-5 formation and combined well with Sailen Manna to help India win the gold medal in the 1951 Asian Games. He was also a member of the Indian team in both the 1948 London Olympics (the first from south Kerala) and the 1954 Manila Asian Games though he did not play a match. He shifted to Mumbai and regularly played for the Indian Gymkhana team. He was a member of the Mumbai team that won the Santosh Trophy for the first time in 1954, beating Services 2-1 in the final in Chennai.

In the 1956 Olympics, coach Rahim made India play with three backs in a 3-2-5 system. Kerala's Rahman played as a gritty left-back in the semi-final against Yugoslavia. He had shifted from Kerala to Rajasthan Club Kolkata in 1955 but joined Mohun Bagan a year later and was a regular in their team for a dozen years. Rahman, renowned for his tight marking and biting tackles, was a crowd favourite. It was often observed that if Mohun Bagan were being troubled by an opponent, defender Jarnail would grind his teeth and say 'Rahman ise dekh le'. In football lingo this meant that Rahman was being instructed to closely mark and intimidate the troublesome opponent with some fierce tackles, if required.

I heard this command myself when watching the Mohun Bagan vs SRC pre-quarter-final Durand match in 1964. The dashing Gurkripal Singh of SRC was troubling Jarnail with his speed and thrust, till he was put off his stride by Mohun Bagan's left-back. Rahman's man marking and biting tackles were exceptional. His defensive skills resembled those of the Italian legend of a later generation, Claudio Gentile. Rahman also distributed the ball well and was very committed. A voracious eater, he enjoyed the local cuisine and relished his Malabar biryani and Thalassery biryani.

Right-back O. Chandrasekhar Menon from Thrissur also moved to Mumbai to earn a living from football. He helped Caltex win the 1958 Rovers Cup. After this prestigious tournament was held, East Germany came and played 3 matches against an Indian XI. This launched Chandrasekhar's international career and for the next five years he became a regular in the Indian team. He played in the 1960 Rome Olympics, the 1964 pre-Olympics, the 1960 and 1964 Asian Cups, and was a member of the gold medal-winning team in the 1962 Asian Games.

He considers the Olympic qualifier against Indonesia in 1960 as his greatest match. India had won the first leg 4-2 in Kolkata. However, in the return game in Jakarta, the home team piled on the pressure in the first-half but were twice denied by goal-line saves by Chandrasekhar. In fact, in the early stages of the match Peter Thangaraj was beaten by a long and high chip but Chandrasekhar, sensing that his goalkeeper was in trouble, darted back and headed the ball to safety. A graduate in economics with a first division, Chandrasekhar was a cerebral player who curbed many attacking moves by his excellent interceptions and reading of the game. He was also captain of Maharashtra, which won the Santosh Trophy for the first time (after the name change from Bombay) in 1964 in Chennai.

S.S. Narayan, who was from the Malabar region, grew up in Mumbai, and started his career with the Indian Gymkhana team in 1952. Next, he played for Matunga Athletic Club and Caltex, and finally joined Tata Sports Club in 1958. He played for thirteen years for Tata and declined offers to join the Kolkata clubs, as he was a favourite of J.R.D. Tata and was always well paid and given a good position in the company. Tall and lanky, Narayan was also a quality basketball player. He represented Mumbai in the 1954 national championships in basketball. However, once he was selected for the Indian team for the 1956 Melbourne Olympics, he focused entirely on football. His basketball skills helped Narayan in leaping upwards and collecting hard, rising shots. Narayan excelled in the 1956 Olympic semi-final against Yugoslavia and in the bronze medal-winning match versus Bulgaria by making several daring saves. First-choice goalkeeper Peter Thangaraj was injured in the 4-2 win over Australia in the quarter-final, and Narayan, in his first major international tournament, proved to be an able deputy. Besides featuring in two Olympics, he was also a member of the squad in the 1964 Asian Cup in Tel Aviv in which India finished as runners-up to Israel.

~

Apart from the Olympians, Kerala has consistently produced a number of great players. In 1960, C. Mustafa impressed for his home state Kerala in his first senior national championship, the Santosh Trophy in Calicut. He had quicksilver reflexes that enabled him to deflect goal-bound shots and is rated as one of the most agile goalkeepers in Indian football history. He represented India at the 1966 Bangkok Asian Games and five successive Merdeka Tournaments, 1964–68.

Another batch of quality international players from Kerala emerged in the latter decades of the twentieth century. These were defenders C.C. Jacob and M. Dayanand, both members of the Indian team which finished joint winners in the 1974 Asian Youth Championships in Bangkok. There was also M.M. Jacob who represented India in the 1976 Merdeka Tournament. Until the 1990s a host of renowned internationals like crafty inside-forward Xavier Pius (known for his quick turning with the ball), bustling striker Najeeb, the tall, imposing and reliable defender V.P. Sathyan, solid right-back Sharaf Ali, skilful winger C.V. Pappachan, goalkeeper Feroz Sherif, solid central-defender Jiju Jacob, left-back K.V. Dhanesh, and the brilliant duo of I.M. Vijayan and Jo Paul Ancheri emerged at regular intervals from Kerala. Ancheri, who first played for India in 1994, and was seen as a better prospect than Bhaichung Bhutia, was the last real superstar from Kerala.

K.V. Dhanesh first came into the limelight playing for Kerala in the 1995 Santosh Trophy in Chennai. Dhanesh impressed the then national coach Rustam Akramov of Uzbekistan with his tackling, aggressive approach, calm temperament and good positional play. He made his international debut in the 1st SAFF Coca-Cola Cup in Colombo in 1995. Since then he was in and out of the national team. Dhanesh was considered a reliable and competent defender and played as either right- or left-wing-back for the national team and for his club sides, FC Kochin and ITI Bangalore. The highlight of his career was being chosen for the 1998 Bangkok Asian Games as a reliable left-back, by erstwhile national coach Syed Nayeemuddin.

In the new millennium Kerala has produced reliable defender and renowned international Muttah Suresh. A schoolboy prodigy, Suresh first played for India in the pre-Olympics in 1999 in both Bangkok and Kolkata. He was especially noticed in the Santosh Trophy in April 2000, when the hosts, Kerala, reached the final but lost 0-1 to Maharashtra. Kerala's success was largely due to some excellent defensive work by the twenty-one-year-old Suresh. He made his senior India debut in the Four Nations Tournament in the Maldives in May 2000. He then joined Mohun Bagan. A cultured left-back, he could also play as stopper-back and on the left side of midfield. His anticipations, timing of tackle and distribution were quite exceptional and made up for his lack of speed. A year later he moved to Mahindra United and from 2002–03 to 2010 played for East Bengal. His career blossomed under the coaching of Subhash Bhowmick and he played as central-defender during East Bengal's glory years, when they won back-to-back NFL titles in 2003 and 2004, and the prestigious ASEAN Cup in July 2003. He was also a regular in the national team for several years.

Other talented international players to emerge from Kerala were roving striker Mohammed Rafi, midfielder-cum-defender K. Ajayan, N.P. Pradeep, who scored the match-winner for India against Syria in the 2007 Nehru Cup final in Delhi, and the dashing SBT forwards Asif Saheer and Abdul Hakim, who played sporadically for India. Unfortunately, none of them have become household names across the country or got the adulation and respect that I.M. Vijayan, Ancheri or the late Rahman and Sathyan received. Only Pradeep enjoyed brief stardom after his match-winner in the Nehru Cup. There is a major fear that the talent pool in Kerala is drying up, which would be a big blow to Indian football.

Till the end of the twentieth century, football reigned as the number one sport in Kerala, just as in Goa and Bengal and the North-east. But the Sourav Ganguly impact in Bengal and that of international fast bowler Sreesanth in Kerala led to a change in outlook, and cricket began to gain the upper hand in these states. There was a sudden downward spiral in football and it caught everyone ball-watching. From 2012 to 2016, there were no players from Kerala in the Indian football team, nor has there been a team from Kerala in the I-League.

However, unlike Hyderabad, active efforts are being made to ensure that the legacy of a glorious football past is maintained in the state. The ISL has acted as a catalyst for the revival of Kerala football. The club Kerala Blasters is the most popular ISL team in terms of crowd attendance and has launched some noteworthy developmental programmes to nurture young talent. These grass-roots-level programmes have created an impact and children are coming to train in large numbers. In 2016, southern cinema superstars Chiranjeevi and Nagarjuna, and two others, agreed to partner with Sachin Tendulkar to own the club. Substantial investment is expected from the new partners. The former Manchester City and Republic of Ireland defender Terry Phelan was in charge of their talent hunt and youth development programmes in 2015, and feels that the future looks promising.

The KFA has also tied up with the UAE Football Association and there will be exchange programmes for junior boys as well as senior-level teams. At the time of writing, infrastructure development is under way for the all-important U-17 World Cup to be held in India in October 2017. Six new grounds are being developed adjacent to the Nehru Stadium in Kochi just for training purposes, including an artificial one from FIFA.

Kerala is marketed around the world as 'God's own country' for its breathtaking natural beauty. However, now there is a distinct difference on the roads of Kochi, with hoardings of a beaming Sachin Tendulkar saying that Kerala is 'Football's own country'. With due efforts, the KFA and other parties may yet be able to prove the truth of this advertisement line.

See in 'Hall of Fame': I.M. Vijayan (forward) and Jo Paul Ancheri (forward/defender).

5

Punjab

Sturdy Sons of the Soil

Football in undivided Punjab started in 1932 but it was mostly confined to the regions and states that are now in Pakistan. The body that controlled football then was known as the North-West India Football Association (NWIFA), headquartered in Lahore. Sir Sikander Hyat Khan was its first president, and H.A. Soofi, sports teacher at the famous Government College in Lahore, its first secretary. Legendary players like Jumma Khan, Bacchi Khan and Kale Khan emerged around this time from the north-west region, but rose to fame playing for Mohammedan Sporting, Kolkata (for details, see Chapter 1: 'Bengal'). The NWIFA became affiliated to the AIFF in 1937.

Prior to Independence, wrestling, kabaddi and hockey were the popular sports in the state, and Bengali migrants like S.D. Chatterjee and S.M. Sanyal made pioneering efforts to create interest in football. Chatterjee had started clubs like Ambala Heroes in 1935 and later Aryan Club, Ambala. In 1941, competitions like the AI V National Challenge Shield and A1 Heroes Ambala tournament were started, in which teams from all over the country, including Frontier Club Peshawar and Sandemoniums Quetta took part.

As Ambala was a garrison town, the game became popular there; today there is even an S.D. Chatterjee Football Chowk located near the War Heroes Memorial Stadium. The football lover S.M. Sanyal popularized the game in Rohtak, where he taught in a local college. Punjab began taking part in the Santosh Trophy from its first edition in 1941, at which time all the players were Muslims from West Punjab, except for Gurdeep Singh.

After Independence, the NWIFA was dissolved and the game in the Indian Punjab region (including modern-day Haryana) came to be governed by the East Punjab Football Association, with Sanyal as its first president. This too was dissolved and finally the Punjab Football Association (PFA) was formed in 1951 with M.C. Jolly as president.

The PFA was affiliated to the AIFF the same year, but it took another decade for organized football to take root in this state. It was the formation of Leaders Club Jalandhar in 1960 that really ignited the interest for football in Punjab. Founded by a football enthusiast, Lala Dwarka Das Sehgal, the club was a pioneer of sorts. It gave an opportunity to young, talented players from universities in Chandigarh, Amritsar and Patiala to seriously develop their career. Some joined Leaders Club straight out of school, like the precocious Inder Singh. Dwarka Das Sehgal was a generous man and, to develop his players, sent them on long trips to tournaments in Kerala, Goa and Hyderabad. It was in these matches that Leaders Club gained expertise and became the most popular team in Punjab in the 1960s.

Several good players emerged: goalkeeper Ravi Kumar (also played for Junior India in the 1963 Asia Youth Cup), defender K.K. Bakshi, wingers Nirmal Singh Sahota and Nirmal Singh Bains and, of course, the strikers Sri Kishen and Inder Singh, who had a telepathic understanding. Their swift wall passes and combined moves were delightful. Another club, Punjab Police, had existed as an institutional side since the 1950s, but their focus was more on hockey. Although they were Punjab's oldest institutional club, their football team gradually became strong only in the 1960s, when they defended in depth and played the long-ball game.

The 1962 DCM Trophy in Delhi featured many strong teams from around the country. Leaders made their debut with a 3-0 thrashing of Howrah Union, a first-division Kolkata side, before squeezing past Punjab Police 3-2 in the quarter-final. Mumbai's powerhouse Mafatlal Mills proved too strong in the semi-final beating Leaders Club 2-1, but the latter still managed to clinch the third spot with a 4-1 mauling of Mysore XI. The performance of Leaders in the DCM Trophy created a frenzy in Punjab as it was the first time a club from that state had excelled in an all-India tournament. Within the span of a decade, Leaders were a force in Indian football, and striker Inder Singh an inspiration.

In 1966 Punjab Police annexed the DCM Trophy, in the first all-Punjab final in a major tournament in India. They beat Leaders 2-0 in the final. Punjab Police were regarded as tough opponents for any team, especially in the Delhi tournaments, although Leaders were the stronger side. The latter, however, did not win many trophies and folded up by the early 1970s. Other teams from the state soon rose to prominence, of which BSF and JCT were the strongest.

These teams and Punjab football came to be known as a formidable force across India due to the outstanding talent the state produced. There was the home-grown legend Inder Singh, brilliant midfielder Parminder Singh, the courageous and daring striker Manjit Singh, and ace defender Jarnail Singh who, though, played mostly for Mohun Bagan. However, Harjinder Singh is arguably the most talented footballer to have emerged from Punjab even though he could not live up to his immense potential due to injuries. P.K. Banerjee considers him one of the best left-footed players India has ever produced.

Harjinder's finest hour was the 1974 Asian Youth Soccer Championships in Bangkok when India emerged joint champions with Iran after the final ended in a 2-2 draw. For his superlative displays in this tournament, Harjinder, just seventeen years old, was chosen for the Asian Youth All-Stars team. He soon became an important member of the Indian team, from 1974–83. Harjinder's sublime skills and calm temperament helped him excel in international matches. In the 1981 Merdeka Tournament he was adjudged the best midfielder of the competition. He scored a brace against Malaysia and with this win India entered the semi-finals. He often told me later, 'The convincing win [6-0] against Bengal in the 1974 Santosh Trophy made football very popular in Punjab, especially amongst students and in rural areas.'

Harjinder started his club career with Leaders, shifted to JCT and later joined Manjit Singh at East Bengal in 1979, where he remained till 1981 before rejoining JCT.

Unfortunately, he was compelled to retire at the young age of twenty-eight due to a niggling injury that could not be fixed despite surgery. He told me that in sheer frustration he led a negligent life for some years. But then he shook himself out of it and took his coaching-licence degrees; he became chief coach of the Chandigarh Football Academy that started in 2000.

At his peak, Harjinder Singh was a brilliant ball player, with a magical left foot. He created openings with his dribbling skills and set up attacks with exquisite passes. His touch and control were impeccable. Harjinder and Surajit Sengupta were the best ball players in India during the late 1970s and early 1980s.

Border Security Force

BSF, one of the five Central Armed Police Forces of the Union of India, came into being after the 1965 India–Pakistan War. It is a paramilitary force whose duty is to guard India's land border during peacetime and prevent transnational crime. Legendary sports administrator Ashwini Kumar, who also served as president of the Indian Hockey Federation and as member of the IOC, was associated with BSF sports from its inception. He insisted that BSF focus on a few sports, which would help developing team spirit and physique. So BSF set up teams in football, hockey, basketball, volleyball, athletics and wrestling.

The BSF football team came into the limelight overnight especially in the DCM and Durand tournaments in Delhi. They poached players from Punjab Police: wingers Surjit Singh and Nazar Singh, goalkeeper Charanjit Singh and inside-forward Joginder Singh Sangha. Some of the leading players from Punjab were recruited into BSF. They had long training camps with a focus on fitness. Within a year BSF became a formidable team which could match the best in the country.

They started the 1968 Durand Cup as an unfancied team but made history by becoming unexpected champions. They won in grand style, defeating three former champions: Andhra Police, Mohun Bagan 0-0 and 2-1 in the replayed semi-final, and

East Bengal 1-0 in the final. In the final Surjit Singh scored the match-winner in the eighty-fourth minute, with a crisp left-footed volley off a cross to the far post by left-winger Nazar Singh. BSF's rugged defence and hard-working midfield pair of Kesho Kripal Singh and Ajaib Singh were the key factors in their triumph. On the basis of his performance in the 1968 Durand Cup, Ajaib was selected for the national team and played for India in the 1970 Asian Games in Bangkok, when they bagged a bronze medal. Both were box-to-box midfielders, who were good interceptors and initiated attacks with quick long-passes. Ajaib's better ball control and support play made him a more complete midfielder.

BSF heralded a new era in Indian football. Their 1968 Durand success sparked off a new rivalry, Punjab vs Bengal in Indian football. After Rahim's death in 1963, Hyderabad football started declining, so BSF and Leaders became the new rivals of the Kolkata clubs. From 1968 till 1990, the Bengal vs Punjab rivalry was the main focus of the domestic tournaments in India. It was also a clash of football ideologies. Both Mohun Bagan and East Bengal played a short-passing game. Individual dribbling skills were used in developing attacks as well as clever through or angled passes. In contrast, BSF replied on a more robust approach: hard tackling, first-time clearances, long ball, quick crosses from the flanks and first-time shots at goal. Matches between BSF and either East Bengal or Mohun Bagan became a fascinating contrast of styles and tactics. Some of the BSF players—especially defenders Gian Singh and Lehmber Singh—were intimidating in their tackles. The referees had a tough time controlling such matches.

For nearly half-a-dozen years, BSF became the nemesis of Kolkata clubs at the Delhi Gate Stadium. From 1968 to 1974, no Kolkata club in either the DCM or Durand tournament defeated them. During this time they won the Durand Cup thrice: in 1968, 1971 and 1973. This winning spree ended in a dramatic quarter-final league match in December 1974. They led star-studded East Bengal 3-1 till ten minutes before the final. Then East Bengal's brilliant forward line of Subhash Bhowmick, Mohammed Akbar,

Mohammed Habib and Surajit Sengupta played inspired football. Habib and Bhowmick used wall passes to perfection to bisect the BSF defence and scored 2 quick goals. The scores were tied at 3-3. Just before the final whistle Bhowmick chested down a diagonal cross from the left and Surajit scored with a stiff, angular volley. East Bengal won 4-3 after a dramatic fight-back.

BSF's brand of direct football based on running, hard tackling and quick release of the ball attracted a new generation of fans to the stadiums, who were more interested in action than the subtleties of the game. BSF were also a hardy and cohesive team. In 1971, they won a match in the Durand Cup and the same evening travelled by bus to Karnal to play in the All-India Police Games the next morning. After spending two days there, they returned to Delhi for their next Durand match, emerged victorious and went back to Karnal to win the All-India Police Games title. This hardiness endeared them to many fans and they had a large following amongst the Punjabi Hindu and Sikh communities of Delhi, many of whom in the 1970s had improved their status due to sheer diligence after having suffered from the dislocation caused by Partition.

In 1976, BSF were joint winners of the DCM and Durand tournaments, bagging the 'Delhi double', a feat achieved only by mighty East Bengal in 1952 and 1960. After 1976 too, no team won the DCM and Durand tournaments in the same year. In the DCM final and replay that year, they held formidable Hanyang University of South Korea to goalless draws on both occasions. A year earlier, Hanyang had beaten an East Bengal side—that included Sudhir Karmakar, Shyam Thapa, Subhash Bhowmick and Gautam Sarkar—2-0 in the DCM final. After the 1976 DCM final, the South Korean coach praised the brilliant Manjit Singh's shielding and passing skills.

BSF's recruitment policy changed after Ashwini Kumar's retirement. An all-India force, they recruited footballers from all over India, so several players from North Bengal and the North-east joined BSF. The best among them was the talented ball player Narender Gurung. He was a revelation for BSF from 1978 to 1983. Gradually their approach play also changed and for many years they relied on Gurung's skills to initiate attacks.

After this period, the rugged BSF football team gradually declined. Although they got talented players from other states, they were unable to combine well, as all the players had different playing styles. Besides, when they were an all-Punjab team their immense regional pride and commitment had resulted in a strong, cohesive side. Another reason could be that they did not get the same encouragement as Ashwini Kumar had given them to practise the entire year.

Many talented players from BSF, however, went on to represent India; like Ajaib Singh, Narender Gurung, goalkeeper Bibhas Saha, defender Jagmohan Singh (son of Jarnail Singh), striker Darbara Singh and the charismatic Manjit Singh.

JCT

Jagatjit Cotton and Textile Mills Football Club, formerly known as JCT Mills FC, and famously known as 'The Millmen', came into existence in 1971. Established by renowned industrialist M.M. Thapar, JCT became a major force in Indian football as the years ticked on. The club built a reputation of grooming young talent and developing professional footballers.

There have been three defining moments in the history of the club. The first was when they snatched lethal international striker Inder Singh from Leaders in 1974. Suddenly JCT, till then a relatively unknown corporate team from remote Phagwara, became a force to be reckoned with in the domestic circuit. Inspired by Inder, they reached the final of the 1974 Durand Cup, losing narrowly 2-3 to Mohun Bagan.

JCT soon earned renown for their speed and attacking prowess, and reached the Durand final for four successive seasons—1974–77—becoming joint champions in 1976 with BSF. Several internationals emerged from JCT during the mid-1970s and 1980s: goalkeeper Surjit Singh (1978 Bangkok Asian Games), sturdy defender G.S. Parmar (also vice-captain of the Indian side in the 1982 Delhi Asiad), dynamic midfielder Parminder Singh, skilful Harjinder Singh (1982 Delhi Asian Games), striker Narender Thapa, later coach Sukhwinder 'Sukhi' Singh and defender Jagir Singh. JCT won India's oldest tournament outright in 1983, 1987, 1992 and 1996. In the 1980s they beat Mohun Bagan in the final on both occasions. During this period they followed the 'sons of the soil' policy and inducted players from Punjab or neighbouring Haryana in their team.

After the 1987 Durand victory, four JCT players—Deepak Kumar, Parminder Singh (Jr) and forwards Kuljit Singh and Narinder Kumar were selected for the Indian side for the 1988 Nehru Cup at Siliguri. Incidentally, Narinder scored the winning goal in both the 1987 and 1992 Durand triumphs of JCT.

The second crucial moment in their history came in 1992 when Sukhwinder Singh replaced G.S. Virk as coach. Sukhwinder had been assistant national coach under the Serbian Milovan Ćirić and the Hungarian József Gelei, and inducted modern coaching methods. A good tactician, with an eye to spot talent, Sukhwinder revamped JCT and a new crop of exciting young players emerged. He chose four newcomers from colleges in Mahilpur and Hoshiarpur, two regions in Punjab where football is very popular. Central-defenders Manjit Singh and Amrik Singh impressed by curbing Bagan's lethal Chima Okorie in the 1992 Durand semi-final. Tejinder Kumar, a live wire in midfield and an astute passer of the ball, became a regular international, as did another midfielder Harjinder Singh, son of the legendary Inder Singh. Sukhwinder's JCT played slick one-touch football with constant mobility, making them difficult to beat. He brought back the winning streak to JCT when they won the 1992 Durand Cup in grand style beating all three Kolkata clubs—East Bengal, Mohammedan Sporting and Mohun Bagan—on the way to their success. They also reached the Rovers Cup final that year, losing 0-2 to Mohun Bagan.

During this era, JCT started recruiting outstation players. International striker Kiran Khongsai and two other Manipuri midfielders joined the team for the 1992 season. In the 1994 season JCT imported players for the first time: striker Chaukrat from Uzbekistan and midfielder Pedro Ricoy from Australia. International striker Bhupender Thakur joined from Himachal Pradesh in 1994.

The third milestone was in 1995 when JCT became the first team in India to lure players from Kolkata. They successfully poached I.M. Vijayan and Ancheri from Mohun Bagan and Carlton Chapman from East Bengal. It was coach Sukhwinder Singh who had initiated these transfers. In December 1994, both Vijayan and Ancheri were playing for Mohun Bagan in the Rovers Cup in Mumbai. One day whilst they were watching a match, Sukhwinder approached them and asked if they would be keen to join JCT if offered a large sum of money. Vijayan replied that they had left their home state to play professionally and did not have any emotional attachment to Bagan. Sukhwinder promptly conveyed this to JCT's executive director and sports enthusiast Samir Thapar, who sanctioned the money. Vijayan and Ancheri thus joined JCT in 1995–96, reportedly for Rs 15 and Rs 12 lakh respectively for the season. Chapman came to JCT reportedly for Rs 10 lakh. These were record sums in the Indian transfer market in those days. These transfers created a sensation as suddenly the financial might of the Kolkata clubs in recruiting top-class professionals had been challenged.

With the presence of the three internationals, JCT improved considerably and, in the 1995 season, they won the Federation Cup for the first time in nineteen years. JCT's Federation Cup victory that season was also an indication of changing times. For the first time Kolkata clubs were vanquished in their home state. JCT beat Mohammedan Sporting 2-1 in the semi-final in Siliguri and East Bengal 7-6 on penalties in the final at the Salt Lake Stadium. Both matches were played on slushy, slippery surfaces on which the Kolkata teams had always excelled. But JCT bearded the lion in his den. JCT became the most formidable team in the country as five of their players—Amrik, Tejinder, Vijayan, Ancheri and Chapman—were regulars in the Indian squad.

In the 1996–97 season JCT created a sensation, recruiting Bhaichung Bhutia from East Bengal and classy foreigners

Stephen Abarowei, Christopher Kem, Musa Aliu, Bernard Oparanozie and Shaheed Akinsanya. They became one of the finest Indian club teams of all time and befittingly won the inaugural Philips NFL. That season they also won the Federation Cup a second time, and both the IFA Shield and the Durand Cup, beating Iraqi club teams in the final with Abarowei scoring match-winners on both occasions.

Sukhwinder Singh emerged as Punjab's most solid and renowned coach and won a number of trophies. His man-management skills were exemplary as he thought up simple yet innovative ways to develop team spirit. For instance, he emphasized eating together to make the outstation superstars and local Punjabi players feel comfortable with each other. He also consulted senior players before taking crucial decisions.

Sukhwinder was also good at handling a crisis. At one stage in the 1997 inaugural NFL, fancied JCT were struggling and were third in the table behind Churchill Brothers and East Bengal. On 16 February at the Salt Lake Stadium, East Bengal beat JCT 1-0. For their next match in Delhi, Sukhwinder made a crucial selection decision that proved he could be a tough coach if required. On the morning of the match on 23 February, during the routine team selection, he dropped a bombshell. After intense discussions with his think tank, manager Inder Singh and assistant coach Parminder Singh, he relegated superstar I.M. Vijayan to the bench and revamped the side. Sukhwinder wanted greater pace in midfield and attack. Hence the nimble Chapman moved from midfield to Vijayan's usual position, the left flank. JCT played in the 4-3-3 system; Abarowei was the right-winger and Bhaichung the striker. The midfield trio consisted entirely of Punjab players, whose box-to-box mobility gave JCT greater control.

It was a gamble to drop India's star striker Vijayan before such an important game. But the JCT coach was spot on. The move clicked and JCT won 2-0. Vijayan, who had scored just 1 goal in the 9 earlier matches, was jolted out of his complacency and JCT peaked at the business end of the league to emerge champions. Sukhwinder's successful handling of a star-studded team and strategic ability helped him become national coach during 1999–2002 and again in 2005. He also guided India's U-23 team to success in the 6th SAFF Cup in Dhaka, 2009.

With the decline of both BSF and Punjab Police, JCT was north India's sole representative in the NFL and I-League. They were runners-up in the 11th ONGC NFL and third in the inaugural I-League in 2007–08. Goalkeeper Virender Singh, strikers Hardip Gill and Surjit Singh, midfielders Hardip Sangha, Hardip Saini, Sukhjinder Singh and Sukhwinder Singh, and defenders Prabhjot Singh, Daljit Singh, Harpreet Singh, Narinder Singh and Anwar Ali were some of the prominent internationals from JCT in the new millennium. Amongst other famous players, Sunil Chhetri, Renedy Singh and Deepak Mondal too played for the club.

In 2007, JCT opened an academy in Hoshiarpur for training young players, including a training complex and football ground, which functions well. They became trendsetters by tying up with English first-division club Wolverhampton Wanderers in May 2008 for the exchange of coaching personnel at the academy level. With the tie-up JCT hoped to fulfil their desire of popularizing football amongst the youth of Punjab. The Chandigarh Football Academy, started by the former governor of Punjab, Lt Gen. (Retd) J.F.R. Jacob in 2000, also did yeoman service in developing quality players.

However, in 2011 JCT were relegated to the second division as the forward line did not perform as per expectations. The club management was hurt at this loss of status. They also felt that Indian football did not get enough visibility for it to be a sustainable business. Their decision to close down in May 2012 was a major shock to their numerous fans all over India and a jolt for the development of football in the state. It marked the end of an era.

With the AIFF having made club licensing a prerequisite to play, the institutional teams from Punjab—BSF, Punjab Police and Punjab State Electricity Board (PSEB)—have faded away. The opportunity that JCT and these clubs had provided to the talented and sturdily built players of Punjab and Haryana to showcase their talent is now no longer available. Also, sadly, there is no team for north Indian fans to identify with.

However, players from that region continue to emerge. The tall and lanky Gurpreet Singh Sandhu and well-built Amrinder Singh are highly rated goalkeepers. Gurpreet, who made his youth state-level debut in 2006, developed his football talent in AIFF's experimental side Pailan Arrows—formed in 2010 in Kolkata. He is the first-choice goalkeeper for the national team and has played as a professional for three years in Norway for Stabæk. At the time of writing, he had joined Bengaluru FC for over Rs 1.5 crore, which makes him the most expensive Indian player in the ISL.[1]

Amrinder initially started as a striker at his sports academy, but on the prompting of his coach, changed his position. Excelling as a goalkeeper, he helped Punjab win the B.C. Roy Trophy for the junior national football championships in 2012. He has played with distinction for Pune FC, Atletico de Kolkata and Bengaluru FC. Amrinder represented India at the 2014 Asian Games in Guangzhou.

Like Gurpreet and Amrinder, midfielders Sehnaj Singh and Bikramjit Singh too are from Punjab; their talent was developed in Pailan Arrows, and they have played for Mohun Bagan. Fortunately for the talented players from Punjab, a new club team, Minerva Academy Football Club, was formed in 2005. They developed the team with foresight, focusing first on an academy for a decade and then making their I-League debut. In their inaugural appearance in the second-division I-League in 2015, they topped the Western Conference, ahead of more established clubs like Dempo. Striker Sehijpal Singh was their top scorer with 5 goals while midfielders Arashpreet Singh and Manvir Singh also impressed.

In the 10th Hero I-League in early 2017, Minerva FC became the first team from north India to play in the I-League since JCT shut down their team in 2011. Coached by Surinder Singh, Minerva FC relied on youthful exuberance and had several teenagers in their playing eleven, such as the talented strikers Krishna Pandit and Baoringdao Bodo (just seventeen years old and the youngest to play in the I-League) and midfielders Anirudh Thapa and Uttam Rai. They took time to settle down but played exhilarating attacking football in the second-half of the I-League. They held both the I-League champions Aizawl (2-2 draw at Ludhiana) and Federation Cup champions Bengaluru (1-1, away), and notched up 13 points from 18 matches.

Minerva FC is doing a good job in trying to revive the interest in football in Punjab by attracting youngsters to watch their home matches at the Guru Nanak Stadium, Ludhiana. They also give a lot of emphasis on youth-training programmes. In light of these developments and with the rise of sports academies in the state, there is hope yet that football's rich legacy in Punjab will be carried forward. The AIFF too needs to lend its support to ensure that football in the land of the five rivers flourishes again.

See in 'Hall of Fame': Inder Singh (forward), Manjit Singh (forward), Parminder Singh (midfielder).

6

Delhi

Football in Shahjahanabad and Beyond

In these days when cricket reigns supreme it is difficult to imagine the grip that football had on the Shahjahanabad region of Delhi, also known as the walled city. Renowned today for its mouth-watering cuisine, old-style perfumeries, textile shops and jewellers, Old Delhi was once a hub of football. The first parent body of Delhi football was formed in 1926 with Mohammed Zubair Qureishi as secretary, with the help of Sardar Sobha Singh and Youngmen FC secretary R.B. Sen, known as Adu Babu. The local league was yet to begin but clubs participated in private tournaments organized by soccer enthusiasts.

Footballers were admired and encouraged by the people of this region, which primarily comprised Bengali and Muslim residents. The Dilliwallahs witnessed the historic 1940 Durand Cup—the first time it was played in this city and won by an Indian side—and watched the DCM Trophy that was held regularly after Independence. Each mohalla supported a local football club, and in the summer months the conversations would be about the chances of the Old Delhi teams in the Delhi League. However, for the rest of the year they were about the performances of the iconic Mohammedan Sporting and Hyderabad City Police in the popular domestic tournaments. Leading teams from Delhi also participated in these tournaments, but players from these two clubs were treated like demigods.

My formative years were spent in Chabi Gunj, Kashmiri Gate, which in the 1960s was not the centre of a motor-parts market as it is now. It was more of a well-connected middle-class residential colony with spacious gardens like Nicholson Gardens and Qudsia Bagh. The aura of the colonial era still hung in the main market that had charming little shops with English names. Ours was the first Parsi family to settle in Delhi. Though my community and family encouraged sports, nobody had played football, so my passion for the game started more by accident than design. In my area there was a club house called the Bengal Association (the space for the local adda) and they had a football team called the Young Bengal Association that played in the local league. As a child, I used to watch them practise at the erstwhile St Stephens' College grounds, now the ISBT grounds, and was fascinated. In later years I played for this club and even became their captain in 1974–75.

Many talented players emerged from the walled city area, largely because there was lots of playing space. The green patch outside Red Fort would be teeming with youth either playing football or flying kites. They would also play on the vast stretch of green opposite Raj Ghat, the Feroz Shah Kotla ground near the Indian Express Building, and nearby places. Red Fort was the breeding ground of champions. The great players of Hyderabad City Police (later Andhra Police) and the 1966 Durand champions Gorkha Brigade all practised here.

Some famous Old Delhi clubs are Youngmen (the capital's oldest club, formed in 1898), Mughals (started in 1905 and the first Delhi team to play in boots), Simla Youngs, City Club, Indian Nationals, Moonlight, Crescent and Union, amongst others. Mughals were a formidable team and won the local league title in 1944–45 without losing a point or conceding a goal. In 1944, Delhi also won the Santosh Trophy for the first and only time till now, beating mighty Bengal 2-0 in the final. Skipper Usman Jaan, who had played for the all-conquering Mohammedan Sporting in the 1930s, was originally from the popular Crescent and later Youngmen. After Partition, several members of this Delhi team—including a trio from Mughals—migrated to Pakistan and started a Mughals Club in Karachi. Right midfielder Afzal from Mughals Karachi was selected for the Pakistan team that participated in the 1954 Asian Games in Manila, Philippines. Usman Jaan was a legend in the subcontinent for his daring goalkeeping, and after his death the Usman Jaan Memorial football tournament was started in Karachi.

During the 1950s, clubs from Delhi frequently crossed the Wagah border and played either tournaments or exhibition matches in Pakistan. Amongst these were Frontier Club, mostly consisting of players whose families had migrated from Lahore and Rawalpindi. Apart from playing football, this would also be a nostalgia trip to renew old acquaintances and visit familiar localities. Sturdy defender O.P. Malhotra who went on those trips recalled that their board and lodging were taken care of by local Pakistani clubs. The hospitality was immense. The team would be invited to *daawat* (feasts) at various houses and be presented gifts as well. Breakfast consisted of lassi, eggs and fruit, and a stream of visitors would come afterwards to gossip. For the three-week tour, Malhotra would carry just Rs 10 as pocket money and could not spend all of it.

The Delhi League was suspended during the turbulent years of Partition. From 1948 onwards the Delhi Football Association got better organized and the league took a particular shape. The local Bengali population played a major role in the development of the game as players and officials. They also came in hordes to watch matches at the Delhi Gate Stadium. The kick-off was often at 6 p.m. and, till the 1960s, entrance tickets cost just 10 paise, which was affordable for common people.

It was essentially an amateur era. Except for transport allowance, kit and refreshment, there was no payment to the players. Even refreshments were meagre: jalebis dipped in a glass of warm milk in the winter months and nimboo pani (lemonade) in the summer. However, club officials would strive to get their top players jobs in important public-sector organizations.

As the city expanded and government housing colonies spread all over south and central Delhi, the popularity of football also increased. A rivalry developed between Old Delhi and New Delhi clubs and the involvement of the crowds was intense. For a decade after Independence, Youngmen were the only formidable team from Old Delhi, winning the league thrice. Goalkeeper Hardev Sahai from Crescent Club and Youngmen was one of Delhi's star players and was hired by the renowned Rajasthan FC in Kolkata.

New Delhi Heroes became the strongest side from this part of Delhi, winning the local league for six years in the 1950s (four consecutively). Some of the stalwarts of this side were centre-forward Amba Suri, inside-forward Krishan Thapar (later chief football coach), sturdy full-back Trilok Nath Lau (later a national referee), midfielder Ram Swarup and former state captains A.N. Jayaraman and V.P. Suri. The 1948–56 Olympic hockey gold medallist, defender Randhir Singh Gentle, also played football for ND Heroes.

It was in the 1960s that the popularity of the Delhi League reached its zenith. Although Raisina Sporting, a team supported by the local Bengali population, won the league twice in the early 1960s, it was City Club that emerged as the most popular in this decade. They comprised some veterans and a talented group of school and college players, all of whom resided in the narrow lanes near Jama Masjid. They had a large support base and were financed by the local butchers.

Indian Nationals, also based in the walled city, had their own committed supporters and were the first Delhi club to pay money to purchase players for the season. They had a fine forward line with striker Nirmal Singh Sahi from Lucknow, wingers Durga Prasad and Ken Matthews, and playmaker Som Nath, all of whom played at the state level. Burly centre-forward Sahi was the most sought-after player in local football for his goalscoring ability. The rivalry of Indian Nationals with City Club was intense. The Delhi Gate Stadium became a veritable cauldron of frenzied supporters when these arch-rivals clashed in the local league. Crowds of 15,000–18,000 witnessed this Old Delhi derby, mostly held on Fridays or Sundays.

Their most memorable clash was on an overcast Sunday evening in July 1964. It was a return-leg match and City Club trailed Indian Nationals 0-3 at half-time. The confident officials of Indian Nationals ordered boxes of sweetmeats for distribution after the match. But an inspired City Club spoiled their party. Spurred by Aziz Qureishi and gutsy wing-half Mohammed Iqbal, City Club rallied to win 6-3 amidst scenes of great joy. Aziz, the hero of that triumph, was given free glasses of milk by happy supporters for the rest of the year; for a fortnight after the match the team was invited for sumptuous daawats by delirious fans. Aziz later acted in popular TV shows like *Hum Log* as well as some films.

Delhi twice won the junior national championships (Dr B.C. Roy Trophy), in 1963 and 1965. Several distinguished players from the city were hired by bigger clubs: crafty inside-forward Shujaat Ashraf (Mohammedan Sporting and East Bengal), goalkeeper Manzoor Ahmed and skilful striker Surender Kumar (Mohammedan Sporting), and lanky stopper-back Dev Raj Katyal and dashing striker Shanker Mukherjee (Mafatlal Mills Mumbai). Surender Kumar had helped his Delhi club Simla Youngs reach the Durand semi-final in 1972 and played for an India XI vs USSR XI test match in 1977.

Over the years, a number of players from Delhi represented India Juniors in the Asian Youth Championships: Aziz Qureishi (1965), left-winger Arunesh Sharma (1969), sturdy left-back G. Bernard (1973), attacking midfielder Anadi Barua (1982), defender Laxman Bisht (1986) and midfielder Trilok Bisht (1992).

In the 1986 Nehru Cup there were Anadi Barua and striker Tarun Roy from Delhi. Tarun had also toured the West Indies with the national team in 1984. Midfielder Santosh Kashyap, noted for his silky skills and sharpshooting, represented the all-India combined universities team in 1985, and later joined Mahindra & Mahindra in 1986. He played in the 1989 Nehru Cup and the 4th South Asian Federation (SAF) Games. Santosh is the only coach from Delhi to have earned his Pro-Licence coaching degree, which he got from Japan. He has trained several I-League clubs including Mohun Bagan, Salgaocar and Mumbai FC. He was named Best I-League Coach at the Football Players Association of India awards in 2015. Speedy winger Gurinder Pal Singh joined Churchill Brothers and played in the 1996 World Cup qualifying matches.

Left-back Rishi Kapoor was the first Delhi player to have won an NFL title (in 2001–02), as part of Mohun Bagan. Delhi's most famous player is the Indian national team's all-time top scorer and skipper as of 2017, Sunil Chhetri, who started his career with City Club in the local league.

Until the 1990s, crowds from Old Delhi thronged the stadiums when their favourite clubs played in either the local league or Durand and DCM tournaments. Attendance at the Central Secretariat, Chanakyapuri, or President's Estate grounds was lower. The passionate support for the big Kolkata clubs continued unabated. With the rise in standards of the Punjab teams, Sikhs and Punjabis started attending football matches too.

In the twenty-first century Delhi football has become a paradox. Leading European clubs organize annual camps to scout for talent here, but football clubs in Delhi have nowhere to play. The calendar of the Delhi Soccer Association (DSA, name changed in 1992) varies depending on the availability of grounds, which has been affected due to infrastructural changes and exorbitant rents. This is in sharp contrast to the well-organized season, which stretched from April to December, from just after Independence up to the 1990s.

In Delhi, which has a rich club culture unsurpassed in northern India, many old clubs are either struggling or are defunct in this era of nascent professionalism. Old Delhi clubs used to be financed by rich patrons. For instance, Students Club was supported by hotel owner Mohammed Rais, and Youngmen was looked after by the Qureishi family, famous butchers of the area. Due to rising costs and escalating players' fees, it has become impossible for a single family to maintain a football club. Expenses for the season are now in the range of Rs 15–20 lakh and the returns are negligible. Indian Nationals (winners of the league in 2008 and 2014) were taken over by the Amity Group but their support base in Old Delhi has dwindled as the team is now based in Gurgaon.

A good beginning was made in 2013 by former DSA secretary Narinder Kumar Bhatia and other officials like Liaqat Ali and

Bachi Ram, to revive football in Old Delhi by holding a training camp for schoolchildren during the summer holidays.

Due to hectic lifestyles, expanding residential colonies and the withdrawal of Mohun Bagan and East Bengal from the Durand, the attendance in domestic tournaments and the local league too has considerably declined, especially for matches that start in the afternoon. The ISL club Delhi Dynamos does not yet have a local identity, like the Kerala Blasters or NorthEast United FC, as the club has no north Indian player.

7

The North-east
The Rising Sun of Indian Football

As in many regions in India, Christian missionaries and the East India Company personnel introduced the sport in North-eastern India. The game was always popular in this region but the immense potential of players first came to light in the Subroto Mukherjee Cup tournaments for schools in Delhi. In both 1979 and 1980, school teams from the North-east contested the final. In 1986, for the first time, three schools from the North-east reached the Subroto Cup semi-finals. Since then, every year a team from this region has reached either the semi-finals or the final in this tournament.

The Subroto Cup's greatest contribution was to bring talent from the North-east to the foreground, though for most of the twentieth century there was a lack of adequate infrastructure or competitive state leagues. Due to this, several players who performed well in the Subroto Cup tended to stagnate or fade away at the senior level.

In the mid-1980s, the newly formed SAI sought to nurture this talent. The director of the Special Area Games (SAG) scheme, the far-sighted B.V.P. Rao, started a residential academy for players from the North-east and the Andaman and Nicobar Islands in Delhi in 1987–88.

Coached by Anjan Chowdhury, who had qualified in Germany, these students played in tournaments around the country as SAG (Red) and SAG (Blue). The idea was excellent. Within a couple of years three players—Kiran Khongsai (Manipur), midfielder Jewel Bey (Assam) and defender Emmanuel (the Andaman and Nicobar

Islands)—became internationals and represented India at the 1989 SAF Games in Islamabad.

Now clubs made a beeline to sign them, and soon Air India (Mumbai) and Churchill Brothers had a majority of players from the North-east in their squads. Bimal Ghosh, the Air India manager, also made annual trips to Manipur, Assam and Meghalaya to select upcoming players. His role in spotting and nurturing talent from Manipur in particular was exemplary, as a number of players later became established internationals. In the mid-1990s, Bimal Ghosh's Air India was often jocularly called Air-Manipur.

The commencement of the Super Soccer series, which led to São Paulo FC (Brazil) touring India in 1984, was an eye-opener and spawned new ideas about football youth development. The house of Tata—the sponsor of the Super Soccer series—started a residential academy in Jamshedpur.

Since its inception in 1987, TFA has been at the forefront of developing young footballers. The recruits receive regular exposure in Germany and earlier went to Brazil as well. Realizing the potential of teenagers from the North-east, the TFA scouts also started recruiting from this region. The skills of many North-eastern players were honed at the TFA and they became renowned internationals from 1996 onwards.

Sikkim produced the first major star of Indian football in the era of colour television, the 'Sikkimese Sniper' Bhaichung Bhutia. He first played in the Subroto Cup tournament and his precocious talent was evident even then. He joined the illustrious East Bengal in 1993 and two years later debuted for India. A pioneer in Indian football, Bhaichung reached unprecedented heights and has been the torchbearer for players from the North-east.

Amongst other trendsetters was diminutive Manipuri midfielder Somatai Shaiza, popularly known as Soso. A product of TFA, Soso created quite an impact in his first few years and was purchased by Churchill Brothers at a very high price. With his accurate crosses and deft through-passes, Soso excelled in their 1st NFL campaign in 1997 and also played for India in the 1997 SAFF Cup.

Within a decade, Bhaichung and several others became role models for aspiring players, and football in the North-east had a promising start in the twenty-first century. Every club team in the I-League or the ISL now has players from the North-east. The Indian squad in the final rounds of the 2004 Asian U-17 Championship qualifiers in Japan had seven players from Mizoram. The squad for the 2017 U-17 World Cup has a majority of players from this region, especially Manipur.

Manipur

The game was introduced in the Imphal Valley in 1899 by a Christian missionary named Reverend William Pettigrew. He popularized football at the John Stone School where he taught. In a decade's time, the school's football team became active and regularly played matches with the Maharaja Team formed by the Maharaja of Manipur, Sir Churachand Singh. In 1920, a Bengali settler in the valley and a few local football enthusiasts formed the Manipur Town Club. They organized tournaments in Imphal and this club even took part in outstation tournaments.

Initially a Union territory under the jurisdiction of the Assam Football Association, Manipur was granted affiliation with the AIFF in 1973 once it became a full-fledged state. Subsequently, Manipur participated in the junior national championships (Dr B.C. Roy Trophy) in 1973 and in the 30th Santosh Trophy in Ernakulam. The All-Manipur Sports Association also played a major role in developing football in this region. They organized training camps and hosted the Dr B.C. Roy Trophy in 1975.

After he became a coach, renowned striker Sheoo Mewalal did yeoman service in developing football standards in Manipur in the early 1960s. Popular clubs Mohun Bagan (1954 and 1959) and East Bengal (1971) also played exhibition matches in Imphal.

Basanta Kumar Kabui was the first Imphal Valley player to represent India in the Asian Youth football tournament in 1964 in Saigon (it's now known as the AFC U-19 Championship). From the 1990s, star players emerged regularly from this state and excelled for clubs in Goa and West Bengal, as well as for Air India (Mumbai).

Dashing winger Bijen Singh became a regular in the senior Indian side in 1999. He was fast and tricky enough to play as an orthodox winger but was also comfortable through the middle, where his quick reactions and snap shots made him effective as a roving forward.

P. Renedy Singh, a product of TFA, was also a regular in the Indian team from 1999. Renedy's range of passing was creditable and he initiated attacks by the clever use of wall passes and short passes. Later he became a dead-ball expert for India. His most memorable goal was the delectable free kick in the 2009 ONGC Nehru Cup final. Renedy scored in extra time and India won the title beating Syria on penalties. Former national coach Sukhwinder Singh was always impressed with his work rate and proficiency, and he was also highly rated by national coach Stephen Constantine.

Discovered by Bimal Ghosh, Tomba Singh was noted for his work rate and ability to chip, charge and harass. Hours of practice with Ghosh made him an excellent crosser of the ball. He was a member of the Indian team that won the LG Cup in Vietnam in 2002. He performed well in the 2002 Asian Games and excelled for India in the 2003 Afro-Asian Games.

Bimal Ghosh also developed the game of Manitombi Singh, an excellent utility player who functioned as defensive midfielder, wing-back or even attacking midfielder. He too played in the LG Cup in Vietnam in 2002 and in the 2002 Asian Games. Accomplished left-back Rattan Singh was a graceful player who excelled in interceptions and read the game well. He debuted for India in the Sahara Millennium Cup in 2001. Right-back or right-sided midfielder Surkumar Singh, again a product of TFA, debuted for India in a World Cup qualifier in 2001. For the next few years he was the first-choice right-back for the national team, and with East Bengal he won the ASEAN Cup in 2003.

Midfielders Gunabir Singh, Dharamjit Singh and Bungo Singh too were established internationals. Within a decade, over eighty players from this tiny North-eastern state were registered in different top clubs of the country. These players were trendsetters and inspired many to take to the game seriously.

At the start of the new millennium, players from Manipur had become famous but the state did not fare well in the Santosh Trophy as their stars were all on duty for either West Bengal or Goa. In 2002, the AIFF secretary Alberto Colaco applied the domicile rule, and the results were instantaneous.

On 5 November 2002 a dramatic final was played before a large and vociferous crowd. Striker Tiken Singh had put Manipur ahead in the seventh minute but Kerala equalized through Abdul Naushad three minutes before the final whistle. Just four minutes into extra time, Tomba Singh scored the golden goal to make Manipur's football dream come true. They beat Kerala 2-1 to lift the 58th LG Santosh Trophy, their first senior national championship title. Midfielder James Singh was chosen as the most valuable player of the tournament.

Manipur's Santosh Trophy triumph further popularized football in the state. The state government declared a holiday to celebrate this grand success. It also marked a significant shift as Manipur became the first North-eastern state to challenge the supremacy of West Bengal, Goa, Kerala and Punjab in Indian football.

Soon afterwards, another crop of talented Manipuri players emerged like central-defender Gouramangi Singh, striker Sushil Kumar Singh and several others. Three players from Manipur have been chosen as Indian Player of the Year: Tomba Singh (2003), Surkumar Singh (2006) and Gouramangi Singh (2010).

Sushil Kumar Singh was captain of the Indian team that won the 8th SAFF Championships in Dhaka in December 2009; this was particularly creditable as India had fielded an U-23 squad. At the 2011 Asian Cup in Doha, there were four Manipuri players in the twenty-member squad. The India captain designate for the 2017 U-17 World Cup, Amarjit Singh Kiyam, is from Manipur.

Manipuri players are highly respected as professionals all over India as they effortlessly adjust to the demands and playing styles of the clubs they join. They are also mentally tough, as they have learnt to adapt to new cultures.

Credit for the emergence of Manipur as a powerhouse in domestic football also goes to the AIFF. Due to insurgency and lack of industries or financial support, local football clubs were not establishing themselves well there. The AIFF selected it as one of the two states in India for the AFC Vision India Pilot Project on 28 March 2005. By following the strictures of the project, Manipur improved its basic football activities, management, youth projects and development of coaches. Above all, it helped in the formation of clubs all over Manipur.

Amongst these is Neroca FC, supported by local businessmen and hotel owners. They provide training and have become an outlet for young Manipuri players to showcase their skills. Neroca finished runners-up in the 2016 Durand Cup, came third in the 2016 I-League second division and won the Manipur State League title in 2016. They then won the I-League second division in May 2017 and qualified for the main I-League in 2017–18.

Mizoram

Unfancied Aizawl FC scripted history by winning the I-League in April 2017, becoming the first club from the North-east to win a major club trophy in India. Their story is similar in many ways to Leicester City, the surprise winners in the 2015–16 Barclays Premier League. Remarkably, they did this on a shoestring budget of just Rs 2.5 crore, five times less than that of the big clubs. Their young coach Khalid Jamil, an old-fashioned disciplinarian in the mould of Syed Nayeemuddin, shaped Aizawl FC into a cohesive, fighting team that played with great intensity. With Jamil's astute coaching, Aizawl FC won their home matches and avoided defeat in away matches to gain 25 of 37 points. Relegated the previous season, Aizawl FC were reprieved by the AIFF and played in the I-League for the second time.

In 2016, Aizawl FC had a dream run to the final of the Federation Cup. For the first time, a club from the football-crazy state was noticed in India's premier knockout tournament for their fluid, short-passing game. They created a sensation by upsetting

I-League champions Bengaluru FC in the quarter-finals and fancied Sporting Clube de Goa in the semi-finals, before getting routed 0-5 by Mohun Bagan.

The passion for the game in Aizawl is unprecedented. The sale of tickets for their opening home match against Bengaluru FC in the 2016 I-League started four days in advance. There were serpentine queues at all the different outlets. The tickets were priced at Rs 200, 500 and 1000, way above the average price at the other I-League venues. This was in part due to the limited capacity of 10,000 at the Rajiv Gandhi Stadium. Bengaluru FC too received a royal welcome in Aizawl. The colourfully dressed fans created a festive atmosphere in the stadium with songs, banners, musical instruments (mostly drums) and cheerleaders.

Football was always a passion in Mizoram but the game got a boost when the AIFF started a development programme in the state in 2010. It was initiated by Rob Baan, the renowned Dutch football coach and technical director of the AIFF till 2014. The Mizoram Football Association (MFA) implemented the FIFA–AIFF project effectively and won the AIFF award for 'Best Grass-roots Development'.

But it was the commencement of the Mizoram Premier League in late 2012, with a ceremonial kick-off by Bhaichung Bhutia, that marked a turning point. The efficiently run eight-team franchise league in the state offered the local talent a rare chance to showcase their skills. Months before the league started, the state association had roped in a local cable network as a major sponsor. Live telecasts of all the matches created a football boom in the state.

'After that, the story has been very encouraging,' said young MFA secretary and former journalist Lalnghinglova Hmar, 'the footballers are local heroes, they endorse local brands, and some of the young ones even have a huge female fan following. The frenzy is at par with the English Premier League.'[1] He added, 'The players hail from almost all parts of Mizoram, so all the villages have some reason to support a team in the tournament.'[2]

The passion for football in Mizoram can be gauged by the following anecdote. Lalvulliana, a government primary-school teacher in the remote Khuangleng village, was an ardent fan of the Brazilian legend Zico, or 'White Pelé'.[3] He would travel nearly 240 km to Aizawl to watch Brazil play on a television in the early 1980s. Like other football fanatics, he named his first born Zico. The young Zico Zoremsanga says that though he started playing football at an early age, 'like any other child in Mizoram', he took up the game seriously only as a teenager. He admits, 'It took me some years to understand who Zico was.'

History was made in the 2014 Santosh Trophy when Zico scored twice in the final, helping Mizoram defeat Railways 3-0. It was the first time this tiny North-eastern state had won a senior national championship. The victorious team were greeted with much fanfare in Aizawl. Watching the procession, an elated Lalvulliana wept with joy and pride.

Along with national recognition the Santosh Trophy victory also brought glory to the community. One of Mizoram's well-known players, Lalrindika Ralte says, 'Our community is a small one, but we are close-knit. We are trying to help younger players. Whenever we are home during the off-season, we play friendlies to raise funds for the junior and village teams.'

At the turn of the century, Mizo players were relatively unknown in Indian football. The trendsetter was junior international Shylo Malsawmtluanga, a TFA product who in 2002 was recruited by East Bengal. For two seasons—2002–03 and 2003–04—East Bengal became the best in the land: winning back-to-back NFL titles, the Durand Cup in 2002 and 2004, and the coveted ASEAN Cup in 2003. Popularly known as 'Mama', Malsawmtluanga played a pivotal role in all these triumphs. He played in every match of the 2004 SAF Games and helped India win the silver. Another Mizo player, Vanlal Rova, was also in this team.

The football star Jeje Lalpekhlua says, 'Until Mama donned the East Bengal jersey, we did not think we could play professional football. He inspired us, helped us find clubs and also planned our roadmaps into professional football.'

Mama inspired a whole generation of Mizo footballers, including Lalrindika Ralte and Jerry Zirsanga. In a decade's time, more than twenty players from Mizoram began to play football professionally in top I-League clubs.

In the 2015–16 SAFF Suzuki Cup, eighteen-year-old Mizo winger Lallianzuala Chhangte was given an international debut by national coach Constantine and the speedy winger impressed with 2 goals against Nepal in the semi-finals. In mid-2016 there were four Mizo players at Constantine's national camp in Guwahati.

Like Hyderabad of the 1950s and 1960s, and Manipur of a decade ago, Mizoram is now the biggest exporter of football talent.

Meghalaya

Vikram Buragohain's documentary *Kicking from the Corner* (2015) gives an insight into the passion for football in Meghalaya. The film shows the public screenings of the 2014 World Cup semi-finals which the state hosted, women discussing their favourite team while doing housework and fans praying at the beginning of a game.[4] Over the years, the love for football has spread like wildfire and there are now seventy-one clubs active in Shillong, the 'Scotland of the East'.

St Anthony's School, Shillong was the first team from the North-east to win the Subroto Cup in 1978. Shillong Lajong FC was formed in 1983 and enjoys a massive following. Amongst other significant landmarks, they were the first club from the North-east to qualify for the main I-League in 2009 and the first to reach the Federation Cup final in 2009–10. The match against East Bengal ended in a draw, but Shillong Lajong eventually lost 0-3 on penalties.

According to the club owner Larsing Ming Sawyan, also the secretary of the Meghalaya Football Association, the club is associated with the pride of Meghalaya. In the Khasi language, *lajong* means 'our own'. In all their home matches, capacity crowds of about 20,000 vociferously cheer their favourite team with fans singing the club theme song:

Hoi Kiw
Hoi Kiw
One voice we'll stand
It's the very name
Come lads come
In Lajong's name we'll cheer

The Shillong Lajong club academy has been functional since 2007 and several of the academy graduates have played for their senior team.

From 2007 onwards, Shillong has established itself as a major football centre of India. The reason for the popularity of football in this scenic town is that 'Shillong is an education hub and a lot of young [boys] come here for their studies,' says Larsing Ming.[5] The Shillong-based clubs get a regular supply of players from Meghalaya, Mizoram and Manipur.

The first North-east derby took place in 2013, when Shillong Lajong met newly promoted Rangdajied United in the 7th I-League. International defender Gourmangi Singh, who was representing Rangdajied United that season, was amazed at the turbulent crowds and the festive atmosphere at the Nehru Stadium in Shillong.

In the 8th I-League another Shillong club, Royal Wahingdoh, played with great spirit and gusto. Coached by Santosh Kashyap (for details, see Chapter 6: 'Delhi'), they had an excellent collection of players from the North-east, including Jackichand Singh from Manipur (chosen as best player of the tournament). They were the giant-killers of the league and finished a creditable third. Under Kashyap's guidance, their comeback 3-2 win against ultimate champions Mohun Bagan was one of the best matches of the tournament. Later, they played a thrilling 3-3 draw with Bengaluru FC.

Many star players have emerged from this hilly region due to well-organized club football. Midfielder Ongnam Milan Singh, a junior international, excelled for Delhi Dynamos in the 2016 Hero ISL and is highly rated by coach Gianluca Zambrotta. Another midfielder to shine in the I-League is the 'David Beckham of the North-east', the dead-ball expert Boithang Haokip, who honed his skills at the TFA. Phlegmatic defender Aiborlang Khongjee is a regular in the senior Indian team. Defender Zodingliana Ralte and dashing striker Seminlen Doungel are other classy players to emerge from Shillong Lajong, now ably coached by Thangboi Singto, the most well-qualified coach from the North-east. All of them played in the 2017 I-League, though Ralte had shifted to Aizawl FC that season.

The case of the star attacking midfielder Eugeneson Lyngdoh is different from the rest. Leaving his engineering degree midway, Lyngdoh of Shillong made a relatively late entry into professional football. Santosh Kashyap noticed him at Rangdajied and made him captain after seeing his excellent work-rate and great composure with the ball. Lyngdoh is considered India's Steven Gerrard and was the AIFF Player of the Year in 2015.

~

Santosh Kashyap is an expert on North-eastern football as he has spent considerable time in the region and coached a number of clubs there.[6] According to him, there are important socio-economic reasons behind the popularity of the sport. Explaining the reasons for the players' natural athleticism, he said, 'Kids don't have regular transport to reach school from homes, need to do a lot of walking along the slopes . . . Football is played everywhere from childhood,' and on all kinds of surfaces.

Like talented players from Africa, the young footballers from the North-east also realize that football is a way of upward social mobility. Observing life in several places in the North-east, Kashyap said, 'Life is hard for families. There is little incentive to stay at home.' So parents encourage their talented children to follow their chosen career path. 'Getting into a top club anywhere provides a way out.'

Ironically, the isolation of the North-east from mainstream India, which is cricket-crazy, may be a factor in their passionate attachment to football. A week after Sachin Tendulkar retired from international cricket, I was in Shillong to commentate for Ten Action for the first

North-east derby in the I-League. In the rest of India, the popular discussions in the media were about Sachin's career and Bharat Ratna award. In Shillong, the atmosphere was entirely different. The picturesque hill station was alive with passionate arguments about the forthcoming derby match. Sachin got a brief mention in the local media and the craze for cricket seemed light years away.

However, North-eastern football still has a long way to go as there is not yet enough private or public-sector investment in football, and local clubs find it difficult to retain quality players. The lack of industry and multiple insurgencies in the region contribute to this phenomenon. So far, Meghalaya, Mizoram and Manipur are the only three states from the region to have made steady progress on all fronts. Assam produced a few quality players from the 1950s to the 1980s, including defender Deka Raja and midfielder M. Kubai who represented India in the 1976 Merdeka Tournament, but football has not taken off in the state. After the 1948 Olympic captain Talimeran Ao, the next Naga player to represent India was Imliakum in the 1983 Nehru Cup.

The ISL club NorthEast United FC offers a ray of hope, as nine to ten of the players are from this region. Owned by popular film star John Abraham, it is the only ISL franchise that is closely connected to the local community. In an interview with Marcus Mergulhao in the *Times of India* dated 5 June 2015, he said, 'NorthEast [United] is one club where we want to create our own stars and retain them. This is the only non-corporate team and we are working from our hearts . . . Everyone knows the North-east is a football nuclear bomb in the making. This is a gold mine.'

The club has popular support from all the seven states of the North-east, and it appears football has managed to do in this region what governments could not for many decades—create a shared identity.

See in 'Hall of Fame': Bhaichung Bhutia (forward), Jeje Lalpekhlua (forward), Talimeran Ao (midfielder).

8

Bengaluru

Football in the Garden City

A suburb in Bengaluru called Gowthampura has a full-size statue of the legendary Pelé. At the unveiling ceremony of this statue about two decades ago, the legends of the Indian football team, including Bhaichung Bhutia and I.M. Vijayan, were present. Often known as the Garden City or the 'Information Technology capital', Bengaluru has produced several stalwarts of international cricket; from spinners E.A.S. Prasanna, Bhagwat Chandrasekhar and Anil Kumble, to batsman Rahul Dravid and wicketkeeper S.M.H. Kirmani. However, it is less known that in certain areas of Bengaluru, football was very popular.

The famous Bangalore Muslims became the first Indian club to win the prestigious Rovers Cup in Mumbai in 1937. The *Bombay Chronicle* of 1 September 1937 wrote about the club's performance: 'Bangalore Muslims treated 20,000 spectators with their brilliant display of first-class football and many a time held their audience spellbound.'[1] Laxmi Narayan—who had scored the winning goal—and Murugesh were the first outstation players to represent East Bengal. The Bangalore Muslims defended the title the next year, beating a British regimental team for the first time in a Rovers Cup final. They won the Cup again in 1948.

The Bangalore Football Association was formed in the 1920s, and in 1946 became the Mysore Football Association. The erstwhile Mysore state was renamed Karnataka in 1973 and since then the Karnataka Football Association looks after the game in the state.

Twelve Olympians in football have emerged from this city. In the 1948 London Olympics, six members of the Indian squad were from Bengaluru: goalkeeper K.V. Varadaraj, centre-half S.A. Basheer and forwards B.N. Vajravelu, M. Ahmed Khan, S. Raman and K.P. Dhanraj. Varadaraj and Ahmed Khan (the latter as vice-captain) were part of the Olympics squad again in Helsinki in 1952, as were skilful right-winger P. Venkatesh and crafty inside-forward M.A. Sattar. In the 1956 Melbourne Olympics team, tireless midfielder M.A. Kempaiah and winger Kannaiyan were from Bengaluru; the indefatigable Kempaiah also played in the 1960 Rome Olympics.

Varadaraj and midfielder T. Shanmugham were members of the gold-medal-winning Indian team at the 1951 Asian Games. The gold-medal-winning team at the 1962 Asian Games had midfielder Ethiraj (from the Army unit team MEG Bangalore) and speedy left-winger Arumainayagam—then representing Mohun Bagan and nicknamed 'Baby Taxi' for his blistering pace. Striker Damodaran represented India at the 1958 Asian Games in Tokyo; midfielder Krishnaji Rao played for India at the 1966 Asian Games in Bangkok, the 1967 Asian Cup qualifiers and the 1968 Merdeka Tournament; and inside-forward Sadatullah Khan played in the 1968 Merdeka Tournament.

The Khans of Bengaluru are famous as, over three generations, eleven members of their family played first-class football for clubs in Bengaluru and Kolkata, and some represented India as well. These include the five brothers Mehmood, Ameer, Nawab, Rahman and Saboo, and their brother-in-law Fazlulla Khan, from the first generation, who played from the 1920s to the 1940s. The four sons of the eldest, Mehmood (also known as Baba Khan)— Ahmed, Latheef, Amjad and Sarmad—played between the 1940s and 1960s. From the third generation, Ahmed's son Majid Khan, also had a brief football career.

Players from Bengaluru were known for their impeccable technical skills and a neat, short-passing game. They played possession football and wore down their opponents. This style of play probably developed out of necessity. During the British Raj, most local sides played barefoot against the better-built British soldiers. To match the pace and strength of the British players, the Bengaluru players developed excellent ball control, dribbling skills, step-overs and body feints.

This distinctive style came to be known as the Bengaluru school of football. T. Shanmugham went to Goa around the 1980s and coached Salgaocar for nearly a decade, so their approach play clearly reflected the Bengaluru style.

In the 1960s and 1970s, it was the public-sector institutions, seen as the bulwark of the Indian economy, that supported football in Bengaluru. The club teams had lost their appeal and could not garner enough finance or sponsorship to build competitive sides. It was CIL, ITI, HAL and Electronics and Radar Development Establishment that recruited talented players from the city, provided them job security and enabled them to play football. In 1977, ITI Bangalore won the inaugural Federation Cup in Ernakulam upsetting star-studded Mohun Bagan 1-0 in the final. The superior players from these teams often took the plunge and shifted to Kolkata or Goa for better financial prospects.

The professionalism of the Bengaluru teams was, however, beneficial to players only during their active footballing years. This is best exemplified by the plight of defender Mohan Kumar of ITI. A sturdy right-back, he represented India at international tournaments in Malaysia, Afghanistan and South Korea in the mid-1970s. He was part of the ITI team that reached the Stafford Cup[2] final in 1980 and lost a memorable match 2-4 to the powerful Iraqi Youth team. After retirement, he tried to become a coach but did not succeed. Cast aside and forgotten, today he works as a security guard and survives on fond memories of playing internationally. He says sportingly, 'I don't look at [my job] as something that is below my dignity. It's still a job and I enjoy it.'[3]

The city has regularly produced several classy internationals. Crafty midfielders Pushpraj Kumar and D. Devaraj were members of the Indian team that finished joint champions with Iran at the

1974 Asian Youth Championship; they also played in the 1978
Bangkok Asian Games. In the 1982 Asian Games, sturdy left-back
Aslam Khan was part of the national team. Since then skilful
winger Babu Mani, wing-backs Ilyas Pasha and Rahmatullah,
midfielders Carlton Chapman and Noel Wilson—all of whom
started their careers in Bengaluru—went on to represent India.
From Aslam Khan to Wilson, all the later-generation Bengaluru
players made their mark in outstation teams. Even in the 1950s,
several star players like Venkatesh, Kempaiah, Kannaiyan, Ahmed
Khan and Sattar represented the Kolkata clubs during their
international career. However, Bengaluru's reputation as a great
nursery of football talent is not as renowned as that of, say, Kolkata
or Hyderabad.

In the new millennium, the character of Bengaluru changed. It
became the hub of information technology companies and a new
generation of young, upwardly mobile people flocked to the city.
The football lovers amongst them were unaware of Bengaluru's
football culture. It is this vacuum which Bengaluru FC has
successfully filled.

Bengaluru FC

On 28 May 2013, the AIFF awarded the Bengaluru franchise of
I-League to JSW Sports. They soon signed on Ashley Westwood
as coach as well as ace striker Sunil Chhetri. The club Bengaluru
FC was officially launched on 20 July 2013, with only twelve
players. In their first season, the team consisted of a number of
young players like Thoi Singh and Siam Hanghal who were trying
to become established in domestic football. Westwood made wise
selections and honed the skills of his players, making Bengaluru
FC one of the strongest clubs in Indian football.

When Rino Anto joined the club in 2013, his career had
come to a standstill.[4] With Westwood's encouragement and
astute coaching, he became a hard-tackling right-back, effective in
overlapping. A TFA product, Anto improved by leaps and bounds

in the professional atmosphere at Bengaluru FC, and by 2015 made his international debut.

One of the best strikers in the country, C.K. Vineeth was on the verge of giving up football when he was picked by the club. From early on in his career Vineeth had played as a winger but Westwood persuaded him to play as a striker, to utilize his speed and thrust. Now a versatile player, Vineeth plays a roving game. He drifts to the flanks to shake off his marker and, when required, charges into the box to score goals with crisp volleys and angular placements. He is the first player from Bengaluru FC to score a hat-trick, a feat achieved against Mumbai FC in 2017 in a third-round match of the I-League. Vineeth made his international debut against Palestine in 2012. He is at peak form and very prolific, so national coach Constantine used him well for the Asian Cup qualifiers in 2017.

The dynamic Eugeneson Lyngdoh joined Bengaluru FC in July 2014. Westwood transformed him into a box-to-box midfielder who also excelled in taking all the free kicks and corner kicks. Westwood said, 'Eugeneson's work rate is admirable. He runs 12–14 kilometres in every match, similar to the distances covered by some of the best midfielders of the English Premier League.'[5] A late developer, Lyngdoh has become a reliable player and an established international. He was the best midfielder of the 2014–15 I-League and was auctioned for over a crore for the ISL in 2015.

Former footballer and coach Englishman Ashley Westwood spotted the potential of these players, developed their skills and, above all, instilled self-belief in them. Under Westwood—who had played for the Manchester United youth teams—Bengaluru FC developed as a modern, professional side. He brought in methods that are commonplace in European clubs and saw to it that his players got the best possible care with professional training and facilities. Their diet was well-regulated with proper nutrition and fitness levels being consistently monitored. Following strict discipline, the players were trained to be responsible and professional off the field as well.

Bengaluru FC also used social media to interact with the local community and 'made going to the stadium cool'. The club have been able to garner a dedicated group of young supporters who replicate the English Premier League atmosphere at the Sree Kanteerava Stadium, waving banners and chanting catchy team songs. These supporters, comprising a number of women, have come to be known as the West Block Blues and they travel to away matches as well. Their witty banners—like 'We are not out of the Westwoods yet'—enhance the atmosphere during matches and have added a new dimension amongst football supporters in the country.

Debutants Bengaluru FC wrapped up the 2013–14 I-League with a round of matches still to be played. They won it in grand style finishing with 47 points from 24 matches, 4 points ahead of their nearest rivals East Bengal. Bengaluru also won the maximum matches (14) and scored the highest number of goals (42), largely due to their trio of attackers: internationals Sunil Chhetri, Robin Singh and the Australian Sean Rooney.

Having achieved stupendous success in their first season, Bengaluru FC have since grown from strength to strength, surpassing the expectations of their fans and management alike. They finished runners-up to Mohun Bagan in the next I-League in 2014–15, but in 2015 they annexed the Federation Cup in Goa, beating Dempo 2-0 in the final. In 2015–16 they won the I-League again, finishing 2 points ahead of runners-up Mohun Bagan. In 2017, they annexed the Federation Cup a second time, beating their main rivals Mohun Bagan 2-0 in the final in Cuttack. It is no mean feat that in the first four years of their existence, Bengaluru FC won four major domestic trophies and also performed well internationally.

Bengaluru FC's achievement in reaching the 2016 AFC Cup final can be ranked amongst the best in Indian club football, as the Cup is the equivalent of the Europa League. The club won their semi-final, convincingly beating holders Johor Darul Ta'zim (JDT) (Malaysia) 4-2 on aggregate and 3-1 at home. Over 21,000 delirious fans watched them upstage JDT at the Sree Kanteerava Stadium. The performances of strikers Sunil Chhetri, C.K. Vineeth, young

defender Nishu Kumar and newly recruited Spanish defender Juan
González were rightly lauded. This victory was very significant as
the previous year JDT had broken the west Asian clubs' monopoly
over the AFC Cup since its inception as a club tournament in 2004.
Additionally, Indian clubs had twice before stumbled at this stage.

In the final on 5 November 2016 in Doha, Bengaluru FC
battled Iraq Air Force, one of Iraq's most successful clubs. They
had won ten national titles and four Iraq FA Cups, including the
latest edition in 2016. The single-leg final was a tough match as
both teams sought their first-ever continental trophy. Bengaluru
FC's goalkeeper Lalthuammawia Ralte (known as Mawia) and
central-defender John Johnson played an outstanding game and
thwarted numerous attacks by Iraq Air Force. Bengaluru FC
eventually lost 0-1 in a closely fought final.

The unsung hero of Bengaluru FC is their owner, Parth Jindal.
An Arsenal fan, Jindal set up this club and has allowed it to be run
professionally, not interfering with day-to-day management. Their
first coach, Westwood, and the recently appointed Albert Roca
(former assistant manager of Barcelona) were given a free hand
in the players' selection and training. This is unique and novel in
Indian football, and the success of the club shows the path ahead.

As of June 2017, Bengaluru FC have moved to the ISL for the
2017–18 season, as they desire more sustained exposure on TV.[6]

See in 'Hall of Fame': Sunil Chhetri (forward).

PART II

BATTLES FOR SUPREMACY

9

Historic Clashes

1911 IFA Shield Final: Mohun Bagan vs East Yorkshire Regiment

In 1910, the legendary Indian *pehalwan*, or wrestler, known as the 'Great Gama' was declared world champion (*Rustom-e-Zamana*) in freestyle wrestling. In front of a capacity crowd at the Shepherd's Bush Stadium in London on 10 September, Gama dominated the bout of over two hours against reigning champion Stanislaus Zbyszko of Poland. The gigantic Zbyszko was on his feet only thrice in the entire bout. A return bout was scheduled a week later, and it was a walkover for Gama, who who were declared champions. The British celebrated Gama's victory as the triumph of a British subject over an uppity European wrestler. Little did they know that their own supremacy would soon be challenged.

In 1911, Kolkata's oldest Indian football club, Mohun Bagan, were invited to play in the prestigious IFA Shield. Coached by the disciplinarian Sailen Basu, the barefooted players had a great run in the tournament. They triumphed over St Xavier's Institute 3-0 and Rangers FC 2-1 in the first and second rounds, defeated Rifle Brigade 1-0 in the quarter-final, and Middlesex Regiment 4-1 in the semi-final. They reached the final in top form.

The craze for the final was such that Mohun Bagan fans travelled to Kolkata from the outlying districts and from neighbouring Assam and Bihar. The East Indian Railway ran a special train for the purpose. Additional steamer services were also introduced to ferry spectators from rural areas to the ground. Tickets originally priced at Rs 1 and 2 were sold in the black market for Rs 15. Refreshment vendors too made good use of the opportunity. The total number of spectators in the final was estimated at 80,000–1,00,000. This was truly remarkable, as the population of Kolkata and its suburbs was then a little over 10 lakh.

The crowds were at fever pitch. Two sides of the ground were kept open for assembled spectators. Touts provided wooden boxes to help them get a view of the match and charged money per box, depending on its proximity to the playing area. There was no space even on treetops. The members' seats were fully occupied and the enclosed side of the ground had been booked by B.H. Smith & Company for British fans. As many Bagan supporters did not have a good view of the match, volunteers devised an ingenious method to keep them informed of the progress of the game—they flew kites with the club's colours and the score written on them.

The final was goalless at half-time. Sergeant Jackson scored with about fifteen minutes left in the match. Mohun Bagan equalized immediately afterwards through skipper Shibdas Bhaduri. The equalizer led to an explosion of kites in the sky, all coloured maroon and green. The burly centre-forward Abhilash Ghosh scored the winning goal. On 29 July 1911, Mohun Bagan made history by defeating a British regimental team East Yorkshire Regiment of Faizabad 2-1, and becoming the first Indian team to lift the coveted IFA Shield.

The victory established Kolkata as the nerve centre of football in India and heralded the city's long-lasting love affair with football. It also had massive political and social implications. Coupled with Gama's victory, Bagan's win had exploded the myth that the British or Europeans were a superior race, something that the Congress Party and proponents of Swadeshi had been unable to do. The victory was seen as a symbol of hope for a subjugated nation.

It challenged the notion of Bengalis as an effeminate race and reconstructed a more masculine and sprightly image of them. Bagan's historic win was chronicled in newspapers outside Kolkata (the *Times of India*, Mumbai, and the *Pioneer*, Lucknow) and internationally as well. It found mention in British newspapers—the *Times, Daily Mail* and the *Manchester Guardian*. The news agency Reuters reported it too.

The entire Mohun Bagan team played barefooted, which has led to the myth that boots cramped their style of play and playing barefoot improved ball control and dribbling skills. However, economic conditions are a more plausible reason for this. At the turn of the twentieth century, hand-sewn football boots cost Rs 7 and 4 annas, a lot of money in those days.

Amongst the legendary playing eleven, the trio of tricky left-winger Bhaduri, muscular centre-forward Abhilash and left-back Sudhir Chatterjee became really famous because of some fascinating anecdotes.[1] For instance, Abhilash's parents did not want him to play this tournament as they feared he would get hurt. However, he defied his parents to impress his girlfriend, who lived in the same locality.

Sudhir Chatterjee, a Christian, worked as a teacher at Bhowanipore College. There is a popular story that before the first- and second-round matches, his opponents tried to prevent him from reaching the venue. They influenced the British college principal to trap Sudhir in work. Sudhir was known to be a cerebral defender and without him Bagan's rearguard would not have been so well organized. In both the matches, Sudhir made it to the venue just in time. In the final too, the same ruse was tried but Sudhir was alert and slipped away early.

A film called *Egaro* (meaning 'eleven' in Bengali) was released in 2011 to commemorate the centenary of this match. According to the film, Sudhir's popularity with the opposite sex probably caused envy amongst his British colleagues. Similar to scenes from the popular movie *Lagaan*—an attractive young British girl would cheer every time Sudhir cleared the ball and when Mohun Bagan scored. Apparently, this young student admired the lean, lanky and smart Sudhir, and there were even rumours of a passionate relationship.

It is believed that on the morning of the final match, Bagan players had gone to Kalighat temple to pray in front of the goddess Kali. The players stepped into the field with red tilaks on their forehead and sacred flowers in their pockets. Even Sudhir, a devout Christian and later a priest, followed the same rituals as his teammates. It was gestures like these which made him a living legend amongst Bagan supporters.

MOHUN BAGAN TEAM IN 2-3-5 FORMATION, 1911 IFA SHIELD FINAL, KOLKATA

Goalkeeper: Hiralal Mukherjee

Defenders: Bhuti Sukul and Sudhir Chatterjee

Half-Backs: Manmohan Mukherjee, Rajen Sengupta and Nilmadhav Bhattacharya

Forwards: Kanu Roy, Habul Sarkar, Abhilash Ghosh, Bijoydas Bhaduri and Shibdas Bhaduri (**Captain**)

1940 Durand Cup Final: Mohammedan Sporting vs Royal Warwickshire Regiment

The 1940 Durand Cup was held in Delhi for the first time. Due to the onset of the Second World War, the capital of the British Raj did not shift to Shimla that summer. At this time, almost 50 per cent of Delhi's population consisted of Muslims. In the Old Delhi region, football was quite well established and a number of local clubs were flourishing. Consequently, there was palpable excitement that an Indian football club had the ability to challenge and overthrow a team of the colonial rulers.

On their way to the final, Mohammedan Sporting trounced Collegians Sports Club 5-0 (Rashid [2], Saboo [2], Rashid Khan) and Hussars 3-0 (Saboo, Karim, Rashid) in the first and second rounds. In the quarter-finals they eclipsed Union Club 2-0, and conceded their first goal in the semi-finals when they beat the powerful Welsh

Regiment 3-1 (Rashid, Saboo, Rashid Khan). They played in the 2-3-5 system and their burly defenders Jumma Khan and Bacchi Khan were tenacious tacklers and tough to beat. Behind them in goal was the tall Usman Jaan, a dominating figure with excellent gripping, agility and courage. He was a 1930s version of Manuel Neuer. The best attacks in India floundered against this defensive trio.

The final was played on 12 December 1940 at the Irwin Amphitheatre, an enclosed polo ground, and now the site of the Major Dhyan Chand National Stadium built as the venue for the 1st Asian Games held in 1951. Nearly 50,000 people witnessed the match in this amphitheatre-like stadium with seating on only one side. Eminent Muslim politicians such as Muhammad Ali Jinnah, Khawaja Nazimuddin (later prime minister of Pakistan), Huseyn Shaheed Suhrawardy (chief minister of undivided Bengal) and A.K. Fazlul Haq attended the final. Fans came in trains from far-off Kolkata, Dhaka, Hyderabad and Bhopal.

For the first time, an Indian referee, Captain Harnam Singh, was going to supervise a Durand final. At the ground, a tricky situation awaited him. The British linesmen—Warrant Officers Oliphant and Greene—refused to officiate as they said it was below their dignity to be linesmen under a comparatively junior referee like Harnam Singh. The DFTS organizers tried but failed to persuade them. As per tradition the then Viceroy of India, Lord Linlithgow, arrived at the stadium to inaugurate and attend the final. When informed of the crisis, Linlithgow threatened to court-martial the two officers. Sensing trouble, the reluctant duo relented.

Musing on the incident, the late Harnam Singh said, 'This tension only added to my prematch nervousness. I felt better when Major Porter gave me a hot cup of cocoa laced with brandy.' The match went off smoothly and Harnam later recalled, 'I must say that the British linesmen, once they had agreed, did a competent job and gave me full cooperation.'

Whilst this furore was taking place, Harnam went to the Mohammedan Sporting dressing room to tell the players that the match may be slightly delayed. He saw senior players like goalkeeper Usman Jaan and defender Jumma Khan urging their teammates to be inspired by Mohun Bagan's 1911 IFA Shield victory, and not get overawed by the British team. All the morning newspapers, whilst previewing the final and in the match report a day later, also had several references to the historic 1911 final.

Mohammedan Sporting's centre-forward Hafiz Rashid had started his career in Ajmer and later went to Delhi to play for Youngmen. During his stay there, Hafiz became friendly with former international referee, the late K.G. Kakkar. Years later Kakkar would love to talk about Hafiz's dedication and how he trained twice a day. The training included running on the sand on the Yamuna river's banks, to improve strength and stamina; and sprints to develop sudden acceleration and hit the ball on the volley. He would also kick from a stationary position at a target on a wall to improve his shots. Rashid reportedly said that he was motivated by Bagan's 1911 IFA Shield triumph and trained this hard as he wanted to play in Kolkata. Rashid had never seen Abhilash Ghosh of Mohun Bagan play, but while growing up in Ajmer he had heard stories about his power and his winning goal in 1911. Ghosh thus became Rashid's childhood hero and he wanted to become a complete centre-forward like him. The glories of Bagan's win had spread by word of mouth all over India, with senior players and coaches using it as a reference point of excellence for aspiring young footballers.

The 1940 Durand final became the second-most historic triumph in the chronicles of Indian football. The famous black-and-white-shirted team, Mohammedan Sporting, ended the winning streak of British units in India's oldest football tournament. They beat the Royal Warwickshire Regiment 2-1 in the final, with goals by Hafiz Rashid and the slick inside-left Saboo. The formidable defence of Mohammedan Sporting repelled the speedy attacks and crosses from the flanks of Royal Warwickshire Regiment. Saboo—who scored the match-winner—and Rahim were crafty inside-forwards noted for their clever passing and dribbling skills. The combination amongst the forwards was almost telepathic and gave them a cutting edge. Above all, they were a very fit and cohesive team.

This victory by a team consisting of eleven Muslim players was a massive boost to the Muslim national movement and it also marked the start of Delhi's abiding love affair with this club.

When Mohammedan Sporting arrived by the Kalka Mail to challenge for the Durand Cup, Delhi was not the sprawling metropolis that it is now. Some expansion had taken place once it became the capital of India in 1911, but it was not yet an overcrowded city. The population was below 10 lakh and public transport barely existed.

Mohammedan Sporting's victories against British regimental teams in the Calcutta League and in the Rovers Cup had caught the imagination of the people of Delhi, who now wanted to witness such victories on their soil. From the first round onwards, people came in large numbers to witness Mohammedan Sporting in action. The late Gama Qureishi, former owner of Youngmen and a prosperous butcher and meat exporter, used to recall the excitement on the day of the matches. Conversations in many houses in Old Delhi would be about Mohammedan Sporting's prospects in this tournament. Gama Qureishi and his brothers were warned that if they did not behave themselves they would not be taken to see the matches. There was no regular bus service to the venue in those days, so the fans either walked, or went by cycle, or took tongas to the stadium.

Another old-timer and ardent Mohammedan Sporting fan, the late Mohammed Taki (who made toys for a living) was too young to be taken to the final. But he remembered the festive atmosphere after the historic victory in the final. He grew up on stories about this triumph and they remained embedded in his psyche.

Mohammed Taki witnessed every Durand final once the tournament restarted in Delhi, but his favourite team never repeated their 1940 success. They reached the final on three occasions but lost. Mohammedan Sporting next won the Durand Cup in September 2013, beating ONGC 2-1 in the final, but ironically their most ardent fan Mohammed Taki had died a few months before in April.

MOHAMMEDAN SPORTING TEAM IN 2-3-5 FORMATION, 1940 DURAND CUP FINAL, DELHI

Goalkeeper: Usman Jaan

Defenders: Jumma Khan and Bacchi Khan

Midfielders: Noor Mohammed (Sr), Noor Mohammed (Jr) and Abbas

Forwards: Rahim, Rafiq, Hafiz Rashid, Saboo and Mehmood

1956 Melbourne Olympics Quarter-Final: India vs Australia

It was a historic day on 1 December, when India destroyed the hosts Australia 4-2 to become the first Asian nation to reach the Olympics semi-final. Centre-forward Neville D'Souza scored a hat-trick: the first Asian to achieve this feat in the Olympics.

India's glorious 1956 Olympic journey happened almost by a miracle. The IOA initially refused to sponsor India's entry for the 1956 Melbourne Olympics. Under pressure, the IOA was forced to send India's entry but refused to pay the national football team's expenses, and demanded a deposit of Rs 33,000 at a certain date with the threat of cancelling the entry.

K. Ziauddin, secretary of the WIFA, used his contacts in Mumbai—including football-loving actors like Dilip Kumar—to collect the required sum. The AIFF was also forced to make its own transport arrangements for the airlift to Melbourne. AIFF president Pankaj Gupta arranged credit facilities from Messrs Mercury Travels by hypothecating his house in Kolkata. The Indian team left Mumbai by air on 18 November and played some practice games in Melbourne before their opening match on 1 December. India had got a walkover in the first-round match as Hungary withdrew in protest against the Soviet invasion of their country.

Except for P.K. Banerjee (originally from Bihar), skipper Samar Banerjee and Neville D'Souza, the remaining eight players were from either Hyderabad or Bengaluru. Of the eleven that beat the Aussies in Melbourne, only P.K. and Samar Banerjee are still alive. The baby of the squad, nineteen-year-old Tulsidas Balaram, was to start on the left flank, but on the morning of 1 December, coach S.A. Rahim felt it would be risky to expose an untried youngster in such a crucial Olympic match, and so opted for the experienced M. Kannayan. In the semi-finals, Balaram replaced Kannayan and from then on until he retired in 1963 due to illness, Balaram was always in India's playing eleven.

Centre-forward D'Souza, who played for Caltex Mumbai, created a personal record in his maiden appearance in Olympic football. On a hard and dry ground and against robust opponents, D'Souza—noted for his instinctive ability to drift into scoring positions—opened India's account in the ninth minute with a firm header. Skipper Samar Banerjee took a stiff shot that rebounded off the bar, and following up, D'Souza headed the ball in. Australia equalized eight minutes later when Morrow headed in a free kick. In the thirty-third minute P.K. sped down the right and whipped in a low cross, which an onrushing D'Souza tapped in. Morrow equalized for Australia again three minutes later.

However, the second-half belonged to India. Accelerating down the left, Kannayan cut in and was foiled by goalkeeper Lord. Then an onrushing D'Souza, following up, bundled the ball into the net to complete his hat-trick. The fourth goal was scored by vice-captain J. Kittu in the eightieth minute. The diminutive Kittu who played for East Bengal scored after a 25-yard solo dash and a curling shot from the edge of the box.

Neville D'Souza had been particularly motivated for this match due to an off-the-field incident. Before the matches began, he was travelling by local bus on a sightseeing trip in Melbourne. When some passengers learnt that he had come from India to participate in the Olympics, they thought he was a hockey player. They were astonished when he told them that he was a football player, as they believed that India did not play this game. They also laughed when he said that India could beat Australia in football. Ultimately, D'Souza had the last laugh at the Aussies.

The versatile D'Souza had an uncanny game sense and was always in the right position at the right time. With his deceptive speed, sudden acceleration and close dribbling, he resembled a Brazilian forward with his superb control. During his student days at St Xavier's College, Mumbai, he played both football and hockey, but later opted for football.

The selection of Mohun Bagan's Samar 'Badru' Banerjee as captain had also caused a controversy. Due to their 1911 IFA Shield win, Mohun Bagan had a nationalist appeal, so it was customary in the early post-Independence years for India's captain to be from this historic club. Thus in both the 1948 London Olympics and the 1952 Helsinki Olympics, the Indian captains were from Mohun Bagan: T. Ao and Sailen Manna. They were established internationals and nobody objected to their appointment.

However, the nimble-footed Samar Banerjee was a newcomer to the side, which included seasoned internationals, defender S.K. Azizuddin and left-half-back Noor Mohammed, both of whom had played in the previous Olympics. Due to Bagan's pressure and certain communal feelings within the AIFF, Azizuddin was denied the captaincy. A few disgruntled AIFF officials said that with Ziauddin as manager and Rahim as coach, if Azizuddin were chosen as captain, it would appear to be a team from Pakistan instead of India. Thus Samar Banerjee became a compromise captain for the side. Aziz declined the offer of vice-captaincy which was then given to Kittu.

India's performance in the 1956 Melbourne Olympics should be evaluated from the perspective of Asian football during that era. The other two Asian countries flopped in these Olympics. Japan lost in the first round 0-2 to Australia. Thailand was routed 1-9 by Great Britain. Compared to them, India performed creditably and coach Rahim fielded the team in an embryonic 4-2-4 formation with Samar Banerjee and later Nikhil Nandy playing as withdrawn forwards. Renowned soccer critics and officials like Willy Meisl and

Sir Stanley Rous lauded India's performance and said the display was a revelation. They congratulated Rahim for making India play modern football. The Duke of Edinburgh, who witnessed this match, also conveyed his message of appreciation.

INDIA'S TEAM IN 3-5-2 FORMATION, 1956 OLYMPICS QUARTER-FINAL, MELBOURNE

Goalkeeper: Peter Thangaraj (Hyderabad/Services)

Defenders: S.K. Azizuddin, S.A. Salaam and S.A. Latif (all Hyderabad)

Midfielders: M. Kempaiah (West Bengal), Noor Mohammed (Hyderabad)

Forwards: P.K. Banerjee (Bihar/Railways), Neville D'Souza (Bombay), Samar 'Badru' Banerjee (**Captain**), J. Kittu and Kannayan (all West Bengal)

1964 Asian Cup Final Rounds

India reached the final rounds of the 1964 Asian Cup in Tel Aviv fortuitously as all the teams in their qualifying group withdrew. The team was coached by Englishman Harry Wright, who had come to India to train coaches at the National Institute of Sports (NIS) Patiala. Wright lacked Rahim's instinctive understanding of the abilities and weaknesses of a player. He also changed India's playing style, reverting to the five-forward attack. Since the 1956 Melbourne Olympics Rahim had made India play with a withdrawn centre-forward. Wright was a hard taskmaster on the field, but discipline in the camp at Delhi was slack.

The brilliant T. Balaram had retired by then. There were some talented newcomers like defender Syed Nayeemuddin and forwards Inder Singh, Sukumar Samajpati and Appalaraju.

India's 1964 squad lacked the instinctive understanding of the 1962 squad but was still formidable and performed creditably.

Prior to their opening match against South Korea on 27 May, the Indian team was jolted by the news of the death of the country's first prime minister, Jawaharlal Nehru. The team manager K.K. Ganguly and the players were reluctant to play and requested a postponement. The organizers prevaricated, but coach Harry Wright also wanted the team to play, as immediately after the final round of matches India had to fly to Tehran to play in an Olympic qualifier against Iran. India finally played wearing black armbands and emerged triumphant beating South Korea 2-0, with goals by Inder Singh and Appalaraju. But two days later India lost 0-2 to hosts Israel.

On 2 June, in their final round-robin league match, India easily beat Hong Kong 3-1 to finish second overall with 4 points from 3 matches. Inder Singh, Samajpati and Chuni Goswami scored for India. It is India's best performance to date in the prestigious Asian Cup and their attacking football was much appreciated.

India finished runner-up to Israel.

INDIA'S FULL SQUAD IN 3-2-5 FORMATION, 1964 ASIAN CUP, TEL AVIV

Goalkeepers: Peter Thangaraj (West Bengal) and S.S. Narayan (Maharashtra)

Defenders: Syed Nayeemuddin (Andhra Pradesh), O. Chandrasekhar (Maharashtra), Jarnail Singh (Punjab), Arun Ghosh and Mritunjoy Banerjee (both West Bengal)

Midfielders: F.A. Franco (Maharashtra), Prasanta Sinha and Ram Bahadur (both West Bengal) and Kajal Mukherjee (Railways)

Forwards: P.K. Banerjee and Appalaraju (both Railways), Inder Singh (Punjab), Chuni Goswami, H.H. Hamid, Arumainayagam and Sukumar Samajpati (all West Bengal), Yousuf Khan (Andhra Pradesh) and B. Narayan (Maharashtra)

1973 IFA Shield and DCM Finals:
East Bengal vs North Korean Clubs

In the early 1970s, there was an aura of mystery about the North Koreans, who were regarded the best in Asia after their 1966 World Cup success. They had reached the quarter-finals after beating Italy 1-0 and led Portugal 3-0 before conceding 5 goals. In the 1973 IFA Shield final, Pyongyang City Club had five World Cup players in their ranks. P.K. Banerjee, East Bengal's coach that season, later said, 'Not much was known about their players, but it was only seven years after the North Koreans had shocked the world by entering the 1966 World Cup quarter-finals, so we all knew it would be a formidable side.'

The North Koreans always attacked with great speed and cohesion. So P.K. decided to use surprise tactics and jolt the opposition by launching a quick blitzkrieg. Winger Subhash Bhowmick, nicknamed 'bulldozer', was in peak form and almost unstoppable in this match. He scored East Bengal's second goal after dribbling past four defenders and finishing from an acute angle. He provided the assist for Akbar's opening goal and also scored the third goal in a delectable 3-1 win. The powerful North Korean club could not cope with East Bengal's clever passing game and variety of attack.

Next was East Bengal's performance against Dok Ro Gang in the 1973 DCM final, considered the finest display by an Indian club side in the history of Indian football. Dok Ro Gang had six players who had taken part in the 1966 World Cup and were considered a tougher side than Pyongyang City Club. In the quarter-final league they trounced the Inder Singh-led Leaders Club Jalandhar 7-0. Dok Ro Gang were so dominant that ace striker Inder Singh at his peak was rendered ineffective. At the half-time of that match, Dok Ro Gang led 6-0 and it seemed they would win by a double-figure margin. Some DCM tournament officials asked me to accompany them to the North Korean dressing room and be their spokesperson. I, along with a couple of the tournament officials, requested the North Koreans not to score many more goals and humiliate one of

India's best clubs. I also fabricated a tale that the owner of Leaders Club supported the socialist movement. Our persuasion prevailed and Dok Ro Gang played at a lesser tempo in the second-half and scored just one more goal.

By the display against Leaders Club it was evident that the speed and power of Dok Ro Gang's approach play was devastating and intimidating. East Bengal were the underdogs in the final. P.K. Banerjee used the two days' rest before the final to plan a strategy and motivate his players. Even the normally committed and fiery Mohammed Habib was resigned to defeat in the final. P.K.'s first task was to revive confidence and self-belief amongst his players. He resorted to a clever psychological ploy. On the roof of the Duke Hotel in Daryaganj where the team stayed, P.K. used to take theory classes with the team. In one of the sessions he brought glass bangles and gave them to Habib, Akbar and some other players, and told them that if they did not want to fight, they could wear bangles like sissies. The players were incensed and got charged up.

In the evening P.K. visited the houses of some Leaders club supporters, known as the L-Club or the Banarsi Das gang, and over drinks requested them for a match to switch their allegiances and support East Bengal for nationalistic reasons. Swayed by P.K.'s persuasion, the L-Club supporters decided to cheer for East Bengal in the final. This attention to detail made a big difference. The roar of the crowd that greeted East Bengal when they entered the field for the final was deafening. The crowd acted like the twelfth man and inspired East Bengal to play their best-ever football on Delhi soil.

In the final, East Bengal out-thought the North Koreans by using a flexible 4-5-1 system. Mohammed Akbar and Subhash Bhowmick alternated as the lone forward and East Bengal's packed midfield enabled them to dominate play. Sudhir Karmakar, Ashok Lal Banerjee, Shyamal Ghosh and Probir Mazumdar marshalled the defence and Arun Banerjee was agile and brilliant in goal.

This match and its replay both ended in a draw. Dok Ro Gang refused to play extra time and so East Bengal were declared winners.

East Bengal's victories against the North Korean clubs were historically very significant. The North Koreans were so impressed

with the club's display that their embassy in Delhi made recordings
of the Kolkata team's matches and sent them back to their capital,
Pyongyang, for careful study and analysis.

**EAST BENGAL TEAM IN 4-2-4 FORMATION, 1973 IFA
SHIELD FINAL, KOLKATA**

Goalkeeper: Arun Banerjee

Defenders: Sudhir Karmakar, Ashok Lal Banerjee, Shyamal Ghosh
and Probir Mazumdar

Midfielders: Gautam Sarkar and Samaresh 'Pintu' Chowdhury

Forwards: Subhash Bhowmick, Mohammed Akbar, Mohammed
Habib and Swapan Sengupta (captain)

Habib would frequently play in midfield, so East Bengal would
switch to the 4-3-3 system.

**EAST BENGAL TEAM IN 4-5-1 FORMATION, 1973 DCM
TROPHY FINAL, DELHI**

Goalkeeper: Arun Banerjee

Defenders: Sudhir Karmakar, Ashok Lal Banerjee, Shyamal Ghosh
and Probir Mazumdar

Midfielders: Swapan Sengupta, Gautam Sarkar, Mohammed
Habib, Mohammed Akbar and Samaresh 'Pintu' Chowdhury

Forwards: Subhash Bhowmick

Akbar would frequently link up with Bhowmick upfront.

2003 ASEAN Club Championship Final:
East Bengal vs BEC Tero Sasana

East Bengal scripted history on Saturday, 26 July 2003. They became the first Indian club to win any officially recognized international football tournament by demolishing Thailand's BEC Tero Sasana 3-1 in the ASEAN LG Cup final. It was heralded as a major triumph as BEC Tero were finalists in the inaugural (2002–03) AFC Champions League and had defeated East Bengal 1-0 in this tournament's first league match. The Gelora Senayan Stadium in Jakarta was again a happy hunting ground for Indian soccer. At this same venue, India had won the 1962 Jakarta Asian Games gold medal, beating South Korea 2-1 in the final.

East Bengal, as the NFL champions of India (2002–03), had been invited to play in the ASEAN Club Championships in Indonesia from 12–26 July. This tournament was played on a league-cum-knockout format. In the group stage, East Bengal lost their opening tie 0-1 to the Thailand League champions on 14 July. Two days later they bounced back in style. Playing exhilarating attacking football, with most of the moves initiated by Brazilian midfielder Douglas da Silva, East Bengal beat Armed Forces FC Philippines 6-0. Bhaichung Bhutia scored all 6 goals, the first Indian to achieve a double hat-trick in international football.

In the quarter-finals on 21 July, the NFL champions overcame Indonesia's top club Persita Tangerang 2-1 in a battle of attrition. Bhaichung put East Bengal ahead in the fifty-fourth minute but Ilham Jaya Kusuma equalized in the sixty-sixth minute. Winger Bijen Singh scored the match-winner in the seventy-seventh minute.

On 24 July, East Bengal took on Indonesia's league champions Petrokimia Putra in the semi-final. The local club had massive support and curtailed East Bengal's fluency. Petrokimia led by a twenty-third-minute goal by M. Jaezal Ichwan. At half-time, pep talks by both coach Subhash Bhowmick and Bhaichung revived East Bengal's morale. The team played more attacking football and Bhaichung equalized at the hour mark. The match ended 1-1 after extra time. In the resultant penalty shoot-out, the scores were tied 4-4.

There was mounting tension in the sudden-death session. East Bengal took their kicks first, so Petrokimia was always playing catch-up. Douglas, Irungbam Surkumar Singh and M. Suresh converted for East Bengal. Goalkeeper Sandip Nandy made a heroic save of the third penalty kick and East Bengal prevailed 7-6 in sudden-death penalties in the semi-final. The Kolkata club had some misfortune as defender Mahesh Gawli was ruled out of the final with a double yellow card, and Debjit Ghosh was injured.

The final was on 26 July. Bhowmick's tactical planning and Bhaichung's mental toughness gave East Bengal confidence. On the eve of the match, Bhaichung set about convincing his teammates that they could in fact win the final. Bhowmick's dilemma was whether to include striker Mike Okoro in the playing eleven in the final. Okoro had missed most of the matches due to sickness, but had by then fully recovered. Bhowmick felt his blistering pace could give East Bengal a cutting edge. He proved quite clairvoyant.

In the twenty-sixth minute of the final, Alvito D'Cunha gave a delectable through ball and Okoro surged past the BEC Tero Sasana defence and scored. Bhaichung played the game of his life in that final and scored what I consider one of his best goals. He shoulder-charged an opponent to gain possession, evaded a defender and placed past the advancing goalkeeper just three minutes into the second-half. At that stage East Bengal led 2-0 and an upset win was on the cards.

The Thailand team started dominating possession, with their superb passing and running of the ball. They reduced the margin in the fifty-eighth minute. Bhowmick was fretting in the dugout as his team was getting overrun in midfield. He replaced defender Deepak Mondal with Shlyo Malsawmtluanga to stem the midfield domination of his opponents. Still the Thailand team surged forward and it was only some heroic work by skipper Suley Musah, M. Suresh, Surkumar Singh and Douglas that helped East Bengal survive.

Bhowmick was contemplating further changes when Alvito scored a miraculous goal in the sixty-ninth minute. A predominantly

left-footed player, Alvito only used his right foot as a balancing
factor. He received a ball on his right foot at the top of the 18-yard
box. Realizing he had no time to relay the ball to his favourite left
foot, Alvito let fly with a crisp low right-footer which bulged the
net. This was the turning point of the match as East Bengal held
on for a memorable 3-1 win. Bhaichung Bhutia emerged as the top
scorer of the tournament with 9 goals and was declared man of the
match in the final. East Bengal received $50,000 for winning this
coveted championship.

On their way back after the final, East Bengal had a stopover in
Singapore. The players went shopping and sightseeing to relax after
their strenuous win. Bhaichung, a consummate team man despite
his superstar status, treated the entire squad to a sumptuous lunch
at a famous restaurant in the Little India market.

East Bengal's 2003 ASEAN Cup victory had a triple benefit
for football in India. It revived the mass hysteria for football
in Kolkata, increased the following of the game in India, and
enhanced our image in Asian football. Thousands of delirious
East Bengal fans thronged the Kolkata airport to greet their heroes
when the team landed clutching the ASEAN Cup. The squad was
felicitated and hailed in the local media. In the national media
too, there were programmes on several TV channels highlighting
this victory. The Internet had just taken off in India and this
victory was highlighted by East Bengal's fans via emails all over
the world.

Foreign clubs now sought Indian players. Bhaichung Bhutia
went briefly to Malaysian league champions Perek. Besides paying
Bhaichung, the Malaysian club also gave East Bengal $10,000 as
compensation. BEC Tero tried to procure the services of young
defender Surkumar Singh and striker Mike Okoro. Mahesh Gawli,
M. Suresh and goalkeeper Sandip Nandy were snapped up next
season by Mahindra United with lucrative salaries. Thus East
Bengal's 2003 ASEAN Cup triumph heralded the start of big
money transfers in Indian football in the twenty-first century.

Like professional clubs in Europe, East Bengal had emphasized
on pre-season training to improve fitness levels. Watching cricket

on TV, Bhowmick saw how fit the Indian cricket team was. He made inquiries and realized that it was due to the work of Andrew Leipus, their physiotherapist and trainer. Leipus recommended fitness expert Kevin Jackson to Bhowmick, who made the 2003 East Bengal squad the fittest-ever football team in India. They set a trend and soon other clubs including rivals Mohun Bagan invested in physical trainers and high-quality facilities. Every club in the I-League has since emulated East Bengal.

I had the privilege of doing the commentary of East Bengal's matches in the ASEAN Cup and the quality of football they displayed in the final has remained unsurpassed. For many of us it seemed that Indian football had at last got over the hump. But India had to wait another thirteen years before a club made a mark in international football.

EAST BENGAL TEAM IN 3-5-2 FORMATION, 2003 ASEAN CUP FINAL, INDONESIA

Goalkeeper: Sandip Nandy

Defenders: Suley Musah (Captain), Deepak Mondal, S. Malsawmtuluanga (59th min.) and M. Suresh

Midfielders: Surkumar Singh, Sasthi Duley, Douglas da Silva, Alvito D'Cunha and Bijen Singh

Forwards: Bhaichung Bhutia and Mike Okoro

Two Socially Significant Durand Matches: 1950 and 1965

1950 final, Hyderabad City Police vs Mohun Bagan

After ten years in the wilderness, the Durand Cup was revived in independent India in December 1950. It was historic in more ways than one. For the first time it was held in the capital and it was also the first time when clubs and institutional teams comprising only Indians (a total of twenty) took part.

In 1950 East Bengal had the formidable forward line of the Pancha Pandavas and had become the first Indian side to win the coveted IFA Shield trophy back to back. Earlier that year, Hyderabad City Police had won their first major trophy, the Rovers Cup, by beating Aryans Kolkata 1-0 in the final. Until then Hyderabad City Police had been relatively unknown outside south India. Their famous coach S.A. Rahim brought them on par with the best Indian clubs. Both these teams and the historic Mohun Bagan started this tournament as favourites for the title.

The final was played on 31 December at the Delhi Gate Stadium. Delhi witnessed Hyderabad City Police's cohesive, attacking football, using a mixture of cross-field and short passes. They trailed Mohun Bagan 0-2 till ten minutes before the final whistle but equalized in the last seconds. Rahim had been unable to get leave for this tournament and was listening to the live commentary on AIR. He fainted in sheer joy when he heard that Laiq had equalized and his team had staged a magnificent comeback. The first day of the final had ended in a dramatic 2-2 draw.

Coach Rahim was very far-sighted and gave more importance to fitness during an era when many Indian club teams valued skills over stamina. Hyderabad City Police's ability to play at the same pace in the closing stages of a match gave them a cutting edge in many crucial encounters. This also enabled them to recover quickly and do well in replayed matches. The myth about their invincibility in replays started after the 1950 Durand final. As Mohun Bagan were the more renowned team then, experts predicted that they would triumph due to better skills. But in the replay the next day, it was Hyderabad City Police which triumphed 1-0. For thirteen years after that, Hyderabad City Police never lost a replayed match in a major domestic tournament.

Some of the Hyderabad City Police players like defender Azizuddin, midfielder Noor Mohammed and outside-right Moin became legends after the 1950 Rovers Cup and Durand triumphs. During 1950–56 both Aziz and Noor were certainties in the Indian team. Moin had exceptional speed. He was a medal-winning sprinter who often clocked below 11 seconds in 100 metres, without regular practice. On the right flank he was greased lightning and difficult to contain. He had thighs like tree trunks and could take swerving corner kicks as well as deliver accurate crosses.

In the inaugural 1951 Asian Games, which India won, three of this squad played in the final at the National Stadium in front of a large and appreciative crowd. The sports-loving Prime Minister Pandit Jawaharlal Nehru was part of the audience.

The social ramifications of Hyderabad City Police's 1950 Durand Cup triumph were also immense. It was just after Partition and refugees from West Pakistan were still pouring into the capital. The population had almost doubled since 1940 when the previous Durand was held. Delhi was slowly limping back to normality. William Dalrymple, in his essay 'The Great Divide', wrote: 'Partition is central to modern identity in the Indian subcontinent, as the Holocaust is to identity amongst Jews, branded painfully on to the regional consciousness by memories of almost unimaginable violence.'[2]

As the demography of Delhi changed, Muslims were reduced to a minority. They restricted themselves to the crowded by-lanes of Old Delhi, as there was safety in numbers. The refugees started residing in some of the new colonies of west Delhi. Interaction between the new and old residents was limited, and tension prevailed. Mohammed Taki, the toymaker and football lover in Old Delhi, recalled that people would start drifting back to their homes before sunset. The football fan and famous meat exporter Gama Qureishi remembered being told to come home before dark, even if it meant neglecting business.

It was in such an environment that the Durand Cup took place. As Mohammedan Sporting, the champions of 1940, did not participate, the local Muslim population supported Hyderabad City Police who were making their debut in the capital of independent India. Their attacking style of play was much appreciated but even their ardent fans felt they would succumb to Mohun Bagan in the final, as the Kolkata club had more experience of big matches, and had India's captain and fine defender Sailen Manna in their team.

There was also a lurking suspicion amongst the Old Delhi supporters that in the replay, the referee and Durand organizers would favour Mohun Bagan as it had players mostly from the majority community. However, these apprehensions were belied as the match was supervised impartially, and people of all communities cheered the victory of the underdog. Mohammed Taki succinctly summed up the mood when years later he told me, '*Hamein pata laga ki insaniyat hai*' [We realized that humanity still exists.]'

HYDERABAD CITY POLICE TEAM IN 2-3-5 FORMATION, 1950 DURAND CUP FINAL

Goalkeeper: Eraiah

Defenders: Norbert Andrew Fruvall and S.K. Azizuddin

Midfielders: Anthony Patrick, Sheikh Jamal and Noor Mohammed

Forwards: S.K. Moinuddin, G.Y.S. Laiq, Doraiswamy, Sussey (Jr) and Mehmood Ali

---

1965 Durand semi-final, Mohun Bagan vs Andhra Police

The 1965 Durand Cup involved a lot of personal upheaval for me, as on the morning of a crucial Mohun Bagan quarter-final I had lost my grandmother (for details, see the introduction to 'The Major Tournaments'). It was this match, in particular, that affected my life and way of thinking hugely. In hindsight, I can say it jolted me out of the innocence of childhood into the harsh realities of life in India.

It was a match that was eagerly anticipated. Mighty Mohun Bagan had some of the best players in the land. Apart from the Calcutta League victory, they had not won a single trophy in knockout tournaments that year. But they were on the threshold of making history by achieving a hat-trick of Durand victories.

Several players of Andhra Police (known as Hyderabad City Police before 1960) had played in the 1963 Durand final and lost 0-2 in the replay to Mohun Bagan. They were aching to get even. Legendary coach Rahim, who had nurtured many of the senior players, had expired unexpectedly in 1963. Andhra Police had won the DCM Trophy some months ago so they were also keen to win the 'Delhi double' in memory of their beloved coach. A lot of pride was at stake for both teams.

The match took place in the first week of January 1966 and Delhi was agog with excitement. From noon onwards, football fans streamed into the Delhi Gate Stadium. Outside, tickets worth Rs 5 cost Rs 25, and tickets worth Rs 10 went for Rs 50. Both sets of fans automatically occupied their own half of the stadium. It was a tense match that ended in a goalless draw. The replay was the next day. Andhra Police forged ahead in the first-half and defended well. It seemed the holders would be beaten.

The match changed dramatically in the last quarter. Chuni Goswami had the ball in the inside-right position and dribbled across the face of the Andhra Police goal. Talented young left-back Nayeem clung to him like a leech and denied him an opportunity to shoot goalwards or enter the 18-yard box. Taller and stronger, Nayeem shoulder-charged Chuni off the ball. The wily Chuni, realizing he had lost this opportunity, took a dive and stumbled across Nayeem's foot into the box. Referee B.S. Chauhan of Delhi promptly awarded a penalty kick.

The Andhra Police supporters were incensed at Chuni's 'dive'. They jeered at the decision, abused the referee, and chucked objects from bottles to small stones on to the ground. The Military Police, always in attendance at the Durand Cup, cleared the ground of debris and restored order. Mohun Bagan's Jarnail Singh, who that year had been appointed as captain of the Asian All-Stars team, kept his cool and converted the penalty kick with aplomb.

Years later both Chuni and Nayeem became great friends of mine and we often discussed this incident. Both bore each other no malice and I too realized that it was an act of gamesmanship. More famous players have done worse on a football field. However, on that day I, a callow teenager, believed that Chuni Goswami had cheated and the referee had been unfair.

As the match restarted Mohammed Yusuf lost his composure and attacked Chuni with a raised foot in the groin region. Referee Chauhan sent him off the field for unprovoked violence and ungentlemanly conduct. Andhra Police had to play with ten men. Mohun Bagan, realizing they enjoyed numerical advantage, went for the kill. Chuni gave a defence-splitting through-pass to outside-left Arumainayagam, who ran in and scored from close. Bagan won 2-1 and were through to the final, to be played after two days. They duly won the final 2-0 against Punjab Police and achieved their cherished dream of becoming the first Indian team to lift the famous Durand Cup for three successive years.

However, after the semi-final there was utter chaos. I witnessed my first full-scale riot. The Andhra Police supporters chanted slogans against the Durand organizers and accused them of bias. When police resorted to a lathi charge, mayhem took place. The incensed supporters attacked the Durand office with stones and fights broke out. The police finally fired tear-gas shells and everybody retreated.

The events after the match were an eye-opener for me. Since I had started attending the two Delhi tournaments, I had seen fans from all communities gathering in groups outside the stadium to discuss the match. Football was a great leveller, where class and religious differences dissolved. It was considered natural that Bengalis would support either East Bengal or Mohun Bagan, while Muslims would support either Mohammedan Sporting or Andhra Police. There would be good-natured banter between both groups of supporters but no malice. I used to cherish these discussions and long walks as I learnt a lot of oral history about Indian football from older fans.

However, on that day I witnessed bitterness and bigotry from both sides. The Muslims, huddled on one side, shouted themselves hoarse that they were victims of injustice. The Bengali Hindus, in groups on another side, smirked about the win and considered it a victory of brains over brawn. They branded the Muslim supporters as hooligans who had been needlessly violent. It was just months after the India–Pakistan War in August–September 1965 and feelings were hardened.

I was aghast and did not know what to do, which group to join for the post-match discussion. Both groups were indulging in communal stereotypes about the other community. A friend from the Bengali group told me not to join the 'other lot as they were traitors and the enemy'. The Andhra Police supporters talked about conspiracy theories, and decades of animosity resurfaced between the two major communities of India.

In my naivety I believed these feelings would gradually disappear and turn to banter about the referee's decision. It never happened. As a neutral fan I felt the penalty decision was harsh but also that speedy winger Yusuf's show of petulance was unwarranted and that he had let his team down.

But there was nobody to talk to. The bonhomie of football fans was gone. Friends ignored each other. I went home alone that night plunged in thought. Suddenly all the values of sports that had been drilled into me at school, of playing in the spirit of the game, to accept defeat sportingly and appreciate the winner, seemed shallow.

At the dinner table that night, I raised several uncomfortable questions about Hindu–Muslim relationships, the existence of divine providence (if a God existed then why did blatantly wrong decisions take place on a football field), and, above all, why a certain community were being called the enemy. Like many middle-class people, my parents were hesitant to directly answer such queries, and told me to sleep and forget what I saw. But I could not forget the incident easily and that night I went to sleep without saying my prayers. It started my journey towards being an agnostic.

MOHUN BAGAN TEAM IN 3-2-5 FORMATION, 1965 DURAND CUP SEMI-FINAL

Goalkeeper: Pradyut Burman

Defenders: B. Debnath, Jarnail Singh (Captain), T.A. Rahman

Midfielders: Nitya Ghosh, Bimal Chakravarty

Forwards: Dipu Das, Amal Chakravarty, Ashok Chatterjee, Chuni Goswami, Arumainayagam

10

The Great Rivalry

'East Bengal vs Mohun Bagan

The famous rivalry between these two clubs started when they first met in a Calcutta League match on 25 May 1925. Particularly after Partition, when Mohammedan Sporting's traditional support base and catchment area were both diminished, these two came to dominate the Kolkata football scene. There have been periods when clubs from other parts of the country like Hyderabad and Punjab gained prominence, but these two clubs have maintained their superior position. The adulation of the fanatical fans and lucrative monetary rewards by both Mohun Bagan and East Bengal have secured Kolkata's place as the nerve centre of Indian football.

This has seen a slight change in the new millennium, with the rise of clubs in Goa, Bengaluru and the North-east, and the start of the ISL. Debashis Majumder, in his well-researched book *The History of the Football Clubs in Calcutta*, provides some very interesting details of their long-running rivalry during 1947–85. Due to the constraints of space, I offer here a few select—but fascinating—stories about these titans of Indian football.

Until recently, it was widely believed that whenever East Bengal first met Mohun Bagan in any major domestic tournament in India, they would be the more motivated side and emerge victorious. East Bengal met their arch-rivals in the IFA Shield for the first time in the 1944 semi-final. They expectedly won 1-0, with V. Rao scoring the winning goal. After their 1943 victory, they were favoured to win the title a second time, but lost 0-1 to EB Railways in the final.

The two teams met for the first time in Delhi in the 1957 Durand Cup semi-finals, thirty-seven years after East Bengal was formed. The first match ended in a goalless draw. In the replay on 28 December 1957, Mohun Bagan led 2-1 at half-time with goals by inside-left Chuni Goswami and striker Krishna Chandra 'Kesto' Pal. At half-time in the dressing room, East Bengal officials, led by their secretary J.C. Guha, begged, pleaded and cajoled the players to raise their game as it would be an insult to lose to their arch-rivals in their first meeting in India's oldest football tournament.

T. Balaram, in his first year with East Bengal, was amazed at the sheer passion of the club officials. He said officials touched his feet and, on bended knees, requested the players to make a comeback so that the pride of the Bangal (East Bengalis) all over India was not hurt. Balaram later told me that before the players left the dressing room, a small prayer was held and the players were blessed. Whatever the reasons, East Bengal's star-studded forward line became highly motivated. They scored twice in the thirty-five-minute second-half, with goals by Balasubramaniam and Moosa, to emerge victorious 3-2.

They used up so much emotional energy in this comeback win that they were flat in the final against Hyderabad City Police two days later. Despite leading by a goal by outside-right Ibrahim, East Bengal lost 1-2 in the final. Balaram later said the officials were sad to lose the final but were overall satisfied as they had overcome arch-rivals Mohun Bagan in their first-ever meeting in Delhi. In fact, for the next fifty years, this jinx of losing the final of a tournament after beating Bagan continued.

In the Rovers Cup, the arch-rivals first met at the Cooperage Stadium, Mumbai, on 29 November 1960 in the semi-finals. East Bengal beat Mohun Bagan 2-1 with goals by defender Arun Ghosh and inside-right B. Narayan. However, the inevitable happened— East Bengal lost 1-2 to Andhra Police in the replayed Rovers Cup final. On the first day, the match had ended in a thrilling 2-2 draw.

Mohun Bagan were able to beat East Bengal in their first meeting in a major domestic tournament only in 1993. In the 2nd Scissors Cup tournament on 31 August 1993, Mohun Bagan beat

East Bengal 2-1 in the final with goals by Vijayan and midfielder Christopher (penalty). Sanjay Majhi reduced the margin for East Bengal in the seventy-seventh minute.

East Bengal too overcame their hoodoo by winning the 2007 Federation Cup tournament for the fifth time—their first since 1996—after beating Bagan 3-2 in the semi-final.[1]

In India, throughout the twentieth century, there has been greater interest in club football, rather than the national team. This could be due to the fact that even when India played abroad in competitions like the Olympics (1948, 1952, 1956 and 1960) or the Asian Games, there was no television coverage and commentary on AIR and media reports were invariably agency stories, which were quite elementary. For instance, there was no Indian reporter when India narrowly lost 1-2 to mighty Hungary on the outskirts of Rome in the 1960 Olympics. Many experts consider this India's finest match against a European side. Towards the end of the match the Hungarians were body-checking the free-flowing Indian attacks spearheaded by T. Balaram, Chuni Goswami and P.K. Banerjee.

In contrast, AIR regularly gave running commentaries of the important IFA Shield and Calcutta League matches. From the 1960s onwards AIR would broadcast all the league matches in Bengali and English. People would remain glued to their transistor sets, much as fans did for cricket until some years ago (now fans get updates on their mobile phones). During the 1970s, the print media also played a major role in turning the players of Kolkata's big three clubs—Mohammedan Sporting had started hiring non-Muslim players in the 1950s and regained some of their dominance—into demigods. Special columns like 'Math Maidan' were introduced in popular newspapers like *Anandabazar Patrika*. All the leading Bengali newspapers had separate pages for local football. Important sports magazines like *Khelar Kagaj* also popularized the sport.

Before wide coverage of international football on television and print media began, it was the Kolkata derby that was the most important match for football lovers in this city. Kolkata would be split into two distinct camps. After the result of this match, one half of Kolkata would be jubilant and celebrate whilst the other half would be plunged into sadness.

The fans also had different dietary preferences. Mohun Bagan fans would celebrate their victory by eating chingri (prawns), while East Bengal fans ate the hilsa river-fish when their team triumphed over their arch-rivals. The fans of the losing team never bought their favoured fish after a derby match, which sometimes left fish sellers—within and outside Kolkata—in a quandary. In the early 1960s in Delhi, the wily fishmonger Goreram of Lodhi Road—a Bengali hub (as Chittaranjan Park did not yet exist)— thrived on Mohun Bagan's successes in the Durand Cup. Bagan won the Durand three years in a row (1963–65) and on the day of the final Goreram would stock up his shop with prawns. He would then carefully listen to the live commentary on AIR. As it became evident that Bagan was winning, he would promptly raise the price of prawns.

When the 1963 Durand final between Mohun Bagan and Andhra Police ended in a goalless draw, Goreram was worried about his excess stock. However, in the replay held the next day, Mohun Bagan prevailed 2-0 (Chuni Goswami scored a brace) and Goreram made a killing selling prawns at inflated prices. He knew that delirious supporters would not refuse to pay extra money. To encourage the Bagan supporters who thronged his shop he would say, 'Aasche bacchor abar hobe [It will happen again next year].'2

The passion of fans sometimes bordered on mania. One such incident occurred after Mohun Bagan's 0-5 loss to rivals East Bengal in the IFA Shield final on 30 September 1975. An ardent Bagan supporter called Umakanta Paloudhi could not face the humiliation of his favourite club losing by the biggest margin ever. He took the extreme step and committed suicide. In his suicide note he wrote that in his next life he wanted to be a good footballer and avenge Mohun Bagan's 0-5 loss. An East Bengal fan of the 1970s known as Baghada never missed a single match of his favourite team in Kolkata. His love for his club was so intense that he came to the ground to cheer for them even on the day of his son's death. Such fierce loyalty is rarely found anywhere else in the world. For some ardent fans in Kolkata, the love for their club is akin to religious fervour.[3]

Club identification was used for political ends in independent India as well, just as the Muslim nationalist movement had used the successes of Mohammedan Sporting in the 1930s and 1940s. Reportedly, in the early 1970s the former chief minister of Bengal, Siddhartha Shankar Ray, wrote to the then prime minister Indira Gandhi requesting that the Kolkata-based players be spared from international duty.[4] The Calcutta League was then held from June to August and the Merdeka Tournament in Malaysia, in which India regularly participated, in July–August.

During this period, insecurity, corruption and unemployment had led to the Naxalbari movement gaining momentum. Meanwhile, the fan base of East Bengal had increased due to the influx of refugees from Bangladesh after the 1971 war. The children of the 1947 refugees had now grown up and they too supported this club. A number of these fans were attracted by the ideology of the Naxal movement because of the terrible hardships they faced. However, as former international winger and now erudite columnist Surajit Sengupta has said, even during the years of turmoil, people's enthusiasm for football and affection for their clubs did not decline.[5]

As a diversionary tactic, Ray wanted the Kolkata players to participate in the local league. He intended to wean away revolutionary students from their extreme-left politics. East Bengal were at their peak during 1970–75, and their fanatical supporters hero-worshipped the star players. Thus the Indian teams for the 1973 and 1976 Merdeka Tournaments were deprived of several key players, but the ploy was successful as large crowds came to witness their heroes in the Kolkata league. This set a trend in Kolkata football—club before country—which led to a major controversy before the 1982 Asian Games.[6]

As desire, passion and money increased in Kolkata football, the transfer season would turn into a fortnight of intrigue and suspense. There were many shady tales, lots of rumours and incidents of subterfuge. Star players were often smuggled to safe hideouts, secluded bungalows, or resorts outside Kolkata, and guarded by henchmen. In some cases, temptations were used. One such case during a mid-1980s season involved the brilliant midfielder Sudip Chatterjee, who played for Mohun Bagan. He wanted to marry a girl whose family were staunch East Bengal supporters. East Bengal's officials persuaded him to join their club, saying they would coax the girl's family to agree to the marriage. Once Sudip joined East Bengal, the girl's father gave his assent to the marriage and it all ended happily for them.[7]

In the late 1990s, the rivalry between the coaches P.K. Banerjee and Amal Dutta was India's equivalent of the bitter contest between Sir Alex Ferguson (Manchester United) and Arsène Wenger (Arsenal). Both used the local media to spark off impassioned debates before a derby match, which added to the excitement and whetted the interest of Kolkata fans.

P.K. Banerjee's finest act of motivation came prior to the 1997 KBL Federation Cup semi-final. P.K. was coaching East Bengal and Amal Dutta was in charge of Bagan, and the match was being billed as the clash of the coaching titans. Dutta was making Bagan play exciting, attacking football, using the diamond system in midfield. Bagan had crushed all opposition on the way to the final, including Goa League champions Churchill Brothers 6-0 in the quarter-finals. They were favourites to win the match. The regional newspapers and magazines had created a lot of hype and built up great expectations with their detailed reports, and Kolkata was in a frenzy. As a tactical ploy, Amal Dutta in his columns and interviews with the local newspapers had been scornful of East Bengal's main striker and star player Bhaichung Bhutia. Dutta had even suggested that Bhaichung was overrated and just a flashy youngster who would not trouble his experienced team.

On the eve of the final, the astute P.K. Banerjee invited Bhaichung to dinner and gave him a detailed account of all the scorn being heaped on him in the vernacular Bengali media by the rival coach. This made Bhaichung livid and he was all charged up for the match. P.K. Banerjee's subtle psychological tactic worked wonders. A highly motivated Bhaichung guided East Bengal to a memorable 4-1 victory before an Asian record crowd of 1,31,000 at the Salt Lake Stadium, Kolkata, on 13 July 1997.[8] He even scored a hat-trick—the first-ever in the derby match, and seventy-two years after it had first been held.

This match was the turning point for the revival of the craze for the Kolkata clubs. Briefly, in the late 1980s and early 1990s, it had seemed to decline due to various factors, including new exposure to international football and some very violent episodes in stadiums, particularly the terrible one on 16 August 1980 at Eden Gardens.[9] It has now taken on a new dimension, with supporters travelling with the team to away matches to cheer them on.

The most unique person amongst this new generation of fans is Bapi Majhi, a tea-stall owner in Paikpara, north Kolkata.[10] For the last thirty years, he has been following his favourite team Mohun Bagan wherever they play—in Mumbai, Goa, Bengaluru, Shillong or Delhi—wearing their famous maroon and green colours. A commerce graduate, he refused to take up a full-time job as it would tie him down. Instead he became a self-employed tea-stall owner who can shut up shop and travel whenever he wishes to. Such is his dedication that when short of money in 2013, he and his wife Sipra mortgaged the few ornaments they had so that he could travel to Kochi to watch Bagan play. Some years before that he had sold some of his property.

His love for the club started when he was ten years old. Despite having fever, he was taken by his father to see an important match. The atmosphere was gripping; the supporters were mouthing expletives at any missed pass by their favourite players, and puffing furiously on their bidis. That match turned him into a lifelong Bagan fan. His recent moments of joy were when Bagan won the 8th I-League in 2014–15 and the Federation Cup in 2016.

The passion for the Kolkata derby has survived despite the incessant telecast of quality European and English football matches on satellite TV. The attachment for these two clubs has grown in the twenty-first century. In 2003, when East Bengal returned after winning the ASEAN trophy, large crowds thronged the airport to get a glimpse of their heroes. In 2015, there were spontaneous celebrations for Mohun Bagan in Kolkata when it won the I-League trophy. And after Bagan's Federation Cup victory, over 30,000 fans gathered at the airport in May 2016, despite the torrential downpour.

The Kolkata derby match is amongst the highest-watched derbies in the world. Other Asian countries have tried (and failed until now) to create such an intense rivalry between clubs, which attracts massive crowds and generates public frenzy, ticket sales, sponsorship and passionate discussions in the local media. In the changing scenario of Indian football, it would be nothing short of a catastrophe if these two clubs and therefore this derby match declines.[11] As this chapter shows, attachment to a football club comes after years; it is not an overnight crush. Sanjoy Sen, Mohun Bagan's coach (2014–present) rightly said that in Kolkata nobody is neutral when it comes to these two clubs.

Indian soccer's Herculean task at present is to get some of the country's historical clubs into the mainstream, after making them thoroughly professional. Indian football with a downgraded or non-existent East Bengal and Mohun Bagan would be like Agra without the Taj Mahal.

PART III

THE HALL OF FAME

11

Forwards

Sheoo Mewalal

Legendary striker Sheoo Mewalal will have a permanent place in the annals of Indian football history for two reasons. He scored the winning goal in the 1951 Asian Games final, with an acrobatic volley against formidable Iran. However, he nearly missed the final on 10 March at the National Stadium, Delhi. A day before the final he received a telegram about a family bereavement and wanted to rush back to Kolkata. When coach S.A. Rahim's persuasion did not work, Prime Minister Jawaharlal Nehru intervened and Mewalal agreed. The sports-loving Nehru, a fan of Mewalal's, ensured that an IAF plane was on the tarmac at the Safdarjung Airport waiting to take off. Mewalal was whisked away immediately after the medal ceremony and joined his bereaved family the same evening. In 1952, he scored the first hat-trick by an Indian player in the 1st Quadrangular Tournament in Colombo. India defeated Burma 4-0.

Sheoo Mewalal was born on 1 July 1926, the son of a migrant worker from Bihar. He had no formal education and started playing football at age seven, inspired by soldiers at Fort William. Sergeant Barnett became his first football coach and helped him join the Morning Star club as an outside-right. His talent was spotted by J.C. Guha of East Bengal, but Mewalal's dream was to play for the club he had supported as a child, Mohun

Bagan. In the 1940s, value systems were very different and Guha informed Mohun Bagan's coach, B.D. Chatterjee, of Mewalal's wish. He played for his dream club for one season alone before Independence. As remuneration in Kolkata football was limited in those days, in 1947 Mewalal joined Eastern Bengal Railways (EBR) and stayed there for most of his career.

He played for India in the 1948 London Olympics. He was a prolific scorer in some of the exhibition matches India played and finished as the top scorer on that tour with 18 goals. India's most notable win was against Ajax FC of Amsterdam 5-1. Mewalal scored twice in that match.

In the 1951 Asian Games he scored a goal in all 3 matches that India won—3-0 vs Indonesia, 3-0 vs Afghanistan and 1-0 in the final vs Iran—finishing as top scorer. His performance was remarkable for sheer speed and agility, as he played barefooted against all the opponents in the Asian Games, who wore boots.

Mewalal had an uncanny ability to drift away from his marker and position himself in a free zone, and take prompt shots and volley with both feet. He had a goal poacher's instinct. Despite not playing for the top clubs he was top scorer in the Calcutta League four times. For EBR he was top scorer in 1949 (32 goals), 1951 (18 goals), 1954 (29 goals), and later for BNR in 1958 with 16 goals.

No exact statistics have been maintained but Mewalal was a goalscoring machine. It is believed that he scored 1032 goals with 32 hat-trick in official and exhibition matches—a rare feat.

Mewalal died on 27 December 2008, not having received any recognition in India, and as a forgotten figure.

Chuni Goswami

Subimal 'Chuni' Goswami was the first glamour boy of Indian football. East Bengal's general secretary J.C. Guha was so impressed by him that he even offered to buy him the new Fiat car that had hit the market in the 1960s. But Goswami refused and stayed with his first love Mohun Bagan. This added to his charisma and mystique as he remained a one-club man throughout his career. His entertaining football delighted fans from all over India, who gathered to applaud and felicitate him wherever he played. Always immaculately dressed, if Goswami had played in the present era, he would have been a marketeer's delight and endorsed numerous products.

What made Goswami special? His superb speed with the ball, excellent trapping and shrewd passing had made him a household name, but it was his dazzling dribbling and body swerves that ultimately set him apart from the other greats of his era. His idol was Ahmed Khan of East Bengal, also renowned for his mesmeric ball skills. Former East Bengal coach Subhash Bhowmick maintains that Chuni could dribble as well as Ronaldinho, Robinho or any of the great Brazilians.

Born on 15 January 1938, and named Subimal, Goswami joined the Mohun Bagan junior team at age nine. He first played for the senior side in 1954. It was a lucky debut. Mohun Bagan were missing their two Olympian inside-forwards, Runu Guha Thakurta and Abdus Sattar. It was still thought that Goswami may not get his chance. But Goswami, on the advice of his mentor and coach Balaidas Chatterjee, wore the club jersey as soon as he entered the dressing room. Mohun Bagan had a superstition that once a player wore the club jersey he could not be dropped. Interestingly, Goswami started playing as inside-left only with this match, and till he retired he was considered the best inside-left inside-forward in India, and ranked amongst the best in Asia.

He first played for West Bengal in the Santosh Trophy in 1955. In the final he provided an astute through-pass to enable dashing winger P.K. Banerjee to score the winning goal against Mysore. Goswami was not selected for the 1956 Olympics, but by 1958, his prowess could not be ignored. He played in the Tokyo Asian Games and from then on became a regular for the Indian team. As captain of the Indian side, his greatest triumph was winning the gold medal in the 1962 Asian Games. He also led the side that finished runners-up in the 1964 Asian Cup and the Merdeka Tournament.

In his prime, Goswami received an invitation to train with Tottenham Hotspur. Back then, Tottenham, managed by the legendary Bill Nicholson, were the biggest club in London. In 1960–61, they won the first league-and-cup double of the twentieth century, and soon after became the first British side to lift a European trophy, trouncing Atlético Madrid 5-1 in the European Cup Winners Cup final.

Goswami, who also played Ranji Trophy cricket for West Bengal, was apparently unaware of just how good the 'Spurs' were. He has admitted in interviews that he had little or no information about English football, and that he never took the offer seriously.

In domestic championships, his greatest triumphs were in the Durand Cup. In 1963 Mohun Bagan beat Andhra Police for the first time in a Durand final. In 1965, as the second President of India, Sarvepalli Radhakrishnan, walked into the Delhi Gate Stadium to watch the Durand final between Mohun Bagan and Punjab Police, he spotted Chuni Goswami warming up with his teammates. The philosopher President smiled and said, 'So I see Chuni again. You seem to have become a permanent feature of the final.'

Chuni Goswami always narrated this anecdote with a note of pride in his voice. Radhakrishnan's words were quite accurate, as 1965 was Mohun Bagan's third Durand final in a row. They became the first team in independent India to bag this coveted trophy for three successive years, and on all three occasions Goswami was the captain.

In his fifteen years for the Mariners (a nickname for Mohun Bagan given by the fans), Goswami led the team five times and was part of their six Durand victories and ten Calcutta League wins.

Goswami was an all-round sportsman and played cricket for both West Bengal and East Zone in the Ranji Trophy and Duleep Trophy. He captained West Bengal in the 1972 Ranji Trophy final. In a first-class match for the combined East and Central Zone team in 1966–67, he took 8 wickets in both innings against the Gary Sobers-led touring West Indies team—the only match the mighty West Indies lost on the tour. The P.K. Banerjee, Chuni Goswami and T. Balaram trio is still considered the best-ever in

Indian football as the three had telepathic understanding, dazzling ball skills and great finish.

T. Balaraman

The legendary Tulsidas Balaraman is arguably the greatest Indian forward of all time, and at his peak, from 1956–62, was considered one of Asia's finest. Popularly known as Balaram, he was born on 4 October 1937 in a small village in Secunderabad and learnt football in nearby playfields. He went against his father's wishes to constantly play the game in his adolescence. Balaram was from a humble background, and recalled that even after intensive practice there were days when he went to sleep hungry. It is believed that if he had had a more nutritious diet in his formative years and a longer career, he would have been spoken of in the same breath as Park Ji-sung, Shinji Kagawa, Hidetoshi Nakata and other Asian greats.

Like many Indian sportspersons, he was discovered by accident. Legendary coach S.A. Rahim saw Balaram play in a local tournament and realized he had immense potential. He invited the precocious eighteen-year-old to attend trials for the Santosh Trophy. Balaram was hesitant as he lacked the funds to travel daily from Secunderabad to Hyderabad. Rahim sensed his difficulty, and gave him the sum of one rupee and twenty-five paise daily to hire a bicycle and attend the trials. That is how an Indian football legend was born.

Figures do not do justice to Balaram's genius and charisma. Overall, he was capped just 26 times and scored 8 goals for India. Yet he is counted amongst the all-time greats because of his ability on the field. Balaram's ball control and pace were exceptional, distribution immaculate, and his capacity for unexpected invention phenomenal. Above all, he had the knack of scoring crucial goals. He first played for India on 4 December 1956 in the Melbourne Olympics semi-final against Yugoslavia, and for the next six years was always first choice in any Indian team.

Balaram's finest hour in international matches was against Hungary in the 1960 Rome Olympics. The Hungarian side was

248 Barefoot to Boots

almost the same team that went on to beat England—with legends like Bobby Moore, Bobby Charlton and Jimmy Greaves—at the 1962 Chile World Cup. Yet in 1960, Balaram tormented the Hungarian defence with his incredible speed and ball control. Following a Chuni Goswami pass, he scored the memorable reducer for India with a flick. In the closing minutes of the match, the desperate Hungarians were tugging at his shirt or body, checking him to break his flow.

He excelled in both the 1958 and 1962 Asian Games, and in the 1959 Merdeka Tournament when India finished unbeaten runners-up. In 1962, he scored in India's victories against both Thailand and Japan; and in the final, he combined with Chuni Goswami and P.K. Banerjee, who scored the first goal against South Korea. In 1958, he shone in the quarter-final match with Hong Kong which went to extra time, with the score line 2-2. Balaram was at his brilliant best, assisting 2 goals and scoring once as India ran out 5-2 victors. He played on with a bandage despite getting injured.

Chuni Goswami had more flair in his play but Balaram had more variety and versatility, as he could play anywhere on the forward line. In the 1956 Santosh Trophy final against Bombay, Balaram first played as outside-left and later in the replay as inside-right. Within the first quarter of the match, Hyderabad launched a blitzkrieg and, with Balaram scoring twice, closed the match 4-1. Those watching at Ernakulam knew a genius had arrived.

Balaram started his club career with City College Old Boys, Hyderabad in 1955 and shifted to East Bengal in 1957. For five years he was like a demigod for the club's legions of supporters. As a token of gratitude, some fans would take turns to accompany him when he went for the national camps, and wash his clothes and run his daily errands.

He won numerous trophies with East Bengal and scored 104 goals for the club. In 1959, he was the highest scorer in the country with 39 goals. In 1961 he won the Golden Boot of the Calcutta League with 23 goals. As captain in 1961, he helped East Bengal win the league by scoring an incredible goal. Balaram outfoxed Mohun Bagan's tenacious stopper-back Jarnail Singh, slid into the penalty box from the left, and scored with the outstep of his right boot from an almost zero-degree angle.

He played during an era when there was little money in football, and so in 1963 he switched to BNR for financial security. In two years, he scored 13 goals for BNR and won two titles, before retiring on medical advice. Later, he became coach of the Kolkata mayor's team; internationals Sangram Mukherjee, Mehtab Hossain and Chandan Das were initially trained by him.

Balaram's genius is acknowledged by many greats of football. Chuni Goswami once said, 'Balaram's shooting and ball control was art of the very highest class.' Arun Ghosh described Balaram as a man who had two eyes on the back of his head, who was at the heart of any team, directing every attacking move. Jarnail Singh regarded Balaram as his toughest opponent because he was the only forward who remained undeterred by his hard tackles.

Renowned coach Subhash Bhowmick has often said that Balaram was like Thierry Henry, with his ability to fall back, retrieve the ball and attack at full speed. P.K. Banerjee once said, 'Balaram's improvisation, industriousness and ability to hit curling shots were second to none.'

If Balaram had played in the present day, he would have undoubtedly been a millionaire. However, perhaps more than the lack of money, Balaram remains deeply hurt at being sidelined by football authorities and not being duly recognized. Old and bitter, he stays alone in a small flat in Uttarpara, Kolkata, has never owned a vehicle, and his only compensation is the continued adulation of fans.

Inder Singh

It was the exploits of Inder Singh that helped Punjab football take off. Within the span of a decade they became a force in Indian football. Generations of young Punjabi boys in the Mahilpur and Phagwara region were inspired by Inder Singh's success playing within the home state.

Inder Singh was born on 23 December 1942 in Phagwara, and was interested in football from his schooldays. He would practise for hours after school, even when it became dark. His goalscoring prowess was evident at a young age when he finished as the top scorer at the All-India School Games in 1960–61. Impressed with his talent, Leaders Club Jalandhar signed him on as a guest player. He soon came into the limelight as a promising, tearaway striker.

The 1962 DCM Trophy launched Inder's international career. He was spotted by the Englishman Harry Wright, who was attempting to rebuild the Indian team for the 1964 tournaments. Inder impressed the English coach with his speed, quick turning ability and an ice-cool finish. Inder never got rattled by hard-tackling defenders and scored goals with deft placements and first-time angled shots. Wright felt he could use him as a suitable target man or as a speedy winger in the national team.

Inder Singh scored in his debut in the 1964 Asian Cup, and was joint top scorer for the tournament's final rounds, having scored 2 goals in 3 matches. He was selected as best outside-right of the tournament. By the mid-1960s Inder Singh became a regular fixture in the national team. This was a remarkable feat in an era when football was well established only in West Bengal, Hyderabad, Karnataka, Mumbai or institutional sides.

Inder participated in the 1966 Asian Games in Bangkok, where he scored in the 2-1 win over Malaysia in the group stage. He continued to represent India till 1978, captaining in 1969, 1973 and 1975. Some of Inder's best international performances were in the Merdeka Tournament. He was selected for Asian All-Stars XI in 1967 and the next year as well. In 1969, Inder was conferred the Arjuna Award—the first footballer who was not part of the 1962 Asian Games team to win it, and only the second after the great Yousuf Khan to receive the award despite never playing for the big Kolkata clubs.

Punjab football got an additional identity due to Inder Singh. He inspired a supporters' club in Delhi known as the L-Club, an abbreviation for Leaders Club, where he started his club career before moving to JCT. The loyalty Inder commanded was awesome to behold.

L-Club comprised mostly Punjabi Hindu or Sikh men, who were shopkeepers or small businessmen. They would unfurl the L-Club banner whenever Inder played. The raucous cheering of this group added to the jovial atmosphere at the Delhi Gate Stadium. The leader of the gang was Banarsi Das, who ran a canteen at the National Stadium. Banarsi had a loud voice and his cheers and insults would reverberate around the stadium. Invariably, at half-time or at the end of the match, he would shout from his seat, 'Time Up!' in a distinctly Punjabi accent that made it sound more like 'Tiem hup'.

Inder could not participate in the 1970 Santosh Trophy due to an injury. Four years later when Punjab hosted the trophy again, Inder was at his lethal best. Playing attacking football rarely seen in the long history of this tournament, Punjab scored a massive 46 goals. Inder was thirty-two years old but scored an incredible 23 goals—still a national record—and a hat-trick in the final.

Inder was thirty-four in the 1976 Durand Cup, when in the quarter-final he scored what he considers one of his finest goals ever—a testimony to his fitness. He was playing for JCT against star-studded Mohun Bagan. Just after half-time he put his team 1-0 ahead. Then came the magical goal. He trapped a forward pass, turned and beat midfielder Prasun Banerjee, then surged past the other midfielder international Gautam Sarkar; in full cry, he evaded the lunging tackles of international central-defenders Subrata Bhattacharya and Pradip Chowdhury and scored with a crisp placement. Inder's sheer speed and dribbling skills left the Bagan defence mesmerized. This was truly a Maradona-like goal. JCT won 2-0 and at the end of the match several Bagan players stood near the touchline and applauded Inder as he walked out. At thirty-five, he again played inspirational football in the 1977–78 Santosh Trophy in Kolkata and helped Punjab reach the final.

Overall, Inder took part in eleven finals in the Delhi club tournaments, seven in the Durand and four in the DCM Trophy, and on each occasion, it was his brilliance that took his team—either

Leaders or JCT—to the finals. That is perhaps why he is such a cult figure in Delhi and is also seen as the brand ambassador for football in Punjab. It is his self-discipline that enabled him to have a long and distinguished career, spanning two decades from 1962–82. His football skills made him a legend in many states in India, particularly Goa and Kerala. Whenever JCT played in Goa, youngsters on seeing a Sikh player would chant 'Inder Singh'. Punjab football meant Inder Singh. For all his all-round excellence and goalscoring feats he can be safely called the Diego Maradona of Punjab football.

Like the international midfielder Parminder Singh, Inder too preferred to stay back in Punjab instead of capitalizing on his fame by moving to Mohun Bagan or Mafatlal Mills (the offer came in 1970). Inder was seen as a 'son of the soil'. His simplicity and habit of talking to the spectators endeared him to fans all over India. He also turned down lucrative offers from Khalsa Sporting Club in Canada and from the Malaysian Prime Minister Tunku Rahman to play there for five years. After retirement, Inder was manager of the JCT team from 1985–2001.

Even today, Inder has a spartan lifestyle. He rarely goes to the cinema and enjoys reading only sports magazines.

Mohammed Habib

P.K. Banerjee calls the diminutive but gutsy striker and ace playmaker Mohammed Habib the 'king of kings'. What made Habib supreme was his dedication, never-say-die spirit and visionary through-passes.

He played in Kolkata from 1966–84 for East Bengal, Mohun Bagan and Mohammedan Sporting. He always gave 100 per cent effort in every match, which endeared him to fans, and he was popularly known as 'Bade Mian' (big gentleman).

He was spotted as a precocious teenager playing for Hyderabad Telephones in 1965. In the 1965 Santosh Trophy final in Kollam, Andhra Pradesh took on West Bengal. The first match ended in a 1-1 draw and in the replay Andhra Pradesh triumphed 1-0 with Habib scoring the match-winner. What was notable in both these matches was his remarkable tenacity. West Bengal and India's ace defender Jarnail Singh were constantly harassed by Habib. Jarnail had an imperious presence and most forwards kept their distance from him. In terms of size it was a David vs Goliath contest as the short-statured, seventeen-year-old Habib battled with the powerfully built Jarnail for every ball. He never gave up trying and often snatched the ball from the bewildered Jarnail. J.C. Guha, the East Bengal mentor, was suitably impressed and took Habib to Kolkata.

Habib played regularly for India from 1968–75. He was a member of the Indian team that won a bronze in the 1970 Bangkok Asian Games and the Merdeka Tournament.

P.K. Banerjee narrates a wonderful instance of Habib's never-say-die attitude. During the tour to the USSR in 1971, India was being outclassed by a top-level Soviet club. The Indian players struggled to retain possession of the ball as the Soviet club led by 4 goals. According to P.K., all the other Indian players were resigned to their fate but Habib battled for every ball with the powerfully built Russian defenders. He was finally able to snatch the ball and score a consolation goal.

In the exhibition match against New York Cosmos in September 1977, most of the Mohun Bagan players were overawed by the legendary Pelé, but Habib treated it like just another match and kept motivating his players to excel. At the end of the game the great Pelé appreciated his inspired display.

Whenever Habib played against foreign clubs in local tournaments, he excelled. He always said, 'When I went out to play, I did not worry about the size of the defenders marking me, I had to be mentally tough to outwit them.'

Born on 17 July 1949, Habib—like Balaram before him—was amongst the few real professionals in Kolkata football. He often practised twice a day and remained committed to the game.

The Hyderabad-born striker was a vital cog in the 1970 East Bengal team that won the IFA Shield without conceding a single goal. His work rate was tremendous in the final against the powerful Pas Tehran. Especially during the 1970–74 period when East Bengal were the best club in the land, Habib's sublime through-passes created many goals. His telepathic understanding with younger brother Mohammed Akbar was a delight to behold. During 1967–74, Habib also scored in four winning finals for East Bengal in Delhi (1967, 1970 and replayed 1972 Durand, and 1974 DCM).

His finest hour was in 1973 when East Bengal beat two outstanding North Korean clubs in the IFA Shield and DCM finals. But Habib's finest goal and match-winner for East Bengal on Delhi soil was against foreign opposition, Port Authority of Thailand in the 1974 DCM quarter-final. The match was tied 3-3 and Kajal Mukherjee with his mesmeric ball skills was creating chances for his team. Following one such move, Habib received a cross from the left outside the box. The Bangkok team's defence thought he would head goalwards, but quick-thinking Habib flicked the ball upwards with his head, chested it to the ground and unleashed a left-footed half-volley which bulged the net—a dream goal.

Habib's best period with Mohun Bagan was from 1976–78 when he helped them win the coveted Triple Crown in 1977. He was the kingpin of a star-studded Bagan forward line and would initiate most of the attacks. He opened the scoring in Bagan's 1978 IFA Shield final 2-2 draw with the mighty Ararat Yerevan of the erstwhile USSR.

After retiring from the game Habib became a coach and trained the youngsters of the TFA for over a decade in the 1990s and early twenty-first century. During his tenure as coach, the TFA reached its peak and produced dozens of internationals such as Alok Das, Carlton Chapman, Deepak Mondal, Mahesh Gawli and Renedy Singh to mention a few.

Shyam Thapa

The legendary striker Shyam Thapa was a crowd-puller and entertainer. Lithe, agile and explosive, Shyam's forte was his ability to conjure up goals from seemingly innocuous positions or half chances with deft placements and crisp volleys. His jinking runs with the ball and acrobatic back-volleys, or 'overhead bicycle kicks', were a delight to behold and will linger forever in memory.

Throughout his playing career, Shyam had the charisma to attract crowds. His sporting attitude on the field (such as never diving in the box or retaliating when fouled) and never-say-die spirit made him a fan favourite.

Born in May 1948, Shyam could feature anywhere in the forward line and also play in the midfield or defence, if required. He was first discovered when he scored the match-winner for his school in the 1964 Subroto Mukherjee Cup final. The East Bengal supremo J.C. Guha, who had a sharp eye for talent, signed him up for the 1966 season. Shyam made a memorable debut as a precocious eighteen-year-old in the 1966 Calcutta League, scoring a hat-trick against Rajasthan FC.

Too young to handle the pressure of Kolkata football, he returned to Gorkha Brigade the next season and played for them till 1969. His finest hour in domestic football came in the 1969 Durand final when he scored an opportunistic match-winner in the replay against redoubtable BSF. General Sam Manekshaw witnessed that match and invited the entire Gorkha Brigade team for a party the next day. At that party, Shyam requested Manekshaw, later to become field marshal, to release him from the army so he could pursue football professionally. The general agreed and Shyam Thapa joined East Bengal again in 1970.

From 1970, his career took off. In the 1970 Asian Games, he scored in India's 3-0 win over Indonesia, and also in the 3-1 win over Malaysia in the Merdeka Tournament. India won a bronze in both competitions. From 1970–77, he was a regular in the Indian team.

Shyam's career suffered a setback when his family, worried about the increasing Naxalite violence, asked him to leave Kolkata. He moved to Mafatlal Mills Mumbai and linked up with former Gorkha Brigade players like Ranjit Thapa, Bhupinder Singh Rawat and Amar Bahadur. He stayed with the club from 1971–74.

The glamour and lure of Kolkata football proved irresistible and he rejoined East Bengal in 1975. He was by then an established superstar and had a memorable 1975–76 season with the high-performing club, scoring some delightful goals including a brilliant back volley against Mohun Bagan in the Calcutta League. He became India's most sought-after player and in the 1977–78 season, Mohun Bagan paid a record fee of Rs 50,000 for his services. He became the highest-paid player in India that year and helped Bagan win their historic Triple Crown. In the Durand final, he scored the equalizer against JCT, darting on to a rebound from goalkeeper Surjit Singh and bulging the net.

From 1977–80, Mohun Bagan had a great run and Shyam figured in four consecutive Durand finals, of which they won three. However, after the 1978 Santosh Trophy in Srinagar, he was surprisingly omitted from the list of probables for the 1978 Asian Games. The national selectors claimed he was slowing down and would not be able to cope with the rigours of international football. There was a major hue and cry in the national media at his unfair omission.

Responding to media criticism, Field Marshal Sam Manekshaw, boss of the All India Council of Sports, intervened and invited Shyam to join the training camp being held in Patiala. But the lionhearted Gurkha spurned the last-minute intervention and announced his retirement from international football. Being denied the captaincy of the Indian team in the 1978 Asian Games has been Shyam's greatest disappointment in his otherwise glittering career.

The culmination of his all-round genius was seen in the 1980 Durand when an injury-ridden Mohun Bagan were compelled to play him in the unusual position of right-central-defender in every match. Shyam combined effectively with Subrata Bhattacharya and helped Bagan annex the Durand. His tight marking of Mohammedan Sporting's ace striker Shabbir Ali on a soggy ground in the final tilted the match in his team's favour.

After his playing career was over, Shyam Thapa was technical director at the Williamson Magor Academy in Assam and later at the TFA. Such is Shyam Thapa's fame that Nepal called him to revamp their football system in the twenty-first century.

A man of simple habits, Shyam remains fit and active by doing yoga every morning. His greatest ambition is to revive football in his alma mater and first love, Gorkha Brigade. Dehradun was once a major catchment area for Indian football, and Shyam, a man of great commitment, is the best man to revive it there.

Manjit Singh

With the looks of a film star, Herculean physique, and abundant talent, Manjit Singh could have been the blue-eyed boy of Indian football. At his peak, Manjit—who was 6 ft tall and weighed about 75–78 kg—was a terror for defenders. He had the technique, strength and competitive spirit to cope with the demands of international football.

Born on 10 June 1950 to a retired army man in a village near Punjab's Mahilpur, Manjit learnt the game playing in nearby school grounds. Like many others of his generation, Manjit developed his football skills with incessant practice and occasional guidance from senior players.

Fame came early. As a twenty-year-old he was chosen for the 1970 Santosh Trophy, being held in Punjab for the first time. Tall and broad-shouldered with curly brown hair, Manjit spearheaded Punjab's attack in place of Inder Singh. In the second semi-final against the mighty holders West Bengal, he came of age when he scored the equalizer just before the final whistle. Punjab then beat Karnataka 3-1 in the replayed final to win the Santosh Trophy for the first time.

Manjit was selected for the 1970 Bangkok Asian Games where he scored the winning goal in the bronze medal match against Japan. A cross by Shyam Thapa led to a commotion and Manjit, the poacher of goals, scored the match-winner in the thirty-sixth minute.

For the next six years Manjit was a regular fixture in the national squad. He played for India in the 1972 pre-Olympics, three Merdeka Tournaments, the 1976 Afghanistan tour and the 1976 President's Cup in Seoul. Manjit played at his best in the Merdeka Tournament and considered the Kuala Lumpur stadium his favourite ground. In the 1976 edition, India played a memorable 2-2 draw with fancied Burma. Manjit and his best friend Harjinder Singh scored for India.

Difficult to dislodge when he gained possession of the ball, Manjit never used his bulk or resorted to excessive rough play. He may have lacked explosive speed but his dribbling and passing skills were of a high calibre.

Due to his impulsive nature and forthright views Manjit was seen as the stormy petrel of Indian football. In the aftermath of the 1976 Merdeka Tournament, Manjit—as Indian captain—fought for better remuneration and facilities for his players. Reportedly, several AIFF officials held this against him and he was never picked for India again. He was then at the peak of his performance and had captained India on several occasions.

The unkindest cut of them all came after the 1980–81 Santosh Trophy in Cuttack, which was Punjab's first-ever national championship triumph outside home soil. The watching journalists and the tournament organizing committee unanimously chose Manjit Singh as the 'Outstanding Player of the Championship'. Yet, unbelievably, his name was not included in the list of 120 probables to attend the preparatory camps for the 1982 Delhi Asiad. Manjit considered this as the biggest disappointment of his career and felt he was omitted as he had been branded a rebel.

In domestic football, he is probably the only player to have represented all five leading institutional and club sides in Punjab. Manjit Singh started his career with Leaders Club Jalandhar and played for them from 1968–72. Next, he represented BSF (1973–78) with whom he won the prestigious Durand on three occasions. His best year was in 1976 when BSF were joint winners of the DCM and Durand tournaments. After the 1976 DCM final, the South Korean coach praised Manjit's shielding and passing skills. He then played for Punjab Police and JCT (1980–81) and lastly with PSEB in 1984. During his stint with East Bengal club in 1979, Manjit became a victim of interregional rivalry and quit midseason. Till the end, he

INDIA'S GREAT COACHES

The legendary S.A. Rahim, under whom India became the 'Brazil of Asia'

Rahim's grave in Hyderabad (Courtesy: Saptaparno Ghosh)

Amal Dutta, India's first professional coach

P.K. Banerjee, former double Olympian and India's most successful club coach

Syed Nayeemuddin, captain of the 1970 Asian Games bronze–winning Indian team and outstanding coach

Dhyan Chand awardee Shabbir Ali captained India to victory in the 1974 Asian Youth Championship

Armando Colaco, India's most successful coach in the twenty-first century

Subhash Bhowmick, former international and cerebral coach

Derrick Pereira, who won the Federation Cup both as a player and as a coach

The formidable East Bengal team that won the 1950 IFA Shield, with the brilliant 'Pancha Pandavas': P. Venkatesh, Ahmed Khan, Appa Rao, K.P. Dhanraj and P.B. Saleh. (Courtesy: Gautam Roy)

The 1950 Hyderabad team who were runners-up in the Santosh Trophy. Most of these players were part of the historic five Rovers Cup–winning team. (Standing, L to R) Sussey (Jr), Pandhari, Asghar Hussain, Eraiah (goalkeeper), Doraiswamy, G.Y.S. Laiq and S.K. Azizuddin. (Sitting, L to R) Mohammed Jamal, Fruvall, S.A. Rahim (coach), Maqdoom Sabir (jt secy of HFA and manager), S.K. Moinuddin and Noor Mohammed. (Courtesy: S.S. Hakeem)

Double Olympian Noor Mohammed, numero uno left-half who also played three Asian Games

1951 Asian Games gold medallist G.Y.S. Laiq, who retired as DCP, Hyderabad (Courtesy: Mustafa Pervez)

Peter Thangaraj, who, at his peak, was India's and Asia's greatest goalkeeper

Tulsidas Balaraman, arguably one of India's greatest ever forwards

The baby of the team in the 1956 Melbourne Olympics, Zulfiqaruddin had the most powerful shots in India
(Courtesy: Saptaparno Ghosh)

Crafty inside-forward B. Narayan, member of the Indian side that finished unbeaten runners-up in the 1959 Merdeka Tournament

Yousuf Khan, India's Ruud Gullit and 1962 Asian Games gold medallist. Seen here as a guest of honour at the Subroto Mukherjee Cup.

1960 Olympian Habibul Hasan Hamid was greased lightning with the ball
(Courtesy: Saptaparno Ghosh)

Excellent winger Sukumar Samajpati, known for his accurate crosses
(Courtesy: Achyut Roy)

The 'Bade Mian of the Maidan', Mohammed Habib, known for his defence-splitting through-passes

Sudhir Karmakar, chosen as Asia's best defender after the 1970 Asian Games

The charismatic Shyam Thapa, renowned for his razor-sharp reflexes and superb back-volleys

1970 (Eden Gardens): East Bengal shocks Pas Club in the IFA Shield final

Goalkeeper Peter Thangaraj denying an Iranian forward in the 1970 IFA Shield final, in which East Bengal beat the mighty Pas Tehran. (Courtesy: Gautam Roy)

The jubilant East Bengal team after beating Pyongyang City Club of North Korea in the 1973 IFA Shield final. (Courtesy: *Anandabazar Patrika* archive)

Newspaper article by the author in the *Weekend Review* about Mohammedan Sporting's win over Bank of Seoul and Trust Co. in the 1980 DCM final.

Prime Minister Smt. Indira Gandhi inaugurating the first Nehru Cup in 1982 with AIFF Secy Ashoke Ghosh. (Courtesy: Nilanjan Datta)

Midfielder Parminder Singh in action at the 1982 Nehru Cup in Kolkata. (Courtesy: Nilanjan Datta)

The 'Black Pearl' of Kerala, the incomparable I.M. Vijayan (Courtesy: Sukhwinder Singh)

Jo Paul Ancheri, a fine utility player with a powerful left foot (Courtesy: Noel da Lima Leitao)

Sikkimese sniper and trailblazer Bhaichung Bhutia (Courtesy: Sandeep Mahankal/IANS)

P. Renedy Singh, India's David Beckham, known for his quality free kicks (Courtesy: David M. Mayum)

Sunil Chhetri, India's present captain and all-time top scorer in international matches (Courtesy: Bengaluru FC)

The Mizo 'wonder boy' Jeje Lalpekhlua, a lethal striker (Courtesy: AIFF Media)

(Left) India celebrating the 2009 Nehru Cup victory, after beating Syria at the Ambedkar Stadium, Delhi. (Right) Bhaichung Bhutia being felicitated by Philipp Lahm after his farewell match with Bayern Munich, 2012. (Courtesy: AIFF Media)

Goa celebrating after winning the Santosh Trophy outright for the first time in 1983–84.

Brahmanand Shankhwalkar, the first Goan to captain India and win the coveted Arjuna Award. Seen here receiving the award from President K.R. Narayanan.

Joseph Rathnam, the Dempo coach who patented their short-passing and possession style of football

T. Shanmugham, the Salgaocar coach who revolutionized football at the club

Mauricio Afonso, excellent box-to-box midfielder and now coach of Dempo

Former India captain Bruno Coutinho, renowned for his powerful shots

Former international Samir Naik, who played for Dempo for eighteen years

Former international Mahesh Gawli, a cool, calm and composed defender

Salgaocar celebrating after winning the 1999 NFL.

The Dempo squad after winning their record fifth NFL/I-League title in 2012.

Churchill Brothers with club founder Churchill Alemao and CEO, Valanka Alemao, after winning the 2013 I-League. (Courtesy: Valanka Alemao)

Bengaluru FC playing an I-League match in front of their passionate supporters. They have won the I-League twice and were runners-up in the 2016 AFC Cup. (Courtesy: Bengaluru FC)

West Block Blues (supporters of Bengaluru FC) with banners at the 2016 AFC Cup, Sree Kanteerava Stadium.

The thrilled Aizawl FC celebrating after they became the first North-eastern team to win the I-League in 2017.
(Courtesy: PTI)

The victorious Atletico de Kolkata team lifting the 2016 Hero ISL trophy after defeating Kerala Blasters FC in the final.
(Courtesy: Indian Super League)

The Indian team that won the 2008 AFC Challenge Cup by beating Tajikistan 4-1. This enabled them to reach the Asian Cup final round in 2011. (Courtesy: AIFF Media)

Unveiling the logo of the FIFA U-17 World Cup India 2017. (L to R) AFC president Shaikh Salman bin Ebrahim Al Khalifa, FIFA president Gianni Infantino, Union Sports Minister Vijay Goel and AIFF president Praful Patel. (Courtesy: AIFF Media)

lamented what he considered the lack of sympathy and the misunderstandings that led to his early exit from Kolkata. An eye operation in 1984 terminated his career.

With his charismatic personality and dashing play, Manjit Singh had the credentials to become an Indian football icon. However, when he died in a car accident in December 1992, he was a forgotten man. He was then working with the SAI, Patiala, having completed a football coaching course there.

Recalling the happy days they had spent together, his close friend Harjinder Singh said, 'Manjit was basically an introvert, who enjoyed outdoor life, good food and listening to music but was a fierce competitor on the field and always wanted his team to do well.'

I.M. Vijayan

In Indian football, there would be few stories as fascinating and incredible as that of Inivalappil Mani Vijayan. He was born on 25 April 1969 in a thatched mud hut in Thrissur and could not afford even a pair of shoes. His father, a farm labourer who survived on daily wages, died in an accident when Vijayan was twelve. His mother worked as a floor cleaner and a scrap collector to earn a meagre income. To supplement his family income, Vijayan sold soda water bottles or groundnuts at the nearby municipal football stadium. This also gave him a chance to watch football matches, which was his childhood passion. He soon began to practise barefoot with neighbourhood children in the streets, using a ball made of cloth rags. During those difficult days he survived on kanji (rice gruel). George Blues, the Scottish coach of FC Kochin in 1997–98, had said that if I.M. Vijayan had been born in Europe and exposed to a nutritious diet, supplements and professional training at a young age, he could have become an international star.

Vijayan's intuitive football skills and intelligence were amazing. Realizing that education was not an option as he had failed thrice in class eight, he decided to pursue a career in football. Vijayan has always acknowledged the Good Samaritans who helped him in his journey, like his kind-hearted class teacher Prabhavati, and a football official, the late Jose Parambu, on whose prompting he went for trials conducted by the District Sports Council (DSC). Vijayan's sublime skills were noticed and at the age of fifteen he was enrolled in the three-year football camp in Kerala.

T.K. Chathunni, who guided Mohun Bagan to their first-ever NFL title in 1997–98, was Vijayan's first coach. The DSC secretary M.C. Radhakrishnan generously arranged food for Vijayan at a nearby hotel during the camp.

Vijayan excelled as a crafty inside-forward with deft dribbling skills and lightning footwork in his first major tournament, the 1990 Federation Cup. Creditably, he had a big-match temperament and never got overawed by the occasion. His amazing skills enabled Kerala Police to annex the coveted title for the first time, and then again the next year. These performances launched his career and in the 1990s Vijayan became one of India's most successful forwards.

Vijayan is the only Indian with two hat-tricks in international football. Both these hat-tricks were scored in the 8th SAF Games in Kathmandu in 1999, against Pakistan and Bhutan. He was first selected for the senior team in 1991 for the tour to Tanzania and after that became a regular in the national team. He was the first Indian to play in three pre–World Cup campaigns—in 1993 at Beirut and Seoul, in 1996 at Doha and in the 2001 Group 8.

For sixteen years, Vijayan played for leading clubs Mohun Bagan (which he joined at age twenty-two), JCT, Kochin, Churchill Brothers and East Bengal. He had the unique distinction of being a part of the team that won the Federation Cup eight times, and except for the DCM Trophy, he has been a part of the winning team at major tournaments in India more than once.

Nicknamed the 'Black Pearl' of Indian soccer, he thrice won the Player of the Year award (1992, 1997 and 2000). He also received offers to play professional football in Malaysia and Singapore but turned them down as he was hesitant about adjusting to other cultures. The money offered was also not lucrative enough.

At his prime he was one of India's wealthiest footballers. In transfer fees alone he earned over Rs 1 crore. Thanks to his football skills he now lives a comfortable life in a three-bedroom house in a posh area in Thrissur. He stays there with his wife, Raji, and three children. His old mother, Kochammu, also stayed with him until her death in 2015.

The way he wooed his wife, Raji, makes for a very romantic story. During the 1994 Federation Cup Vijayan was on duty in Goa for the holders Mohun Bagan for over two weeks. In the days before mobile phones, a long-distance call was the only way to stay in touch. Vijayan is genial and affectionate by nature, and he would call up Raji—whom he was courting then—daily, and have hour-long chats with her. The owner of the STD booth was elated as his income escalated during that fortnight, so he bought Vijayan a drink on the day after the final, which Mohun Bagan won.

Cherian Joseph directed a documentary feature titled *Kalo Harin* (The Black Stag) on the life of India's famous No. 10, I.M. Vijayan.[1] Such is Vijayan's popularity in his home state that he started acting in Malayalam films, debuting in *Shantham* directed by Jayaraj.[2]

Vijayan, who idolizes the Brazilian legend Zico, was noted for his sublime ball skills, superlative free kicks, visionary passing and work rate. But above all, his sheer unpredictability and unexpected goals made him a defender's nightmare and a spectator's delight. There was a buzz of excitement whenever he touched the ball and fans always expected magic from him.

Former national coach Syed Nayeemuddin has said that Vijayan looked casual but attacked like a panther when he had the ball. Renowned coach Subhash Bhowmick considers him the most talented Indian player of the last few decades.

Vijayan now runs a football academy, I.M. Vijayan Sports Foundation, in Thrissur and in March 2017 the Government of India designated him National Observer for football.

Bruno Coutinho

Bruno Coutinho is a Salgaocar and Goan football legend, for his exciting, attacking football and unexpected, powerful shots. With his pleasing smile and mop of curly hair, the rugged Bruno was once a teenage prodigy and the pin-up boy of Goan football.

His skill, big-match temperament and potential were recognized early. He had impressed in the 1986 Subroto Mukherjee Cup final rounds and as a fifteen-year-old was selected for the Indian Schools squad for the World School Games in Brunei. Under the watchful eye of coach Salvador Fernandes, or 'Salu' (an ex-Sesa Goa player), Bruno honed his shooting skills, spending hours after practice developing his shots.

Bruno had just played one season in club football when he made his debut for the national team at the 1989 President's Cup in Dhaka. He was just nineteen and played for both the junior and senior Indian teams. Bruno became captain of the senior team for the 1995 SAF Games and 1999 SAFF Cup. In both tournaments, India emerged victorious. In the latter, Coutinho scored the winner against the Maldives in the semi-finals and then scored the first goal in the final against Bangladesh. He was also captain of India in the Asian Cup in 1996 and the Nehru Cup in 1997, and member of the Indian team that won the 1997 SAFF Cup in Kathmandu.

He was, however, severely disappointed when he was left out of the Indian squad for the 1998 Asian Games. It was one of the most frustrating moments in his career; this had been his only chance because at both the 1990 and 1994 Asian Games, India did not participate in football.

Bruno was named the AIFF player of the year in 1996, and in 2001 he became the second Goan player to get the coveted Arjuna Award.

Bruno Coutinho started his club career with Dempo in the 1987–88 season. He then joined Salgaocar and stayed there (except for one season with Dempo in 1990) till 2002. Salgaocar experienced their most successful era with Coutinho in the team.

He helped his club win the Federation Cup (1997), three Rovers Cup titles, Taca Goa (1989), the Durand (1999) and the NFL in 1998–99.

His greatest hour and claim to eternal fame was the 1997 KBL Federation Cup final. Unfancied Salgaocar started as underdogs against East Bengal at the Salt Lake Stadium, which had a capacity audience of 1,20,000 people. East Bengal were on a high as they had overcome arch-rivals Mohun Bagan in a thrilling semi-final. Coached by T.K. Chathunni, Salgaocar adopted clever tactics and bottled up Bhaichung who was not at his agile best in that match.

Playing as a roving midfielder, Bruno put his team ahead with a powerful rising shot in the twenty-third minute. East Bengal equalized in the eighty-third minute and the match went into extra time. Bruno once again rose to the occasion as he scored the golden goal from a Savio Medeira pass in the second minute of the extra time. His 'finger on lips' celebration after scoring the golden goal is still remembered by fans across the nation. It is one of the defining moments in Indian football of the 1990s, and he was deservingly named the Player of the Tournament. Salgaocar felicitated Bruno after the match and he continues to be an icon for young Goan players.

Bruno also mesmerized fans whenever he turned up for Goa in the Santosh Trophy, having represented his state more than ten times. In the 1999 Santosh Trophy he was named the Player of the Tournament even though Goa lost the final.

In a career spanning around twelve years, the stockily built striker-cum-roving midfielder terrorized rival defenders with his skill, clever distribution and unexpected but powerful shots. Bruno was a consistent goalscorer on the domestic scene, scoring 9 goals in the 3rd NFL that Salgaocar won. His combination with the fleet-footed Roy Barreto was both telepathic and devastating, not unlike that of the brothers Habib and Akbar in the 1970s.

After retirement, Bruno worked for the Sports Authority of Goa and also as an expert TV commentator.

Jo Paul Ancheri

Born in 1973, Jo Paul Ancheri started his career with SBT. He first came into the limelight during the 1993–94 Santosh Trophy in Cuttack. In the semi-final Kerala trounced the hosts Odisha 5-1, with Ancheri scoring twice. In the final against West Bengal, Ancheri with his speed, thrust and powerful shots created havoc on the left flank. He gave Bengal's international right-back Ilyas Pasha a harrowing time, and in a rare occurrence, even eclipsed his senior I.M. Vijayan.

It was a breakthrough year for Kerala's latest sensational player who was chosen to represent India in the Independence Day Cup in Doha. The well-built Ancheri excelled as a striker and was chosen as the 'Best Player of the Tournament' in Doha.

On Vijayan's initiative, Ancheri joined Mohun Bagan for the 1994 season and helped them become the most successful club in the country, as they won numerous domestic tournaments. The Vijayan and Ancheri combination was lethal and a delight to watch. Ancheri with his blistering pace, power, and powerful shots was the perfect foil to Vijayan's unpredictable genius. The talented Ancheri was very consistent throughout his Kolkata debut season and was rightly chosen as the AIFF Player of 1994.

India's finest multipurpose player of the 1990s, Ancheri played for Mohun Bagan, JCT, Kochin and East Bengal in the NFL and other domestic tournaments. After the great Yousuf Khan in the 1960s, Ancheri is the only Indian to play in defence, midfield and upfront in international matches.

It was at the 1995 Nehru Cup training camp that the national coach Rustam Akramov saw the versatility in Ancheri's game and persuaded him to switch over to defence. A crippling knee injury soon after, during the 1995 SAF Games final, was to sideline him for nearly a year. The Nehru Stadium in Chennai, where the matches were held, was full of potholes since athletic events were also held there. For Ancheri the unfortunate injury in the semi-final against Nepal was the worst moment in his career and he is still bitter about it.

After this, Ancheri lost his sudden acceleration which had made him a lethal striker. He had to reinvent his game to remain an international player, and Akramov's advice to play in defence proved to be a boon.

On his return to the Indian team after recovery he played in either defence or midfield. National coach Syed Nayeemuddin used Ancheri as a central midfielder in the 1997 Nehru Cup and 1998 Asian Games. However, in whatever position he played, Ancheri, a free-kick expert, became famous for his powerful left-footed shots. He was nicknamed the 'poor man's Roberto Carlos'. His two goals in the away match against Yemen in the 2001 World Cup qualifier in Sana'a are an example of his mighty long-range shots. The second goal against Yemen from 35 yards was a world-class effort.

Ancheri played regularly for India from 1994–2004 but after that was not considered for selection. After retirement, he has been involved in coaching young players and served briefly in the Mohun Bagan SAIL Football Academy in Durgapur.

Bhaichung Bhutia

Bhaichung Bhutia is Indian football's Neil Armstrong, a true pioneer. Born on 15 December 1976 in a small village five hours away from Gangtok, Bhaichung set new trends in Indian football. His desire to improve his game by playing abroad set him apart from other Indian players. He had trials with a number of leading clubs in England and then became the first Indian to play professional football in Europe, on a three-year contract with English second-division club Bury FC in September 1999. Towards the end of his first season with Bury, Bhaichung became the first Indian to score in the English professional league, against Chesterfield.

In May 1999, he became the first Indian to be chosen as Asian Player of the Month by the AFC for his scintillating performances in the SAFF Coca-Cola Cup, which India won, beating Bangladesh 2-0 in the final at Margao, Goa. There are many other feathers in his cap. Playing for JCT in the 1996–97 NFL, Bhaichung finished top scorer with 14 goals, the highest by an Indian and that too in only 14 games. He is also the first to score a golden goal in Indian football after FIFA introduced this rule in the 1994–95 season.

In 1997, he became the first Indian footballer to be sponsored by a multi-national company, Reebok, and later he appeared in advertisements for a number of other Indian and international products. All this, combined with his immense talent, made him Indian football's pin-up boy. He contributed hugely in generating interest in football amongst the Indian middle class and became a role model for younger players.

Popularly called 'Twinkle Toes from Tinkitam', Bhaichung was a product of the National Sports Talent Contest scheme conducted by the SAI. As a prodigious fifteen-year-old, he scored 16 goals for his school in 3 matches in the 1991 Subroto Mukherjee Cup. He was chosen as one of the five best players of this prestigious tournament.

After being spotted by East Bengal's former international goalkeeper Bhaskar Ganguly, Bhaichung joined them in 1993 on a monthly stipend of Rs 4000. The turning point in his playing career came in the 1993 Durand semi-finals against rugged BSF. East Bengal struggled to break through their tenacious back four and the match drifted goalless into extra time. Coach Shyamal Ghosh felt that his team was in a rut and needed some original approach play. Instinctively he took the plunge and introduced the seventeen-year-old Bhaichung as a substitute attacking midfielder. With two minutes to go for the final whistle, Bhaichung scored with an acrobatic mid-air reverse kick reminiscent of the great Brazilian Pelé. Initially the stadium was stunned into silence but then erupted into tumultuous applause. Bhaichung had arrived. Since then, scoring spectacular and decisive goals became a feature of his career.

In October 1995, in a pre-Olympic match in Peshawar, India and Pakistan were tied at 1-1. Bhaichung trapped a high ball on his chest and then spun around and scored with a booming volley into the roof of the net. The then national coach, Rustam Akramov, has always praised this wonderful display and said, 'Even the partisan home fans vociferously applauded this amazing goal.'

Bhaichung admits that his most memorable goals were the hat-trick against Mohun Bagan in the 1997 KBL Federation Cup semi-final (for details, see Chapter 10: 'The Great Rivalry').

Though just 5 ft 7 in. tall, Bhaichung's aerial ability and courage against tall defenders was exemplary as was his running off the ball. His goalscoring skill has always earned him high praise from discerning players. P.K. Banerjee said, 'Bhaichung was extremely agile and a quick thinker.' Nayeemuddin often said, 'Bhaichung's reflexes in the box were the best I have seen amongst any Indian players.' Nigerian striker Chima Okorie has said, 'Bhaichung could be quite electrifying on the field. He had the ability to be at the right place at the right time and stick the ball into the net.'

Bhaichung says, 'I matured as a player under the professional playing conditions [in England]. Playing for Bury FC was more technical in nature. It was like being on a job. Playing under organized, professional conditions for three years did wonders towards improving my game.'

After returning from England, Bhaichung was a complete professional in attitude and proved a true leader as captain of the Indian football team. This was best exemplified in the pre–World Cup qualifiers in April-May 2001. Prior to the home match in Bengaluru against the favourites, UAE, the Indian team were travelling to a practice session. The entire squad had their eyes glued to the television set, watching the crucial fifth One Day International cricket match between India and Australia. Bhaichung, with his back to the TV set in the bus, chastised his teammates and told them to bring their focus back to their game.

During his peak he was the best striker in South Asia and the most feared Indian player in Asian football. He scored 4 goals in one Asian Games in Busan in 2002, a feat only P.K. Banerjee had achieved before, in the 1962 Asiad. Bhaichung had the reflexes of Shyam Thapa or Sheoo Mewalal in the box, and the sudden speed of Inder Singh. His consistency in international football made him special.

Despite the fame, riches and adulation that came with being the best-known football player in South Asia, Bhaichung has remained affable and approachable.

Sunil Chhetri

At first glance Chhetri does not look like a lethal striker but what he lacks in height and physique he makes up with stealth. He shields the ball well, turns sharply and takes quick shots at goal. Chhetri has a great ability to peel away from his markers and is a silent assassin in the box. He has a good spot jump and finds space in a crowded penalty box to head decisively. He knows his limitations, plays to his strengths and has kept himself injury-free during a long career of fourteen years. His mental toughness has enabled him to score a record 54 goals in 94 international matches. He is the first Indian to score over 50 goals and may become the second after Bhaichung to play over 100 times for the country.

Sunil Chhetri was born to Nepalese-origin parents on 3 August 1984 in Secunderabad, and was first noticed as a precocious teenager playing for a Delhi school in the Subroto Mukherjee Cup. A prolific goalscorer, he was snapped up by Delhi's popular City Club for the local league. Soon, his reputation as a clever striker with nimble feet led to many offers by outstation clubs. In 2002, Mohun Bagan chose many players for their squad from north India including Chhetri.

Chhetri adapted well to Kolkata football's demanding atmosphere. In the 109th IFA Shield final, Bagan took on arch-rivals East Bengal before a packed Salt Lake Stadium. The thrilling match ended in a goalless draw and during the penalty shoot-out, both teams were level at 3-3 when nineteen-year-old Chhetri stepped forward to take the fourth penalty kick. There was a palpable groan from the Bagan supporters as they thought he was too inexperienced. Many experts and seasoned journalists also thought that Bagan's coach Alok Mukherjee had gambled heavily.

Cool as a cucumber, Chhetri stepped up and calmly placed the ball past East Bengal's seasoned international goalkeeper Sangram Mukherjee. This proved to be vital and Bagan eventually won the 2003 IFA Shield.

After this match, Chhetri became a hero amongst the Bagan fans. After a successful first season with the club, he got selected for the Indian team that participated in the 2004 SAF Games in Islamabad, held for the first time as an U-23 competition. Chhetri played in all the matches and scored twice in the 4-1 demolition of Bhutan in the semi-final. In the final, though India lost 0-1 to hosts Pakistan, Chhetri was not overawed by the hard-tackling and experienced defenders, and his ability to drift into vacant space to receive the ball and take quick shots was noticeable.

On the flight back to Delhi, I was with the Indian coach for SAF, Alok Mukherjee, who analysed Chhetri's performance and offered some perceptive observations. He said, 'If he [Chhetri] concentrates, he can have a good international career.' Mukherjee was worried about his constant interaction with friends over the mobile phone, which was then a novelty. But Chhetri was mentally strong and never let anything distract him from excelling as a professional footballer. He has an amiable temperament and enjoys travelling and mixing with people, but knows where to draw the line. He has also been conscious of diet, fitness and training.

In international football Chhetri first came into the limelight in the 2007 Nehru Cup, in Delhi, which India won for the first time ever. His combination with the experienced Bhaichung Bhutia was devastating. Chhetri was India's top scorer in the tournament with 4 goals.

Chhetri went abroad in 2010, when he signed for the American club Kansas City Wizards, becoming the third Indian to play outside South Asia and the first Indian to play MLS. Peter Vermes, the club's head coach, described Sunil as a 'crafty player' saying, 'Technically he's very sharp, and he's a guy who has good attacking tendencies.'

Chhetri's finest hour was during the 2011 SAFF Cup at the Nehru Stadium, Delhi. India emerged champions and he finished with 7 goals in 5 matches—a record for a single SAFF Cup tournament. He had the unique distinction of scoring in every match. The previous record was held by Vijayan with 6 goals in the 1997 edition. Selected as captain of the national team for 2012, Chhetri thrived on responsibility, and his role as a mentor and motivator of young talent is acknowledged by all.

In August 2013 Chhetri shifted to Bengaluru FC, and finished as joint top scorer (along with Darryl Duffy of Salgaocar) in the 7th I-League with 14 goals. He helped Bengaluru become I-League champions in their debut season and again in 2016. Bengaluru allowed their players to be available for the 2nd ISL in 2015. At the 2015 ISL auction, Sunil Chhetri became the highest-paid Indian player, bought by Mumbai City FC for Rs 1.2 crore.

Jeje Lalpekhlua

Jeje Lalpekhlua excelled at the 9th SAFF Suzuki Cup in 2015–16, scoring 3 goals—a brace in the semi-final (when India beat the Maldives 3-2) and once in the final (India beat holders Afghanistan 2-1). This was India's 7th SAFF Cup win since the tournament started in 1993.

Jeje—often compared with Argentine forward Carlos Tevez owing to his stocky physique—was born on the same day as Chelsea and Belgium's legend Eden Hazard.[3] Jeje's football career started well as he scored 4 goals in 3 matches in the first five days of playing internationally. He has been adding to that tally ever since. He is now unanimously acknowledged as one of India's best and most promising players in the current era.

Born in 1991 in Mizoram's Lunglei district, Jeje rose to fame from a small town just like his idol Bhaichung Bhutia did in the 1990s. He took to football due to the passion for the game in Mizoram. Recalling his youth Jeje once said, 'There was a small ground near my house where I had my first tryst with football. I used to go there whenever I had the time to. But we mostly played only on Saturdays and Sundays, after we had finished homework.'

Jeje's life changed after training at the Ari Benjamin Football Academy in Aizawl, where he was converted to a striker from a central-defender or a left-back and was chosen for the India U-19 team after representing Mizoram in local tournaments. Soon, the confident seventeen-year-old was playing for the I-League second division, and later the top league clubs. In the ISL he played three seasons for Chennaiyin, helping them win the title in 2015.

Just as his career was taking off in 2013, he suffered a knee injury, which took a year to heal. He returned a stronger and more mature player. He stayed calm even when he was pressurized by opposing defenders and started shielding the ball well. Gradually he improved his running off the ball, distribution to the flanks and stealthy moves into scoring positions. During his stint with Chennaiyin he benefited from Marco Materazzi's coaching. He says, 'My aim is to be at the right place at the right time.' He has become a lethal goalscorer and realizes that in international matches scoring opportunities are rare. *'Jab bhi chance milega, goal marna hai* [Whenever a chance comes, you have to score].' Till July 2017, he had scored 18 goals in 41 international matches.

Having made it big, the small-town hero does commendable charitable work for the local community and trains youngsters during his spare time. He has cajoled the Football Players Association of India to support his initiative by providing boots and other football gear.

Along with his childhood friend Lalrindika Ralte, Shylo 'Mama' Malsawmtluanga and another prominent Mizo player Robert Lalthlamuana, he donates money and football kits to the HIV-affected in Mizoram. Jeje's motivation in such matters is simple: 'It is not the amount that matters . . . As a Christian, I feel whenever I am helping poor people, I am helping myself.'

12

Midfielders

Talimeran Ao

A biopic on independent India's first captain Talimeran Ao (from the Ao tribe whose homeland was Mokokchung in Nagaland) would be both revealing and sensational. He was a man of many facets—captain of the first Indian team in the 1948 London Olympics, captain of Mohun Bagan, a practising doctor, director of Nagaland Health Service, and a humanist who during the Naga insurgency in the 1970s gave medical treatment to both the injured rebels and the soldiers. The soldiers asked him why he was helping those classified as 'undergrounds'. Talimeran is said to have replied, 'I am a doctor, I have taken an oath and I have to operate on all human beings, whether they are over ground or underground.'[1]

He was above all an ardent patriot. Talimeran's confidence, education and knowledge of English made him an obvious choice for captaincy for the 1948 London Olympics. One evening, on the ship bound for England, the bandmaster asked if the Indian football team wanted any special tune to be played. Most of the players were uncomfortable in an unfamiliar environment and remained silent. Talimeran, who was 5 ft 10 in., stood up majestically and in a booming voice said, 'Yes, play for us the "Song of India",' a popular contemporary Tommy Dorsey jazz composition. He also named his younger son Indianoba, which means 'one who led India'.

Talimeran Ao was born in 1918 at a hilltop village at Changki, Assam (now Nagaland). His father, Baptist Reverend Subongwati Ao, moved his family to Impur as part of his missionary work. Talimeran, at six years of age, became fascinated by football in the mission's compound. For hours he played not with a real ball but one made of cloth scraps, or sometimes with a wrapped-up pomelo—a grapefruit variant. As this ball lacked pace and bounce, he developed instinctive control, on small grounds that had a number of teams playing simultaneously after school.

In the All Assam Inter-School Football Championship in 1937 he was chosen as the best footballer. He graduated from Cotton College, Guwahati, where his football career took off. The famous Maharana Club of Guwahati trained at his college grounds. He joined the practice session and soon became a regular member of their team. They made him play as defensive midfielder. Talimeran was successful at other sports as well, and won trophies in athletics, volleyball and football, most of which he could not carry back home due to the arduous journey.

After graduation, he went for medical studies to Carmichael Medical College—now known as the R.G. Kar Medical College—in Kolkata. He was determined to become a doctor and serve his people, to fulfil his father's last wish. His teammate from Maharana Club, Sarat Das, helped him join Mohun Bagan in 1943, where he paid a 'joining fee' and was soon a regular player.

A strapping young man, he excelled as a roving centre-half in the old 2-3-5 system. Within a year of becoming Bagan's captain, he became India's captain for the London Olympics and for a short tour of Holland. Talimeran was a man of sharp wit. During the Olympics when a British journalist asked him why his team didn't wear boots, he reportedly said, 'It is football, not bootball.' India nearly won against France in their first match, before losing 1-2 by missing two penalties. But the game of the 'barefoot wonders' was appreciated by all.

In Holland, India beat Ajax Amsterdam 5-1 and against English clubs, they won 3 and drew 2 matches. During a friendly match, Talimeran heard the English club manager remark that if the Indians defeated his team, he would eat his hat. After the Indian team won, the captain was invited to say a few words. According to his son Talikokchang, Talimeran said, 'I will only speak after the manager eats his hat.'

Talimeran was an elegant player renowned for his skill, ball control and accurate passing with both feet. After his excellent display in the Olympics, he was offered a one-year contract by Arsenal, which he refused saying he had to return to Kolkata to complete his medical studies. He earned his MBBS degree in 1950.

His adolescent years were spent during the struggle for Independence when serving a cause was more important than individual glory. He imbibed the ethos of the age, which was evident in the football field. In the 1950 Durand final against Hyderabad City Police, Mohun Bagan's goalkeeper Manik Sarkar got injured. Substitutes were not allowed those days so Talimeran volunteered and became the goalkeeper for the rest of the match.

After his football career was over he returned home to Kohima where, in 1963, the state of Nagaland was created. In 1970, in recognition of Talimeran's exemplary work, the government granted him five acres of forest land. He became the director of Nagaland Health Service in 1978. After retirement he became a cultivator and a hunter.

He died on 13 September 1998 and like many greats of the past, his achievements have not been fully recognized. The new generation of football enthusiasts are barely aware of his remarkable achievements. In 2009 the North Eastern Council launched the Dr T. Ao Memorial Football Tournament, which is now a major football event in the region.

Noor Mohammed

It was the opening match of the 1957 national championship, i.e., the Santosh Trophy. With only seven minutes to go, Hyderabad, the holders, were facing the ignominy of being knocked out in the first round itself by Punjab, who were leading 2-1. The home team's supporters began to pray for at least 1 goal and a chance to remain in the tournament, to try their luck in the replay. Their prayers were answered with not one but 2 goals. The home team ultimately won the championship and retained the Santosh Trophy.

The 2 goals, both off spot kicks, were obtained by Noor Mohammed, Hyderabad's left-half. The air was tense with excitement, but the cool-as-a-cucumber Noor did not falter and beat the goalkeeper twice.

Noor Mohammed was the younger brother of Hyderabad's centre-half Sheikh Jamal. Born in 1924, Noor played left-half for his school and briefly for other clubs. Unsure of his performance in football, he turned his attention to other games and found himself better at vollcyball and basketball. When he joined H.E.H. the Nizam's District Police in 1940, he did not even try for a place in the football team. He was beginning to make a name in basketball, but Jamal urged him to take up football again. Noor's game improved and by 1942 he was in the District Police football team.

Noor was loaned by District Police to the Hyderabad City Police to help them win the Ashe Gold Cup in 1943. Attracted by their frequent outstation tours, Noor shifted to the City Police in 1944 and donned their colours with distinction till 1958.

Between 1951 and 1958, Noor represented India several times. He played in the Olympics twice: 1952 Helsinki and 1956 Melbourne (where he was India's oldest player). He played in the Asian Games (1951, 1954, 1958) and toured the Far East with India in 1951. He was in the Quadrangular a couple of times and went with the Indian team on their tour of the Philippines (1954) and Russia (1955). In 1958, on a Far East tour, he captained the All India XI against the Malayan XI in 1 match.

People seeing Noor for the first time would never have thought he was a footballer, for he was rather lean and weakly built. However, his skill was second to none. Highly talented, his sense of anticipation and positional play were exemplary. Famous coach S.A. Rahim once said about Noor that he would appear suddenly in front of a rival player, almost by magic, and snatch the ball away. Ex-Olympian and former national coach P.K. Banerjee who often played against him in domestic tournaments, endorsed these sentiments. He said, 'Noor was a difficult opponent to get past.' Former national captain Syed Nayeemuddin, who is also from Hyderabad, said that he learnt positional play by watching Noor Mohammed in action.

Noor was the first Indian player to realize the value and utility of the long throw. He could tackle, man mark and pass accurately with both feet with equal felicity. His intelligent interceptions and clever diagonal passes were a treat to watch. At his peak, he was rated the best in Asia in his position.

Noor symbolized the ethos of the decade after Independence—the will to sacrifice, the ability to overcome great odds and work for greater ideals. Noor and Jamal even played a state league match for their team on the same afternoon that their mother expired. Like Aziz, he remained loyal to Hyderabad Police, even though financial rewards were meagre. Even during his bright international career he earned only about Rs 150 per month. Noor maintained high fitness levels by his dedication in practice. Despite lack of facilities, he overcame all hurdles and succeeded due to sheer willpower.

Unshakeable faith in his own game was another one of his strengths. An illustration of this is his performance in the 1956 national championship. Before the matches commenced, it was made known that older players would be omitted from the Indian team for the Melbourne Olympics. Noor was on the wrong side of thirty and was, from all accounts, out of the reckoning. But he would not take matters lying down. His performance was so consistently good that he could not be ignored. When he was included in the thirty-two selected to undergo training, Noor knew he would go to Melbourne. 'I never thought that at thirty-two I was old enough to be omitted. I was keen to show the selectors that my skill had not yet been blunted,' he said later.

Noor played briefly in domestic tournaments as captain of CPL in 1960, and retired the next year. For some years after that, he served as the official coach of the Andhra Police football team. He always acknowledged his debt to Rahim, who helped him become a classy player and later a coach. Noor was also a Provisional Class I referee.

Unfortunately, he suffered in old age and survived on charity. Two days before the start of Euro 2000, on 8 June, Noor Mohammed died in a small two-roomed house in Osmanpura in the old city of Hyderabad, unsung and uncared for. He was eighty years old and suffered from tuberculosis. His funeral was attended by officials, coaches, players and referees.

Yousuf Khan

The lanky, bearded man who was hoisted on the shoulders of supporters at the Old Delhi railway station in 1961 before the Durand Cup was Yousuf Khan; international midfielder who played in the 1960 Rome Olympics, the Asian Games (1962 and 1966), the Asian Cup (1960 and 1964), and was also in the Asian All-Stars XI both 1965 and 1966. A regular in the Indian team from 1959 onwards, he was one of Asia's best midfielders. He represented India in the pre-Olympics (1960 and 1964) and Merdeka Tournament for three years as well. He scored 5 international goals for India.

Yousuf Khan had unfailing loyalty and commitment to the national team. In 1964, he was with the Indian squad in the Asian Cup final rounds when his father expired. His mother did not inform him immediately as he was on national duty. He came to know later but stayed on to play for India.

When I watched him play in the early 1960s, he was my hero, and I wanted to become a player like him. Tall with a serene face and neatly trimmed beard, Yousuf was the poor man's Ruud Gullit. Long before total football was dreamt of, he exemplified this concept. He could play in any of the ten outfield positions. For India and for his team Hyderabad City Police—later Andhra Police—he played as an inside-forward, withdrawn centre-forward and even in midfield. Indefatigable, with his long strides he was all over the field, helping in defence and attack and always passing intelligently. He would surge into scoring positions and finish with accuracy. He tackled with the same calm temperament and rarely got ruffled.

At his peak Yousuf comfortably ran 11–12 km, the same as a Premiership footballer, in each match. His versatility and work rate were astounding and far superior to any contemporary Indian player. Gautam Roy, the East Bengal media manager and India's leading football statistician, has often said whilst conversing with me, 'If players [of that era, including Yousuf Khan] had played in the ISL era, they would have retired as millionaires.'

Born on 5 August 1937, Yousuf learnt and developed his football skills by playing with a tennis ball. His ball control, trapping, positional play, clever passing and fitness were exemplary. As a talented sixteen-year-old he played for City College Old Boys in the 1953 Hyderabad League. Three years later, he joined the legendary Hyderabad City Police and started as a midfielder. He joined them as an ordinary constable on Rs 120 per month. By contrast, when India's current wing-backs Narayan Das and Pritam Kotal were nineteen, they each earned close to Rs 50 lakh per season.

Yousuf Khan's amazing adaptability was on display in the 1963 Rovers Cup in Mumbai. He was compelled to play as a stopper-back for his team as the regular defender Kaleemuddin was injured. Yousuf played with aplomb and helped his side win, beating East Bengal 1-0 in the final. He was chosen as the best defender of the tournament ahead of Jarnail Singh (Mohun Bagan) and Arun Ghosh (East Bengal) who regularly played in this position for India.

In December 1963 in the replayed Durand Cup semi-final, I watched Yousuf scoring twice against East Bengal, enabling the Hyderabad cops to win 3-0. After the match I stood outside the dressing room and, though awestruck, timidly asked him, as he emerged, the reasons for his magnificent display. Modest and soft-spoken, he just chuckled and said, 'Khoob bhaga' [Ran a lot].'

In December 1967, in the twilight of his career, he gave another majestic display in the Durand Cup. By then knee trouble had slowed him down and he played as a central-defender in the 4-2-4 system. Andhra Police defeated the fit MEG Bangalore 3-2 and holders Gorkha Brigade 3-1, before losing to mighty East Bengal 1-0 in the replay. Yousuf cleverly directed play, becoming the poor man's Xavi in these matches, so that Andhra Police bowed out but were not disgraced. Yousuf and many of his teammates left the lush green surface of the Delhi Gate Stadium with their heads held high. Even the fans of East Bengal clapped incessantly as he walked down the tunnel to the dressing room, realizing that a page of history had turned forever. That night I did not know whether to cry or laugh. As a player, I was enchanted by East Bengal's display, but was sad that there was no fairy-tale ending for the man who inspired me to love this beautiful game.

A contented individual, he never hankered after wealth and adulation. Yousuf said that both Mohun Bagan and East Bengal had made lucrative offers, but he had declined them out of loyalty for Andhra Police and he was happy with life in Hyderabad.

In the 1990s he often came to the annual Subroto Mukherjee Cup tournament in Delhi as a talent spotter. But, unfortunately, he contacted the dreaded Parkinson's disease soon after.

In 2003, I had gone to Hyderabad as a Doordarshan commentator for the Afro-Asian Games and went to his house to meet him. His health was rapidly deteriorating. Several of us made an appeal to the chief minister of undivided Andhra Pradesh, Chandrababu Naidu, who promptly responded, and Yousuf got financial help from the state government. He did not live much longer and died on 1 July 2006 aged just sixty-nine. The 2006 World Cup was in full swing then, so his death went mostly unnoticed. Yousuf Khan is yet another story of a former football legend who was neglected in his later years.

Parminder Singh

Football was not popular in many schools in Punjab during the 1960s and 1970s, but some players made an impression in the Subroto Mukherjee Cup inter-school tournament. One such was the stripling Parminder Singh who in the 1973 Subroto Cup created a stir with his long strides and powerful shots. He later excelled for BSF, JCT and India.

Born on 5 May 1957, Parminder first played internationally at the 1976 Asian Junior Championships in Bangkok. On his return, he was snapped up by BSF. In the summer of 1978, Parminder encountered difficulties in travel while heading to Kolkata for an international match. This made him take the decision to leave BSF and join a club side. Therefore in 1978 he joined JCT.

Parminder's career and fortunes took an upswing in JCT due to some strange circumstances. He played as a striker for JCT in the 1978 Durand. In a quarter-final league match, JCT were outclassed 0-3 by East Bengal.

By their spirited performances since 1974, JCT had developed a massive fan following in Delhi. The fans—which included the famous L-Club, a group of vociferous Punjabi and Sikh supporters who waved banners and chanted loudly throughout the match—were stunned by JCT's capitulation. Coach G.S. Virk and skipper Inder Singh were pressurized to make changes and Parminder was made to play as a midfielder. It was believed that with his work rate, long-range shots and hard tackling he would be more effective in midfield.

Parminder took to his midfield role like a duck to water. He played the game of his life against mighty Mohun Bagan in the semi-finals, and eclipsed Bagan's legendary international midfielder Gautam Sarkar; the match ended in a draw.

Parminder was now a transformed player. Though passed over for the 1978 Bangkok Asian Games, he became a permanent fixture in the national side from 1979 onwards. He toured UAE with the Indian squad in 1979 and played in the 1980 pre-Olympics. This was a new-look Indian team, led by Prasun Banerjee, which started playing in the 4-3-3 system, and Parminder gradually became a first-choice right-sided midfielder. His speed, quick passes and powerful shots were a contrast to Prasun's guile and the positional play of Devraj Doraiswamy of Karnataka. Parminder was admired by coaches P.K. Banerjee and the late G.M.H. Basha. The midfield combination of Parminder, Prasun and Prasanta Banerjee excelled in international tournaments, and were the established trio for India in the 1982 Asian Games. Both Parminder and Prasun were selected for an Asian All-Stars team.

Till the mid-1980s, Parminder Singh was Indian football's Steven Gerrard, a box-to-box midfielder with a powerful shot and good ball-winning ability. Parminder played regularly in the Nehru Cup from 1982–86. He considers the performance of the Indian team in the 1984 Nehru Cup as one of the best in his career. The dashing midfielder also has fond memories of the Merdeka Tournament, where he played thrice, and especially of the 1981 performance, when, according to him, the Indian team was outstanding.

Parminder last played for India in the 1986 Nehru Cup in Trivandrum. He sadly became a victim of India's poor performances in that tournament and was surprisingly overlooked for the 1986 Seoul Asian Games.

His mobility and commitment made him an exciting player to watch. In the 1983 Durand Cup, JCT and rugged Punjab Police were locked in a hard-tackling semi-final. Parminder broke the deadlock with a blistering right-footer from the top of the box, which thudded into the roof of the net. Such a goal became a Parminder speciality. In both the 1983 and 1987 centenary Durand Cup finals, he played a stellar role in helping his side win against a well-knit Mohun Bagan. Parminder always recalls JCT's memorable triumph in the 1987 Durand, 'We played effectively as a team and beat all three Kolkata clubs . . . This makes this Durand win very satisfying and it is one of the best performances by a team consisting entirely of players from Punjab in any tournament in India.' During this period, Parminder also helped Punjab win the Santosh Trophy twice in a row, in 1985 in Kanpur and 1986 in Jabalpur.

Another remarkable attribute of Parminder's game was his fitness and disciplined lifestyle, due to which he had a long and satisfying career. In 1990, the national coach, Hungarian József Gelei, chose Parminder as one of the probables for an international tournament but was shocked to hear

that the Punjab midfielder was over thirty-five years old.
Parminder has no regrets about not joining the glamour clubs
of Kolkata, although he was approached several times by both,
because he was content with JCT and wished to remain in a
familiar environment.

Parminder got a coaching degree from NIS, Patiala, and worked
as assistant coach to Sukhwinder in JCT. In Sukhwinder's absence
from 1999–2001, it was Parminder who looked after JCT with
reasonable success in the NFL matches. One of the highlights of his
coaching career was guiding a new-look Punjab side to the final of
the 2004 Santosh Trophy in Delhi, where they lost narrowly 2-3 to
Kerala in extra time.

13

Defenders

S.K. Azizuddin

When the international match between India and Pakistan at Hyderabad's Police Stadium in 1959 ended, all the spectators spontaneously rose to cheer and applaud the dazzling display of one of their favourites—Syed Khwaja Azizuddin. It was his last match for the country. He was bowing out of international soccer after having represented India on twenty-two different occasions during a ten-year period. It was then a record for an Indian footballer, as India played limited international matches in the 1950s.

Aziz, as he is popularly known, means 'dear' in Urdu. True to his name, Aziz was admired by football enthusiasts wherever he played. He was a great crowd-puller, with his tough tackling, man marking, accurate and booming kicks, and powerful headers. A modest man, he was one of the greatest full-backs the country has seen in either the 2-3-5 system or even the three-back system of 3-2-5.

Broad-shouldered, squat and strongly built, Aziz never resorted to rough tactics and was called the 'gentle giant'. His timing for the tackle was impeccable. He excelled in shadowing a rival forward away from goal into a tight corner and then dispossessing him. He was also commanding in the air and had a tremendous spot jump. Aziz could kick powerfully and accurately with both feet and was an asset as a goalscorer in dead-ball situations. He would often move up and score vital goals, with powerful, well-directed headers, during corner kicks and free kicks. It was remarkable but he rarely wasted a pass. His defence-splitting diagonal passes to the flanks helped his team quickly counter-attack.

Aziz had a phlegmatic temperament and kept a cool head even under pressure. His positional play was extraordinary and his understanding with Hyderabad City Police's left-back S.A. Latif was perfect. They both covered each other very well. Aziz was quick while Latif was a solid defender with powerful kicks and exceptionally good volleys. When they came to play for the Durand in Delhi, the Hyderabad Police players stayed in simple conditions in the Karim Hotel, near Jama Masjid. Though Aziz was a regular international by then, he never complained or demanded special treatment.

In the two-back system, Aziz and Latif were a formidable combination and the best in India in that era. Aziz assisted India in winning the first Asian Games in Delhi in 1951, toured the Far East with the national team, and played in several Quadrangular Tournaments in the following years. The year 1955 was another milestone in his career when he was selected as India's captain for the Quadrangular at Dhaka. Aziz led the side magnificently. India won the tournament played on a round-robin league basis, comfortably beating Ceylon (as Sri Lanka was then known) 4-3, Burma 5-2 and Pakistan 2-1.

Aziz played in two Olympics: Helsinki 1952 and Melbourne 1956. A jovial man with an amicable temperament, he was deeply slighted at being passed over for captaincy in 1956. Later in life, Aziz told me that initially he wanted to withdraw from the team but S.A. Rahim scolded him and told him to play. Aziz bore no grudges and played with great aplomb, but he always said that being deprived of captaincy for the Olympics was the saddest day in his football career.

Two years later, he was captain of India in the 1958 Tokyo Asian Games. If not for the hectic schedule, the talented team led by Aziz could have got a medal, but India finished fourth.

Born on 12 July 1930, Aziz was fortunate to have his talent recognized early on by his physical instructor Thakur Rao at school. 'I am greatly indebted to him for putting me on the road to football fame,' Aziz used to say. Later he came under the care of the state coach Rahim, under whose guidance Aziz learnt more about tactics and techniques.[1]

Aziz considered his debut for Hyderabad in the semi-finals of the 1949 Santosh Trophy in Kolkata as his greatest match. Hyderabad was trailing by 2 goals to Bombay. In the second-half, Bombay nearly scored twice again. Hyderabad's goalkeeper was beaten but young Aziz made goal-line saves on both those occasions. That prevented Bombay from increasing their lead to 4 goals. Ultimately, Hyderabad scored thrice to win the match. Soon after, Aziz was included in the Indian team that visited Afghanistan that year. For the next ten years he was first choice either as full-back or centre-half in every Indian team.

After retirement from national and state-level football, Aziz continued to play for the Police team till 1963. Having undergone training under Rahim as a coach, he went to the NIS, Patiala, for further training. Later he was transferred from Hyderabad to Karimnagar, where he coached the district football team. He helped them reach the final of the inter-district zonal tournament for the first time. Aziz was also a Class I referee.

Aziz passed away in 1998 at his daughter's house in the US.

Jarnail Singh

The 1962 Jakarta Asian Games gold medal is Indian football's finest hour, because of the difficult circumstances in which it was won. India's ace defender Jarnail Singh's courage, versatility and determination played a major role in this memorable victory. Due to his head injury, Jarnail could no longer play as stopper-back, so Rahim made a bold tactical switch, putting him as a centre-forward. The burly Jarnail played his role to perfection as a battering ram, a striker who held up the ball and allowed his inside-forwards Chuni Goswami and T. Balaram to link up play. Jarnail also scored one of the 2 Indian goals.

Jarnail was the first Indian to be selected as captain of the Asian All-Stars team in 1966, and again the next year—a rare feat. He was arguably the greatest defender India has ever produced.

Jarnail Singh Dhillon was born in 1936 in undivided Punjab. His family was a victim of Partition and it was perhaps his horrific experiences as a child that instilled courage in him. Creditably, he never held grudges against players of a particular community and was professional in attitude.

An example of his mental toughness was evident in the 1960 Rome Olympics, when India was due to play Hungary. Though Hungary did not have players of the calibre of Ferenc Puskás and Nándor Hidegkuti, they were still a powerful team. P.K. Banerjee and others were discussing the merits of the Hungarian players and they warned Jarnail that he was up against a formidable centre-forward, the incomparable Flórián Albert.

Jarnail listened quietly and then intervened just once, 'Albert also has two hands and legs and I also have the same. Why should I be afraid?' Jarnail never feared reputations or past records. Irrespective of their fame, players from opposing teams were subjected to his fearsome tackles. He wore size twelve boots, was powerfully built, and tackled ruthlessly but with perfect timing. In the match against Hungary, Jarnail was admirable as he prevented Albert from touching the ball for long periods. Only once did Albert escape his marker to score a goal.

An intimidating defender and a perfectionist, Jarnail improved his technical skills—trapping, shooting and heading—with hours of intensive practice. He would tie a football to a tree branch and spend hours jumping and heading the ball. He could also kick powerfully with both feet.

Jarnail was first spotted in the DCM Trophy whilst playing for the Khalsa Sporting Club of the Sri Guru Gobind Singh Khalsa College, Mahilpur. In 1957, he made the dream move to Kolkata, joining Rajasthan Club. Rajasthan Club were one of the giant-killers in the Kolkata circuit at that time. Funded by local Marwari business families, the club bought players from all parts of India. Jarnail's start in Kolkata football was not smooth. He was used as a centre-half, which was not his natural position, and his boisterous and tough tackling style was initially not appreciated by viewers who nicknamed him 'Jaguar Singh'.

But Arun Sinha, the Mohun Bagan coach, noticed his raw talent and knew he could mould Jarnail into a top-class player. In 1959, Jarnail Singh began his legendary career donning the green-and-maroon jersey. Arun Sinha started playing him as a stopper-back. In the beginning Jarnail had a difficult time coping with the crowd pressure, but he rose to the challenge in an all-important Kolkata derby match that season. After that there was no looking back. He stayed with Bagan till he returned to Punjab in 1968.

Chuni Goswami and Jarnail formed one of the most memorable partnerships in Indian football. These two were diametrically opposite players in terms of style but combined well on the field. They excelled for Mohun Bagan, an unstoppable force in the 1960s, as well as for the country. Such was Jarnail's aura and confidence that after he had thwarted some attacks by an opposing team, Bagan's fans would make witty remarks punning on his first name. They would chant 'Ab Jarnail-General ko field marshal bana do [Now make Jarnail-General the field marshal].'

Jarnail Singh was a man of simple habits. When playing for Mohun Bagan in Kolkata he always stayed at Broadway Hotel. When visiting Delhi, he enjoyed eating dinner at the famous yet modest Kake Da Hotel at Connaught Place. Jarnail enjoyed the goat brain curry, keema-mattar, dal fry and chicken curry with naans at this restaurant. After retirement, he also enjoyed regular liquor sessions with friends.

Overall, Jarnail's fame in the 1960s was incomparable. In a poll organized by the *Indian Express* in 1963, he was elected as the most popular sportsperson in India, ahead of tennis star Ramanathan Krishnan, athlete Milkha Singh, and famous cricketers Chandu Borde and Polly Umrigar. House-full boards would be removed in cinema halls to accommodate him. After his return to Punjab, he captained the state team, which won its first Santosh Trophy in 1970. Four years later with him as the coach, Punjab steamrolled every other team in these national championships.

Jarnail was one of the select few Indian football players who enjoyed a star status even after leaving the game. He was bestowed with the Arjuna Award in 1964, and was the deputy director (1985–90) and director (1990–94) of sports for Punjab. Players from later generations, such as Subrata Bhattacharya and Mahesh Gawli, also admire and respect him, and people in his village Parnam still speak of him fondly.

Unfortunately, Jarnail's son Jagmohan, who was a promising football player, committed suicide in 1996, which had a crushing psychological effect on the indomitable Sikh. Jarnail Singh breathed his last on 14 October 2000. A large number of football personalities paid their tribute to one of the greatest and bravest players of Indian football.

Arun Ghosh

Lean and lanky Arun Ghosh has been considered one of India's all-time great defenders. He played forty-five times for India, including the Asian Games in 1962 and 1966, the Asian Cup in 1964 and 1967 (as captain), the pre-Olympics in 1964, and the Merdeka Tournament several times—in 1968 as captain. He excelled in the 1962 Asian Games and in the 1964 Asian Cup final round. In 1968 he was chosen for the Asian All-Stars XI.

Above all, the soft-spoken and stoical Arun Ghosh was a very cerebral defender. He excelled in tight marking, impeccable anticipation, hard tackling and timely clearances. His distribution of the ball was unmatched, even better than the famous Jarnail Singh. An anecdote best illustrates this. For the 1982 Asian Games, he was an assistant coach to national coach and former teammate P.K. Banerjee. During a practice match, India's main defender Monoranjan Bhattacharya was indisposed and declined to play. The other central-defenders were also injured. P.K. was thinking of reshuffling his back four when Arun Ghosh opted to play.

Arun Ghosh had retired from first-class football a decade ago. Yet he turned back the clock and by dint of sheer anticipation of the crowd, excelled in that match, curbing the opposing forwards.

After the match, all the Indian players complimented him, and Monoranjan even said, 'I will play the next practice match because the way you are playing, you may replace me in the Indian team.'

Like many in Indian sports in those days, the 1939-born Arun Ghosh's prowess was discovered fortuitously. In 1957, he was recommended to Chuni Goswami who was captain of the Calcutta University team for the inter-university football championships. Arun Ghosh excelled in practice matches; he was chosen for the team and helped them become all-India inter-university champions. Two years later he joined Mohun Bagan, after an impressive showing for Howrah Union in the 1958 season. In the 1959 Durand Cup, the famous club's regular full-back T.A. Rahman could not make the trip to Delhi due to an injury. Arun Ghosh got his chance and excelled, especially in the final against a classy Mohammedan Sporting side that included the brilliant forwards Oomer and Moosa. His display in the final impressed the national coach S.A. Rahim who always watched important tournaments to discover new talent. Immediately afterwards, the soft-spoken Rahim asked Arun Ghosh to join the national camp. Rahim moulded Arun Ghosh into a complete defender and selected him for the 1960 Rome Olympics.

From 1960–62 Arun Ghosh played for East Bengal and became a legend. His finest hour for East Bengal was in the 1960 DCM final, when he helped them triumph 3-1 against a rampaging Mohammedan Sporting. His commitment was remarkable. In the return leg of the 1961 Calcutta League against Mohun Bagan, he played despite having a high fever. After the match he became unconscious and had to be hospitalized.

Arun Ghosh represented West Bengal in the Santosh Trophy from 1959 to 1961, and then from 1963 to 1972 he played for his employers, the Railways. He was brilliant in the 1971 Santosh Trophy final in Chennai. Railways led 1-0 and West Bengal's star-studded attacking quartet that included Subhash Bhowmick, Mohammed Habib, Swapan Sengupta and Sukalyan Ghosh Dastidar launched numerous attacks, but they were all thwarted. This was one of the best games of Arun Ghosh's career. Till the last quarter of the match, West Bengal could not score and an upset seemed imminent. Bhowmick was getting increasingly frustrated and kept muttering in Bengali, 'We cannot play as this old man is blocking all our moves.' Eventually, Arun Ghosh got injured and limped off. West Bengal went on a rampage and won 4-1. This final was one of those matches in which the score line does not reflect the true nature of the game.

Later, as a coach, Arun Ghosh was gentle but firm and helped to improve the technical skills, positioning and football acumen of his players. If he found any player slackening, he would have a quiet word with and urge him to be professional.

Arun Ghosh's most successful year was in 1978 when he guided a young East Bengal team to a resounding 3-0 win over star-studded Mohun Bagan in the Durand final. He also guided East Bengal and later Mohun Bagan to Federation Cup victories in 1978 and 1980 respectively (for details, see Chapter 1: 'Bengal'). Under him, Bagan won the 1980 Durand beating Mohammedan Sporting 1-0 in the final.

In 1978, Arun Ghosh was appointed as chief coach of the Indian team for the Asian Games; also in 1985 when India played in the World Cup qualifiers for the first time; and again in 1993 for the 1994 World Cup qualifiers. He was assistant coach to P.K. Banerjee for the 1982 Asian Games.

14

Goalkeepers

Peter Thangaraj

In any imaginary all-time great Indian eleven, Peter Thangaraj is always the first-choice goalkeeper. Scribes, experts and former players all unanimously rate him the finest goalkeeper India has ever had, and the best in Asia in the 1960s. Born in 1936 in Secunderabad, he was from the Trimulgherry-Cantonment Board stretch that produced some of the other stalwarts of Indian football. Ironically, Thangaraj started his career as a centre-forward for Praga Tools Corporation in the local league. He later played for other clubs, before joining MRC Wellington, in 1953, where his career blossomed. He made the switch to goalkeeper at the behest of their commanding officer, mentor and football buff Col. Rajarathnam.

Peter Thangaraj's international career ranged from 1955–67, the longest span ever by an Indian goalkeeper. He made his international debut in the 1955 Quadrangular Tournament in Dhaka as the second choice to Sanat Sett. Ever since then he was always first-choice goalkeeper for the country. According to Thangaraj, 1956 was the turning point in his football career. It was the year he first played in the Santosh Trophy and his sterling performances led to his selection for the 1956 Melbourne Olympics, where India reached the semi-final. He played in the next Olympics in 1960, in three Asian Games including the 1962 final, the Asia Cup in 1964, and several

Merdeka Tournaments. Thangaraj was also in the Asian All-Stars in the 1960s.

At 6 ft 3 in., Thangaraj cut an imposing figure and could intimidate opposing forwards. He was commanding in the air and with his large hands, safely plucked crosses from both flanks. Despite his burly physique he was also very acrobatic and famous for his dramatic reflex-action saves. Attracted by his charismatic personality, crowds came in large numbers to see him perform. His long one-handed throws to set up quick counter-attacks were always a delight to watch. Another Thangaraj special were his booming kicks, which landed near the opposing 18-yard box.

Nicknamed the 'lamp post' during his playing days, Thangaraj felt that the sense of team spirit was India's forte during the successful era from 1956–66. He once said, 'We shared responsibilities. We understood each other very well. If I had left charge, Arun (Ghosh) and Jarnail (Singh) let me get the ball even though we rarely said anything to each other. And the moment I shaped up for a goal-kick, P.K. (Banerjee) would start running and I knew exactly where to land the ball for him.' In the Santosh Trophy, Thangaraj holds a unique record as the only player to have led two different outfits to victory. In Calicut in 1960, Services won against a star-studded West Bengal team—with Chuni Goswami and T. Balaram in the ranks—for the first time, and without conceding a goal. Under him, Railways had a memorable triumph against Services, in the 1966 Santosh Trophy in Hyderabad. For two spells, he also played for Bengal in these national championships.

During Thangaraj's seven years with MRC, the club twice won the coveted Durand Cup. He considered the 1958 Durand triumph as one of the great moments of his career when they ousted East Bengal and Gorkha Brigade in the final rounds.

In 1961 Thangaraj began his eleven-year association with Kolkata football, first with Mohammedan Sporting, then Mohun Bagan, and the longest with East Bengal. With these famous clubs, he won all the major domestic tournaments more than once, but the Durand always had special memories for him. Thangaraj hung up his boots after another season with Mohammedan Sporting in 1971–72. He played top-level football in India for two decades, a testimony to his fitness and dedication.

After retirement, Thangaraj became a qualified coach and trained the Aligarh Muslim University team and Vasco Goa, where he played as well. Then for two decades he served Bokaro Steel Plant as a coach and administrative officer and was also adviser to their football academy.

Thangaraj's life was dedicated to football and nurturing young talent, but apart from the Arjuna Award in 1967 he did not get any other form of recognition or accolades in India.

At the close of the twentieth century, a poll was held to choose Asia's goalkeepers of the century. Despite India's low profile in Asian football during that time, Thangaraj still polled enough votes to finish fifth overall in the all-time great Asian goalkeepers' list. Saudi Arabia's 1994 and 1998 World Cup custodian Mohamed Al-Deayea won the contest. Former East Bengal coach Subhash Bhowmick feels that Thangaraj had the talent and physique to play professional football in Europe, but Indian players earlier used to be content with the public-sector jobs and did not like to venture abroad.

Peter Thangaraj breathed his last on 24 November 2008.

Brahmanand S.K. Shankhwalkar

Lean, lanky and reserved, Brahmanand Shagun Kamat Shankhwalkar is the philosopher king of Goan football. He overcame adversity, injuries and setbacks to have a long, illustrious career in which he won numerous honours. He represented Goa in the Santosh Trophy for a record seventeen times and saved six penalties in regulation time, which is unique. He also created a record in the 1983–84 senior national championships for not conceding a goal for 576 minutes.

The AIFF honoured him by declaring Brahmanand the 'Player of the Decade' for 1985–95, and he became the first Goan to be bestowed with the coveted Arjuna Award in 1997 for his distinguished service to Indian football. He also received the highest Goan state honour, the Kerkar Award. Born on 6 March 1954, he first played for India in the 1977 Jasson Celebration Cup tournament in Kabul and became captain for the first time in the 1983 Nehru Cup at Kochi. His international career ended in 1990. Earlier, he had played for the junior Indian team in 1975 at the Asian Youth Championships in Kuwait. His biography is included in textbooks in Goa to inspire children.

Brahmanand's affair with the game started when his neighbourhood family doctor Alvaro Remigio Pinto encouraged him to play football. Dr Remigio also guided him to play as a goalkeeper due to his lean frame and height. He devised exercises for him and also taught him to concentrate for long durations. Brahmanand's playing career started accidentally in 1971 when he had to replace the missing custodians for Panvel Sports Club on New Year's Day. The club's management were hesitant to play him but after seeing his performance, they signed him up the very next day. Under his captaincy in 1974 the team won both the Bandodkar Trophy and the Goa League. Brahmanand joined Salgaocar in 1974. He stayed with them for seventeen years before shifting to Churchill Brothers for a brief period. He retired in 1995 from the little-known Anderson Marine Sports Club, from his ancestral village Sancoale, having played first-class football for twenty-five years.

The high point of his career was on his birthday when he played with guts and conviction to thwart West Bengal's rampaging attacks in the 1982–83 Santosh Trophy final in Kolkata. The final and replay ended in goalless draws and for the first time this title was shared. After this victory, an elated Brahmanand proclaimed, 'We have proved tonight that football is played elsewhere too, not merely in Bengal.' Calm and composed, Brahmanand had motivated his team, telling them not to get overawed by the internationals in the West Bengal side or their vociferous supporters.

In 1984, Goa won the Santosh Trophy outright for the first time beating Punjab in the final 1-0. Brahmanand was again captain and the coach was again T. Shanmugham. Brahmanand did not concede a goal in the entire championship that culminated in Chennai. Completely committed to Goan football, he had tears of joy rolling down his cheeks when he stepped up to receive the glittering trophy.

The Santosh Trophy victories were really significant for Brahmanand as he had made a comeback after a career-threatening injury. In 1981, he had fractured his hand at a preparation camp for the 1982 Asian Games. It was sheer grit and endless hours of strengthening exercises that enabled him to regain his place in the Indian squad. Brahmanand's quiet self-belief helped him prolong his career, serve India in many international tournaments, and become the greatest goalkeeper Goa has produced so far.

After retirement Brahmanand continued to serve football as a specialized goalkeepers' coach with the national team from 1997–2005, having completed his training under AFC. He also became the technical director of GFA's Youth Football Development programme.

15

Legendary Coaches

A country with a foreign coach has never won a World Cup title or a major international tournament, except Greece in Euro 2004, when Otto Rehhagel of Germany was their coach. Yet, many countries—especially in Asia and Africa—opt for foreign coaches as they believe their expertise, acumen and experience can rapidly improve standards. Those who disagree believe that a local coach has a better understanding of the psychology of his country's players and so is more effective. Foreign versus local coach is a perennial debate in international football.

India's first foreign coach was Harry Wright of England who came in the early 1960s, when the Indian squad was considered the best in Asia. Wright's strict training methods were not appreciated and he did not gel with the players. In the 1964 pre-Olympics, India lost 0-3 and 1-3 to Iran and got eliminated. There was discontent and newspaper headlines appeared that said, 'Wright is not always right'.

From 1981 till the conclusion of the Asian Games in Delhi in December 1982, India had Dietmar Pfiefer of the erstwhile German Democratic Republic as technical director. Bob Bootland of England was briefly the national coach in 1983. From 1983–85 came the late Milovan Ćirić of former Yugoslavia who had also coached Red Star Belgrade. József Gelei of Hungary followed from 1990–91. Next was the Czech, Jerry Pesek, from 1993–94. Rustam Akramov of Uzbekistan succeeded him in 1995 and remained till 1996. Islam Akhmedov (Uzbekistan) was briefly national coach for the Sahara Millennium Cup in 2001.

In June 2002, the AIFF appointed a thirty-nine-year-old Englishman Stephen Constantine, a qualified FIFA instructor, as national coach. During his tenure India won the LG Cup in Vietnam in August 2002. They also finished runners-up in the inaugural Afro-Asian Games in Hyderabad in October 2003.

The experienced Englishman Bob Houghton was the longest-serving and most successful foreign coach in India, from 2006–11. He guided the national team to three successive international tournament successes, the Nehru Cup in 2007 and 2009, and the AFC Challenge Cup in 2008. By winning the AFC Challenge Cup, India qualified for the Asian Cup final rounds in Doha Qatar in 2011. It was India's third appearance in the Asian Cup final rounds after 1964 (runners-up) and 1984.

The next foreign coach Wim Koevermans, a member of the Netherlands team that won Euro 1988, made the Indians play possession football and build attacks from defence. In his first tournament India won the 2012 Nehru Cup in Delhi, edging past Cameroon (second-string squad) via the penalty shoot-out in the final. However, after that it went downhill.

In February 2015, Stephen Constantine was again appointed national coach. He gave debuts to thirty-three players and, with scientific coaching, has helped India improve from 173 (March 2015) to 96 in the FIFA rankings list (as of July 2017).

Balaidas Chatterjee, Bagha Shome, Saroj Bose, Sheoo Mewalal, S. Langcha Mitra and Arun Ghosh (Bengal), G.M.H. Basha and J. Kittu (Karnataka), Mohammed Hussain (Bombay), Jarnail Singh and Sukhwinder Singh (Punjab), M.A. Salaam (Hyderabad), Anjan Chowdhury (SAI) and Savio Medeira (Goa) are the Indian coaches to have coached the national team.

However, the quartet who achieved the maximum success with their clubs and country are: the late Syed Abdul Rahim, Syed Nayeemuddin (both from Hyderabad), the late Amal Dutta, and P.K. Banerjee (both from Bengal). For nearly half a century—from 1950 till the late 1990s—this famous four shaped the destiny of Indian football with their dedication, inspirational coaching and tactical innovations. In the twenty-first century, impressive Indian coaches have been Armando Colaco and Subhash Bhowmick. For two decades, 1991–2012, Bimal Ghosh and Shabbir Ali also had remarkable records as club coaches. Recently, Derrick Pereira, Sanjoy Sen, Khalid Jamil and Santosh Kashyap have been noteworthy.

S.A. Rahim

In Hyderabad, the city of the Nizams, India's most successful and revered coach Syed Abdul Rahim was born on 17 August 1909. He grew up during the 1920s when football flourished in this city. B.K. Iyengar, Riasat Ali, Aftab Ali, Sher Khan and Mehboob Khan were famous players of that era and Rahim also played with them. Football in this region received the patronage of the royalty, especially the Nawab of Tarband. S.A. Rahim, who as a coach guided India to two Asian Games gold medals, was the secretary of the HFA from 1943 till his death on 11 June 1963.

Rahim started coaching at a time when formal coaching was almost non-existent. A teacher by profession, he was a well-read person, a practical psychologist, great tactician, motivator and disciplinarian. He achieved glory as coach of Hyderabad City Police, the most successful team of the 1950s, and also successfully coached Hyderabad/Andhra Pradesh in the Santosh Trophy, as well as the Indian team on various occasions.

Rahim's coaching was very methodical. Moves planned for a match were first theoretically explained on a blackboard and were later rehearsed on the ground till the players perfected them. Rahim ensured that his players' conduct on the field and dedication were impeccable.

Like the late Sir Alf Ramsey, Rahim was always fiercely loyal to his players and, as was typical of his times, had a very paternalistic attitude towards those he coached. In that respect he was cast in the mould of authoritarian figures like Sepp Herberger (West Germany, 1954 World Cup) or the legendary Herbert Chapman (Arsenal, 1930s). Rahim discouraged his players from playing cards (as he felt it upset team spirit and marred concentration and discipline) or even having an occasional drink. For entertainment, he encouraged them to read or analyse and discuss the game. Watching films was the only luxury permitted.

But he was also pragmatic in his approach to man management. Once Rahim was coaching the Hyderabad team for the 1959 Santosh Trophy held in Nagaon, Assam. The team included Saleh (Jr) who, like Socrates the legendary Brazilian skipper, was a chain-smoker. During the tournament, the frail but tenacious midfielder became desperate for a smoke and begged his teammate S.S. Hakeem, Rahim's son, to ask his father for a few cigarettes. Ironically, Rahim always smoked Charminar cigarettes and carried packets with him wherever he went. Hakeem said, 'I hesitantly approached my father . . . At first he said no, but then realizing Saleh's plight he gave him two cigarettes, with a warning that he should give up this habit, especially during tournaments.'

In international football, Rahim's achievements are numerous. Even before Brazil popularized the 4-2-4 system in the 1958 World Cup, Rahim used this playing system with the Indian team. In the 1956 Melbourne Olympics, instead of a deep-lying centre-forward he used Samar 'Badru' Banerjee in the withdrawn, playmaker's role. According to Hakeem, 'No country in the world had even attempted that formation then.' India trounced Australia 4-2 to reach the semi-finals.

Rahim also guided India to success in the South East Asian Quadrangular Tournaments in 1952 and 1954. In the 1959 Merdeka Tournament, India finished as unbeaten runners-up in the four-team final-round group league.

But it was in the Asian Games that Rahim achieved his greatest success and glory. He guided India to two gold medals—the inaugural 1951 edition in Delhi and later in 1962 in Jakarta. It was only under Rahim's coaching that India established their supremacy as the best in the continent.

On their way to the 1962 Asian Games final, India beat Thailand 4-1 and Japan 2-0, and then South Vietnam 3-2 in the semi-finals. The semi-final victory came after a titanic struggle, as Vietnam had a formidable team. Coach Rahim had instilled great team spirit and self-belief in the Indian squad. The fitness levels of the team were also exemplary—and probably the best-ever—as Rahim put a lot of emphasis on power training and cohesiveness.

The Indian side showed remarkable dedication and adaptability to win the final 2-1 against the favourites, South Korea. Incidentally, in an earlier preliminary league match the Koreans had beaten India 2-0. Due to injuries, coach Rahim improvised with the playing eleven (see Prologue for more details). It was this ability to get the best out of the available resources that has made Rahim a legend amongst Indian coaches.

Hyderabad will remember S.A. Rahim for popularizing the game in the city with his innovative coaching methods. His son Hakeem recalled:

> He organized non-dribbling tournaments so that teams could improve one-touch passing and combination. There were also weaker-leg tournaments where a player was only allowed to kick and tackle with his weaker foot. This enabled players to become two-footed. For juniors he organized height-restricted tournaments, five-a-side and seven-a-side games in local parks. Thus the flow of talent in Hyderabad football was consistent for over three decades.

Each year at training camps he gave intensive coaching to the promising players seen in league matches. Rahim also started age-group tournaments and gave specialized training to teenagers long before these trends became fashionable. Always meticulous, he set different goals and tasks for various age-group teams. All these initiatives ensured that while Mumbai and Kolkata lured away many top Hyderabad footballers, the city was able to replace them with several new talents, who regularly represented India.

Rahim also conducted a number of coaching classes for footballers and trained scores of coaches and referees. He was a visionary and did more for Indian football than any coach, before or after.

Amal Dutta

India's first-ever professional coach, Amal Dutta, may be called India's Brian Clough. He was renowned for his tactical acumen, innovations, and development of young talent, but famous for his acerbic remarks and critical comments against the establishment. Due to this his tenure with the national team lasted barely a year and he was never made coach of India's age-group teams—a loss for the game in the country.

A trendsetter, Dutta was made technical director of the Indian squad with Syed Nayeemuddin as chief coach in 1987. Planning meticulously, he introduced the Indian team to a new 4-4-2 formation, becoming the first to make them play with either retracting wingers or all-purpose midfielders. At the Salt Lake Stadium in Kolkata, India won the 1987 SAF Games gold medal beating Nepal 1-0 in the final. In the 1988 Nehru Cup at Siliguri, India played inspired football, drawing with Poland 1-1 with tenacious central midfielder P. Vijay Kumar scoring the goal. Against Hungary too India took the lead, with Tarun Dey scoring a penalty kick before losing the match. The four midfielders moved effortlessly into scoring positions and the overlapping left-back provided thrust on the flanks.

Amal da, as he was popularly known, was a highly successful club coach, winning thirty-nine major trophies with Mohun Bagan (26), East Bengal (10) and Mohammedan Sporting (3). He was renowned for spotting and nurturing young talent and rescuing a team in adversity. As he once jocularly told me, 'I am known as a Harley Street specialist. When the patient (losing football club) has been treated by all doctors and not recovered, they come to me.'

Born on 4 May 1930, Amal Dutta was an iconoclast and was willing to explore new territories. A competent midfielder in the mid-1950s, he represented India in the 1954 Asian Games. He took a one-year coaching course at the FA in England and worked

under the renowned Walter Winterbottom. Soon after his return
and coaching his former club East Bengal successfully, he gave up
a cushy job in the Indian Railways to become a full-time football
coach—the first one to do this. This was a bold step as in those
days income from football was meagre. He once told me he took
the plunge as he was confident of his knowledge of the game.

Dutta coached in Odisha and Kerala for some years and returned
to coach Mohun Bagan in the 1969–70 season. He introduced them
to the 4-2-4 formation at a time when most Indian teams played in
the 3-2-5 formation. The central idea of the 4-2-4 is that both wing-
backs overlap to lend width to the attack. Initially he faced intense
opposition, particularly from the legendary defender Sailen Manna,
but Dutta was persuasive and patient. He spent hours with the Bagan
officials and former players showing them videocassettes of world
champions Brazil playing in the 4-2-4 system and the effectiveness
of the formation. Finally, they relented, and Dutta became famous
as the man who brought 4-2-4 to Indian club football. Bagan were
immediately successful and the system became a craze in Kolkata.

From the 1970s to the 1990s, the P.K. Banerjee–Amal Dutta
rivalry as club coaches of either East Bengal or Mohun Bagan was as
intense as the celebrated contemporary rivalry of Pep Guardiola and
José Mourinho. Their verbal jousting through their football columns
often heightened the suspense before an important derby match.

In the 1997 season, Amal Dutta created a sensation with his
tactical innovation the 'diamond system', that is, a 3-4-3 formation
with a defensive midfielder playing as a screen ahead of the stopper-
back. There were two attacking midfielders on the flanks, who would
also backtrack to help in the defence. The attacking midfielder at the
tip of the diamond would link with the three front-runners and also
defend if required. Dutta's new system aroused spectator and media
interest especially after Bagan's 6-0 demolition of Churchill Brothers
in the KBL Federation Cup quarter-finals. The crowds flocked back
and the semi-final against East Bengal attracted a record attendance
of 1,31,000 at the Salt Lake Stadium.

Bimal Ghosh, chosen as the best coach in the 1998 Philips
National League, rated Amal Dutta 'as the best reader of the game

in Indian football. His substitutions were always very good'. A perfectionist, dreamer and visionary, Amal Dutta is recognized as the finest thinker of the game in India. A voracious reader, his knowledge and analysis of trends in world football were always insightful. He had multifaceted interests and read widely from Shakespeare to Salman Rushdie; he relaxed by playing musical instruments.

At least in death, Amal Dutta got the respect and honour often denied to him during his illustrious career. The eighty-six-year-old Dutta died on 10 July, the day of the Euro 2016 final, suffering from Alzheimer's. Creditably, fans and former players braved the showers for his final journey around Kolkata, his body draped in the tricolour. His last rites were performed with full state honours and a gun salute.

P.K. Banerjee

In the 1970s there was a popular saying, 'Where P.K. goes the trophies go.' Pradip Kumar Banerjee, popularly known as P.K., became India's first superstar coach. The brilliance of great coaches before him, like Rahim and Amal Dutta, was recognized in football circles alone. It was P.K. who made the role of the coach indispensable by utilizing the media effectively.

Born on 15 October 1936, P.K. was a prodigy. A dashing but tricky right-winger with a blistering shot, he became an Olympian in 1956 at age twenty and later captained India in the 1960 Rome Olympics. He scored in the final against South Korea in the 1962 Asian Games and was chosen as Asia's best winger. For over a decade he was the regular first-choice right-winger for the Indian team, and was awarded the FIFA Centennial Order of Merit in 2004.

In the national team P.K. had invariably played under coach Rahim, who noted P.K.'s astute match analysis and encouraged him to take up coaching. P.K. underwent several courses at home and abroad and took to coaching like a duck to water.

P.K.'s tenure with the national team started with a bang in the 1970 Bangkok Asian Games. He and the late G.M.H. Basha guided India to win a bronze medal, the last medal won by India in a major international competition. P.K. coached India in four Asian Games—including 1974 Tehran, 1982 Delhi and 1986 Seoul—the maximum ever for any Indian coach. India performed creditably at the 1982 Asian Games as well, losing by a ninetieth-minute free-kick goal to Saudi Arabia in the quarter-finals. In the 1986 Merdeka Tournament, P.K. guided India to the semi-finals, including a memorable 4-3 win over South Korea.

P.K. was involved with club coaching for nearly three decades, and his first major club assignment was with East Bengal in 1972. This squad became the first and till now the only team post-Independence to win the Calcutta League without conceding a goal. In addition, they annexed three other major domestic tournaments and displayed all the trademarks of P.K.'s coaching: a well-organized defence, quick breaks from defence to attack, variety in attack, and tactical awareness coupled with emphasis on individual skill.

An effervescent person, P.K. was unafraid to gesticulate and show his emotions during matches as he urged his team to victory. Fans were delighted with his open involvement and the media lapped it up. He also set the trend of providing crisp analysis, juicy quotes and invigorating comments that exhibited self-confidence and control.

Like his mentor Rahim, the wily P.K. also made subtle use of human psychology to motivate his protégés. For instance, in the 1975 DCM final East Bengal were trailing Hanyang University (South Korea) 0-1 at half-time, in front of a capacity crowd at the Ambedkar Stadium. P.K. strode into the centre of the field with the East Bengal club flag in his hand. Recalling that incident he said, 'I made the players form a circle around me and spoke passionately to them. I made them all touch the flag and pledge that they would strain every sinew to bring glory to their club.' It was a remarkable gesture that whipped up a frenzy amongst the crowd. P.K. would later use this tactic often, and the crowd's roar would rouse the players to excel.

Another example is how he raised the game of two of the hardest kickers in Indian football in the 1970s, wingers Subhash

Bhowmick and Swapan Sengupta. By taunting them that they could not kick the ball as powerfully as he did in his heyday, he got 'both of them to spend long sessions after practice to improve the power in their shots'.

In club football, P.K. has won every major tournament in India as a coach. He guided Mohun Bagan to their first-ever triple crown triumph in 1977, and with East Bengal demonstrated his astute game reading particularly in the 1973 DCM tournament. In the initial stages of the 1973 DCM semi-final, East Bengal struggled to find their rhythm against the hard-tackling Leaders Club. P.K. realized that their frail playmaker Samaresh 'Pintu' Chowdhury was being repeatedly body-charged, so he substituted Samaresh with junior international Chandan Gupta.

Many East Bengal fans and media personnel were aghast as only two substitutions were allowed in those days. The fans muttered and even shouted, '*P.K. da ki korchis?* [What is P.K. da doing?]' P.K. had the last laugh. The combative and stocky Chandan Gupta coped with the physical challenge, and slowly East Bengal regrouped and dominated play. This East Bengal squad went on to have a memorable win against a leading North Korean outfit in the final, a match P.K. considers the best of his career (see 'Historic Clashes' section).

P.K.'s rivalry with the quiet but shrewd Amal Dutta is well-documented, as these coaching titans dominated Kolkata club football for nearly two decades. His finest act of motivation was before the 1997 Federation Cup semi-final when Dutta was coach of Mohun Bagan (for details, see Chapter 10: 'The Great Rivalry').

Time could not diminish P.K.'s appetite for coaching. He has been involved with the Indian team at every age group, was technical director of TFA (1993–96), and even in 2002 at age sixty-six, he was technical director of the Indian U-16 team.

Syed Nayeemuddin

During his playing days, Syed Nayeemuddin, born on 11 February 1944 in Hyderabad, was one of the most accomplished and artistic defenders in the country. Nayeem—as he was popularly known—was a versatile player and had a glittering international career. He represented the senior national team regularly from 1964–71, including as captain in 1970. In 1967, he was chosen for the Asian All-Stars team.

He learnt his football skills under S.A. Rahim in the Andhra Police team which he joined in 1963. From 1966 till the end of his playing career, Nayeem played in Kolkata for all three big clubs, starting with East Bengal. A trendy dresser and classy player, he was nicknamed the 'Dev Anand of football'.

The soft-spoken but serious Nayeem plunged into coaching after injury terminated his playing career in the mid-1970s. A perfectionist, he took coaching courses all over the world, often at his own expense, after completing a course in India. He firmly believes that a coach never stops learning.

In the early 1980s Nayeem started coaching Mohammedan Sporting and made an impact, before becoming assistant coach to the national team in 1983. From 1987–89 he was national coach for the Nehru Cup, the SAF Games (when India won the gold medal) and the Asian Cup. His first stint as national coach was not too memorable, as he tended to be rigid in his game plans and was also overshadowed by Amal Dutta (technical director from 1987–88), who often planned the coaching sessions and the playing formation.

It was in his second stint as club coach, which started in 1990, that Nayeem blossomed. He became renowned as the man for a crisis. Nayeem's seriousness during preparation and his tactical acumen transformed the floundering fortunes of East Bengal. They remained undefeated for the rest of the season and won the triple crown for the first time. Nayeem brought a new dimension to Indian football by introducing weight training and even sand running into regular training sessions. This particularly helped skilful playmaker Krishanu Dey, whose career got an extra lease of life once he toughened up under Nayeem.

The next season East Bengal again won three titles, including their third successive Durand victory. Nayeem coached Bagan from 1992–94 and they annexed ten trophies in two seasons.

Nayeem's greatest hour in club football was in 1994 when he again took over East Bengal, just two days before the prestigious Rovers Cup. East Bengal had not won a single trophy that season, but within the space of a month, Nayeem helped them annex both the Rovers Cup and IFA Shield. Realizing that his midfield was fragile, he opted for the 4-4-2 formation instead of the customary 4-3-3 system.

Nayeem had the Midas touch from 1990–95, when he won twenty-five trophies with both East Bengal and Mohun Bagan, and guided West Bengal to three successive triumphs (1993–95) in the Santosh Trophy. His trademarks as a coach were emphasis on fitness, nutritive diet, proper rest and adequate medical care. Any team under Nayeem's charge would become the fittest in India.

In 1997, he was given charge of the national team which he developed into a physically fit, tactically alert and cohesive side. India won the SAFF Championships trouncing the Maldives 5-1 in the final, reached the semi-finals of the Nehru Cup for the first time, and the quarter-final league phase in the 1998 Asian Games, despite limited exposure. After the match with Japan, their manager Philippe Troussier complimented Nayeem and said that the team had a great future.

A strict disciplinarian, Nayeem's attention to detail and analysis of a player's ability are unique. He has transformed the careers of many players, including the Nigerian international Emeka Ezeugo. Nayeem made Emeka realize he lacked the necessary speed to succeed as a striker and transformed him into a midfielder. The rest is history. Some of Nayeem's coaching methods were both unique and innovative. In 1997, he made the national team stay on the top floors of the hotel and insisted they climb the stairs instead of taking the lift. In the 2000–01, he took the East Bengal squad to Darjeeling in north Bengal for altitude training.

As a coach, Nayeem is in the mould of Argentina's national coach Daniel Passarella. With his focus on players' well-being, he insists they drink only mineral water and receive the best diet, so he has been branded an expensive and demanding coach. True to his beliefs, Nayeem has often bought dry fruits, chicken and fruits for his players even if officials demurred at the extra cost.

He pithily observed, 'Just as a car needs petrol to run, so a player needs rest and good food to perform well.'

On 2 March 2006, Syed Nayeemuddin was sacked as national coach. The only man to have won both the Dronacharya Award as a coach (1992) and Arjuna Award as a player (1970), he then went through the worst phase of his career. Nayeem, who won thirty-five tournaments as a club coach and three international titles as national coach (including the 2005 SAFF Championships), found all doors shut to him. With no other source of income, he became financially dependent on his sons, which hurt his pride. He has only an old scooter, which he calls his 'old friend'. Dismayed, he even remarked, 'I have turned from national coach to national beggar.'

Shunned in India for over a decade, Nayeem was appointed by Bangladesh in 2007–08, becoming the only Indian to be national coach of a foreign country. He has also coached two clubs, Brothers Union and Mohammedan Sporting of Dhaka, and moulded young Bangladesh internationals.

Nayeem is the only player to have received both the Mohun Bagan Ratna award (2016) and the East Bengal Lifetime award (2017) for his excellence. But his quest for perfection and taciturn nature have made him more sinned against than sinning. He remains a much-maligned coach, whose invaluable services have not been fully utilized.

Armando Colaco

India's most successful club coach in the twenty-first century, Armando Colaco has guided Goa's Dempo to win the NFL twice (2004–05 and 2006–07), three I-League titles (2007–08, 2009–10 and 2011–12), the Federation Cup (2004), the Super Cup (2008 and 2010) and the Durand Cup (2006). Armando Colaco took over as Dempo's coach in 2002 and transformed the fortunes of this club that was on the verge of being closed down.

Given the freedom to develop a team within a limited budget, Armando revamped Dempo in his very first stint as a club coach.

Like the great Liverpool team of the 1980s, he chose players who fitted into his style of playing based on possession, quick interchange of positions and clever passing. He built a reputation of being a good judge of a player's ability and character. Under his guidance, Brazilian Beto and Nigerian Ranti became a lethal combination. Armando did not believe in spending lavishly to recruit glamorous names but would splurge when required, as in the case of Mahesh Gawli. Gawli became the first Indian defender to get Rs 1 crore, and at the peak of his career, helped Dempo win three I-League titles. From 2005–12, Dempo, nicknamed the 'Barcelona of India', were a delight to watch.

The hallmarks of Armando's coaching have been his excellent management skills and ability to create a family-like, cohesive atmosphere with a settled squad. He was also secretary of Dempo and ensured his players got a fair deal from the management.

After his success with the club, Armando was chosen as national coach in June 2011. During his brief stint he got India to play cohesively and rely on quick short passes. He also gave debuts to striker Jeje Lalpekhlua and midfielder Lalrindika Ralte. His greatest triumph was India's 2-1 win over higher-ranked Qatar in a friendly match on 17 July 2011.

Armando then committed a huge blunder during a tour to the Caribbean Islands in August 2011. He did not let his team play a friendly match in Barbados as the players had not had enough time to rest. Not realizing the protocol involved in being national coach, he created an embarrassing situation for both countries. The AIFF gave Armando only a year's contract, and feeling piqued, he left in a huff. The Goan coach said that like foreign coaches, he had expected to be given more time to 'work with players and . . . develop a national squad'.

After a couple of seasons with Dempo and a fallout with the management, he was recruited by East Bengal in 2013. As their style of play was very different, he was unable to revamp the side, and during his brief tenure they excelled only in patches. After some years in the wilderness, he is back as coach of new Goan club Bardez FC.

Subhash Bhowmick

Esteemed international of the mid-1970s, Subhash Bhowmick was a versatile right-footed winger, equally comfortable on either flank. He made his debut as a coach with the national team before getting established with any club, a rare occurrence in any country. His debut for the President's Gold Cup in 1989 was not very successful and Bhowmick's coaching ambitions were thwarted for nearly a decade.

He was more successful in his first stint as East Bengal's coach in 1999–2000, but his greatest hour came in his second stint with the club, from 2002–05. He returned to coaching after heart surgery and was on a restricted diet, but worked methodically to get results. He won eleven trophies with East Bengal including back-to-back NFL titles, the Durand Cup in 2002 and 2004, and two trophies on foreign soil—the San Miguel Cup in Nepal and the LG ASEAN Club Championship in Jakarta.

Bhowmick created a family-like atmosphere in the team and ensured his players got the best treatment. He improved their game by cajoling, coaxing and sometimes even shouting at them. An excellent analyst, he would give very precise instructions to his players before each match.

His eye for talent is exceptional, as was seen in his moulding of Syed Rahim Nabi. Bhowmick converted Nabi from a prodigal striker into an attacking left-back, and made him a fine utility player for the national team as well. Bhowmick was the first Indian coach to experiment with a three-back system. Teams coached by him were always attractive to watch, as they used the flanks to attack, either through retracting wingers or attacking wing-backs.

Bhowmick's finest hour was when he led East Bengal to remarkable success in the inaugural ASEAN Club Championship in July 2003. At the start of the 2003–04 season, he recruited several established internationals and retained most of the previous year's squad, which had won five major tournaments.

Bhowmick changed the pre-season training of East Bengal, and like professional clubs in Europe, placed emphasis on improving fitness levels. The players stayed in a five-star hotel in Kolkata, with access to a gymnasium and sauna baths for six weeks. The rigorous training by Kevin Jackson made this squad the fittest-ever football team in India (see 'Historic Clashes' section for details).

Bhowmick was hailed as a visionary for his meticulous planning, eye for talent and team-management skills. Performing unremarkably in the domestic tournaments, East Bengal were able to retain their NFL title in 2003 and also became the first Indian club to enter the AFC Cup quarter-finals in May 2004. Bhowmick's stock as a coach was soaring high.

His coaching career got stalled as he was falsely implicated in a case in December 2005. He then coached or was technical director of Mohammedan Sporting, Salgaocar, East Bengal and Mohun Bagan. His next big success was as technical director of Churchill Brothers in 2012–13, when he helped this family-owned club win the coveted I-League title for the second time (for details, see Chapter 3: 'Goa').

His greatest contribution was reviving the confidence of Sandip Nandy, Tomba Singh and Chhetri who had been rejected by other clubs. During his successful season with Churchill Brothers, Bhowmick played the role of father figure to perfection, mediating with the management and offering both solace and guidance. It was no wonder that the players began calling him 'Papa'.

~

The diversity of coaching experience that Shabbir Ali has is unmatched in the annals of Indian football. The former international from Hyderabad is the only person in India to have coached eleven different clubs, including glamorous teams like Salgaocar, Mohammedan Sporting and Mahindra United. He justifiably became the first Indian footballer to receive the Dhyan Chand Award in 2012 for lifetime service to the game. Shabbir is a sound tactician, who continually updates his knowledge by staying abreast of international trends.

He is noted for his man-management skills and philosophy of coaching. Shabbir has often said, 'Each player has to be treated as an individual. Some can get motivated by persuasion and some by coercion.' He has always been liked by his players as he treated them like adults, giving them individual responsibility and freedom. His most successful tenure was with Salgaocar, winning eight trophies and also helping them become the first Goan club to win the coveted NFL title in 1999.

Shabbir Ali's tenure as a technical director of the national team was very successful. He functioned as an adviser to coach Rustam Akramov of Uzbekistan from 1995–97. An amiable person, Shabbir developed a great rapport with Akramov and they would exchange ideas about Indian players and their potential. The Shabbir–Akramov duo steered the Indian team to the gold medal in the SAF Games in December 1995, runners-up in the South Asian Gold Cup in Colombo in April 1995, and creditable performances in the 1995 pre-Olympics, when Jo Paul Ancheri was first used as a central-defender instead of as a striker. Shabbir Ali also guided West Bengal to victory in the Santosh Trophy in 2010 and 2011, after a gap of ten years, and was duly honoured by the Bengal government.

A man of pleasant demeanour but a sound tactician, Derrick Pereira of Goa is a promising coach. He can manage iconic players and develop young talent with equal ease. His greatest hour as a club coach was helping Mahindra United win the grand double of the Federation Cup and the NFL in a single season in 2005–06.

Looking Ahead

On 14 February 2017, Union Sports Minister Vijay Goel tweeted an infographic under the 'Transforming India' programme. According to its stated mission, the government aims to reach 1.1 crore children and 'make them play football on a regular basis'. It intends to 'reach out to over thirty-seven cities and 12,000 schools across twenty-nine states' and incentivize schools to encourage the game amongst students.[1]

Such efforts are laudable and there is a gradual awakening towards developing football talent in India. Middle-class interest in the game, primarily due to watching European football on satellite television, has been on the rise, which is reflected in the mushrooming of academies all over the country.

Nurturing Young Talent

For decades, there was no system in Indian football to nurture and develop talent. Some nursery clubs like Aryans, Kidderpore, Wari AC and Howrah Union (Kolkata); Vasco FC (Goa), BB Stars and Young Boys (Delhi); Hyderabad Arsenal, Hyderabad Rovers, City College Old Boys (Hyderabad) and several others played a pivotal role in developing young players. But it was not done systematically.

The Super Soccer series that began in 1984 and featured São Paulo FC (Brazil) was the catalyst for football development in the country. It led to the setting up of India's first football training centre, the TFA. Since 1987 the TFA has contributed hugely to the nurturing of young football talent. In the last three decades, over 125 TFA recruits have represented India in international competitions, and over 175 have represented the country in age-group national teams.

TFA's scouting of promising players is broad-based and includes all social categories. For instance, the graduation batch of 2012 had defender Sanjay Balmuchu, from a village in the iron-ore rich region of Jharkhand, and suave striker Karan Sawhney, the son of a wealthy Mumbai-based businessman. TFA is egalitarian in its treatment of players. All share the same modest facilities, staying in rooms without air-conditioning, no matter what their backgrounds are. TFA set the trend but for nearly a decade had no imitators.

After some years, other academies came into existence. Some of the prominent ones are the Chandigarh Football Academy, the Sesa Football Academy (Goa), the Sikkim Football Academy (Gangtok), the Mahilpur Football Academy, Gorkha Training Centres in Shillong and Sikkim, the Dalbir Football Academy (Patiala), the Young Challengers Football Academy (Rajkot), Sambalpur Football Academy, Jodhpur Football Academy, the Mohun Bagan SAIL Academy started in 2003, the JCT Football Academy (Rurka Kalan), the Simla Youngs Football Academy, DDA Academy (Delhi), the Hindustan Football Academy, the Premier Indian Football Academy (Mumbai), the Kenkre Football Academy (Mumbai) which started in 2000, Sports and Education Promotion Trust, and the Rahman Coaching Centre (both Kerala). The Bhaichung Bhutia Football School has centres in Delhi, Ghaziabad, Chandigarh and Mumbai. The future generations of Indian footballers are being developed in these academies.

Later, the AIFF took major steps for long-term development by setting up an academy in Goa in 2007 to nurture and develop talent. Irish coach Colm Joseph Toal's diligence made it successful.

In 2010, trainees from Colm Toal's AIFF Academy in Goa were inducted into a developmental squad known as the AIFF XI, and later as the Indian Arrows. The name of the developmental side was changed to Pailan Arrows on 15 June 2011 after the AIFF reached an agreement with Pailan Group to sponsor the team. On 29 August 2013, it was announced that Pailan Arrows had been disbanded by the AIFF as the club sponsors, Pailan Group, could not financially support the team. This concept lasted only for three seasons but it provided many outstanding players, who have represented India.

Club Academies

Another welcome change is that existing I-League teams are realizing the importance of youth development and have an allocated budget for their age-group academies. The now-defunct Pune FC started this trend about a decade ago.

DSK Shivajians have a flourishing youth academy in collaboration with Liverpool; Shillong Lajong from Meghalaya, a low-budget team, rely on developing promising players from the North-east in their academy. Debutants in the 2017 I-League, Minerva FC (Punjab), are also doing yeoman development work in Punjab.

Salgaocar's youth development programme, introduced in 2003, is amongst the best in the country. Unlike any other club, Salgaocar FC have eight junior teams from U-10 to U-20. There is also Salgaocar FC's annual Community Outreach Programme which started in 2013. Held over twenty Sundays between October 2016 and March 2017, the programme saw the registration of more than 600 children from and around Vasco.

Reliance Foundation

A big effort is being made by the Reliance Foundation to spread the game in the country and provide systematic training to talented players at a young age. To select such players, ISL club grass-roots festivals were held across the country in the initial months of 2015. The final trials for all the ISL franchises were held at Father Agnel's Sports Centre, Navi Mumbai. Twenty-four footballers in the 11–14 age group were named in May 2015 and scholarships awarded by the Reliance Foundation and Football Sports Development Limited chairperson Nita Ambani, movie icon Amitabh Bachchan, and Maharashtra Chief Minister Devendra Fadnavis, at the Jio Garden in Bandra Kurla Complex. They are being given systematic training and education at the Reliance Foundation School in Kopar Khairane, near Mumbai.

Piet Hubers, technical director of the ISL Grass-roots Programme, is a noted grass-roots coach, having worked at Dutch club NEC Nijmegen. Brazilian striker José Barreto, who excelled for Mohun Bagan at the turn of the century, is the assistant coach.

Twenty-two players from the Reliance Foundation Young Champs programme got their first international exposure in May 2016 when they travelled to England and played against U-12 and U-13 teams of Southampton, Crystal Palace, Manchester City, Reading, Aston Villa and Liverpool. In 2017, at last count, the Young Champs have forty-eight talented boys scouted over three seasons.

In July 2017, the enthusiastic owner of the NorthEast United franchise of the ISL, Bollywood actor John Abraham, announced the launch of a residential youth academy. Started in collaboration with Shillong United and named Centre of Excellence, it will be based in Shillong to focus on developing talented players from the eight North-eastern states. Abraham said, 'We have already charted a well-defined and competitive pathway for the fantastic talent pool of the North-east. We want to showcase all this on the biggest footballing stage in India.' He also said he wished to recruit up to 60 per cent of players for his club from the academy.2

Foreign Academies

For nearly a decade now, foreign clubs have been scouting for young hopefuls in India. Arsenal, in collaboration with Tata Tea, has organized inter-school tournaments in different metropolitan cities to scout for talent since 2007. The chosen players are taken to Arsenal's academy for specialized coaching. Mark Seagraves, who was associated with Arsenal Soccer Schools, then branched off on his own and set up an academy with an Indian business partner to train young players in Goa. Seagraves has three decades of playing and coaching experience with top English clubs. His Indian business partner is Sushila Tiwari, a young entrepreneur with expertise in business development, marketing and advertising.

Following Arsenal's example, many renowned foreign clubs like Barcelona, Liverpool, Everton, Crystal Palace, Bayern Munich, Sporting Lisbon and Celtic have started academies or training schools or begun selecting players for training in their academies.

New Initiatives by the AIFF

In August 2016, three U-19 players of the AIFF Academy, Anirudh Thapa (Dehradun), Prosenjit Chakraborty (Bengal) and Jerry Lalrinzuala (Mizoram) were selected to train with French club FC Metz. 'The three boys already have international experience and we hope to develop them into better players. We want to give them an opportunity to train and see European football from close quarters,' Denis Schaeffer, the director of FC Metz had said.

The long-term preparation of age-group national teams is now a regular feature in Indian football and can lead to more confident players. For the U-17 World Cup to be held in India for the first time, in October 2017, a squad of talented youngsters including eleven from Manipur have been training for two years.

The AIFF has left no stone unturned to prepare them for the event. Former chief coach Nicolai Adams had chalked out an extensive training schedule. On exposure trips to Dubai, South Africa, Brazil and Europe; as well as training camps, tournaments, kits and diet; the AIFF spent nearly Rs 8 crore in two years since Adams took over in July 2015.

Tournament experience was provided in 2016. In the AIFF Youth Cup in May 2016, they competed against quality teams like South Korea and the US. Pitted in the 'group of death' in the AFC U-16 Championships in September 2016, alongside the UAE, Saudi Arabia and Iran, India lost narrowly to Saudi Arabia, and held UAE to a thrilling draw, but lost 0-3 to Iran and failed to reach the semi-finals.

Adams's commitment was evident as he did not return home to attend his father's funeral during the Asian U-16 championships. However, in February 2017, Adams and the AIFF agreed to part ways by mutual consent. There were over a hundred applications for the vacant post including famous former international from England, Stuart Pearce. However, the AIFF finally opted for the sixty-three-year-old Portuguese coach Luís Norton de Matos who has coached the Benfica B team and the national team of Guinea-Bissau from 2010–12, and was strongly recommended by José Mourinho, the manager of Manchester United. India's U-17 team has good potential and is playing possession football, relying on speed and building from the back.

In the second decade of the twenty-first century, academies and coaching centres for football are flourishing in India, along with visits to foreign countries by age-group teams. Corporate sponsorship too is increasing. However, long-term objectives and patience are required. Owners seem to think that success and crowd support can be obtained instantaneously.

A classic example is Pride Sports of Madhya Pradesh. They joined the I-League second division with much fanfare in January 2017 but did not fare well and were bottom of the group before the penultimate round of matches took place in the last week of February 2017. Disappointed at the mediocre results, the club owners left their outfit in the lurch and did not pay their players and the Portuguese foreign coach Paulo Pedro.

Money in Sports

Successful sportsmen and women get many opportunities for making money. Apart from the salaries that players receive, sportspersons earn good money through endorsements. In the present day, the importance of sports in the country has gone up significantly and subsequently, sportspersons earn a lot more than their predecessors.

Though professionalism in Indian football is still in its embryonic form, under-the-table payment to players continued for nearly five decades, primarily in Kolkata and later in Goa, and was tacitly tolerated by the authorities. Previously institutional clubs such as Air India or JCT hired players by giving them jobs. The Kolkata clubs too helped their players get jobs in nationalized banks or public-sector companies.

For instance, the 1952 Helsinki Olympics skipper and Mohun Bagan's stalwart defender Sailen Manna was never paid by his club. He played for nearly two decades from 1942 onwards but only received travel expenses. His primary source of income was a job with the Geological Survey of India. Similarly, superstar of the next generation Chuni Goswami, who was India's captain from 1962–65 and Mohun Bagan's inside-forward from 1955–68 was not a paid professional. During his playing career he initially worked for Indian Aluminium, and later in 1961 joined the State Bank of India, from where he retired as an officer.

East Bengal's brilliant quintet of forwards in the 1950s—P. Venkatesh, Appa Rao, K.P. Dhanraj, P.B. Saleh and Ahmed Khan—played for a pittance of Rs 3000–5000 per season. They lived together for the sake of companionship in Anand Bhavan, a hotel in central Kolkata. Asian All-Stars defender Jarnail Singh moved to Mohun Bagan from Rajasthan Club for just Rs 6000 in 1959. At his peak in the 1960s, Jarnail was the highest-paid player in India and got Rs 25,000 for the season.

In the lesser-known Kolkata clubs, payments during the 1970s were very basic. International winger Surajit Sengupta, who joined Kidderpore as a promising young player in 1970, got only expenses and Rs 10 as remuneration. When he withdrew from the club in 1971, he was given a Favre-Leuba wristwatch (a prized possession in those days) as a token of appreciation.

As neither the clubs nor the players were officially professional during the 1970s, payments were not methodical. Players got paid during the club transfer period or towards the end of the season to retain their loyalty. Promises made by the clubs were often broken. Sometimes transfers took place by sheer coincidence. Younger

players struggled to get their dues. Prasanta Banerjee, who joined
East Bengal as a promising midfielder in 1975–76, was paid Rs
5000 for the season which was given in instalments.

During this decade, the established stars got their payments
on time but the money was not huge. Mohammed Habib who
played in Kolkata from 1966–84 and was called the 'king of
kings' by coach P.K. Banerjee, never got more than Rs 40,000
for the season. The first player to receive Rs 50,000 per season
was Shyam Thapa when he left East Bengal for Mohun Bagan in
1977. The first to get Rs 1 lakh was Iranian international Majid
Bishkar (1978 World Cup) who came to study in India but joined
East Bengal in 1980; he got this amount for the 1981 season.

It was a decade later, in 1987, that burly Nigerian striker
Chima Okorie became the first player to get Rs 3 lakh per season
when he left Mohammedan Sporting for East Bengal. Later Chima
shifted from East Bengal to Mohun Bagan for a record sum of
Rs 5 lakh in 1992.[3]

In 1995 JCT became the first team in India to get players from
Kolkata by using money power, going as high as Rs 10–15 lakh
per player (for details, see Chapter 5: 'Punjab'). Unfortunately,
JCT soon fell behind in business and there was an exodus of big
players from the club. In the 1997–98 season, the young prodigy
striker Bhaichung Bhutia became the highest-paid player when he
received Rs 15 lakh for switching from JCT to East Bengal. The
Kolkata clubs, realizing that their monopoly had been challenged,
then worked overtime to obtain more sponsorship. They again
became the richest in the land by persuading Vijay Mallya's United
Breweries Group to join their management. Bagan and East Bengal
each got Rs 2.5 crore per season, and the latter paid Bhaichung
Bhutia Rs 24 lakh. Chima Okorie and I.M. Vijayan both got Rs
27 lakh each and Jo Paul Ancheri got Rs 20 lakh from Mohun
Bagan.[4] Boasting of the most lethal line-up that season, Bagan's
president proclaimed that it was like getting 'Shah Rukh Khan,
Aamir Khan and Salman Khan to act in the same movie'.

During those years, Churchill Brothers changed the payment
trends in Goa football as well by starting the system of annual

contracts, instead of offering players well-paid jobs like the top Goa clubs did. They also recruited players from the North-east and even from Kolkata. The annual contracts varied from Rs 7 to 15 lakh per season for foreign players.

By the beginning of the twenty-first century, payments to players increased by leaps and bounds as other clubs also began to work with a huge budget. Established internationals like goalkeeper Sandip Nandy, and defenders Mahesh Gawli and Irungbam Surkumar Singh, left East Bengal to join Mahindra United in the 2005–06 season for a generous monthly cheque. In the 2012–13 season, the average salary of India's professional footballers—especially those in Kolkata—increased between 40 and 62 per cent. Nilanjan Datta, the AIFF's media manager who was tracking these changes said, 'Any average professional player, who played for India last year [2011–12] made anywhere between Rs 40 and 50 lakh per annum. In 2012–13 their salaries have seen a spike and they are drawing anywhere between Rs 65 and 70 lakh.'

The highest-paid player in India in the 2012–13 season was the prolific Nigerian striker Odafa Okolie (Mohun Bagan), who got a whopping Rs 3.25 crore, followed by Prayag United's Nigerian striker Ranti Martins at Rs 1.8 crore, Tolgay Özbey (Mohun Bagan) at Rs 1.5 crore and Costa Rican midfielder Carlos Hernández (Prayag United) at Rs 1.25 crore. They also got perks like accommodation, reimbursement of children's tuition fees and a Mercedes S-Class car.

Leading Indian footballers also got lucrative contracts: Subrata Pal, international goalkeeper (Prayag United) got Rs 1.1 crore, while Gouramangi Singh, central-defender for the same club, earned Rs 1.05 crore. In Goa, football had by now become a thriving industry, and when Dempo won the 5th I-League in 2012 their budget was about Rs 12 crore. Goan international midfielders Climax Lawrence and Clifford Miranda, and defenders Samir Naik and Mahesh Gawli had annual contracts worth Rs 1 crore.

The money for Indian footballers spiked even further with the advent of the ISL. Payments and transfers also became more transparent and the shady deals of the past were almost eliminated. During 2014–16, Indian players who were not established stars but got contracts with teams in both the ISL and I-League, earned in the range of Rs 40 to 70 lakh. This was more than the average Ranji Trophy player who earned about Rs 20–30 lakh per season.

In July 2017, when the ISL draft was held in Mumbai, the ten franchise clubs spent Rs 37.33 crore on 134 players. Including the money spent on retained players, the total expenditure was Rs 48.85 crore. This was a massive increase from the Rs 24 crore spent by the eight ISL franchises in the first ever players' draft in 2014. For the first time, seven Indian players were paid over Rs 1 crore.[5]

However, the paradox was that those who did not make the cut at the players' draft found themselves facing an uncertain future. At a time when Indian football needed more established clubs to grow and prosper, traditional clubs like Salgaocar, Dempo and Sporting Clube de Goa withdrew from the I-League in protest against the policies of the AIFF which they believed were flawed and harmful to the future of budding players.

Indian football has not yet created an economic system whereby younger and middle-level professionals do not have to struggle to get a living wage. This is best exemplified by the fate of the talented Milagres Gonsalves. He played in the 1st ISL final for Kerala Blasters, but was unwanted in 2017; he gave up the game in disgust and migrated to England to work in a courier company. Similarly, many Goan players have begun to look for alternative employment.

It is also true that due to a shortage of quality players, clubs compete in a limited market, and so players' prices get needlessly escalated. Former technical director of the AIFF, Scott O'Donnell, once said that many top-level Indian players get overpaid and lapse into a comfort zone. The ambition to go abroad even in Asia and compete with the leading professionals of the continent gets diminished.

But players are now living much better lives thanks to high salaries. Even those who retired a decade ago are not struggling. Some have got enough capital to start a business. Diminutive midfielder Gunabir Singh has a thriving catering business in

Kolkata. Right wing-back Irungbam Surkumar Singh has a transport and hotel business in Manipur. Others, like Noel Wilson, Carlton Chapman, Jo Paul Ancheri and Shankar Lal Chakraborty, have become qualified coaches.

Much-higher income has led to a significant improvement in the lifestyle of the football players. Many splurge on cars and luxury items, a testimony to the impact of consumerism. Honda City seems to be the most popular car amongst them, followed closely by Toyota Corolla and Hyundai Accent. Some of the elite cars they own are Nissan Sunny, Renault Duster (at Rs 11 lakh), BMW 3 series (at Rs 30 lakh), Audi and Toyota Fortuner (at Rs 24 lakh).

Utility player Ishfaq Ahmed from Kashmir, who has been on the circuit for a long time and has played for Dempo, East Bengal and Mohun Bagan, is on to his third car, Honda City, after switching from Hyundai Accent Viva and Volkswagen Polo. His justification for splurging on cars is typical of many youngsters in aspirational India: 'I work really hard every day and my body goes through a lot of strain. Thus, I feel the need to pamper myself and a car is a part of that.'

In contrast, players in the past like the late, great Sailen Manna, Peter Thangaraj and Ram Bahadur, used public transport for daily work and practice sessions. Only on match days they came by taxis. Syed Nayeemuddin still travels on the old Lambretta that he bought decades ago and calls 'my old friend'.

It is not only possessions but also recreational activities that have undergone a change. Players now go abroad on vacation with their family. A vacation for the Kolkata footballers of the 1970s meant an excursion to either Darjeeling or Shimla.

Though it cannot yet compare with cricket, money for Indian football players is on the upswing. Players in the national squad can comfortably earn a salary of Rs 50 lakh per annum. When compared to the international standard, these salaries are low, but are very favourable considering India's low ranking in world football.

Overall, a bright future beckons Indian football, but patience and time are needed for success.

Notes

Prologue: The 'Brazil of Asia'

1. Extracts from a booklet of notes prepared by the late Syed Abdul Rahim in 1961, reproduced by his son, Syed Shahid Hakeem, a 1960 Olympian, as a booklet, *A Guide to The Young Footballer*, 2001.

Introduction

1. Shamik Bag, 'Bend it like Ganguly', *Livemint Asia*, 14 Nov 2014.
2. Mihir Vasavda, 'The Game of their Lives', *Sunday Express*, 7 May 2017.
3. Ronojoy Sen, *Nation at Play: A History of Sport in India* (New Delhi: Penguin/Viking, 2016), 131.
4. Ibid., 132.
5. For more details, see Novy Kapadia, *The Football Fanatic's Essential Guide Book* (New Delhi: Hachette, 2014).

The Major Tournaments

1. As told to me by G.P. Sinha, secretary of the DCM Football Tournament Society (1975–90).
2. Mario Rodrigues, *Golden Eagles: 50 years of Dempo Sports Club (1967–2017)* (Mumbai: Spenta Multimedia Pvt. Ltd, 2017).
3. Praful Patel at a press conference organized by the AIFF, Taj Palace Hotel, March 2016.
4. IANS, 'AIFF rules out I-League, ISL merger for now', *Business Standard*, 6 May 2017, http://www.business-standard.com/article/news-ians/aiff-rules-out-i-league-isl-merger-for-now-117050600828_1.html.

5.   At a press conference, January 2017.

6.   Spoken by Shaji Prabhakaran at the launch of his book, *Back to the Roots: A Definitive Guide to Grassroots & Football Development*, in Delhi in November 2016.

7.   'India is a sleeping giant: Blatter', *Financial Express*, 30 December 2006, http://www.financialexpress.com/archive/india-is-a-sleeping-giant-blatter/188368/.

Chapter 1: Bengal: Indian Football's El Dorado

1.   Debashis Majumder, *The History of the Football Clubs in Calcutta* (Kolkata: Readers Service, 2012), 9.

2.   Ronojoy Sen, *Nation at Play: A History of Sport in India* (New Delhi: Penguin/Viking, 2016), 121.

3.   Ibid., 126.

4.   Statistics compiled by Gautam Roy, India's leading football statistician for the Mohammedan Sporting's Platinum Jubilee celebrations magazine.

5.   Majumder, *The History of the Football Clubs in Calcutta*, xiii–xiv.

6.   The account that follows about post-Partition impact is from Ibid., 5–15.

Chapter 2: Hyderabad: The Fountain of Sporting Talent

1.   Pratibha Karan, 'Hyderabadi Cuisine' in *Hyderabad Hazir Hai*, ed. Vanaja Banagiri (New Delhi: Rupa & Co., 2008), 98–105.

2.   N. Ganesan, 'Hyderabad football', *Sports and Pastime*, 9 July 1964, 18–19.

3.   Karen Isaksen Leonard, *Locating Home: India's Hyderabadis Abroad* (Stanford University Press, 2007), 60.

Chapter 3: Goa: Fiesta, Feni and Football

1.   A lot of the history narrated here has been sourced from James Mills, 'Football in Goa: Sports, Politics and the Portuguese in India', in *Soccer in South Asia, Empire, Nation, Diaspora,* ed. Paul Dimeo and James Mills (Frank Cass: London, 2001), 75–88; and Nirmal Nath, *The History of Indian Football* (Kolkata: Readers Service, 2011).

2.   Marcus Mergulhao, *Footprints in the Sand, History of Salgaocar Football Club (1956–2016)* (Vasco da Gama: Salgaocar FC, 2016).

3.   Armando Colaco, 'Coaching Effect', in Mario Rodrigues, *Golden Eagles: 50 Years of Dempo Sports Club (1967–2017)* (Mumbai: Spenta Multimedia Pvt. Ltd, 2017), 20.

Chapter 4: Kerala: The Many Paradoxes

1. Nirmal Nath, 'Where Football Knows No Bounds', in *History of Indian Football* (Kolkata: Readers Service, 2011).
2. The 1967 KFA Shield souvenir carries this information.

Chapter 5: Punjab: Sturdy Sons of the Soil

1. Dhiman Sarkar, 'ISL4: Sandhu to Be Dearest of Them All', *The Hindustan Times*, 16 August 2017.

Chapter 7: The North-east: The Rising Sun of Indian Football

1. Ratnadip Choudhury, 'A league of their own', *Tehelka*, 29 March 2014, http://www.tehelka.com/2014/03/a-league-of-their-own/.
2. Atanu Mitra, 'Move over Bengal and Goa, the North-East is India's new football powerhouse', Scroll.in, 30 May 2016, https://thefield. scroll.in/808883/move-over-bengal-and-goa-the-north-east-is-indias-new-football-powerhouse.
3. Much of what follows is from Ratnadip Choudhury, 'A league of their own', *Tehelka*, 29 March 2014.
4. Some of the information that follows is from Kanika Sharma, 'Football frenzy in the North-East', *Mid-Day*, 17 December 2014, http://www.mid-day.com/articles/football-frenzy-in-the-north-east/15848163.
5. Ratnadip Choudhury, 'A league of their own', *Tehelka*.
6. Nandakumar Marar, 'North-east footballers make coaches' job easy: Kashyap', *The Hindu*, 31 December 2015, http://www.thehindu.com/sport/football/northeast-footballers-make-coaches-job-easy-kashyap/article8051021.ece.

Chapter 8: Bengaluru: Football in the Garden City

1. Ronojoy Sen, *Nation at Play: A History of Sport in India* (Viking, 2016), 131.
2. Started by the Staffordshire Regiment stationed in Bengaluru in the 1920s. The regiment donated a pure silver cup to the erstwhile Bangalore Football Association as a running trophy, and the tournament was played regularly till the 1980s.
3. Farheen Ayesha, 'Former star player is a security guard now', *Bangalore Mirror*, 24 May 2017, http://bangaloremirror.indiatimes.

com/sports/others/former-star-player-is-a-security-guard-now/
articleshow/58810955.cms.

4. Some of the facts that follow have been taken from Mihir
    Vasavda, 'Bengaluru FC: The antithesis of Indian football',
    Indian Express, 6 November 2016, http://indianexpress.com/
    article/sports/football/the-rise-and-rise-of-bengaluru-fc-afc-cup-
    2016-final-3739235/.

5. In a conversation with me during a match in Bengaluru in
    2015.

6. Club official Mandar Tamhane in a press release of Bengaluru
    FC.

Chapter 9: Historic Clashes

1. See Chapter 1: 'Bengal', in this book, for the story of Shibdas's
    'prophecy'.

2. William Dalrymple, 'The Great Divide: The Violent Legacy of Indian
    Partition', *The New Yorker*, 29 June 2015.

Chapter 10: The Great Rivalry: Mohun Bagan vs East Bengal

1. Statistics courtesy Gautam Roy, *East Bengal Almanac 2015*,
    82–83.

2. Major S. Bhattacharya, 'That Was the Year That Was', in the
    Durand Annual, 2005, edited by Novy Kapadia.

3. Debashis Majumder, *The History of the Football Clubs in Calcutta*
    (Kolkata: Readers Service, 2012), 39–40.

4. Novy Kapadia, 'Club vs Country', *Kindle* magazine, August 2011.
    Facts from conversations with at least three senior journalists who
    do not wish to be quoted.

5. Surojit Sengupta, 'Golden 70s even influenced Naxalbari Days',
    in Nirmal Nath, *History of Indian Football* (Kolkata: Readers
    Service, 2011).

6. See Kapadia, 'Club vs Country' for more details.

7. Personal conversations with the late Sudip Chatterjee and some East
    Bengal officials.

8. Conversations with P.K. Banerjee and Bhaichung and some Bengali
    newspapers of July 1997.

9. For details, see Majumder, *The History of the Football Clubs in
    Calcutta*, 47–50.

10. Mihir Vasavda, 'Bapi Majhi, Mohun Bagan's last man standing', *Sunday Express*, 7 June 2015.
11. See 'The Major Tournaments', in this book, the section on ISL, for details.

Chapter 11: Forwards

1. *Limca Book of Records* (New Delhi: Coca-Cola India Private Limited/Hachette, 1999), 268.
2. 'Soccer star Vijayan makes film debut', *The Hindustan Times*, 12 October 2000.
3. Some of the information is from Aasheesh Sharma, 'Jeje Lalpekhlua: The bold, new face of Indian football', *The Hindustan Times*, 21 August 2016.

Chapter 12: Midfielders

1. Much of the information on T. Ao is from Sharda Ugra, 'Doctor, pioneer, footballer, leader: the remarkable story of T Ao', ESPN.in, 1 November 2016, http://bit.ly/2u387nt.

Chapter 13: Defenders

1. N . Ganesan, 'A Great Full-Back', *Sport and Pastime*, 15 July 1965, 42–43.

Looking Ahead

1. 'Central government pushes for football as sport of choice in India', *The Hindustan Times*, 14 February 2017.
2. 'NorthEast United launch residential youth academy', *The Times of India*, 19 July 2017; and Souvik Roy Chowdhury, 'ISL Draft 2017', Sportskeeda.com, 24 July 2017.
3. For more details read Novy Kapadia, 'It's Got To Be JCT', *Sportsworld*, 21 June–4 July 1995, 56.
4. *Limca Book of Records* (New Delhi: Coca-Cola India Private Limited/Hachette, 2000),410.
5. For details, see Novy Kapadia, 'The paradox of Indian football', *The Week*, 24 July 2017.

Select Bibliography

A lot of the information in this book is from my coverage on Indian football over the span of fifty years in various media, including in the *Indian Express,* the *Asian Age,* the *Week,* the *Telegraph (2005), the Economic Times, Kindle magazine, Sportsworld* (until 1999), the *Durand Annual* (1983 to present), Sportskeeda.com, Indya.com, and commentaries and programmes on television and radio.

Official information is also from press conferences held by the AIFF. Other references are listed below.

AIFF, Souvenir on Seventy Five Years of the AIFF, 1937–2012.

Bandyopadhya, Kausik. *Playing for Freedom, A Historic Sports Victory* (Delhi: Standard Publishers, 2008).

Basu, Jaydeep. *Stories from Indian Football* (Delhi: UBS Publishers Distributors, 2003).

Dimeo, Paul, and James Mills (eds). *Soccer in South Asia: Empire, Nation, Diaspora* (London: Frank Cass, 2001).

Goldblatt, David. *The Ball Is Round: A Global History of Football* (London: Penguin/Viking, 2006).

Kapadia, Novy. 'Blaze of Glory', *The Sunday Express Magazine,* 7 June 2015, pp. 6–8.

———. 'History and Future of the Federation Cup', in *90 Minutes,* Vol. 3, Issue 1, January–March 2011, pp. 29–43.

———. 'History of the Durand Football tournament', in Subhransu Roy (ed.), *90 Minutes,* Vol. 1, Issue 3, July–September 2009, pp. 50–73.

———. 'Mohammedan Sporting's Glory Years in Delhi', Platinum Jubilee Celebrations souvenir, 2010, pp. 22-32.

————. 'Rahim, Amal Dutta, PK and Nayeem: the coaches who shaped Indian Football' in Paul Dimeo (ed.), *Football Studies*, Vol. 5, No. 2, London, October 2002.

————. 'Rovers Cup Twenty Years Ago', in Sunil Warrier (ed.), Bristol Rovers Cup souvenir, 1980, pp. 53–55.

————. 'Syed Abdul Rahim and the Glory Years of Hyderabad football', in Subhransu Roy (ed.), *90 Minutes*, Vol. 1, Issue 1, January–March 2009, pp. 21-41.

————. 'Triumphs and Disasters: The Story of Indian Football, 1889-2000', in Dimeo and Mills (eds), *Soccer in South Asia*, pp. 17–41.

————. 'Unforgettable Moments in the Santosh Trophy', in Novy Kapadia (ed.), Souvenir on the occasion of 59th National Football Championship, Delhi, October 2004, pp. 42–45.

Majumder, Debashis. *The History of the Football Clubs in Calcutta: Bengali Identities since the Partition: 1947–1985* (Kolkata: Readers Service, 2012).

Mills, James. 'Football in Goa: Sport, Politics and the Portuguese in India', in Dimeo and Mills (eds), *Soccer in South Asia*, pp. 75–88.

Mukherjee, Kumar. *The Story of Football* (Publications Division, Ministry of Information and Broadcasting, Govt of India, 2002).

Nath, Nirmal. *History of Indian Football* (Kolkata: Readers Service, 2011).

Rodrigues, Mario (ed) and Marcus Merghulao. *Golden Eagles: 50 Years of Dempo Sports Club (1967–2017)* (Mumbai: Spenta Multimedia Pvt Ltd, 2017).

————. *Footprints in the Sand: History of Salgaocar Football Club (1956–2016)* (Vasco da Gama: Salgaocar FC, 2016).

Roy, Gautam (ed.). A Football Almanac, presented by East Bengal, 2006.

————. East Bengal Club, Football Almanac, Volumes I, II, III, IV and V, 2012.

Roy, Subhransu (ed.). *90 Minutes, A Journal on Different Aspects of Soccer* (Valerian Soccer Association): various Issues.

Sen, Ronojoy. *Nation at Play: A History of Sport in India* (Gurgaon: Penguin/Viking, 2016).

Sengupta, Somnath. 'Legends of Indian Football' series. TheHardTackle. com.

The Grass Is Green in Goa: Celebrating 40 Years, 1959–1999 (Goa Football Association).

Ghosh, S.L. (compiled and edited). *The Indian Football, 1975*, Delhi Football Association, Shaheed Prakashan Press, New Delhi.

Index